Ilex Foundation Series 29

THE ZURKHĀNEH AND ITS MILIEU

Also in the Ilex Foundation Series

On the Wonders of Land and Sea: Persianate Travel Writing
edited by Roberta Micallef and Sunil Sharma

Illusion and Disillusionment: Travel Writing in the Modern Age
edited by Roberta Micallef

Worlds of Knowledge in Women's Travel Writing
edited by James Uden

Poet and Hero in the Persian Book of Kings
third edition
by Olga M. Davidson

Comparative Literature and Classical Persian Poetics
second edition
by Olga M. Davidson

Ferdowsi's Shāhnāma: Millennial Perspectives
edited by Olga M. Davidson and Marianna Shreve Simpson

Global Medieval: Mirrors for Princes Reconsidered
edited by Regula Forster and Neguin Yavari

Erin and Iran: Cultural Encounters between the Irish and the Iranians
edited by H. E. Chehabi and Grace Neville

Dreaming across Boundaries: The Interpretation of Dreams in Islamic Lands
edited by Louise Marlow

The Rhetoric of Biography: Narrating Lives in Persianate Societies
edited by L. Marlow

Ruse and Wit: The Humorous in Arabic, Turkish, and Persian Narrative
edited by Dominic Parvis Brookshaw

Persian Literature and Judeo-Persian Culture: Collected Writings of Sorour S. Soroudi
edited by H. E. Chehabi

Strī: Women in Epic Mahābhārata
by Kevin McGrath

Jaya: Performance in Epic Mahābhārata
by Kevin McGrath

Kṛṣṇa: Friendship in Epic Mahābhārata
by Kevin McGrath

Naqqali Trilogy
by Bahram Beyzaie
translated by Richard Saul Chason and Nikta Sabouri

more at www.ilexfoundation.org

THE ZURKHĀNEH AND ITS MILIEU

A Study of Traditional Athletics in Iran

Philippe Rochard

Ilex Foundation
Boston, Massachusetts

Distributed by Harvard University Press
Cambridge, Massachusetts and London, England

Copyright © 2025 Ilex Foundation
All Rights Reserved

Published by the Ilex Foundation 82 Revere Street, Boston, MA 02114.
cd@ilexfoundation.org

Distributed by Harvard University Press, Cambridge, MA and London

Printed by Gasch Printing, 1780 Crossroads Drive, Odenton, MD 21113.
info@gaschprinting.com

EU GPSR Authorized Representative: LOGOS EUROPE,
9 rue Nicolas Poussin, 17000, La Rochelle, France.
Contact@logoseurope.eu

Production editor: Christopher Dadian
Cover design: Joni Godlove
Printed in the United States of America

Cover image: Untitled drawing by Ahmad Amin Nazar, 2008. Reed pen and liquid watercolor on paper. The British Museum of Art, London

Library of Congress Cataloging-in-Publication Data

Names: Rochard, Philippe, author.
Title: The zurkhāneh and its milieu : a study of traditional athletics in Iran / Philippe Rochard.
Other titles: Study of traditional athletics in Iran
Description: Boston, Massachusetts : Ilex Foundation, [2025] | Series: Ilex Foundation series ; 29 | "Distributed by Harvard University Press, Cambridge, Massachusetts and London, England." | Includes bibliographical references and index. | Summary: "The athletes known in Iran as pahlavāns and the domed structure, the zurkhāneh, where they congregate to practice ritualized martial arts, physical culture, and spirituality, are usually presented as the cornerstone of traditional Iranian masculine identity. However, this idealization does not do justice to the complex history of Iranian society. The author, who has observed the zurkhāneh world for the past thirty years and actually lived in it for over four years, sets out to reveal through his own experience and a reconsideration of the extant historiography regarding the various identities-real or imagined-of the zurkhāneh, its role within ancient and contemporary Iranian society, and the intimate mechanisms of the male societies that frequent it, as well as the moral and social values-real or simply proclaimed-that the athletes embody"-- Provided by publisher.
Identifiers: LCCN 2025004561 | ISBN 9780674298828 (paperback)
Subjects: LCSH: Athletic clubs--Iran--History. | Gymnasiums--Iran--History. | Futuwwa (Islamic social groups) | Islamic orders of knighthood and chivalry. | Nationalism and sports--Iran. | Ethnology--Iran.
Classification: LCC GV204.I712 R64 2025 | DDC 796.06/055--dc23/eng/20250429
LC record available at https://lccn.loc.gov/2025004561

for Shirin and Shadi

Contents

Preface ix

Acknowledgments xi

Introduction.. 1

PART ONE
Anthropological History of the Zurkhāneh

Chapter One
What the World of the Zurkhāneh Remembers 7

Chapter Two
Identity Matters..76

Chapter Three
History of a Professional Practice.. 120

PART TWO
Social and Symbolic Aspects of the Zurkhāneh

Chapter Four
The Time Frames of the Zurkhāneh and *Varzesh-e Bāstāni*.......................... 142

Chapter Five
Big Brother and Little Brothers: Privileges and Constraints of Fraternity 164

Chapter Six
At the Crossroads.. 196

Epilogue 231

Bibliography.. 241

Index... 259

Preface

"WHAT WAS THAT GAZELLE DOING AMONG ALL THOSE LIONS?!" somebody once asked about the research this book is based on. That gazelle had, six years earlier, spent all of 1993 waiting for a visa – in vain. However, I (the gazelle) was more determined than ever to leave in pursuit of a research object that was perhaps rather too romantically and naively chosen. This was the Persian gymnastic traditions, which preserved an ancient martial art practiced by *pahlavān* wrestlers, and that was once the home of the *luti*s, the righters of wrongs, the *javānmard* knights, and lawless ruffians. Happily, once I arrived in Tehran, Iranian society and the real life zurkhāneh provided an accelerated introduction that rapidly brought lucidity and the opportunity to completely revise the central research question. The gazelle was lucky enough to meet the right people and justified in defending a research subject that was considered by some to be hackneyed or superfluous. Professor Michael Gilsenan, author of the famous *Lords of the Lebanese Marches*,[1] clearly told us in a seminar in early 1993: "As far as research is concerned, when everyone points to the valley, I tend to climb the mountain. You should always look more closely at what others neglect or scorn."

This original research on Iran's traditional gymnasiums and their physical and sporting activities between 1994 and 1998 combined two approaches: social anthropology and history. It also involved a comparative dimension that cannot be published here in its entirety. The historical aspect has been published elsewhere,[2] and the comparative elements provided the material for an article.[3] The present book contains the findings of this research that have not yet been published in English, modified and updated by subsequent research.

1. Gilsenan 1996.
2. Rochard 2002, especially from page 324 on. See also Rochard and Jallat 2018.
3. Rochard and Bast 2023.

Acknowledgments

I WOULD LIKE TO EXTEND MY HEARTFELT THANKS to the Ilex Foundation and particularly to Olga Davidson, without whom this book would not exist, to Niloofar Fotouhi for her vigilance and benevolence, to Christopher Dadian for his thoughtfulness and his efficiency, to Nicolas Visanica, who helped me draw up several figures that illustrate this book, and to Katharine Throssell for her hardfought translation of the French text. I owe special gratitude to Houchang Chehabi, who believed in me and has constantly supported my work, in Iran and in France, from my first year as a PhD student in 1994. The current work, form and content, is the culmination of thirty years of friendship and unfailing scientific exchange and commitment. Finally, I would like to thank my wife, Shirin Baniahmad, for her affection, understanding, and support, which have saved me more than once over the course of these long years. In the words of Marguerite Duras, whom Shirin has translated into Persian, she has shown me that "you have to be very fond of men. Very very fond. You have to be very fond of them to love them." This book, in which unfortunately there are too few women, is dedicated to her and to our daughter Shadi.

This research was made possible nearly thirty years ago by my friends and colleagues in Iranian academic institutions and, of course, in the zurkhāneh. I cannot thank them all individually, but I can thank them collectively by expressing my gratitude to the Foundation for the Encyclopaedia of Islam, and Varzesh-e Bāstāni va Koshti-e Pahlavāni Federation, and particularly the man who was then its president, Seyyed Abdollāh Sajjādi, and my friend Behnām Jaʻfari, who helped me to understand what my interviewees were saying through all of the year 1994. I would particularly like to thank all the athletes who welcomed me into their sport and their lives: my guardians Hasan, Abbās, all the big-hearted *mashdi*s, and the kind and generous *pishkesvat*s who helped and guided me, and above all my dear and greatly missed friend Dāvud and his family. I am also grateful for the financial and moral support of several French institutions between 1994 and 1998: the research team at the Monde Iranien de Paris (CNRS – Sorbonne – INALCO) and its former director Bernard Hourcade; the French Ministry of Foreign Affairs and its political, economic, and cultural representation in Tehran; the French Institute for Research in Iran (Institut Français de Recherche en Iran (IFRI)) directed between 1994 and 1998 by Professor Rémy Boucharlat, and its general secretary, Mohammad Akbary; Professor Robert Ilbert, founder of the Maison Méditerranéenne des Sciences de l'Homme (MMSH – Aix-en-Provence), who inspired me to become a researcher. Finally, I am grateful to my thesis supervisor Professor Christian Bromberger and the Institut d'ethnologie Méditerranéenne, européenne et comparative (MMSH – Aix-en-Provence).

After the summer of 2009 I thought that I would never write or talk about Iran again. I would like to express my most sincere thanks to Houchang Chehabi, Oliver Bast, Nader Nasiri-Moghaddam, and Lloyd Ridgeon for having convinced me to reverse that decision and given me the means to do so.

Strasbourg, April 2024

Introduction

"You didn't ask me the right questions." When the veteran of traditional sport I had been talking to for nearly an hour threw in this remark by way of goodbye, I was a little put out. It is true that this rather severe comment came after a discussion a few weeks earlier with a sociologist who had unceremoniously told me that I was wasting my time on this study because everything there was to say about the subject had already been said. But I had been in Iran for six months, I had written an MA thesis (admittedly very theoretical, for want of a visa) on the subject, and I thought I had a handle on it. Nevertheless, it seemed that what I was interested in was secondary, and I was not even doing it right.

A *zurkhāneh* (which literally translates as "house of strength") is a traditional Iranian gymnasium where acrobatic and strength training have been practiced for several centuries. These activities are performed by groups of ten to fifteen men in a sunken hexagonal pit, the *gowd*, at the center of the room, to the rhythm of percussion instruments played by a musician on the edge of the pit. Those who practice this sport say that it teaches a philosophy of life that has its origins in an old moral and spiritual tradition, the *javānmardi*.

Up until the first third of the twentieth century, the zurkhāneh was above all a school for acrobatics and a type of wrestling that was practiced – until the collapse of the empires of the period – from Mongolia to Algiers, and from Istanbul to Calcutta. However, things changed profoundly with the arrival of modern sports in Iran, and the creation in 1934 of the Sāzmān-e Tarbiyat-e Badani (Organization of Physical Education, henceforth STB), which organized different recreational sporting practices in Iran into federations. The new Iranian Wrestling Federation (IWF), created in 1939, adopted the standards of FILA (the international amateur wrestling federation, renamed United World Wrestling in 2014) and trained its members in freestyle and Greco-Roman wrestling in modern gymnasiums. Soon, wrestling was no longer taught in the zurkhāneh. Traditional Iranian wrestling, renamed *pahlavāni* (from the word *pahlavān*, the title awarded to champions in this sport), was put under the auspices of the IWF, as were the zurkhānehs and their gymnastics program. Beginning in 1941, the IWF organized *pahlavāni* championships and the STB unsuccessfully attempted to set up the same thing for zurkhāneh gymnastics, then called *varzesh-e bāstāni* (ancient sport) in reference to the reconstruction, then underway, of Iranian national historiography around the pre-Islamic period.

When I arrived in Iran, this "ancient sport" was hardly a forgotten tradition; it is not as though it was revived by a researcher who stumbled across the last reposito-

1

ries of a dwindling knowledge in a few out-of-the-way mountainous regions of Iran. Zurkhāneh traditional sport was very much alive. At the time I conducted my research in the late 1990s, there were around thirty thousand athletes who practiced it every day within a sporting federation created in 1979, the Federāsion-e Varzesh-e Bāstāni va Koshti-e Pahlavāni-e Irān (Ancient Sport and Pahlavāni Wrestling Federation, henceforth VBKP Federation).

It was this time lapse that led to my first investigations of this subject. The modern sporting movement was launched in Iran in the 1930s but only extended to the zurkhāneh and its gymnastic practices forty years later, following the 1979 Islamic Revolution. Yet the term "traditional sport" and the idea of transforming the physical activities of the zurkhāneh into a sport, with the organization of the first competitions, had been formalized as early as 1940. This was something that called for further investigation. For nearly forty years the world of the zurkhāneh had not felt the need to create an official association – why?

The second question that arose in relation to the zurkhāneh stemmed from my discovery of the substantial exegesis surrounding its supposed origins, its role and place in Iranian history. The first questions that my Iranian contacts asked me when I said I wanted to study the zurkhāneh, were legitimate, although somewhat redundant: what were the origins of this tradition? Was it a resistance movement against the Mongolian invaders (thirteenth century CE)? Or was it inspired by a military organization of Sasanian knights (third to seventh centuries CE)? Or by the alleged initiation rituals of Mithraism? Was its ideology inspired by chivalry or by ordinary people? To what extent can we say these ancient practices and values influenced Medieval Islam? Many of the people I spoke to seemed totally uninterested in any other questions about the zurkhāneh, because between Antiquity or the Middle Ages and today, there have been numerous recriminations against this institution. Whatever their claims to be ancient and venerable schools of chivalry or a noble tradition, since the nineteenth century the zurkhānehs have been accused of many things, including being dens for pederasts indulging in alcohol and opium, who used their strength to steal from honest people and sold their services to the rich, and whose activities ranged from racketeering to the tolerated but socially stigmatized hobby of pigeon fancying. I found the fact that statements about the nobility of the sport's origins and current-day recriminations were often made by the same people and the contrast between them fascinating.

But this research was not about "looking for origins." I set myself the limit of not going further back than the early twentieth century – that already gave me more than enough to do! And the more I was encouraged to study the origins of this tradition by exploring the hypothetically pure practices of the zurkhāneh in remote regions, the more I wanted to listen to athletes in Tehran tell me about what they did in their immediate everyday practices. In the event, I was obliged, in a way, to undertake a veritable rewriting of the history of the zurkhāneh.

Introduction

Both the veteran sportsman and the sociologist left me with insights that were stimulating and beneficial. It was clear that the texts that had been written on the zurkhāneh over the last fifty years had resonated with those who practice this sport. The veteran had come to talk about the philosophy of the sport, but I was interested in the more prosaic aspects of the practice. If I had disappointed him, I wanted to know why. There was indeed something else at work behind this physical training. As for the sociology professor, he laid down a challenge. Much had been written about the zurkhāneh. If I wanted to persevere, I would have to approach the question differently.

This institution of the zurkhāneh had already been studied from philosophical, mythological, military, religious, and literary perspectives, but up until then no one had looked at the history of its practices, the actions and gestures themselves, or what it might mean for an athlete today to go into the exercise pit three times a week. Existing research often provides interpretations of this practice without seeking the input of the athletes themselves. What could they show me and teach me about? I hope to provide an answer here.

I have chosen not to give a linear historical-anthropological account, beginning with the most ancient times and leading up to today, based on the analysis of texts and interviews. Nor did I want to author a disconnected juxtaposition of historical analysis and anthropological monograph. Instead, I wanted to give the reader the possibility to follow the logical consequences of my questions and my choices, which will be presented in two parts. An epilogue will trace the evolution of *varzesh-e bāstāni* in the two decades since my field work.

PART ONE
Anthropological History of the Zurkhāneh

How can we approach and understand the tradition of the zurkhāneh, its present and its past? Part one of this book provides in its first chapter an immediate immersion into the object of study. It aims to adopt the "thick description" approach so dear to Clifford Geertz,[1] to give a perspective of present-day zurkhānehs in Tehran, which has the highest numbers of zurkhānehs in Iran. In other words, it looks at the current state of practice that contributes to the memory of actors. The athletes of the zurkhāneh told me about what was meaningful for them and about the historical figures who marked their experience. From what I learned, I could deduce why no VBKP organization worthy of the name had emerged between 1941 and 1979.

The second chapter of Part one is the logical continuation of the first. In it we glimpse the impact of the identity construction process that began when this traditional sport and the zurkhāneh were given a place within the new national Iranian historiography of the 1930s and 40s. It begins by shedding light on the general context of this identity construction and explores the establishment of a new sporting world in Iran, as well as the place for zurkhāneh within that world. In light of this brief history of sport in Iran and the discourses on the role and function of the zurkhāneh, from its origins to the contemporary period, it offers a new approach. It re-examines the same history by seeking to identify more specifically the users of the zurkhāneh evoked in the earliest sources, and to understand their function in Iranian society from the sixteenth century to the 1930s. However, it would be impossible to meet this objective without having previously established a number of things: first, that the Iranian zurkhāneh were home to activities that other cultures, India and Central Asia in particular, also practiced; and second, that these practices were possibly the fruit of a range of experiences rather than a single source. To succeed in this endeavor, I had to engage differently with well-known sources, to lead them to speak in new ways. It was only after having performed this groundwork, revealing new materials and new questions, that I could hope to establish a sort of "cultural stratigraphy" of the zurkhāneh to learn more about the practices and people that modern traditional sport came from. However, there is a clear hiatus between the traditional practices and those that are documented in the first studies by Iranian authors in the 1940s and 50s. The third chapter of this book sets out to explain this gap.

1. See particularly Geertz 1973 and Geertz 1983. For those who wish to explore the approach I have used in this study further, see Althabe, Fabre, and Lenclud 1992, specifically the notion of ethnology of interaction that Fabre mentions on p. 45. However, my background in history means I have a fondness for the New History school, and particularly the approach of André Burguière to historical anthropology. I also greatly admire the way historian Georges Duby presents knowledge in his famous "Dimanche de Bouvines"; see Duby 1990. See also Le Goff 1978.

Chapter One
What the World of the Zurkhāneh Remembers

Waiting

In hindsight, the way in which I gained access to the zurkhāneh was particularly significant. Well aware that first impressions can be merciless, I did not want to simply descend upon this sphere with an official letter that would have at best gained me a few polite responses followed by a decisive and very "*ta'ārofian*"[1] neutralization. It was important to me that I was accepted by those practicing the sport before approaching the VBKP Federation.

However, the quality of my status and my information would depend on the rank and reputation of the person who would be my initial contact. I therefore had to look for the "right contact," but this approach meant someone had to recommend me to my future guarantor. From the interviews with my contacts at my host institution in Tehran it became clear that this would take some time. On the pretext of giving me time to "discover Iran," they were waiting to get to know me better. Then, suddenly, they decided I was "a nice guy" and everything was sorted out in a matter of hours. One of my contacts recommended me to one of his colleagues who, through his training and position had friends both in the university sector and, through a religious school in Qom, among the bazaaris in Tehran. In addition to his official functions, this colleague was part of a group that through his network and contacts guaranteed the respectability of his institution with regards to the revolutionary authorities – guaranteeing that it was kept "in line," so to speak. After beginning religious studies in Qom, he went on to study at university, while carefully maintaining contact with his old friends. This allowed him to keep a foot in both worlds.[2]

And it was this other world that was mobilized when this man, in front of me, made a call to one of his acquaintances, Hasan, asking him to look after, as he put it, "a nice young man who is interested in the zurkhāneh and *javānmardi*." A meeting was arranged the very next day and I made my official entry into the world of the zurkhāneh three days later. It was 13 May 1994; I had waited four months.

A *Mashdi*

I wanted the man who would present me into the world of the zurkhāneh to be someone of high standing, a real *mashdi*. This term needs to be explained in more detail.

---

1. In Persian *ta'ārof* literally means etiquette or civility, a protocol recognizing status and decorum, and in its broader usage, politeness. See Beeman 1986.
2. On this point, a very interesting read is Mobasser 1991; also Mobasser 1985.

Mashdi normally refers to somebody who has completed the pilgrimage to the Imam Reza Shrine in Mashhad, which is one of the most important pilgrimages in Twelver Shiite Islam. *Mashdi* is a contracted form of the full expression *dāshmashdi*, in which *dāsh* comes from the Turkish *dādāsh*, meaning brother. This term came to refer to people also called *luti* or *jāhel*, the latter literally meaning "the ignorant one."[3] The term *luti* is a synonym for "companion," but until the late nineteenth century it was used for a troupe of performers or jesters known for bawdy tales and low manners. The root of the word is *lut*, suspected of being a direct reference to the prophet Lot and the people of Sodom, and thereby those who practice sodomy. These terms, which were certainly not chosen by those concerned but rather by their many critics in scholarly circles, were therefore initially highly pejorative. However, they have been reclaimed and their meaning inverted to refer to individuals who come from "the people" and who, whether good or bad, are quick, crafty, independent, and "tough," with their own culture, vocabulary, lifestyle, and sense of humor. The most famous literary example is that of the *luti* in the city of Shiraz, Dāsh Ākol, that the writer Sadeq Hedayat depicts in the short story of the same name.

The man who would eventually become my mentor met these standards fully. Hasan was a tall man of few words, his voice a gravelly drawl, a man who was never in a hurry. He was just as sparing with his movements as he was with his words; his head slightly tilted so as to observe from the corner of his eye that the orders he had given were being properly executed. Always surrounded by a childhood friend ready to carry out the slightest task, Hasan was the very incarnation of the traditional *paterfamilias*.

Hasan was born and had grown up in the Chāleh Meydān, which said it all. The name of this neighborhood, now the twelfth district of Tehran, derived from an ice pit. It used to be one of the poorest neighborhoods in Tehran.[4] Being a "child of the ice-pit" meant that one came from a very poor background, and this was looked down upon in good Iranian society. Through a reversal of meaning, it also came to connote an authenticity and connectedness that is the mark of old Tehrani families, who cannot be "hoodwinked" – much like the youngsters of Montmartre in Paris, or those of Five Points in Manhattan.

But Hasan did not start out with nothing. He was the second son of Mirzā Mohammad, a respectable bakery owner. When their father died, the oldest of five brothers, Abbās, a real *luti*, squandered the family's assets to such a point that the other four brothers held a family council to take control of what remained of their father's fortune and set up a printing business, a profession that seemed both more financially advantageous and more noble. This decision bought significant social success to the four brothers, led by Hasan.

Like members of the Tehrani upper class, Hasan left the overcrowded, polluted city

---

3. The term *jāheliyyat* refers to the period that preceded the arrival of the Prophet Mohammad.
4. The "ice pit" square was so named because it was the site of several underground spaces that were used to keep large ice blocks sent down from the mountains north of Tehran.

center in the 1970s for a large villa in the north of the city, near the Qeytarieh park. He also had a small summer house in the mountains towards Chalus, which served as a refuge for the family during Iraqi aerial attacks on Tehran in the 1980s. Hasan's eldest son was studying at a university in the United States. Yet the luxuriousness of the imposing reception room was in stark contrast with the simplicity of the room in which he and his family spent most of their evenings. The two rooms were adjoining but their functions were clearly different. The European-style lounge was for formal receptions, and the Iranian-style lounge for family life, where meals were still served on a *sofreh*, a cloth placed directly on the rug, upon which the food is traditionally served.

He had a large room to himself underneath the terrace that led to the garden. There, he could take refuge from the domestic hubbub to enjoy the view of the flowers in his garden, particularly his magnificent and highly perfumed roses, which were a veritable passion for him. He could also receive his guests, work, or read his most precious books, and practice his *varzesh-e bāstāni* exercises. His workout space and the main tools for the exercises were laid out across from his desk and for many years he followed the early-morning rhythmic and musical exercises broadcast on Iranian radio for training at home. On Thursday afternoons, he would smoke the opium he was prescribed for his increasingly painful joints, but in moderate quantities, at the homes of acquaintances, where the whole family was adept in the art of *bast*, the base measurement of opium balls, equivalent to 1.66g, and the *manqal*, the charcoal brazier used to heat the coals for the pipe.

He worked mainly in the printing district, between Ferdowsi, Sa'di, and Jomhuri Avenues and the old Tupkhāneh Square, which was renamed Khomeini Square after the revolution. In addition to his work at the printers, Hasan, like his peers, had various interests in the bazaar, about which he remained discreet. He was also constantly concerned with cultivating and maintaining his indispensable network of contacts by occupying various functions that were not particularly well paid (at the Tehran Chamber of Commerce, for example) but were a good source of contacts and information that could extend his sphere of influence. To remain up to date about everything that might concern his activities and businesses, he never failed to regularly attend the different *hey'at*s, social circles held by the various members of his network. These relations were based on loyalty to his childhood friends who were born in the same neighborhood, regardless of what fortune had brought each of them. His friends and acquaintances respected him and he could mobilize large sums of money with a simple telephone call and the guarantee of his good word. This proves that he had substantial capital of *e'temād o e'tebār*, trust and credit, the quality required for being *khoshnām*, having "a good name," and therefore being able to conduct business.

His early days as a printer had not been easy, however. Having changed professions, and with a disreputable *badnām* (literally "bad name") brother, he had to rebuild everything and earn respect. For example, he had to go in person to see those who owed him money and who were always asking for extensions for their final payment after the work was completed. When discussion alone was not enough, when all attempts at mediation had failed, having friends and four brothers in the zurkhāneh lent a certain weight to any threats that a different kind of "negotiation" might begin. This meant that the five brothers ended up carving out a reputation for themselves. "I owe nothing to my youth," he said one day with a smile.

A famous anecdote in the family gives us a good idea of what young Hasan was like. It was related to me by his eldest son, Bābak, who had heard it from one of his uncles who had witnessed the scene. For a time his father did not want to go to the bars and cabarets that he usually attended, because several young thugs – also looking to get themselves a reputation – had defied him constantly and even forced him to fight several times. Nevertheless, one of his friends had insisted on inviting him, along with two of his brothers, to have a drink there. They accepted, and his friend promised him that their gathering would be uneventful. Unfortunately, while they were waiting to be served, a young man, probably imagining that this was his opportunity to become well known, and feeling bolstered by his friends around him, stood up and made a loud and clearly disobliging comment about Hasan. The latter, who was listening, looking down at the table, calmly fingering his *tasbih* (rosary of prayer beads), and did not respond. But he did raise his eyes towards the friend who had invited him, with a little fatalistic nod as if to say, "what did I tell you?" Without thinking twice, and without a word of explanation his friend stood up, violently slapped the young man and threw him out of the room, and then came to sit back down with the usual *ta'ārof*, asking his guest to forgive him and promising and that would not happen again. Hasan had not moved, nor opened his mouth, nor had the friends of the would-be top dog.

In spite of having moved out of the neighborhood, Hasan had maintained all kinds of social connections with the people of the area where he grew up, and in particular with the old athletes of the zurkhāneh. As a teenager, presented and protected by his brother Abbās, eleven years his elder, and accompanied by his childhood friend Asghar, he had finally been allowed to join the groups of adult men in the exercise pit.

Abbās was born in 1930 and had practically never left the old southern districts of Tehran where he was born. He went to school until he was twelve and then became an apprentice in his father's bakery. In the early 1950s, he became friends with the brothers of the famous mafioso Tayyeb Hājj Rezā'i. One of the shops owned by the brothers Tāher and Masih was adjacent to the bakery. Abbās remembers these years nostalgically:

> The bakery where I worked was just next door to the Tayyeb's fruit and vegetable shop. They also sold us coal, which is how we met. We liked to have a drink and follow the girls in the street. We knew all of the renowned *mashdi*s in Tehran. During Muharram we were the first in the *dasteh* [procession], and it was not like today, the blood flowed![5]

---

5. Conversation with Abbās, 21 June 1994.

As proof, he took off the hat that he always wore to show me the old scars that crisscrossed his bald head. They were the result of many years of *qameh zādan*, dagger striking, an act of self-mutilation consisting in striking one's head with sharp knives as a sign of communion with the martyred Imam Hoseyn. The scalp bleeds quickly and the self-flagellator wears a white shirt, a *kafan*, like a shroud, to prove he is ready to die for Hoseyn, which shows off the bright red of the ostentatious sacrifice to good advantage. Although it was grudgingly tolerated by religious leaders before the revolution, since their rise to power it has been severely condemned. Today, it is performed at night in closed circles by an official who strikes each head only once. This is a precaution to avoid overly zealous self-mutilation that can lead to serious injury by devotees who have lost control of their actions.

Causing blood to flow, whether one's own or someone else's, is a risk that is acknowledged and accepted in the lifestyle that was described to me. Whether it is linked to the idea of sacrifice or vengeance, it always involves a concern for reputation and constitutes a serious action but no surprise. Much later, many of my contacts in moments of great trust, showed me photos of those who had not survived these neighborhood fights, or who had been condemned to death by imperial courts or later by revolutionary tribunals. These massive, mustached men, who were photographed lounging, with their arms around each other's shoulders, in the *hammām*s after the zurkhāneh, before going off to eat and drink together, almost all died a violent death. Sometimes the photos even showed the future victims arm-in-arm with their future murderers, soon to be condemned to death, but smiling for the photographer, the only one of the group who survived. Alcohol abuse was to blame for much of the excesses of Thursday nights that always left bodies on the streets of the old city in the early morning. In this respect, the Islamic regime brought about widespread pacification. Abbās had his own opinion on this violence:

> We fought and we won because we were right. We were not defending the strong. We were concerned with the family, but when a friend was going to be robbed, we protected him without needing to go to the police. I was respected partly because of my father and partly for myself. We respected our seven neighbors[6] and everyone respected us; and I always respected people as much as they respected me, but Tehran was small back then; now everything is too big, nobody knows anyone, and you do not know who you have to take your hat off to anymore.[7]

Having lived as a *jāhel*, a *luti*, and having been the reason for his family's financial problems, Abbās refused to take a share in the profits when the printing business began to

---

6. This is an old neighborhood law that dictates one must be a good neighbor to the seven houses surrounding one's own, on both sides of the street.
7. Conversation with Abbās, 24 June 1994.

make money. He also refused to take the job that his brothers had reserved for him in the business. When he sunk into poverty, he also refused the financial assistance they were offered him. Even when he lived only in a single room across from their largest print shop, he refused his brother Hasan's offer of accommodation. The only thing that he accepted was a free lunch when his brother would order kebab for himself and the printshop workers; refusing to share a meal with a family member would have been rude.

Abbās Āqā knew absolutely everyone, and thanks to him – because I had been presented by his brother, which effectively put me under his protection – I was able to continue my work peacefully and cover subjects that would have otherwise been off-limits to me. I only needed to say that I was a guest of Hasan and Abbās Āqā and whoever was asking questions, a policeman or young *basij*, would scuttle away and the address books would open.

When I told his nephew Bābak that I would like to thank Abbās Āqā in some way, Bābak, knowing his uncle, led me to understand that it would be difficult: "maybe he would like you to bring him something back from France." When I did finally ask him in a way that I thought acceptable and highly deferent, the response was polite but firm: "the only thing that I ask of you is to help Iranians in France like I help you here." And that was it. When I told some of my Iranian friends about this response, they immediately retorted, "*kāresh javunmarduneh bud!*" It was a "*javānmardi*" response.

But what does that mean? What is *javānmardi*? This notion is inextricably connected to the explanations surrounding the history of the zurkhāneh, so we must try to shed some light on what is behind it.

Javānmardi and *Ayyāri*

Javānmardi is the Persian equivalent of the Arabic word *futuwwa*. Henry Corbin defined it like this:

> The Arabic word *fata*, of which the plural is *fityan*, refers to a young man (between 16 and 30 years old); it corresponds to the Persian *javān* (a cognate of the Latin *juvenis*). Youth, juveniliy, is *fotowwat*, or in Persian, *javānmardi*. That is when we use this word literally in reference to physical age. When it is used figuratively [...] it refers to the spiritual pilgrim (*sālik*, homo viator), he who has arrived at the "stage of the heart," that is the truth of the inner being, and in that way has reached the stage of the inalterable youth of the soul. Through physical youth, the perfections of the external form are fulfilled. However, the fulfilment of human perfection and internal spiritual strength are achieved through the *fata*, the *javānmard*, the "knight."[8]

8. Corbin 1973, 5–6.

Javānmardi is quite simply the distinction between good and evil, a pure altruism and courage to defend one's principles at any cost. At the beginning of his text, Henry Corbin brushes aside any historical consideration, claiming that professional treatises, *fotovvatnāmeh*s "are not notarial acts." In fact, they are, but not the ones that we are used to imagining. Alongside its historical and social origins, *javānmardi* has been and remains a spiritual ideal that demands a certain attitude towards the world that surrounds the man who seeks to practice it. That it has been interpreted and used in different ways by different groups in different periods is beyond doubt. However, ultimately, today there is a moral and spiritual dimension to the respect and admiration paid to those whose lives have followed the way of *javānmardi* that goes beyond the banal appreciation of simple acts of skill and generosity.[9]

We need to immediately make a distinction between two notions, *javānmard* and *ayyār*, which are conflated by some even though the terms have separate histories, as Marina Gaillard demonstrates in her work on *Samak-e Ayyār* and the *Dārābnāmeh*, a twelfth-century epic.[10]

Gaillard shows the evolution of the word *ayyār*, which perhaps initially referred to a profession of itinerant soldiers or mercenaries, and later became, for better or worse, a synonym for actions demanding particular skill and cunning. She also provides an example of the use of the word *javānmardi*, which became a synonym for generosity in its moral and material dimensions. Men described as *javānmard* are always positive heroes, while bad characters are never described in that way. "Baddies" and "goodies" can both demonstrate skill, and ability may be used for good or for bad; this corresponds to the term *ayyāri*, cunning. An *ayyār* will use cunning to win, for example in an eloquent discourse convincing his opponent to come down off their horse for a fist fight, only to take out a dagger at the last moment to gain an advantage over the adversary he has tricked. All the other knights in the army will laugh at this treatment, considering it both unworthy of them but typical of an *ayyār*.

The spiritual descendent of the *ayyār* in Iranian history was clearly the *luti*, up until the 1950s. Yuriko Yamanaka has shown how Iranian storytellers of the nineteenth century, who put the legend of Alexander the Great in writing and also updated it, were inspired by these mischievous thieves, who disrupted the bazaars of their own time,[11] and who were referred to in popular memory as *luti* – forgetting that the term once referred to a profession that sometimes trained in the zurkhāneh (as well as in their own specific *lutikhāneh*) as we will see later on in the book. Interestingly, however, they chose to

---

9. Research on this subject has evolved significantly since this was originally written in 2000, in particular thanks to Lloyd Ridgeon's work. See Ridgeon 2007; Ridgeon 2010; Ridgeon 2011; Ridgeon 2018. See also Karamustafa 2006.
10. Gaillard 2001; Gaillard 1987.
11. Yamanaka 2002. Conference Papers from the IVth European Congress on Iranian studies (ECIS) held in Paris on 6–10 September 1999.

represent these *ayyār*s in their illustrations by reproducing the silhouette characteristic of the *shāter*, the guards and messengers of the powerful who also frequented the zurkhāneh, and who will be discussed in more detail. Being thus associated with the house of an important figure conferred dubious advantages, it would seem.

The ambiguous figure and personality of the *luti*, which can be divided between negative and positive stereotypes, leaves no doubt as to his primary characteristic being cunning, whether it is used for better or worse. However the, *javānmard* does not possess any negative characteristics; if he did, he would simply be denied the right to that title. The term actually implies moral and professional honesty (the latter is important), as well as sincerity, simplicity, humility, and a hospitality not simply reduced to generosity and the amount of money spent on someone. These people, the *javānmard*s, are rare but they do exist; I have had the pleasure and honor to meet some, in spite of what the skeptics might say.

However, the range of implications of the *javānmardi* is such that it can also be summarized as an unattainable but perpetually pursued ideal. We can say that somebody is acting like a *javānmard*, but that does not give him the right to claim the title all the time. Who would dare to say they have achieved perfection? Anyone who claims that they are *javānmard*, in a zurkhāneh or elsewhere, in fact demonstrates a conceit that brings a wry smile to others. So, if you are told in a zurkhāneh or elsewhere that someone or other is a *javānmard*, it is always worth checking the relationship and strategy between whoever is making the claim and the person they are referring to. Even in the zurkhāneh, where the wise men, the veterans – those referred to as *pishkesvat* – often use this word, *javānmard* is generally a reference to an ideal and rarely to a particular individual. When it is a particular person, it is most often somebody who is dead or extremely old; because it is only after one's death that the meaning of one's life can be evaluated and a judgement can be handed down to posterity. Everything else is just strategy.

In light of these considerations, my protector Abbās Āqā was indisputably a *mashdi*, a "real man," but when he was young, he had behaved like a *jāhel*, a street hoodlum, although everyone agreed, he had *mardānegi*, a very strong sense of traditional, virile, male values. All of these social characteristics together were not enough to make him a *javānmard*. However, asking me, as sole payment for his help, to solemnly swear to help others was clearly an act of total altruism, generosity, protection of the vulnerable and the foreigner, all characteristic of a *javānmard*. He nevertheless did not consider himself one, and neither did his friends. But he deserved this title much more than some of the surprising people I met later, who were so taken with their own skills or muscles, more or less discreetly enjoying the accolades of their retinue, and who had – as I learnt at my expense – a surprising understanding of the notion of disinterested service.

THE ZURKHĀNEH-YE JAM

The big day had arrived. My first time entering into the world of the zurkhāneh. It was late morning on a Friday. The zurkhāneh is open at that time because the exercises are above all dedicated to God, the Prophet, and Imam Ali ibn Abi Tāleb, whom Shiites consider to be the Prophet's rightful successor. The *do'ā*, the invocation of God, which is performed standing and is simpler than the complete ritual prayer (*namāz*) is performed at the end of the exercise and accepted as a substitute for the midday prayers. Friday is also the day when one is most likely to meet the protectors and notables that frequent this place. As one of the athletes explained to me one day, "during the week we train, but on Friday we come together and show each other what we have done and talk with our friends." Having perfectly understood what I wanted to observe and understand, Hasan had told me that I could come to speak with "some very important people." He did not give any more detail than that, but he had made it clear that I was invited to attend a particularly formal session.

The zurkhāneh Hasan had chosen, the Zurkhāneh-ye Jam, was symbolic of a certain period in more than one way. Also known by the name of its long-time principal owner, Ahmad Mir-Ashraf, it was in the southeast of Tehran, in a small street in a neighborhood that stretches south from Meydān-e Khorasan. This was a place never visited by the bourgeoisie from the north of the city. The houses in this area were rarely more than a few stories high. Despite the fact that it was Friday I quickly regretted having been chosen as the group's chauffeur, what with the *jub* – large deep gutters that are typical of Tehran – the anarchy of pedestrians, motorbikes, and Peykan cars, and avenues saturated with exhaust pipe fumes from small trucks and buses.

One does not enter into a zurkhāneh without having been presented beforehand in one way or another; and one never goes in alone. Not because it is dangerous in any way, on the contrary, the welcome is always polite, but it is not the done thing. As my protector told me one day, "it is better to have nothing and be rich in true friends than the opposite." Going out is only worthwhile if one is with friends, and the zurkhāneh is indeed an outing. It is as much a club as it is sports training; and as in all clubs, membership is not automatic. Human relations are very uncertain. Who will answer for you? Here, having known someone for "only" ten years is tantamount to admitting they cannot be vouched for; and if there is no one to vouch for you how can you stand alone? Being part of the group saves time, grants strength, and confers prestige. Local notables know how to play on these external signs of influence and power and, when you are young and lack self-assurance, a group allows you to speak with authority, with their protection.

Etiquette and entry

We met up with close friends somewhere in town, and then once that small group had gathered we joined the larger group of more distant friends waiting near the zurkhāneh to welcome us and enter the space together.

Whereas the greetings between the *rafiq* and *dādāsh* in the car had been joyful and excited, with lots of joking and laughing, the meeting with the other group of friends waiting outside the zurkhāneh was much more dignified. Some were still kissed fondly on the forehead but the tone of voice had changed. "Ah ha! Hasan khān, hāletun chetoreh?" (Hey, Hasan Khān, how is your health?) They called out loudly to each other or spoke more intimately. Depending on affinities and how long they had known each other, the two groups greeted each other differently: "Cheh khabar ? - salāmati" (What news? Good health!). Polite questions seemed to follow endlessly on from counter questions and responses that were nothing more than pure etiquette, markers of modesty, which also allowed the person to avoid genuinely responding. One of the members of the welcoming committee moved towards a member of our group and shook his hand and arm, and kissing him on the forehead asked him earnestly if everything was well with his family, his children, while staring intently into his eyes each time he had to respond. This made the object of his attention palpably uncomfortable; smiling, his head tilted to one side, eyes on the ground, he responded to each question with "nokaretam, qorbunet beram, mokhlesam" (I am your servant, may I be sacrificed for you, I am your devotee), and each time he confirmed that everything was well, the other raised his eyes to the heaven and punctuated this with an "alhamdolellāh" (Praise God).

All this, even though we were running late and we could already hear the percussion instruments played by the *morshed*, the music master, who was finishing marking the first exercise program. One of the oldest men made a sign to enter and stood near the door to invite the others to go first: "Āqāyān befarmā'id! – Aslan, na, shomā befarmā'id" (Gentlemen, you lead! No, never, you lead the way!). It was clear that Abbās and Hasan had to go in first, followed by myself, as their guest, but we remained another one full minute outside the door, some even having to have their elbow playfully grabbed so they would accept not to go in last. This was about knowing how to insist or persist just enough to show that, between equals no one is *bi-adab* (ill-mannered), and being temporarily placed before or after others does not prevent one knowing that it was not the recognition of a definitive social hierarchy but, instead, the result of the will of the group that also marks a recognition of social etiquette which is considered good and fair.

Although, among friends, *ta'ārof* is often the opportunity for ironic banter, it must nevertheless not be taken too lightly. One day, I observed the following scene: a young *morshed* who had not been able to mark "the forms" in the zurkhāneh for lack of experience and who had rather nonchalantly neglected to greet an old well-known athlete, was made to pay the price. The group agreed that he had been "very impolite." As the group was on its way to attend a funerary meal in a restaurant after the session, a friend alerted the young *morshed* to his disgrace. In front of the restaurant door, with worried eyes and embarrassed tones, he expressed his respect to all the members of the group (there were fifteen of us). In his ostensible repentance before all the other members of the zurkhāneh (some of whom could not repress a smirk) he insisted to enter the restaurant last of all. As a minor punishment, the members of the group did not once seek to have him go before them through the door, although ordinarily a *morshed*, even a young one, is always worthy of respect and recognition. He was entirely non-existent for the whole evening and no one spoke to him, until the group once again extended their consideration by including him in the general discussion. Nothing was said, but the message was clear and well understood.

A space of integration and discussion ...

Back to my first visit. We therefore bent our heads to pass through the small doorway of the zurkhāneh, and then, having left our shoes in the small space dedicated to this, we pulled back the heavy curtain that separated the entrance hall from the main room and, interrupting the session, made our appearance to a frenetic drum roll and bell ringing, amidst acclamations and resounding "salavāt" (repeated three times): "Allāhoma salla alā Mohammad va āl-e Mohammad!" (Greetings to the Prophet Mohammad and his descendants).

The *morshed*, the music master, was a white-haired old man, seated on the podium, the *sardam*, to our right. There was a *zarb*, a large goblet drum made of stretched hide and terracotta (rather than wood) lying across his knees, and within arm's reach, hanging above his head there was a little bell, the *zang*. He was bare-chested, but wearing a *long*, a traditional garment, red with dark stripes, folded lengthways and draped across his shoulder like a Highlands Scot. He nodded his head in welcome, continuing to signal our entry with a fast drum roll accompanied by several chimes of the bell. The session had been well advertised, the front and the back benches of the zurkhāneh were full of regular attendees as well as certain "important people."

... where it is immediately clear who is who

The whole crowd, spread on both sides around the *gowd*, the exercise pit, rose to welcome us and shake hands in turn, or for those who were too far away, to bow slightly, with their right hands on their hearts in response to our distant salutations and gazes. We moved towards our seats of honor in single file between the first row of spectators and the octagonal pit in which the athletes, already out of breath, the *long* across their shoulders, launched a second *salavāt* in our honor. We went straight up to a white-haired, quite martial-looking man, who sat surrounded and immobile, sturdy in spite of his age. He kissed Hasan and Abbās, and then turned to me with a thunderous "Wie geht's mein Herr?" (How are you, Sir? in German) whilst energetically grinding my hand. I had just been introduced to "the Colonel," a former commanding police officer of His Imperial Majesty.

There was no need to explain who I was or what I was doing there, he knew it all already. He placed me and my interpreter friend Behnām to his right, Hasan to his left, and Abbās to the left of Hasan, so as to be able to talk more freely. The others were left to award each other the remaining positions of honor and were therefore subject to a new round of *ta'ārof*.

The hierarchy of the gowd

It was urgent that the session resume we had delayed it enough. The athletes who wanted to leave had had time to do so, but those who wished to stay to perform the program a second time had no intention of giving up their places to those who now wished to enter the pit. Indeed, as I understood later, many had in fact waited for our arrival to participate in the exercise program where the public discourses would be more important and everybody would be paying close attention. The best athletes had been waiting for this opportunity, but unfortunately the octagonal pit could not hold more than twenty of them. It was therefore necessary to make certain delicate choices according to precedence, without causing vexation, insisting that some consent to leave, and persuading others not to enter the pit. This was based on a combination of seniority, social status, and reputation (Figure 1). In this game, everyone was able to see where he stood in the esteem of others. On this occasion, there were no *seyyed*s (descendants of the Prophet) in attendance, and there was therefore no need to automatically cede them the place of honor under the *morshed*'s podium. The athletes, divided between the veterans who were in the pit and the young ones outside it, now began the game of humility. The best athletes in the *gowd* tried to occupy the least prestigious places out of humility, and their friends tried to pull them, smiling, into the place their status ordinarily conferred upon them. The same thing happened for the choice of the *miyāndār*, the exercise master, who stands in the middle of the pit. Someone had to be pushed, still smiling, into the center for him to accept to lead the exercises.

The athletes spread out in two semicircles in the *gowd* and the *miyāndār*, who was the most experienced athlete in his prime, took his place in the middle. Two semicircles were formed, rather than a full circle, even though ultimately the result resembled a circle, because the hierarchy of the group inside the octagon was organized as follows:

The most prestigious veteran of the group took the high status place under the podium, directly facing the *miyāndār*, who in turn faced the veteran and the *morshed*. Immediately to the left and right of the veteran the other athletes spread out in descending order of status and experience all around the semicircle toward the lowest-ranked place, that of the beginners who face the *miyāndār*'s back, directly opposite the position of the veteran. Thus, according to age, talent, and mastery of the sport, but also according to the identity of those who are present in the *gowd*, athletes will progress from place to place, eventually being able to aspire to the most coveted position in the middle. And perhaps one day, God willing, an athlete might claim the place of honor if he lives long enough to have spent more than forty years in the *gowd*, after which he can aspire to the title of *pishkesvat* (a title that comes from the Sufi tradition) and the position directly in front of the *sardam*. The road to this title is long; the individual must live an exemplary life and have an immaculate *āb-e ru*,[12] (honor), and have a perfect mastery of technique

---

12. This notion, which comes back often in all kinds of expressions in Iran, is translated by "face," literally "water of the face." We will come back to this as it is a key notion relating to a person's honor.

What the World of the Zurkhāneh Remembers

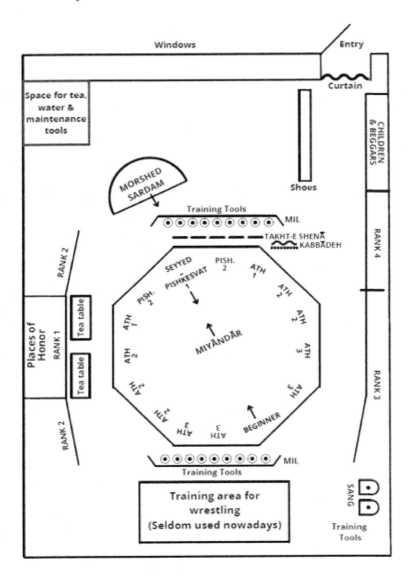

Figure 1. Organization of hierarchical and material space within a traditional zurkhāneh, in this case the Zurkhāneh Jam in 1994. The hierarchy of participants within the *gowd* is based on birth/title (*seyyed*) on age (*pishkesvat* first) and on sportive skill (all the other athletes from the best to the beginner). All of them face the *miyāndār*, the leader of the exercise, and the *miyāndār* looks mainly at the *morshed* to coordinate rhythms. The hierarchy within the audience ranges from the most important seats (rank 1) to those designated for the beggar, the wandering sufi, or young children (rank 4).

as well. As a result, the *pishkesvat* is by custom the guardian of tradition and moral authority.

The *miyāndār*, who had finally taken his position in the center, did not begin the exercises without having asked the others, out of simple protocol, to replace him, and having asked the notables present in the room for the permission to begin. "Rokhsat...? Rokhsat...? (Authorisation?) – Forsat! (This is the moment!) Akbar Khān! Befarmā'id! (Akbar Khan, please proceed!). Clearly the Colonel was losing patience with these politeness rituals and made a brusque gesture with his hand. For our benefit, the *miyāndār* made an unusual demonstration of the *sang* (stone) exercise in the middle of the *gowd*. This is a preparatory exercise that is ordinarily done before entering the pit. The athlete lies on his back, a small pillow under his head, and alternately raises a pair of wooden shields (Figures 2 and 3) that can weigh between 25 and 50 kg each. One shield is raised towards the sky, while the other is parallel to the ground, and then vice versa.

Two men on each side watch over him, while the *morshed* begins the countdown of the movements, forming a melodic litany, and marking the tempo for the athletes to follow. The exercise is done with the legs raised above the ground. Arms, shoulders, chest, and abdominal muscles are all put to a severe test. Normally a friend sits alongside, but on this occasion the role was performed by the *morshed* himself. Once the demonstration was finished, it was time for the exercises. Each athlete took his *takht-e shenā* (literally "swimming board"), which consists of a small wooden board (Figure 4) resting on the ground with two small feet, and lay down to begin several series of stretches on the ground, with numerous variations requiring serious mastery of one's breathing. The *morshed* had chosen to open the exercise program by accompanying his rhythm with a poem by Hafez, then he continued with two poems by Sa'di.

Limited equality

While we watched the athletes and listened to the *morshed*, the Colonel raised his voice to be heard: "Here we are all equals! We are all friends!" If that was so, I wondered, why had Hasan stopped me from shaking hands with an old man a few minutes before, telling me not to shake hands with just anyone? I asked the Colonel, who burst out laughing, openly declaring that the zurkhāneh was a place where people looking for forgiveness or help could come and find or beg for help or support, according to the status of each person. However, the man with whom I had wanted to shake hands was "bi sar-o-pā" (literally "without head and feet," meaning insignificant) Someone in that situation had to behave respectfully and not sit next to the places of honor, but instead near the door and the shoes. There was equality, but only between those who recognized each other as equals. Here, in this room of some sixty people, the equals were sitting in the ten seats of honor.

The Colonel emphasized the fact that those who were in the wrong could find advice here. "Black and white do not exist. All men are grey. Do you know why these men

What the World of the Zurkhāneh Remembers 21

Figure 2. *Sang* exercise. Generally, the assistant close by murmurs a count for the movements, from 1 to 50, then from 50 to 1, and finally from 1 to 17 (Zurkhāneh Tālechi, Tehran, 1995; photo Philippe Rochard).

Figure 3. *Ta'ārof*: "Rokhsat? Forsat!" (Zurkhāneh Honar, Tehran, 1996; photo Philippe Rochard).

Figure 4. *Shenā* exercise with *takht* (Zurkhāneh Nur, Tehran 1994; photo Philippe Rochard).

all respect me? Because I put half of them in jail myself! [gigantic guffaw of laughter]. Him! He got five years!" He pointed out an athlete in late middle-age, still bearing the *tāj*, the imperial crown tattooed on his chest, and a warrior's head on his left shoulder. He told me later that it was a tattoo of Nader Shah Afshar. The Colonel continued, "The one over there, he got ten years for murder! They paid their price, we have to forgive them and help them so that they do not return to those ways; in the zurkhāneh we can give them advice."

The Colonel remembers

We sat beside a large bowl of fruits, drinking piping hot tea – which is sipped scalding from the saucer with a cube of sugar in one's mouth – and eating lots of small cakes, while watching the exercises. The Colonel explained that men like him came to the zurkhāneh to maintain relations and hear the news. This was very useful for him in his work, whichever city he was posted to. I asked him why he chose to be a police officer. His response was sincere, direct, "so I did not die of hunger! I did not have much when I was young, just my daring." He explained how he had had his first moment of glory in the zurkhāneh when, as a young captain, he had unloaded several bullets from his revolver into the ceiling to replace the sound of the bell and drum roll that the *morshed* had been slow in sounding in his honor. He was still laughing about it forty years later, as was his old friend, the retired commander sitting at his side. This was all confirmed to me later on. The Colonel had been much feared and was still very respected. He said, "I always only just passed my exams and I would have nothing today if it was not for my wife's fortune." Like all Iranians of a certain social class, his son wanted to study in America, but, the Colonel recounted, "I told him I forbade it! He is Iranian, not American!"

Later on, in the weeks that followed, the Colonel willingly explained his role in the police, without having much to fear, "because all that is in the past." After a long posting in the Chāleh Meydān district, and then several positions in the provinces, particularly in Zanjan and in Hamadan, he had been appointed to the censorship bureau of the police where he had worked in collaboration with Mahmud Ja'fariān, a former member of the communist Tudeh party who flipped and joined the shah's regime. A former ideologue of the Resurrection party, *Rastākhiz*, the single party created by the shah in 1975, Ja'fariān was one of the senior managers in television and also worked in the censorship office. He was shot a month after the victory of the revolution.

What the Colonel wanted to reveal to me about his last position, which he presented as a simple routine, consisted in positioning his informers in all spheres of life, from the bazaar to small businesses. They would strike up discussions over drinks, identify possible leaders, contact them, frighten them, arrest them, and "flip them" so they became informers in turn. At the time, he was able to count on the support of some religious figures, even those opposed to the regime, because they considered the Marxists to be atheists, *bi-khodā*, which was much worse than being a royalist. He was also able to count on the help from the zurkhāneh athletes close to Sha'bān Ja'fari, former protector and main intermediary between the zurkhāneh and the representatives of the imperial court between 1963 and 1979. Ja'fari had become a "national celebrity" because he had been involved in the assault on Prime Minister Mossadegh's house during the 1953 coup d'état, which was organized by royalist officers and the CIA. As the Colonel put it, "we worked to break up any assembly," their targets being union leaders, or more simply, anyone who was unfortunate enough to be demanding anything.

Sometimes the police had a bit of fun. When an important person had to come into the bazaar for some reason or other, the Colonel and his men had to make sure that all of the bazaaris along his path were wearing ties, which were provided if necessary. The bazaaris were lined up and reviewed to check that their ties were properly knotted, and to ensure that, the Colonel and his men would even put their hands around the bazaaris' necks, which was humiliating for the latter. The bazaaris and the policemen sometimes had to remain in place for several hours, and then, once the illustrious personage had left, the ties would be collected. However, to pass the time while they were waiting, the police officers sometimes obliged them to kiss their hands to see if they would do it properly when they had the illustrious person in front of them. They were obliged to do this several times while repeating after the officers "for the love of the shah and fear of the soldier!" The smallest sign of rebellion was punished with a slap on the face, regardless of age or seniority, and that was enough to smother any attempt of protest. The Colonel's voice changed depending on the anecdotes. This one had been told with no illusions, a nod of the head and a dry little laugh, which left no doubt as to what he thought. The forces of order that he represented believed themselves untouchable, the idiots ... and look where they were now.

How had he survived the purges and lynchings of the first months of the revolution? I did not dare ask him. He had simply been given early retirement, without any other form of trial. Many had suffered much worse for much less. Why had he survived? The answer came several days later, when I understood to whom (apart from the Colonel) I had really been introduced that day.

For the moment, the athletes were finishing their exercises with their wooden boards, and moving onto the stretching exercises, and continuing with the *pā zadan* (literally, foot stomping, kicking) (Figure 5). These exercises involve alternating more or less rapid running movements, knee bending, and high kicks to the side or in front, always to the rhythm of the *morshed*'s drum. The central figure, the *miyāndār*, turns around so that all of the athletes, particularly the novices, can see him and from time to time he gestures to the *morshed* to indicate changes in rhythm, and then the end of the exercise (Figure 6).

The pause that followed was the opportunity for the *miyāndār* to launch a *salavāt* in honor of the *morshed*, which was taken up by the audience, among whom the youngest tried to make their voices heard above the others. "Dast-e shomā dard nakoneh!" "May your hand not hurt!" This expression is used every time you thank someone for serving you something. The athletes got their breath back and the *miyāndār* took the opportunity to show that he was well brought up and not *bi-adab*, by honoring the memory of the elders, living or dead. He also used the time to address a particularly insistent greeting to somebody in the audience – but why? We did not know, but I learnt later, at my own expense, that receiving a compliment from the octagonal pit could be a particularly delicate thing to manage. It could be a simple thanks, a sincere homage, a polite gesture of welcome; but it could also be an implicit request for service, "I have honored you, now help me."

After the sword, the turban. All the notables finally present

The pause was not yet finished when the *morshed* suddenly released a drum roll on the *zarb* and a series of bell rings that heralded the arrival of someone of great importance. I could not yet see him, but the man was clearly a most distinguished guest because those who were seated on the other side of the *gowd* with a view of the door suddenly stood and were already calling out a resounding *salavāt*, though we were not even able to see for whom it was meant. The Colonel, who had been informed some five minutes previously by someone in the crowd, was not surprised and, without a word, gestured for me to stand. A man wearing a large *abā*, the traditional brown garment of the *mollā*, along with the black turban worn by *seyyed*s entered slowly. His bearing and quiet dignity

What the World of the Zurkhāneh Remembers

Figure 5. *Pā zadan* exercise (Zurkhāneh Soleymāniyeh, Tehran, 1996; photo Philippe Rochard).

Figure 6. The *miyāndār* signals to the *morshed* to change the rhythm (Zurkhāneh Soleymāniyeh, Tehran, 1996; photo Philippe Rochard).

were striking. Leaning on his cane, the towering man, bearded and grave-faced, accepted with a friendly gesture the marks of respect from the athletes and certain members of the audience. They kissed the back of his right hand, which bore a single ring of silver adorned with a *kahrobā-ye siyāh*, a piece of jet.[13] Having soberly shaken hands with the Colonel (because that was whom he had essentially come to see) he sat to his left and did not seem to pay the least attention to the fact that the whole line of spectators had to reorganize themselves as a result. Hasan preferred to stand rather than to be retrograded. Some who had been waiting near the seats of honor tried to move closer to those they had something to ask of, but there was no point. The brothers and the Colonel had this ability, common in constantly solicited notables, of moving their gaze above and beyond people without noticing their presence in spite of the ostensible attempts of the latter to attract their attention. The gaze of those who had not been noticed remained tense, desperately waiting for the moment in which they could make the connection. I observed that each of them, Hasan and the Colonel, had noticed and listened to a single person in the session in this way, but no one dared approach the *seyyed*.

The man who had served us tea hastily returned with a platter bearing a *manqal* filled with embers on which he had tipped several generous handfuls of *esfand* (wild rue or Syrian rue, *Peganum harmala*, Figure 7). With a fan, he directed the thick and acrid white smoke emanating from the *manqal* towards each spectator. The *seyyed* drew the smoke towards him with the traditional gesture performed at the end of the *do'ā*, the invocation, sweeping both hands from the top of his face to the chin; this gesture was imitated by most of the others present.

The reason for these fumigations was both to cover the odor of the athletes' sweat and to honor those present by performing this act of purification and protection. Wild rue seed is considered a *nazar cheshmi*, it has the power to ward off the evil eye. It is burned on many occasions, including religious festivals; as it burns, it makes a noise like a small firecracker. Still in their shells and strung on threads ornamented with colored shapes, these same seeds also constitute talismans to protect houses. *Esfand* has this virtue because it is the first plant to grow at the end of winter. Its Persian name comes from the twelfth and final month in the Iranian solar calendar.[14]

---

13. According to my friend and colleague Eve Feuillebois-Pieruneck, this stone is not worn all the time because it is also considered to bring bad luck. Following the ancient principle that bad combats bad, this stone is also called *moshkel goshā*, that which "unties the knots of problems," and it is used, for example, when undertaking administrative matters.

14. Henri Massé, who quotes Pietro Della Valle, the Spanish ambassador attending the court of Tamerlan (1336–1405), thus describes the *esfand* festival of 15 February, clearly pre-Islamic, and now no longer celebrated. "As soon as it began to emerge above the ground, they began their solemnity, which consisted of a large number of torches and candles, that they kept alight in their shops all day until the following night, for a mark of celebration that they had made it through winter" Pietro Della Valle (III, 116) in Massé 1938, 162. This seed is also used in several traditional medical decoctions. See Jozani 1994, 143, 155, 207.

What the World of the Zurkhāneh Remembers

Figure 7. Warding away the evil eye, honoring the audience, and masking the smell of sweat by burning *esfand* on hot coals (Zurkhāneh Soleymāniyeh, Tehran, 1996; Photo Philippe Rochard).

A very small inheritance: the consequences of the clauses of a vaqf[15]

Many days later, as I was familiarizing myself with the functioning of the zurkhāneh, I was surprised to learn that the man serving the tea and burning the *esfand* was the son of the (late) founder of the zurkhāneh. Should he not have been sitting with the notables then? Alas for him, no. A few years before his death, Mir-Ashraf had sold half of the business to the *morshed* of the Zurkhāneh-ye Jam. The latter owed a perpetual debt to Shaʿbān Jaʿfari because it was thanks to his protection that he had obtained a position that he had held for the rest of his working life. The *morshed* had invested part of his savings in it. In Iranian law a property is divided into six parts, or *dong*, so there were only three parts left for the Mir-Ashraf family. When he died, each of his children inherited one *dong* each, which was not much revenue in total. Transforming the building into a warehouse – as was the case for many provincial zurkhānehs – would have increased profits tenfold. However, a clause in the will obligated the recipients to continue the same activity at the zurkhāneh for forty years and a municipal decision pronounced by the mayor of the time, Gholām-Hoseyn Karbāschi, prohibited zurkhānehs from being sold for any other purpose. This pushed the "unfortunate" co-owner to try and use the only clause that in either case allowed him to change the activity of the zurkhāneh:

15. A donation in the context of religious law, similar to the idea of "mortmain."

Figure 8. "An old lion is still a lion»," a *pishkesvat* aged 94 (Zurkhāneh Kāshefi, Tehran, 1994; photo Philippe Rochard).

bankruptcy. For this he first had to ruin the zurkhāneh, which he came close to doing, but the *morshed* who had much more at stake and had no desire to change the activity, got wind of the maneuver. No one knows how the matter was resolved between them. The inheritor was not taken to court, but from then on the *morshed* took control of the accounting ... and the inheritor began to run around serving tea to the guests.

Jāvdānegi, the dream of immortality ... [16]

But I did not know any of that yet. I was still contemplating my first vision of the exercise room. Hundreds of photos were hung on the wall. They were divided into three

---

16. I thank my dear friend Amir for suggesting this title.

groups. In the place of honor, in direction of the kibla (*qebleh*, the direction of Mecca) were the usual portraits of the supreme leader of the revolution (Iran's head of state) and the president of the republic, which also hung in all shops. Just below them were photos of several religious dignitaries, and then there were photos of the athletes, the most illustrious *pahlavān*s, first among them Gholām-Rezā Takhti, whom we will discuss in more detail later on. Below that there were countless photos of the athletes, all generations combined, all connected to memories of the people present in the room: photos of groups of friends, some no longer of this world, and athletes who had become *pishkesvat*s; those who died on the battlefront, as twenty-year old *shahid*s (martyrs), young athletes whose loss was felt even more cruelly because they represented the hope for the future of this aging traditional sport that often referred to itself as a dying art. I do not remember a single zurkhāneh in which I was not shown – with lengthy explanations – the portraits of the athletes, and the feats of the most famous among them, the proof that great *pahlavān*s had frequented this zurkhāneh, and the links that bound some of them to each other (Figures 8 and 9) In certain zurkhānehs, the photos provided more information about the friendships and rivalries at work there than any number of interviews would have been able to.

Figure 9. *Jāvdānegi*, the old *pishkesvat* in Fig. 8, is immortalized on the wall (Zurkhāneh Kāshefi, Tehran, 1994; photo Philippe Rochard).

... *transformed into the burden of proof*

These photos were severely narrowed down during the first months of the witch-hunt after the revolution. The photos of the shah, the shahbanu (empress), and the crown prince, were all taken down and replaced with those of the new leaders. In 1994 Khomeini, Khāmene'i, and Rafsanjāni were on display, one triad replacing another. The photo of the former boss of the zurkhāneh world, Sha'bān, was also removed. The only photos of well-known men from the pre-revolutionary period that remained were those of Takhti, who was displayed in all the zurkhānehs, and more rarely the famous mafia boss Tayyeb Hājj Rezā'i. The rare athletes who accepted to talk to me about the revolutionary period all told me the same thing. Surprise raids by revolutionary authorities, all looking assiduously for proof of collusion with the regime. All the photos in which athletes were receiving medals from or shaking hands with state officials could be considered proof of sympathy towards the former regime. Moreover, under the shah, sporting organizations were most often run by military figures, and having their photos in your possession invariably had a negative impact. Zurkhāneh athletes suffered in this respect because of their reputation as royalists, which was due to the famous figure of the zurkhāneh, Sha'bān Ja'fari, who was notorious for having collaborated with the regime. The Islamic left, particularly the Mojāhedin, were the most ferocious. They were the ones with the most scores to settle with the world of the zurkhāneh. So all these photos were destroyed, along with any documents or certificates that bore the signature of Sha'bān or any other general, not without regret because it was tantamount to amputating a piece of memory, and watching the proof of a particular victory disappear forever. Some could not bring themselves to destroy them and instead hid them, even buried them, and quickly put others in their place. One of these in particular was a photo of former "strong men" close to Sha'bān, who had gone to the pains of being photographed alongside Ayatollah Khomeini when he still lived in Qom.[17] Nearly twenty years later, I was shown all those that survived the cataclysm, as so many treasures and testimonies from "before."

Even tattoos on the body could be considered proof. The imperial crown could be a sign of a support of the famous *tāj* football club, but it could also be seen as an unacceptable mark of loyalty to the old regime. Tattoos such as this were therefore removed using acid from car batteries, which leaves a visible scar but enables the bearer to avoid this kind of accusation. Nevertheless, there were a few in the *gowd* of the Zurkhāneh-ye Jam sporting a tattoo on their chests or arms – kings, soldiers, or women, and for one of them, the only imperial crown that I had the opportunity to film in four years.

A traditional way of doing things

No one in the group of athletes, the *varzeshkārān*, of the Zurkhāneh-ye Jam performed the difficult *mil bāzi* (literally *mil* play) exercise (Figures 10 and 11). This consists in juggling two, three, or four wooden clubs, while performing pirouettes, leaps, and other acrobatic movements, and is most often performed by a lithe young acrobat in the tradition of the acrobatic *luti*s. The men in the pit on that day were older, nearing the end of middle age, and the novices were still too inexperienced. The age group from twenty-five

---

17. Photo published in the newspaper *Rokhsat Pahlavān* no. 1, Sunday 11th, (Khordād 1376/May-June 1997): 3.

What the World of the Zurkhāneh Remembers

Figure 10. *Mil bāzi* traditionally performed with two six-kilo *mil* (Zurkhāneh Sherkat-e naft, Tehran, 1996; photo Philippe Rochard).

to thirty-five years old was missing in this zurkhāneh. Agility exercises, which were increasingly popular in the zurkhānehs in Tehran were not in the "house style." Here, the athletes focused on *sangin* (slow and heavy) exercises, and did not necessarily admire those who jumped around all over to get on television. The *varzeshkārān* therefore directly picked up the *mil*s, the massive stone-shaped clubs used for muscle training, each weighing between 6 and 12 kg, the heaviest up to 16 kg (Figures 12 and 13). They rested the ends of these clubs on their shoulders and at the signal from the *miyāndār*, the *morshed* began reciting a poem by 'Attār Neyshāburi (ca. 540–618 h.q./1145–1221). In rhythm with the recitation, they raised the clubs, alternating from one side to the other, sweeping in an arc from their backs to their chests and back again, sometimes with more complicated movements over the shoulder. This lasted a certain time; the *morshed* had stopped chanting and was simply marking the rhythm with a long deep muffled note.

Figure 11. *Javānān* and *mil bāzi* with four *mil* (Zurkhāneh Sherkat-e naft, Tehran 1996; photo Philippe Rochard).

Then, suddenly, he rang the bell and the rhythm accelerated. The clubs reacted instantaneously and were swung higher. No one in the room was talking anymore. The drum beat the rapid rhythm of perfectly coordinated movements. The massive bodies, and the ease of this gesture that thrust these forty *mil*s, each weighing over 4 or 5 kg, into the air over the athletes' heads as though they were made of straw, was indeed a fascinating sight to behold. The spectators were awed, respectful, and silent. This lasted a full minute, while everyone held their breaths. The *morshed* sounded the end of the athletes' performance by ringing the bell three times. "Māshāllāh!" (What God has willed!).

The *varzeshkārān* and the *morshed* were covered in sweat. The audience was manifesting its admiration and pleasure in various ways. They proclaimed the glory of the *morshed*, the athletes, the *pishkesvat*s, the *pahlavān*s; they proclaimed the glory of the

What the World of the Zurkhāneh Remembers

Figure 12. *Mil gereftan* exercise, Tehran, Zurkhāneh Honar (photo Philippe Rochard, 1996).

Figure 13. *Mil gereftan* exercise, Tehran, Zurkhāneh Kāshefi (photo Philippe Rochard, 1996).

miyāndār, who in turn thanked those who had thanked him. The Colonel then made a speech, invoking the memory of the *miyāndār*'s father, whom he had known well. The audience then greeted the Colonel. One of the athletes, the one with the imperial crown on his chest who had been to prison, a man with broad shoulders, bald head, and a white beard, who was over sixty and potbellied, then leaned out of the *gowd* and in the middle of the general hubbub unceremoniously asked the Colonel for money, pronouncing a single word: "pul!" (cash!) rubbing his fingers together in an unmistakable gesture. Thus solicited by one of his former informants, the Colonel was clearly obliged to lean forward to listen. The man said that he wanted to take a new wife, but that the dowry, *mahriyeh*, was high. The Colonel made an exclamation in a voice that was half-amused, half-irritated and then diverted his gaze from the man, indicating with hand gesture that he had heard enough.

Those pouring the tea served certain athletes who were still in the *gowd* and then distributed the *long*s (towels) so they might dry off. The break was going to last. The Colonel took the opportunity to introduce me to the prestigious cleric, *seyyed* Emāmi. This worthy religious figure agreed to answer a few of my questions. After completing his religious studies in Najaf, Irak, where he learned and practiced traditional sport, he was for a time in the service of Imām Musā al-Sadr,[18] before returning to Iran. At that time, he only rarely came to the zurkhāneh, but when he had learned that the Colonel himself would be there on this occasion, he wanted to attend. After my meeting with him, we did some research and I understood who he was. A former sympathizer of Fadā'iyān-e Eslām, the *seyyed* was from a family that had given several militants to this radical Islamic group founded in 1940s by Navvāb Safavi.[19] His family was responsible for two assassinations, that of the judge Ahmad Kasravi on 11 March 1945, and that of the minister of the imperial court, Abdolhoseyn Hazhir, on 4 November 1949.[20] The Colonel was an old friend of *seyyed* Emāmi and it occurred to me, watching them laugh-

---

18. Musā al-Sadr (1928–1978) was a Shiite theologian born in Qom, and a disciple of Muhsin al-Hakim (the spiritual leader of all Shiites from 1961 to 1970). In 1959, this charismatic leader replaced Abd al-Husayn Sharaf al-Din al-Musawi at the head of the Lebanese Shiite community. In 1974 he founded the Movement of the Disinherited, and officially recognized the Shiite militia *Amal* in 1975. His activism was not to the liking of all, and he disappeared between Libya and Italy in 1978. See Ajami 2012.

19. For the events of this period (history of the movement, its program, their victims) see Richard 1985.

20. Ahmad Kasravi was born in 1269/1890 in Tabriz. He was a historian, a legal scholar, a distinguished linguist and a fervent defender of the modernization of Iranian society, founder of the journal *Parcham* (the Flag) and the journal *Peymān* (the Pact). He was the first enthusiastic partisan of the systematic substitution of the Persian vocabulary with the Arabic vocabulary in the Persian language. See Mo'in 1981, 1577. His goal of promoting a new rationalist religion (*pākdini*), made him into an apostate and thus a target. Abdolhoseyn Hazhir, who had been a parliamentary minister several times, as well as prime minister was shot in front of the Sepahsālār mosque during the Āshurā ceremonies. For more details see, "28.000 days of the history of Iran and the world," supplement to the journal *Ettelā'āt* (Tehran: Ettelā'āt, 1355/1976), 870–871; also Mehdiniā 1373/1994; as well as Richard 1985, 30–31.

ing softly together, that they probably helped each other before and after the revolution. Two survivors. They could be on opposite sides and understand each other, they could be religious or military and still drink their tea, go to the zurkhāneh in the same way, and speak the same language. It was a simple question of the rules of the game, manners, and philosophy of life. The Colonel politely avoided my allusions to this possibility and strongly advised that I decline the *seyyed*'s invitations; he knew him well and considered him dangerous.

Public speaking, a matter of precedence, specialists and experts

The break between the *mil* exercise and the main event of the program, the twirling or spinning movements, was too long and lunchtime was calling the men and their stomachs back to their duties as the heads of households. Many had people waiting for them for the midday meal. The master of ceremonies therefore transformed the break into the final speech. Then we proceeded to the *do'ā*, the invocation of the Prophet Mohammed, Imam Ali, and his son Imam Hoseyn, and ended the program with rotation exercises and the *kabbādeh*, a huge metal bow.

It was the *miyāndār* and two veterans who had the honor of making the final speeches in honor of everyone. These things were not decided in advance, their order came about naturally depending on the context and the audience. There is an element of personal responsibility when someone decides to speak publicly and thereby attract the attention of all. If those who are present are mentioned, the speaker must be very careful to respect the hierarchy, the oldest first, then the most deserving, then the next most and so on until the last person. The very fact of being in the *gowd* at seventy years old is a testimony of merit in itself. It is proof that lions are lions even when they are old. The public is called upon to witness this and certain high-status people can respond, which the Colonel, Hasan, and the *seyyed* did several times. In fact, the man making the speech is also honoring himself as much as those he is praising, because he is demonstrating the extent of his manners and breeding and his in-depth knowledge of the reputation of people of worth, all of which consolidates his listeners' favorable opinion of him.

People who are not sure of themselves do not dare to make public speeches such as these. Only twice in four years did I hear speeches that did not make their point. Of course, this delicate task is broadly facilitated by the audience, which does not expect personal reflection from the speaker, but rather the demonstration of his mastery of the genre or particular themes. A balanced tribute is the mark of the great orator, as much as is its style. An audience of connoisseurs of such speeches will listen more to speakers they know will provide a good performance.

There are signals in the speech that rely on a series of conventional phrases that express unwavering unanimity as to appropriate behavior in life and before death. We must act wisely "down below" because everything will be tallied "up above." The older the listeners are, the more this speech is serious, the names of the dead are mentioned, old athletes and friends whose memory is honored. They pray for the sick, the old, those who are in need, and the martyrs of the war. They recall the statements of Imam Ali on different subjects, such as ingratitude for example, drawn from the *Nahj al-Balāgheh* (The Way of Eloquence), the book of sayings attributed to Imam Ali. The metaphors and themes are sometimes chosen for their double meanings, and those in the audience often hunt for these subliminal messages with a secret contentment and discreet smiles.

The *morshed* thanked the last speaker and asked the public to give a *salavāt* in his honor, which was also the signal of the ends of the speeches and the beginning of the *doʿā* in itself. On this occasion it was *seyyed* Emāmi who led it, but it could also have been the *pishkesvat*, the most renowned, or another notable persons in the audience. He recited the invocation, punctuated by the listeners' powerful *Āmin* (Amen) in response. We all turned towards the direction of Mecca, and then in the direction of the mausoleum of Imam Reza in Mashhad, hands held up to the sky, and the *seyyed* called the audience to pronounce another *salavāt*.

The athletes who needed to leave then bent down to touch the ground before bringing their hands to their lips in a sign of respect for Imam Ali, to whom the sacred ground of the *gowd* is dedicated. They put their street clothes over the top of their workout clothes, and took their leave, carefully saying goodbye to everyone they had to. Everything was said in five minutes this time; meetings were arranged, services to be rendered were confirmed, promises were made, and affairs were settled.

The spinning exercises: the moment of truth

Those who remained began their spinning exercises after the same ritual of humility and the same requests for authorization as described above (Figures 14 and 15), except that in the spinning exercises the most *inexperienced* athletes have to go first, for which reason the most experienced, out of politeness but without insisting much, pretend to want to go first, only to be held back. In fact, it is important not to go too far in one's insistence, because some facetious athletes enjoy not holding someone back if they go too far in their protestations of humility. This situation can become delicate when several athletes of the same status and age who are not connected to each other or who belong to different circles of friends find themselves face to face. Without anything being explicitly said, a good *miyāndār* can judge in a few seconds who should take precedence to avoid an embarrassing hesitation. Someone might accept to be the first to start the exercise, but not if they have the impression that the exercise master took too long to make his choice!

In any event, this task immediately dampens ambition. The athletes whirl around themselves with arms outstretched, quickly or slowly, including one, two, or three jumps in the center of the *gowd*, or following a circular trajectory in the pit. This has been the main event of the training session since traditional wrestling is no longer taught here. A legacy of traditional Sufi practices, it is the moment when the athlete demonstrates his self-control, even as he is subject to the forces of vertigo and imbalance.

What the World of the Zurkhāneh Remembers

Figure 14. *Charkhidan* medium speed (Zurkhāneh Nur, Tehran, 1994; photo Philippe Rochard).

Figure 15. The *pishkesvat* corrects the position, the arms were too low (Zurkhāneh Nur, Tehran, 1994; photo Philippe Rochard).

The exercise depends on the athlete's choice of slow or rapid spinning, according to his temperament, age, and body type. It will be judged on grace and harmony with the rhythm of the drum, the posture of the body, which should be strong, and simply the ability to remain upright and not end up on the ground or in the arms of the other athletes, with apologies or laughter depending on the case. In a single moment, it represents the act of integration and evaluation of each athlete within the *gowd* and the group. They challenge and compare each other in joking terms, among friends, or more cruelly and mockingly if there are antagonistic groups present. For example, throwing a towel at an athlete who is not elderly and who was not successful in his spinning exercise is a message that he was not good and should be ashamed, which the recipient never appreciates. When the two exercise masters of two antagonistic groups are obliged to share the same pit for training (which generally everybody tries to avoid), there is a subtle confrontation, which all are immediately sensitive to. I once observed someone simulate a violent pain in the ribs to avoid the humiliation of defeat and save face, without anyone being actually fooled by this.

Invariably, the athlete who fails to complete his performance places his hands on his head and closes his eyes with his head bowed as a sign of ostensible repentance for the *morshed* and for his friends. If the athlete is very elderly, he does not turn but instead makes a figure called "the last step" which allows him to go to the center of the *gowd* and demonstrate a certain skill. The spectators then applaud him lavishly as does the *morshed*, while two athletes then move towards him to accompany him back to the edge of the *gowd*, putting a towel around his shoulders to honor him and avoid any loss of face (Figures 16 and 17). Once again, the spectators were waiting for several athletes who created a sensation by forming a sort of spinning column with arms outstretched horizontally and head upright, so fast their faces were a blur; and yet their movements perfectly coordinated to form a perfect circle.

A gift in parting, as honor commands

In the middle of our lengthy departure, with many ovations and thanks, no one forgot to leave a small sum of money in a cup for the purpose, equivalent to what honor demanded each give. Some people were exempt from payment or participated only symbolically, young people who were not yet established or those in need; but it was the duty of the breadwinners and the notables to leave much more.[21] The *morshed* thanked each of the generous donors, ringing the bell for everyone who had been particularly generous, or to announce the exit of the veterans, the *pishkesvat*s. As the people were leaving, two athletes who were still in the pit took up the great metal bow, the *kabbādeh*,

---

21. The cup, placed within reach of the *morshed*, is covered with a plate, upon each athlete places his money, as honor dictates; for a fraction of a second it remains on the plate before the *morshed* sings a praise (proportional to the donor's generosity!), the plate is tipped, and the money falls into the cup, which is covered by the now-empty plate, so that the next person will not know how much the previous person donated.

What the World of the Zurkhāneh Remembers 39

Figure 16. The veterans honor: *pā-ye ākhar-e pishkesvatān* (Zurkhāneh Honar, Tehran, 1996; photo Philippe Rochard).

Figure 17. To honor him, two athletes cover him with a long and accompany him to the edge of the *gowd* (Zurkhāneh Honar, Tehran, 1996; Philippe Rochard).

which is strung loosely with a chain ornamented with metal discs that make a deafening noise when it is shaken in rhythm over their heads as the exercise dictates. This tool, the vestige of a training exercise for archers, is now the prerogative of certain particularly muscular athletes who have made it their specialty (Figure 18).

Figure 18 *Kabbādeh* exercise (Zurkhāneh Kāshefi, Tehran, 1996; photo Philippe Rochard).

Our time at the zurkhāneh was finished but the outing was not over. Hasan invited us to a restaurant with the Colonel. A good dish of *ābgusht* was waiting for us on Rey Avenue. Breakfast for these athletes is generally eaten early in the morning, often a *kalleh pācheh*, a dish made from the meat of sheep's head and trotters accompanied by cooking stock, with slices of unleavened bread. However, lunch was *ābgusht*, a traditional invigorating and flavorful dish, reputed to be "hot" according to the canons of ancient Galenic medicine still widespread in Iran. The dish is made from potatoes, lentils, chickpeas, and the meat and fat from a sheep's tail. The broth is drunk and then the pulp is mashed using a pestle (a *gushtkub*) in a bowl (the *dizi*, which is another name for this dish). It is eaten accompanied with slices of *sangak* bread, baked over hot stones. Today, Coca Cola and Fanta are often drunk with the meal, as an alternative to the traditional *dugh*, a yoghurt drink diluted with water and mixed with spices. The whole meal is accompanied with numerous glasses of tea, drunk with a cube of sugar between the teeth, *labriz o labsuz o labduz* – a tea that "overflows, burns, and sews lips together" [with its bitterness].

Once served, the meal is eaten in silence. Happily, the concept of a frustrating business lunch, which prevents one from eating correctly or appreciating one's food does not exist in Iran. More tea was brought, along with *pulaki* from Isfahan, sugar discs perfumed with lemon or saffron in the form of coins. They also brought the *qalyān*, a hookah or water pipe filled with Iranian tobacco from Qamsar or Kashan, less expensive and stronger than the fruited tobaccos from Egypt or Bahrain. Once it had been set up, the men took out their own mouthpieces to smoke, and as I did not have one, a plastic one was found for me. The discussions left off in the zurkhāneh could now begin again, to the sound of the gurgling of the pipe and the smoke that contributed to sweet post-prandial lethargy. All around us, and at our table, there were old men wearing hats, who fingered their prayer beads in silence, staring at a point in the distance, puffing on tobacco and listening – in a way that was both pensive and disconnected – to an old friend whom it was impolite to interrupt or to look at directly. Then we took leave of each other, which was much like the greetings but slower and more peaceful. It was already hot and time for a nap.

Asking too many questions would have been unbecoming. Three questions maximum would fit in a discussion like this, and rarely on more than one subject at a time. The reconstruction of the history of the Zurkhāneh-ye Jam and the discussion of a time when this zurkhāneh was one of the last "realms of memory"[22] in Tehran therefore took place through several private discussions on many days, which unfolded in the same way as the one I have described. In these conditions, an anthropologist has to forget certain protocols, like questionnaires or audio recordings. When I thought about my university courses and lectures, I had to laugh. I had to commit to memory as much as possible, braving the effects of opium and/or alcohol, and once I returned home at night, after a cold shower, quickly transcribe everything I had heard or understood, impressions, and ideas, before collapsing into sleep. My mentors and these athletes had introduced me to a world where passion reigned supreme.

The extraordinary in the ordinary

In connection with the zurkhāneh, I very quickly had the opportunity to discuss pigeon fancying, another passion shared by many athletes but about which they remain

22. As used by Nora 1997.

discreet, with good reason. The members of the zurkhāneh have often been stigmatized for this hobby (*kaftarbāzi*), suspected of climbing on the flat roofs of their houses to spy into neighbors' gardens and thus threaten the honor (*nāmus*) of women, or accused of preferring to feed their pigeons rather than their children. Generally, it is a hobby associated with men of a bad sort, with low morals, but the reality is quite different.[23] Pigeon fancying and the traditional sport of the zurkhāneh are both masculine passions, often carved out of periods of hard work. They are moments of personal or collective pleasure, in a system that does not value such things, although it does not prevent them. I will explain this in more detail, but for now it is important to note that the practice of the traditional sport is often frowned upon by the immediate entourage of the athletes, and keeping pigeons even more so. The hobby and its attendant competitions are organized by a group of volunteers, who are also often criticized by their friends and family. Their wives in particular consider this an unproductive expenditure of money, energy, and time, to the detriment of the family. Both the pigeon keeper and the zurkhāneh athlete are aware of the fact that they do something not everyone does. However, of the two, it is the pigeon keeper who is really considered the outsider, although the two occupations make up a world that takes pride in being different from others; those who have broken out of the mold, who cannot be hoodwinked.

Although most of the men who keep pigeons simply take pleasure in seeing their birds fly at sunrise and sunset and accept the practice of "capture and keep" (during flights, any pigeon lured can be permanently captured), others organize races with bets to be won. These bets are not based on chance, which would be contrary to Islamic law, but rather based on the consideration of the animal and its qualities, which supposes an exercise in reasoning and thus allows the gamblers to declare their bets to be entirely lawful. However, for the religious authorities of the holy city of Qom, this argument is only accepted for horse races, which were relaunched in 1997, allowing Iran to save its national and private stables, which were then facing bankruptcy. The richest pigeon keepers therefore rent villas temporarily for the specific purpose of organizing these competitions. The pigeons are released far to the southwest of Tehran and return to the city, and there are various expert techniques to allow the judges to tell whether the animal has in fact covered the distance. Unfortunately the new extension to Mehrabad Airport and its security zones cover the areas used for traditional competition, which mitigates the pleasure somewhat and is a threat to the safety of the pigeons. Bets on these races are substantial, and 1 million *tumān* (equivalent to $3000 in 1994) does not raise an eyebrow. The way I collected this information led me to understand that things are not generally stated explicitly. As was the case for the speeches in the zurkhāneh, the subtle art of implication and innuendo is clearly another major aspect of Iranian culture, and I would have to get better at it. Soon an opportunity presented itself.

23. Goushegir 1997.

The art of understatement

In the course of our conversations, we also talked about business and the way the notables of the zurkhāneh traditionally operated. For example, on one day the Colonel introduced me to a man he presented as a real estate promoter renowned for being a generous benefactor. Glad of the opportunity to talk to one of the private financiers of the zurkhāneh, I naively asked the Colonel if he could arrange an interview for me with him, and after quite a lot of hesitation, he accepted. Through Hasan, who controlled all my contacts in the zurkhāneh, he told me the date and time of the meeting. The discussion would take place after the meal following the training, as usual. The man's name was Changiz, and he was mischievously known to his friends as Changiz Khān – because he was a Turkman, from the northeast Iranian region of Torkaman Sahrā. He was a little over sixty years old and carried a *tasbih* in his hand. Small and potbellied, with a three-day old stubble, he was a respectable revolutionary. His shoes were broken at the heel to be able to remove them more easily for prayer. His voice was high-pitched, characteristic of those who treat their rheumatism by smoking the oldest medicine Iran has to offer. In his style of dress he was identical to the most humble athletes in the room. The only sign that he was really "important" was that he remained immobile in the midst of a whirlwind of people at his service. In the exercise pit, he had obtained the coveted place of *miyāndar* without contestation. However, after the meal, I understood that I was not going to be able to ask any questions. The "interview" consisted in a ten-minute monologue. He was asked to explain to me what the traditional sport *varzesh-e bāstāni* was and in response he gave me a lecture on Islam, Shiism, morals, and Imam Ali, from whom *fotovvat* and *javānmardi* stem.

The Colonel was also listening to the speech. I noticed that he was extremely cautious, preventing me – by a discreet pressure on my knee – from interrupting Changiz, or from asking any questions. He could not repress a smile when Changiz looked him in the eyes for a quarter of a second and then recited a verse from Sa'di as an example of the poetry that could be recited in the zurkhāneh:

> Be pir-e meykadeh goftam keh chist rāh-e nejāt ?
> Bekh^vāst jām-e mey-o goft rāz pushidan

> (The old man in the tavern was asked what is the path to salvation?
> He took his cup of wine and said, "keeping secrets")

He continued by saying, "the principle of discretion and not revealing the secrets of others is one of the qualities of God, who we know is also *Sattār al-oyub* (concealer of faults)." I noticed that the Colonel could not help smiling a little. We took our leave and I understood that I would not see him again – but I did not stay disappointed for long.

In the car that took us back home, one of Hasan's friends who had come with us exploded angrily, "he's playing at being a *pishkesvat*, that *pedar sag!*" [son of a dog]. If Changiz was so rich, powerful, and respected today it is because of him, Ahmad, who did not get anything in exchange when the wheel of fortune turned! It was he who allowed Changiz to enter the zurkhāneh, who introduced him to the right people, taught him to hold the exercise tools, and protected him when others had wanted to take advantage of a chubby-cheeked, beardless young man. He took out a photo in support of his claims – proof if ever there was one – a sepia photo of him protectively holding the shoulder of a young, bare-chested, and chubby Changiz. The Colonel consoled him by saying he could be proud of having remained an honest man.

Changiz indeed came up from nothing, but he was noticed in the zurkhāneh and that allowed him to join the service of a notable from the bazaar. At the beginning, he had to run around in the service of others in the bazaar, but once he had got some money together, he went into business. Thanks to his connections, after the revolution he became a *besāz o befrush* (one who builds [houses] quickly and sells them), which, in Iran generally and in Tehran in particular, is an unmistakable byword for corruption. The recipe is simple for anyone with money and the means to control all elements in the construction business system. Having paid off people in both state businesses and administration, the *besāz o befrush* first obtains construction materials – at state prices – for his project, a housing development, for example. Rapidly built by underpaid Afghan workers, who are protected by no legislation or control, the development is then sold on the private market and he makes 300% profit off it in one go.

But in a world of sharks, only those who bite the hardest survive. Changiz built his reputation by liquidating one of his rivals, Abbās Mohājer, a *luti* from the Darvāzeh Shemirān neighborhood, with his own hands in 1960. He served nine years in prison for it, but that had not prevented him from continuing his business from his cell. As the Colonel tells it, his guards did not know what to do with the sheep heads and opium that his friends kept sending him, and which he liberally distributed among prisoners. That is why hearing him talk about morality produced a smile. I understood much better why Changiz could not refuse the "invitation" from the person who had arrested him – and of course his choice of poetry. In the zurkhāneh, the understated is understood.

Even though he now frequented the zurkhāneh in the north of Tehran, in the old villages in the foothills of the Alborz mountains that were now part of the city itself, Changiz remained faithful to his origins. Although his business affairs were now in the provinces and in Farmāniyeh, one of the more affluent areas of the city, he still returned to his original neighborhood to look for recruits he could trust, primarily from among the athletes, but not Ahmad.

Changiz never failed to attend the *golrizān*, the "flower giving" festivals organized primarily during Ramadan. This festival of solidarity and goodwill (which we will discuss in detail in chapter four) enables the community of a zurkhāneh to come together to help someone in need who is considered worthy. However, for Changiz and others, *golrizān* is also the opportunity to thank friends and show a certain generosity. Thus, unlike the *kot-o shalvāri*s (literally, suit wearers), young entrepreneurs who are easily recognizable by their Western dynamic, close shave, sunglasses, mobile phone, and a brand new 4WD or Mercedes, Changiz remained true to tradition. He continued to eat his *kalleh pācheh* in the morning, dress like his employees, and finance a religious association for the Āshurā festival. He was also meticulously careful to avoid attracting attention or provoking rancor. When underhand affairs and arrests broke out among the *kot-o shalvāri*s (a prelude to the corruption controversy surrounding the city hall, which served as a pretext to bring down the mayor of Tehran, Gholām-Hoseyn Karbāschi, who had been instrumental in the election of the newly elected president Khātami) it was generally accepted that these figures had been altogether too visible. Changiz, on the other hand, had (according to the most recent accounts) managed to slip under the radar and continued to do business with the municipality with full impunity, to obtain his interest-free loans without difficulty[24] – and "play at *pishkesvat* in the zurkhāneh."

Recalling a Bygone Era

Three emblematic figures

Of course, as the Colonel said, the world of the zurkhāneh was not all black or white. Yet the interviews I obtained with the veterans, the *pishkesvat* from the Zurkhāneh-ye Jam, and/or my contacts over the four years of my study, systematically mentioned three very contrasting figures, who had each in his own way marked the world of the zurkhāneh in Tehran from the end of the Second World War until the 1979 revolution. These were the mafia boss of the 1950s and 60s, Tayyeb *Hājj* Rezā'i, the head of the zurkhāneh establishment at the time of the shah, Sha'bān Ja'fari; and the legendary wrestling champion, Gholām-Rezā Takhti. The latter cannot be compared with the first two, but they all lived at the same time and were important for the people of the zurkhāneh, as well as all Iranians who remained connected to activities and lifestyles that respected the norms and values of traditional society. This is a triptych of exceptional destinies that provide a complementary perspective on how public opinion considers the life choices of men who followed the path of strength.

Today Takhti and Tayyeb in particular are subject to a discourse regarding *javānmardi* which should be moderated somewhat. Although Takhti was undoubtedly a *javānmard*, a good man, the same was not true for Tayyeb, far from it. Behavioral ethics cannot dissociate the essential distinction actors make between which actions are "good" and which are "bad" within a given society; between what is inspired by faith and the *javānmardi* and what stems from the idea men have of the simple virile values, *mardānegi*, and the outward signs of power. Yet as I learned from Hasan, and above all Abbās, that Tayyeb's memory was very connected to the Zurkhāneh-ye Jam, I set out to understand why.

---

24. On the interest-free loan societies, see Adelkhah, Bayart, and Roy 1993, 26–27.

Places and men

Although the Zurkhāneh-ye Jam was built relatively recently, in 1963, its past dates back to the 1930s, when a wealthy trader in Tehran known as Asghar Shāter-Rezā, deemed a sympathizer of the pro-Nazi SUMKA Party, founded one of the most important zurkhānehs of his time, the Zurkhāneh-ye Shāh-e Mardān. This club, which was frequented after the Second World War by Tayyeb and his brothers, later came to be known simply by the name of its last owner, Mir-Ashraf. It was located in *Anbār-e gandom*, Wheat Silo Avenue, in the heart of what would later become Tayyeb's territory. Asghar Shāter-Rezā thus hoped to be able to promote his ultranationalist ideas within the bazaar and recruit men for him and the SUMKA.[25]

Asghar Shāter-Rezā, himself an athlete and a *mashdi*, who sported a Hitleresque mustache and had no reservations about tackling his opponents in a knife fight, had many commercial investments, as wide ranging as bakeries, butcher shops, taverns, and cabarets on Lālehzār avenue, where many theaters were located. In 1941 he had been persuaded to finance a newspaper, *Mard-e emruz* (Today's Man), which expressed very violent opinions. It is said that this financial support proved fatal. Several witnesses from this era, including a member of Mir-Ashraf's family, told me that Asghar Shāter-Rezā was said to have been assassinated by men connected with the Communist party. My subsequent research revealed, however, that there may have been confusion in the memories of those who told me about this assassination; as I was not able to find a reliable primary source on this point, it is difficult to tell. Although they do not strictly refute the information, former journalists in the Iranian media of the time reminded me that the only assassination connected to *Mard-e emruz* was that of its chief editor Mohammad Mas'ud, which had been carried out in 1947 by the men of Khosrow Ruzbeh, the leader of the armed wing of the Tudeh, Iran's Communist party. Mas'ud was a particularly virulent journalist, who was regularly banned from publishing. To get around these prohibitions, he used the authorization of publication of existing newspapers, which he bought up for this exact purpose. The murder of the chief editor is well remembered, that of the financial backer not, but the one does not rule out the other.[26]

25. I would like to thank the descendants of the Mir-Ashraf family and of the former SUMKA members for the interviews they gave me. Pursued by the Russians between 1941 and 1946 many former members of SUMKA owed their survival to the auxiliary anti-Communist roles they played at the beginning of the Cold War.

26. When I revisited this issue, which I had not dealt with since 2000, I became aware of another account of this, collected by Sinā Mirzā'i from Hesām Dibā'i, indicating Asghar Shāter-Rezā's date of death in 1333/1954 (at the age of thirty-eight, wealthy (unmarried?) and without an heir), which does not mention a link with the SUMKA and which includes another name for the newspaper associated with him, *Mard-e peykār* (The Fighting Man). Whom should we believe? In my opinion, perhaps everyone. Mohammad Mas'ud's editorial practices can easily explain the difference in the titles in the witnesses' memories, given that Mas'ud successively bought up the rights of many newspapers before he was killed in 1947. The death of Asghar Banā'i (the real name of Asghar "Shāter-Rezā," this last name being that of the tutelary figure of the family that Asghar liked to use as a nickname) is by no means clear but it still raises the possibility of the responsibility of Iranian communists and we can reasonably

The attempt to implant national socialist ideology in Iran through the zurkhāneh was no accident and corresponded to a policy of control in certain neighborhoods (Figures 19 and 20). The SUMKA and the Tudeh did not limit themselves to expressing ideas. They also controlled whole streets that functioned as borders, which it was not a good idea to cross if you were "on the other side." The Tudeh also had its influence in certain zurkhānehs, in particular the Zurkhāneh-ye Pulād ("steel," in reference to Stalin) and the ideological war was mirrored by humiliation and a bloody knife war in the streets of Tehran. The *mahalleh*s (neighborhoods) became territories to be won, in the pure tradition of Middle Eastern and Iranian urban factionalism.[27] SUMKA members were implanted in Hedāyat and Safi Alishāh Avenues (where the headquarters were), Bahārestān, Shāhābād, and Sa'di (not far from the German Embassy), while Tudeh members remained close to the Soviet embassy on Ferdowsi and Nāderi Avenues, where they frequented the famous Café Naderi, which is still open today. The allies of the SUMKA controlled Ekbātān Avenue.

The two militant groups were therefore only separated from each other by Eslāmbol and Lālehzār Avenues. The latter was officially neutral but known for leaning towards the Tudeh. It was the site of most of the city's theaters and cabarets. Rival gangs constantly challenged each other on the pretext of political opposition and sought to extend their influence towards the south. But as they did so, they came up against the bazaar, the fief of Ayatollah Seyyed Abolqāsem Kāshāni,[28] who would play a major role after the Second World War, in the era dominated by Prime Minister Mossadegh in the early

---

wonder if it was not an assassination. Indeed, all accounts converge on the fact that his lifestyle, from the mid-1930s and 1940s, was extremely violent, even by the already fearsome standards of Tehran's street gangs. He was truly feared by all and described to me as "a former staunch SUMKA supporter during WWII." The photos and description of Asghar Shāter-Rezā published by Mirzā'i show a man from two perspectives: either as a man who is extremely well-dressed, with gold buttons on his shirt of expensive cloth, driving one of the first cars in Tehran (a man from a traditional background, but from a rich, religious, and well-educated family); or as a bare-chested fighter in traditional wrestling dress (a sport that he mastered to perfection), sporting a Hitler-style mustache, quite common but in direct competition with "Stalin"-style mustaches from the 1930s and 1940s. Both accounts present him as wanting to play a role in political life via the ownership of a media outlet that provided a platform for his populism and virulent anti-American and anti-British ultra-nationalism, which was the bedrock of the SUMKA during the war, but also of many people at the time, including Mohammad Mas'ud. He continued this fight against those who did not share his opinions, in the street with the men of his zurkhāneh. This is all coherent and plausible, as is the claim he was assassinated after the overthrow of Prime Minister Mossadegh. The hypothesis of communist vengeance against Asghar Shāter-Rezā is unverifiable but still plausible, particularly if, as I suspect, Asghar Shāter-Rezā fought for the shah in 1953, contrary to what Hesām Dibā'i claims. Indeed, Tayyeb and his brothers were already frequenting the zurkhāneh of Asghar Shāter-Rezā in the late 1940s and early 1950s. So how can we believe that a man such as Asghar kept away from the events of 1951 to 1953? In any event, the case remains to be clarified. See Mirzā'i 1381/2002, 45–49 and throughout.

27. An interesting point of comparison can be established with the work of Michel Seurat (Seurat 1985).

28. Seyyed Abolqāsem Kāshāni (1877–1962), the leading political cleric during the critical period of 1941–53. See Rahnema 2012,.

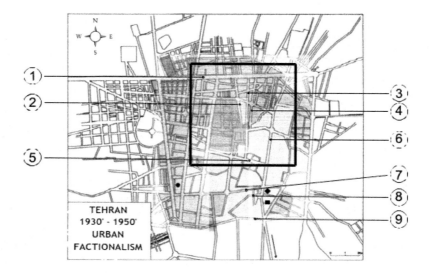

Figure 19. Asghar Shāter-Rezā against Khosrow Ruzbeh hypothesis. Urban factionalism between ultra-nationalists *luti*s (and former partisans of the SUMKA after 1945) and the Iranian Communist party (Tudeh).

① Shāhrezā Ave.; ② Ferdowsi Ave.; ③ Lālehzār Ave.; ④ Sa'di Ave.; ⑤ Buzarjomehri Ave.; ⑥ Sirus Ave.; ⑦ Mowlavi Ave.; ⑧ Bāgh-e Ferdows Ave.; ⑨ Shush Ave.; ● Shahr-e Now ; ◆ The fruit and vegetable market ; ■ Zurkhāneh Shāh-e Mardān/"Mir-Ashraf."

1950s. Eyewitnesses from that time tell us how on several occasions they saw the SUMKA brownshirts running after the whiteshirts of the Tudeh, arresting them, and symbolically cutting off their red tie (when they were party intellectuals) or unceremoniously shaving off their mustache (which Tudeh members generally wore "à la Stalin"). There were scissors and razors, and other more murderous stories. The assassinations of Mas'ud and, perhaps, Shāter-Rezā are part of this same pattern of urban guerrilla warfare.[29]

With Asghar Shāter-Rezā dead, a young cousin of the family, Seyyed Ahmad Mir-Ashraf, managed part of the inheritance on behalf of one of the aunts who had inherited the zurkhāneh in 1954. After he had taken it over for himself, he sold it in 1963 (we will see later that the date is no accident) and exchanged a house for another freshly built zurkhāneh, the Jam. Thus, up until 1963, the veteran athletes whom I met at the Zurkhāneh-ye Jam in 1994 had all frequented the Mir-Ashraf, which was near Tehran's wholesale fruit and vegetable market, the Meydān-e miveh va sabzi, near Amin al-Soltān Avenue.[30]

29. Behzādi 1998, 186–87.
30. The most detailed chapter I could find on the *Meydān-e miveh* is the excellent second chapter of Adelkhah 2004, which overlaps well with the testimonies collected by Sinā Mirzā'i in 2002. However, I do not share her conclusions on Tayyeb's status as a *javānmard*.

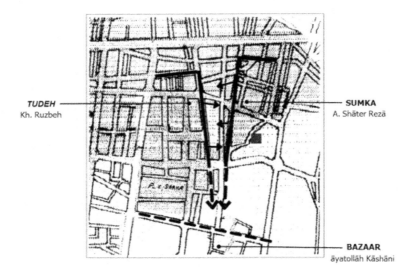

Figure 20. Asghar Shāter-Rezā against Khosrow Ruzbeh, a conflict extending towards the south, Tehran bazaar, fief of Āyatollāh Kāshāni and Tayyeb's area of influence? ■ *Mard-e emrouz* newspaper, Ekbātān Ave.

The fruit and vegetable market in Tehran

This market square, created last century on land given to the city of Tehran by Prime Minister Amin al-Soltān, was a particularly sensitive place, where massive financial interests went hand in hand with the roughness of manners of the laborers working there tirelessly. This place was regularly disrupted by quarrels between traders and would-be racketeers.

Although people from the market went to the bazaar, they also went to the Shahr-e now (New Town), the district surrounded by brothels and shifty cabarets more to the west. There, imprudent farmers could lose most of the income from their market sales in just a few days of drinking, transformed into entry tickets bought in advanced and demanded by the brothel madams before entering the rooms. These "rough" neighborhoods were full of drunken men, people selling pigeons and organizing animal fights, gambling, murders and account settling, theft and looting, swindling, and generally people of "ill repute." Here the police was just another actor on the stage, with whom there could be negotiations, calculations, or even alliances.

Indeed, like all badly paid police forces in the world, they could be temporarily bought. One of the well-known maneuvers to acquire a rival territory was to come to an arrangement with the police officers so that the rival gang leaders were arrested for a few days or a few weeks, just enough time for the other gang to levy the racketeering and replace them. Then one of two things would happen: either the other group recognized the change in situation once they were freed, in which case negotiations were held to find an honorable resolution and a new distribution of territory, or the whole neighborhood had to prepare for a heavy-handed, violent response from the ousted gang. The Colonel thus told me that one day, when he was still a young captain, there was a kind of score settling involving Tayyeb that had put him in an uncomfortable position and forced him to hurriedly obtain an audience with the mafia boss to explain and excuse himself, because the latter thought that he had been defrauded by his enemies and that the Colonel was complicit, which was not the case. The simple idea that Tayyeb may have doubts about one's intentions was enough to make anyone tremble, even police officers.

This in-between world remains rough in the southern neighborhoods, in the bazaar and the fruit and vegetable market area. There was a lack of a strong power figure after the Second World War, and therefore the market became a battlefield between rival gangs, to the detriment of all legal business. It was this precise context that saw the beginning of the remarkable rise of Tayyeb.

In 1946, one of the most influential men in the Meydān, Zeyn al-Ābedin Arbāb nicknamed "Hāji Meyduni," called on Tayyeb Hājj Rezā'i (1912–1963), known later simply as Tayyeb, to get things in order. According to Fariba Adelkhah, who wrote the first serious study on this mafia figure, Tayyeb had made a name for himself for his authority among the lorry drivers of Kermanshah. Our *gardan koloft* (roughneck) hero did not let him [Hāji Meyduni] down and asserted his pre-eminence over the whole market in a short time.[31]

Hāji Meyduni awarded Tayyeb the right to tax all products that left the marketplace. This took place when the products were weighed for sale on the gigantic scales (*qapān*) at the Meydān. Among other things, this money paid for keeping Tayyeb's men in the network of loyalties that he needed to consolidate his power. Tayyeb's brother, Tāher, who was a very good zurkhāneh athlete, provided a direct link between Tayyeb's faction and the sport that provided many of his henchmen.

Friendships were therefore created during this period between Tayyeb and Mir-Ashraf, who became one of his many henchmen. When Tayyeb took control of the big scale, struggles for influence in the south of Tehran and in the Meydān became ferocious because he was contested. Tayyeb was clearly aware, as Sha'bān would be later on, of the importance of the loyalty of Mir-Ashraf's men. They were vital to him in the different fights he had to engage in, particularly against the Yakhi brothers, who were his first real opponents, or against the butchers' corporation, whom he could only control by taking the daughter of one of the most influential bosses in this powerful group as his first wife.

Those who worked in the butcher shops were well-fed, used to blood and death, and handy with a blade; they provided not only the best athletes in the zurkhāneh but also a formidable power in the streets of southern Tehran. It was not an accident that

31. Adelkhah 2004, 39.

Pahlavān Mostafā Tusi, one of the most famous *mashdi*s of Tehran and the first president of the new VBKP Federation created in 1979 was also the owner of Tehran's abattoirs.

During my interviews with athletes, they remembered and recounted epic battles. When Tayyeb was extending his sphere of influence, he drew on the Mir-Ashraf boys in fighting the formidable *luti*s from the city of Rey, which provided the capital's fruit and vegetables. These *luti*s also worked in that city's markets and had developed remarkable combat techniques with the wooden beam of the scales they carried on their shoulders. Other memories were invoked as well, without a precise date but somewhere in the 1950s, of fearsome men wielding metal studded clubs, who forced Tayyeb to negotiate an alliance after a week of tension and two days of bloody battles during which the headquarters of both gangs were set on fire and during which the police did not dare show their faces. Butchers, athletes, and other strongmen were constantly at the ready to fight those who would later regularly attempt to carve a little fiefdom for themselves out of Tayyeb's empire. In any event, this is how the history of the mafia connected with the history of some of these veterans, athletes, or notables who were close to the Zurkhāneh-ye Jam. It is also important to note that although zurkhānehs can be closed, sold, or exchanged, groups of athletes will not dissipate as easily. They migrate, with all their possessions, photos, and equipment, to a new locale when the old is no longer accessible or frequentable. Contrary to popular belief, there is hardly any attachment to the zurkhāneh itself. It is the group that matters.

Tayyeb's story is thus one of a rapid ascension under the protection of a major boss of the Meydān, an almost uncontested decade-long reign with the favor of the shah, and then a brutal fall in 1963. This was the last time the streets had a master with such power, one with whom the authorities could only "deal" and whom they could not dispose of, until the revolution. During the crisis surrounding the nationalization of the oil industry under the authority of Mossadegh, between 1951 and 1953, Tayyeb and another man were to become famous in the world of the zurkhāneh. Sha'bān Ja'fari, nicknamed the "*bi mokh*" (The Brainless), played a role that gained them royal favor when Ayatollah Kāshāni, who protected the Fadā'iyān-e Eslām, broke away from Mossadegh and sent a signal to those with interests in the bazaar that everyone was free to do as they chose.

Tayyeb and Sha'bān, who had both defended Mossadegh's side against the police in 1951, were only looking after their own interests and, knowing they were covered by Kāshāni, sold the support of their men to the shah's faction, who would return in the subsequent military coup d'état. They were responsible for providing popular support for the ruler, organizing "spontaneous demonstrations," and participating directly or indirectly in the repression of those in the bazaar who still dared to support the Jebheh-ye Melli (National Front, Mossadegh's coalition), even forcing it to close, officially as a sign of protest against Mossadegh. On the day of the coup (28 Mordād 1332, 19 August

1953), Shaʿbān was used by conspirators to distract attention,[32] particularly by leading a procession of cars filled with his entourage, his *nowchehs*, parading around the town with the portrait of the shah held high.

When I asked the Colonel why the men of the zurkhāneh had not supported Mossadegh, he (who was perfectly Anglophobic and pro-Mossadeghist like many of his generation) gave me an explanation that summed up the situation: "how long had Mossadegh been in power? Three years! How long had kings held power in Iran? Three thousand years!" Ultimately the risks associated with being on the losing side were much too high to be militant and publicly affirm one's ideas. Loyalty to the imperial regime also took this kind of power relations into account. In working-class and commercial worlds like the bazaar and the fruit and vegetable market, politics was and remains extremely concrete. Political ideologies and the ideas of advisers, who are not ultimately those who pay, remain largely ignored.

Once Mossadegh had fallen, Tayyeb and Shaʿbān were rewarded by the royalists. Tayyeb obtained a monopoly over the market for banana imports, which was a luxury fruit at the time, and this swelled his fortune considerably. As a master of scales in the market, he could dictate minimum and maximum prices, and generally it was his products that had to be sold first. Each year during the gigantic Āshurā festival commemorating the martyrdom of Imam Hoseyn in Karbala, which brings tens of thousands of people it to the street, the procession (*dasteh*) of his religious association was the largest of all, his giant gilded standard (*alam*), was the most beautiful, the heaviest, the biggest, and the highest. His *dasteh* of self-flagellating mourners always went to the Sepahsālār (today called Motahhari) Mosque, where a member of the imperial court was waiting to bestow a prize sash upon him in great pomp, a mark and signal to all that royal protection was renewed. Tayyeb was the strongman of the poor districts. His business prospered and allowed him to invest his sometimes illegally obtained wealth in various legal business activities, selling coal, which was essential for bakers and heating, and even buying a soap factory. No one dreamt of standing in his way or refusing to sell what he wanted to buy. He lived according to the morality of his world, often paying for everyone and building his reputation in the working-class districts by distributing firewood to the poor and demonstrating his great generosity during the Āshurā festival. Ultimately, as a good *mashdi*, he did what honor demanded according to the importance one has or ascribes to oneself.

According to witnesses interviewed by Fariba Adelkhah, "Tayyeb became so dominant that his worst enemies became his friends,"[33] and that by replacing the police he imposed a fairer law. The reality is much more sordid, and more than one of Tayyeb's opponents was found hanging from a butcher's hook, or in the early morning with their belly open in a *jub*, one of the wide gutters that run down Tehran's streets. However, it

---

32. See Abrahamian 1985. Abrahamian talks about an "acoustic diversion" in Abrahamian 1982, 141. See also Nejāti 1985.

33. Adelkhah 2004, 40.

is true that he did impose a "law" – that of his interests – and that he knew how to rule the streets. For example, a famous young hoodlum named Mohammad *por ru*, Mohammad the impertinent, who used to attack people in the street when he was drunk, was summarily executed by Tayyeb, much to the general relief of the population. However, he was only eliminated because he had made the mistake of not paying his gambling debts. Tayyeb himself had to face several assassination attempts, but the way in which he reacted to the first really serious one decisively cemented his reputation:

> Tayyeb became known by that simple name after his victory against the Yakhi brothers. At the time, Tayyeb was young and under the protection of Hāji Mayduni [...]. The latter, who was fond of him, gave him the right to collect one *rial* from all the loads that came through the market doors, the *darbāghi*. Hoseyn Ramazān Yakhi and his brother Taqi came to Tayyeb to ask for their "cut of his cut," and because he refused, they decided to assassinate him. He was followed on his way home, and on the Bāgh-e Ferdows (near Amin-ol Soltān Avenue] Tayyeb was stabbed twice in the back by Taqi Ramazān Yakhi himself. He was left for dead in the *jub* but was then taken to hospital, where he was healed and saved (paid for by Hāji Mayduni). When he left the hospital he took his vengeance himself [he killed Taqi with his own hands and Hoseyn abandoned the fight]. The incident was widely talked of and after that no one dared to contest the *darbāghi*, and he became simply "Tayyeb."[34]

There was no police, nor anyone else; Tayyeb took his vengeance himself, just as Taqi had undertaken to murder Tayyeb without delegating it to anyone else, or at least that is what the tales say. Thus, money, a concrete reality which was systematically denied by all of my interviewees, but which is unavoidably central and a silent motivation, can be seen implicitly in many of these tales. However, it is not enough to gain respect and be obeyed, as Fariba Adelkhah notes in her remarkable chapter on Tayyeb, it was also a question of having the right style. A leader had to be protective and generous, but also fast and implacable. The poor neighborhoods received firewood for free, money spilled from Tayyeb's hands and fell around him as from those of a monarch, a figure who must be a source of abundance. Yet does this constitute *javānmardi*? No, clearly not. It might be called munificence. As Paul Veyne reminds us, "an expression that is too calculated, that aims for the target, misses its effects. True greatness must not skimp, it must flow in overabundance."[35] The attributes of power and might of the master of Tehran's underworld were hardly different from those of the American mafia bosses of the 1930s.

Someone who had first-hand experience of that world and who wished to remain anonymous confirmed to me that:

---

34. Interview with Abbās Āqā.
35. Veyne 1988.

With Tayyeb, it was money, brothel women, gambling, alcohol in drinking houses, and the strength of the *nowcheh*s of the zurkhāneh. That is why he was respected. When he decided someone needed to be removed, it was simple: they arrived with six or seven men, two or three immobilized the victim, Tayyeb was given a knife, he cut him open and then gave the knife to one of his men. That man would go to prison in his place and he would not talk, and all would be done to get him out as quickly as possible, while also ensuring that his family wanted for nothing. Afterwards, he was found a job, and he and his family had nothing more to fear.

Tayyeb owned illicit cabarets and gambling dens where clients had to pay to enter. This allowed him to recoup in the evening what he had given to *bārforush*s (wholesalers) in the morning. His best agents were often the prostitutes who worked for him. One of them, nicknamed "Fari Siyāh," was responsible for gutting one of the butchers from the Jewish community of Tehran who had refused to pay the *bāj*, the racketeering money demanded by Tayyeb. None of Tayyeb's men could get close to such a well-guarded target. The corporation that managed the Kosher butchers and the gangs of Jewish *luti*s, which protected the Iranian Jewish community in Tehran, also had their own specific zurkhāneh, the Hammām Khānum. Fari Siyāh took advantage of the fact that no one would suspect a woman, and she was able to get close to the target, eviscerate him, and escape. The man survived, but the message was sent, Tayyeb was able to set up negotiations. For many, Fari Siyāh's intelligence, her courage, and her loyalty, made her the equal of the men who believed themselves *mashdi*. She was like one of the famous women *ayyār*s of the epic stories.

However, it would be deeply unjust to suggest that the zurkhānehs as a whole were places of ill repute. They were just like the rest of society: there were some with good reputations while others were more shady. The social fabric of the working-class neighborhoods, overall, had to accommodate the "strong." Not being able to identify the source of real power was a source of danger for those who were unaware. Tayyeb and his likes could resolve problems that no public authority at the time was able to address. Thus, in spite of their criticism, the members of the local institutions, professional organizations, or sporting clubs entrusted themselves by necessity to him who could pull the most strings.

The creation of the SAVAK in 1957 was associated with a reinforcement of central power that was less and less tolerant of intermediary, independent, and mafia forces. This new institution never appreciated the *jāhel*s and *luti*s of the Meydān, and progressively acquired the means to take control and finally put an end to the sword rattling of the *jāhel*s who refused to submit to the police.[36] One of them was called Mostafā *divāneh* (Mostafā the crazy) to his back, and *Shirkhān*, the Lion King, to his face. When

36. Gölz 2018, and Gölz 2019. See also Rochard and Jallat 2018, particularly 236, notes 8–10.

he was called to the police station on a serious matter, he did not hesitate to rip all the imperial symbols of the lion and the sun off the wall, much to the bemused stares of the police officers, on the pretext that there was already a lion in the room and that was enough! This same man was also capable of bringing his mistress into the zurkhāneh and introducing her as his younger brother, to the horror of the *pishkesvat*, the *morshed*, and in blatant disregard for tradition and morality.

The veterans I spoke to told me that the world of the zurkhāneh was particularly turbulent at that time. Zurkhānehs were destroyed by rival gangs, there were battles between antagonistic *dasteh* processions during the Āshurā parades, a bar was ransacked because the cabaret singer had sung a satirical song mentioning the misfortunes of a man with a bald head and there happened to be a *luti* named *haft kachal* ("seven times bald") in the room who felt insulted. Although nobody really complained about the end of these exactions, the comments nonetheless conveyed a certain nostalgia for the agitation of these feelings of strength and recognition that were gone. *Those were the days.*

Those who had understood that things were changing quickly fell into line. The others practically all ended badly, through score settling, arrests, and in the first years after the revolution, summary trials and executions. For Tayyeb it all ended in 1963, during the demonstrations that followed the political and agrarian reforms of the shah known as the "White Revolution," to which the clergy was staunchly opposed.[37] On June 2, during Āshurā, Tayyeb's procession was moving along Bahārestān avenue in front of the National Assembly to cries of "yā marg! yā Khomeini!" (death or Khomeini!) amid crowds of people. The next day, the same cries were heard, but this time people were killed amid chases between policemen and demonstrators in the back streets of the bazaar. An athlete, Dāvud, who was young at the time, told me about his personal experience:

> My mother had told me to go look for my younger brother, who was a real idiot, who had gone there. Everybody was running, you could hear shooting and they arrested anyone wearing a black shirt…. So they arrested me too. They asked me if I was against the shah, I swore that I was not, they asked "so why are you wearing a black shirt?" "Āshurā'st digeh!" (But it's Āshurā!) I said. I had the idea of showing them the white buttons on a black shirt to show that I was really for the White Revolution. I was terrified. The soldiers burst out laughing and let me go with a kick in the pants. Which I passed on twice over to my brother when I found him."[38]

Rumor has it that Tayyeb had claimed it was he who had brought the shah to power in 1953, and that ten years later, he could undo what he had done. He was arrested and held responsible, along with his lieutenants, for the riots that had broken out in Tehran.

37. Ansari 2001.
38. Conversation with Dāvud, 23 May 1996.

His enemies saw this as a good opportunity to get rid of him. From that point on there are two different versions. Officially, the prosecutor offered him a deal, he could save his head if he declared that Khomeini had paid him to organize the riots. He refused, accepted death rather than falsely accuse Khomeini, and was executed.

After the Islamic Revolution, Ayatollah Kho'i, the most eminent figure in the Shiite hierarchy, awarded Tayyeb the posthumous title of "Hurr" (freeman), in reference to the man who defected from the Yazid camp to Imam Hoseyn's during the battle for Karbala. Ayatollah Khomeini, however, paid no public homage to him after 1979,"[39] which is perhaps a sign. So much for the golden legend that the current power holders would like to see endorsed in certain post-revolutionary publications.[40]

Another, less glorious version of the story, at least as far it is told in collective memory, is that Tayyeb did indeed use the 1963 protests to remind the governments that he had to be reckoned with, and far from supporting Khomeini for his program, he had thought he would be able to use him to his advantage. Between 1954 and 1962, the power of the state had been considerably strengthened, and it was less and less likely that it would consider the mafia boss as someone who had to be accommodated. Business had been generally very bad between 1960 and 1962, and in early 1963 there were arrests in the ranks of Tayyeb's mafia. He had not understood that things had really changed since 1953. Yet, even once he was arrested, Tayyeb felt invulnerable and did not believe for one second that they would dare to execute him. When the legal machine was launched, Tayyeb continued to deny everything, in one of the bouts of defiance he was prone to. He was waiting for the trial to become bogged down, or buried, but it was not. He was counting on the shah's pardon, as a memory of services rendered, but it did not come. It was finished, the street had lost its last great *luti* chief. Henceforth it would only have the right to provide servile informants to the police. They would be well served.

One of the reasons that many of Tayyeb's former admirers cursed Sha'bān Ja'fari was that he was partly (although wrongly) considered responsible for Tayyeb's death. Rumor, which always needs a script and has to reduce complex facts into a story that can easily be remembered, has it that he was the one who put Tayyeb's name forward as the scapegoat, which hardly seems likely. Anyhow, many note that when Tayyeb's empire collapsed after his death, Sha'bān took control of some of his rackets. All the public transport companies (like the Vahed bus company, to mention only the biggest, where he could mobilize nearly two hundred men, all from the zurkhāneh of the company), mechanics, taxi agencies, certain banks, and even administrative directors were gently encouraged to demonstrate their generosity and pay out more often than necessary. In 1953, the royalists had given Sha'bān land in his original district so that he could build the largest zurkhāneh in Tehran, but that was set afire in the riots of 1963. The standard

---

39. Adelkhah 2004, 36.
40. Tehrānchi 1985, 261.

analysis sees this as a protest against "the King's man." However, it might not be that. Others suggest that a gang of *jāhel*s, rivals to Shaʿbān, simply used the riots as an opportunity to burn his zurkhāneh so he would stop being *por ru* (insolent). But by presenting himself as a martyr to the royal cause, he was able to have his zurkhāneh rebuilt and paid for by the STB. He even received the supreme honor of the shah himself attending the first inauguration session, as he had done in 1954. In honor of the ruler, several hundred athletes performed an exaggerated welcome, lined up along the avenue leading to the zurkhāneh with cries of "zendeh bād Shāh!" (Long live the King!). Today, this zurkhāneh, now named Zurkhāneh-ye Shahid Fahmideh,[41] is the home of the VBKP Federation.

The head of Tehran's zurkhānehs

Shaʿbān Jaʿfari was born in 1920 in Tehran, in the working-class district of Sangelaj. Like all the young people of the period, he was not allowed to enter the zurkhāneh, even though his father and his older brothers were athletes. At age fifteen he finally managed to be admitted into the zurkhāneh Darkhungāh, which was one of the four most well-known zurkhānehs at the time, along with the Mirzā Mahmud, the Pulād and the Hammām Khānum. As we have seen, the Hammām Khānum was frequented, or even controlled by the Jewish community in Tehran's working-class districts. Later Shaʿbān founded his first zurkhāneh by renting a space in the small Kal-Abbās-Ali Bazaar.[42]

In 1944, during the only competitions of the *varzesh-e bāstāni* that have remained famous, he won the *kabbādeh* and the spinning competitions, exercises that no one dared to perform better in public while he was still competing, because doing so would have incurred his wrath. This accounted for his being known among many people as "Tayyeb's [female] dancer" (*raqqāseh*), which dates from the period when he was, according to them, just the *nowkar* (the vassal) of Tayyeb. Unlike the latter, Shaʿbān had organized his business more modestly at the beginning, receiving rent from several properties. After the events of 1953, he emerged as one of the major figures of the zurkhāneh. Royal favor made him the protector of a large clientele, who came to him in the hope of being noticed and finding work, and many of the old *morshed*s and the *pishkesvat*s owe their first job to Shaʿbān. However, he was not to the liking of all the athletes, who were not always happy with his ways of doing things. After the death of Pahlavān Hājj Seyyed Hasan Shojāʿat, known as "Razzāz,"[43] these athletes would have preferred Pahlavān Hājj Mostafā Tusi as their leader, as he was many times champion of Iran in

41. Mohammad Hoseyn Fahmideh was a thirteen-year old child soldier in the Iran-Iraq War, who threw himself under an advancing Iraqi tank, detonating a full grenade belt, thus halting the advance of the column. The Islamic Republic celebrates him as a martyred war hero.
42. Interview with Shaʿbān Jaʿfari by Houchang Chehabi, Santa Monica, 15 May and 2 June 1997. See also Chehabi 2008.
43. Pahlavān Hājj Seyyed Hasan Shojāʿat (ca. 1880–1946) the greatest Iranian wrestling champion of the early twentieth century.

freestyle and *pahlavāni* wrestling. Moreover, in addition to his dignity as *pahlavān* and then *pishkesvat*, Tusi had never (in everyone's opinion) seriously meddled in the illegal activities of Shaʻbān and Tayyeb and had, above all, managed to keep away from the police and the sinister SAVAK. Tusi, along with Habibollāh Bolur, was one of the first champions of modern Iranian wrestling in 1939, while still remaining in the world of the zurkhāneh. Champion of *pahlavāni* wrestling between 1944 and 1946, Tusi was also the boss of Tehran's abattoirs in the mid-1960s, and after Shaʻbān fled to the United States in 1979, he became the first president of the new VBKP Federation in the same year, and held that office until his death in 1359/1980.

Figure 21. Shaʻbān Jaʻfari performing a demonstration of the *kabbādeh*. Zurkhāneh Jaʻfari [now, Shahid Fahmideh] (Partow-Beyzāʻi, 1958).

The world of the zurkhāneh could therefore find itself other protectors than Shaʻbān, and many did so. As an excellent connoisseur of this world, the chief editor of the *Rokhsat Pahlavān* sports newspaper, Ezzat Karimi, explained to me one day (as a young sports journalist at the time he often saw the head of the zurkhānehs): "Jaʻfari had an unparalleled ability to find money and have people talk about him. That was already enough for him to become the best of protectors" (Figures. 21 and 22). Very good at staging his own persona, he knew how to seize the moment to make himself look like a star, to attract the flashbulbs of the media, as we can see in one of the most famous anecdotes about him. When he was arrested on 28 February 1953 for having led

What the World of the Zurkhāneh Remembers

Figure 22. Sha'bān Ja'fari among his men (Homa Sharshār, 2002).

a riot outside the house of Prime Minister Mossadegh, he used his trial as publicity. He refused to speak as long as the portrait of the shah was not hanging in the courtroom, and he constantly interrupted the judge reading the charges against him, on the pretext that he could not be called "*bimokh*" (brainless). He stood on the chairs to protest and have his photo taken by the paparazzi in the room. When the judge declared that the court could not go on like this, that the hearing was suspended and that he "quit" for the day, Sha'bān got down off the chair declaring that he too "quit" being the accused.[44]

Independent of his more or less legal income, Sha'bān was a skilled courtier of the powerful and thus able to obtain subsidies from major companies over which he had no control, the National Iranian Oil Company (henceforth NIOC) in particular. He

44. Behzādi 1998, 188–89.

was even received at the Marble Palace and performed a demonstration for the shah and his guests. In return, he was awarded a sash of honor. He ran his zurkhāneh like a showman, bringing in all kinds of pop stars. Along with the zurkhāneh of the Bank Melli (Iran's oldest national bank), run by Kāzem Kāzemeyni, whom he disliked, his zurkhāneh often received official visits that the press, which had been properly wooed, did not fail to cover extensively. The shah, the crown prince, visiting celebrities, and many ambassadors were photographed there, as well as (to cite just those who are the most decried in the world of the zurkhāneh today), Gina Lollobrigida and Googoosh, the most famous Iranian singer of the imperial period. Many never forgave him for having had these women in the zurkhāneh, from which they are traditionally excluded, and for having the latter two saluted with the *zang* and *zarb* even while the great Tusi was in the room. Having provoked this encounter was equivalent to setting the great *pahlavān* of the period on the same level as the most famous singer in Iran. Many did not appreciate this way of obtaining money and considered that he was "prostituting" the tradition.

These highly charged symbolic moments did Sha'bān a lot of harm. He was considered impolite and without honor, particularly when Seyyed Ahmad Mir-Ashraf, whom we discussed earlier, fell out with him over money. After having collected the *bāj* on Tayyeb's behalf, Mir-Ashraf had moved to the Zurkhāneh-ye Jam and had begun to collect *bāj* for Sha'bān. However, apparently it had not been a success. In addition to other maneuvers, he had officially sent the photo of Sha'bān holding a *mil* on Gina Lollobrigida's shoulder to the religious authorities in Qom, to ask for a moral condemnation.[45] This condemnation was the signal some had been waiting for to provoke his disgrace within the traditional circles of the bazaar and get rid of him. Sha'bān was only able to save his skin by invoking his police protection to the maximum, and against all expectations it was Mir-Ashraf who was summoned by the SAVAK. This incident caused a lot of controversy in the world of the zurkhāneh and publicly revealed what no one could now ignore, that Sha'bān was in league with the political police. Moreover this identification of the zurkhāneh, through Sha'bān, and the SAVAK would have very serious consequences for the athletes during the revolution. Even more so, given that the zurkhāneh lost their best ambassador within the Iranian public opinion very early on.

The last great javānmard in Iran

During my interviews, the figure of Sha'bān was often mercilessly compared to that of the man who was the greatest sports legend in Iran: the *Jahān Pahlavān*, the *Pahlavān* of the world, Gholām-Rezā Takhti.[46] In contrast to the horrible, impure, domineer-

---

45. Many thanks to Hushang Fathi for having showed me the photos in question, which unfortunately I was not able to publish. A photo of Lollobrigida and Sha'bān is reproduced in Chehabi 2019, 405. See also Fathi 1992.

46. For a history of Gholām-Rezā Takhti (1930–1968) see Chehabi 1995. This section is inspired by this article, which draws on Raf'at 1987, and Behmanesh 1979, 9–14.

What the World of the Zurkhāneh Remembers

ing image that Shaʻbān gave of the sport, Takhti gave a positive and heroic image both to Iranian public opinion and the zurkhāneh he came from. In Houchang Chehabi's words, the latter was perceived by Iranians as personifying "kindness, grace under pressure, altruism, generosity, forgiveness, a concern for common people, and inner purity in an environment dominated by greed, duplicity and jealousy."[47] Takhti had political courage as well, and his suicide in 1968 plunged Iran into dismay and disbelief (Figures 23, 24, and 25).[48]

Figure 23. Gholām-Rezā Takhti.

47. Chehabi 1995, 56.
48. Davari and Sohrabi 2021.

Takhti came from a very humble background, the son of an ice maker. At age seven he went through the traumatic experience of seeing his house seized by his father's creditors. His whole family was forced to sleep outdoors for two days before the neighbors took pity on them and took them in.

Figure 24. – Takhti in Khāni ābād Zurkhāneh (Homa Sarshār, 2002).

He was still too young for the zurkhāneh, so Takhti and his friends trained outside, listening to the music, and copying the exercises in the street, like the other children of the bazaar. Then, around sixteen, he began in the Zurkhāneh-ye Pulād. As we have seen, this zurkhāneh was close to the Iranian Communist party. Takhti was a worker for a major oil company, and during his military service he was noticed by an officer belonging to the IWF. His success grew from there. He won a silver medal in the world wrestling championships in Helsinki in 1951, then the silver medal in the Olympic Games in Helsinki in 1952, then a gold medal at the Olympic games in Melbourne in 1956, and another in the world championships in Tehran in 1959, and another in Yokohama in 1961. Between 1957 and 1959 he also won the *bāzuband* (a leather armband worn around the biceps) as the champion of *pahlavāni* wrestling in Iran. Throughout this whole period, he was the most popular public figure in Iran.

But outside his sporting career, Takhti, who was both a sincere believer and close to the working class, became involved in politics in 1951. He joined the "Third Force,"

What the World of the Zurkhāneh Remembers

Figure 25. The statue of a legend: Jahān Pahlavān Takhti, inaugurated in 1997 (Bustān-e Bahārān; photo journal *Hamshahri*, 12 June 1997).

the socialist wing of Mossadegh's National front. This would put him in an increasingly difficult situation. In 1961, Takhti supported the demands of high-ranking wrestlers for social protection. During the Cold War, competitive sport had become an essential international showcase for states, and the iron rules of amateur sports (which at the time forbade athletes from being paid for competing) put high-ranking athletes who did not benefit from "arrangements" to get around the rules, in a very insecure position. The same year, even as Takhti refused to participate in international competitions in Tehran (in the sports hall now known as Sālon-e Haft-e Tir, near Park-e Shahr), on the grounds of this demand for social protection, the crowd heckled the shah's brother, Prince Gholām-Rezā Pahlavi, president of the National Olympic Committee in Iran, and delayed the ceremony by preventing the prince from making his speech. The wild crowd only calmed down when Takhti, whom they had been calling for, stood up on his seat and called out his famous "Forsat!" from the top of the stands, the traditional response and authorization given to the zurkhāneh athletes asking those who count for permission to begin. From that moment Takhti acquired powerful enemies at court.

Takhti did not decrease his political action. On 21 July 1962 students decided to celebrate the tenth anniversary of Mossadegh's return to power. The regime organized a counter demonstration made up of police cadets and bus drivers (provided by Sha'bān) dressed as peasants, who were supposed to demonstrate their gratitude to the shah for his agrarian reform. The clash seemed inevitable when Takhti and other athletes from the National Front arrived. There were two wrestling champions among the police cadets; they changed their attitude and went to greet Takhti, and as they did so they provoked a shift among the police cadets who joined the students in enthusiastically welcoming Takhti. The bus drivers were left on the side of the road, struggling to understand the new turn the demonstration had taken. The students' demonstration thus ended hand in hand with the cadets, who were all severely punished the next day. Takhti had saved the demonstration and prevented confrontation.

Just a few weeks later, there was a major earthquake near Qazvin to the west of Tehran, leaving over 12,000 people dead. Takhti was involved in the relief effort in two ways. First, he made an announcement on the radio, giving a bank account number and an address where people could leave donations without worrying that they would be misappropriated by regime officials. Second, from his famous white VW beetle, he himself oversaw the loading of the trucks that would distribute these donations. It is important to note that as a successful and popular figure, legends were immediately constructed about him. His political involvement was exaggerated, additional details were created and added to well-known anecdotes, and others were entirely fabricated. Whoever had an original tale added it to the shared story (which hardly needed it) but which eventually consolidated his status as a true *javānmard* legend. For example, a shopkeeper who was boycotted because he belonged to a religious minority, was saved by Takhti's ostentatious visit to his shop, breaking the boycott; a car thief who realized that he had stolen Takhti's old white beetle, returned it full of petrol, and in another version of the story, entirely repaired and repainted. Everything tends towards the construction of a modern myth. Even certain historical elements that seem well documented raise questions.

However, the facts are there. The Iranian National Front understood that Takhti was an emblematic figure. He was elected to the high council of the organization. While many National Front leaders were arrested the same year – the shah was preparing his plebiscite for the White Revolution and did not want it spoiled by criticism – Takhti was spared. The authorities feared the consequences such an arrest would have around the country. Nevertheless, they sought to neutralize him through intimidation and seduction. In March 1964 he refused to attend the summons before a court of justice and his salary as an employee of the Iranian railways was suspended. It was suddenly "discovered" that, like almost all high-level athletes of his time, he was a "pseudo amateur" as it was impossible to be openly professional. In addition, officials tried to buy him off by offering a position in the twenty-first Majles which was to be "appointed-elected" in 1964 by the authorities. He refused. As punishment, he was prevented from training and competition, but forced to participate in the Olympic Games in Tokyo in the same year. With pressure from public opinion, he agreed to go, although he would have preferred not to. As a final insult, the Iranian Olympic officials refused to let him carry the flag during the parade. Underprepared and now getting older, Takhti returned from Japan without a medal.

His enemies had hoped that this would lead to the collapse of his popularity and they had also promoted other wrestlers, including Emām Ali Habibi and Mohammad Ali Fardin (who would later become Iran's most popular cinema actor), in the hope that they would take his place. It was a lost cause. They thought that they had brought down an old glory, but they in fact consecrated a hero. A historical (and hysterical) crowd rushed to the airport to celebrate Takhti, now identified with Rostam, the hero of the Book of Kings, the *Shāhnāmeh*, the well-known fundamental work in Persian history and modern nationalism, the old warrior who accepts to fight and risks his life for Iran. He was therefore no longer considered simply as a *qāhramān*, a sporting champion, but as the *Jahān Pahlavān*, the title reserved for a mythical warrior. He had demonstrated abnegation, had many times proved his fundamental goodness, and had not "sold his honor," refusing all tempting commercial propositions and the many propositions of roles made for him in the commercial *jāheli* films.[49] Having himself lived through poverty, he was sensitive to the suffering of others, but never needed to steal for them; he never asked anything for himself, only for others. He was famous for apologizing to his vanquished opponents and lifting them up. As Chehabi notes, "he was a pious man who was an observant Muslim and regularly went on pilgrimages, yet he was a loyal

---

49. The *jāhel* inspired a film genre, in which *Qeysar* and the adaptation of Sadegh Hedayat's short story *Dāsh Ākol* by the director Mas'ud Kimiā'i remain the most significant.

supporter of Mossadegh's secular movement to the end."[50] He represented the middle path, open, progressive, and moderate, but also respectful of tradition.

However, as his own family admits, Takhti was overwhelmed by his status as a national hero. Devastated at the death of Mossadegh in 1967, he was also bitter about the way in which the National Front had used him. He was depressed, and unhappy in his marriage, and on 7 January 1968 in a hotel room in Tehran, he killed himself. The opposition immediately declared that it was a murder disguised as suicide. SAVAK was accused. A *pahlavān* does not kill himself. Yet it was true. His funeral became an event of national mourning and for a long time, at each anniversary, a long funeral procession made its way to the cemetery of Ebn-e Bābuyeh to lay flowers on his tomb. His portrait is often hung on the walls of shops and is displayed in all the zurkhānehs in Iran.

His only son, Bābak, considers that his father owes much of his status to the period and the manipulation of his image by the National Front. He is sad and frustrated at the most recent attempt by the regime to appropriate the image of his father to promote a "javānmardian" orientation in Iranian society. The media have received orders on this point.[51] Half the people in Tehran consider that they knew him well and had dined with him. The world of the zurkhāneh was proud to have had Takhti as one of their own, even though most of his career was devoted to international freestyle wrestling. Although Takhti was responsible for transferring his legend onto the zurkhāneh of the twentieth century, his impact in that world was quite limited. Eleven years later, during the revolution, it was the image of Sha'bān that dominated. The zurkhāneh is marked by these two indissociable dimensions, dignified and disturbing, the good side necessarily linked to the bad.

An ambiguous pre-revolutionary heritage

Sha'bān Jafari's leadership had consequences for the future of the zurkhāneh that proved to be negative in the long term, but their nuances must be considered. It would be incorrect to say that traditional sport declined during his leadership. With him, the world of the zurkhāneh was able to benefit from substantial financial advantages, emanating both from his "personal networks" and his grants officially awarded by the STB, particularly in the context of the construction of new zurkhānehs. Financial assistance was obtained without having to account for activities and without having to organize competitions (a victory in itself!). Paradoxically, after 1961 only three *pahlavāni* wrestling competitions, the initial reason for the existence of zurkhāneh, were organized – in 1965, 1973,

50. Chehabi 1995, 57.
51. Devictor 2004, 87–112 and 155. See in particular the text of cinema regulations in 1995. Having strictly controlled the subjects of films involving *luti*s in the wake of the revolution, the authorities imposed the notion of *javānmardi*. When they are scripted, *luti*s can only be generous, right and good, their reputation as bad boys only being due to social disadvantage and belonging to the poorer classes. Such films will provide the opportunity for moralistic redemption. The essentially moral and positive acceptance of the *javānmardi* is all the more obvious.

and 1975. Today no one remembers the names of the champions of that era. Award ceremonies of what passed for *varzesh-e bāstāni* competitions were simply honorific medal distributions among friends, as denounced by Mehdi Tehrānchi in his book. Nothing serious was organized at the national level.[52]

Paul Vieille and Kazem Mohseni note that between 1956 and 1966, twenty-one zurkhānehs were created, of which twelve were established between 1962 and 1966 with the help of the STB.[53] This brought the official number of zurkhānehs to forty-seven. The end of competitions therefore went hand in hand with the peak in the number of zurkhānehs. The reasons for this peak and the subsequent stagnation are not clear. Aside from a waning "Takhti effect," it seems that the IWF showed little interest in *pahlavāni* wrestling, and that the STB had limited interest in zurkhāneh exercises. According to Ja'fari, matters got worse when General Ali Hojjat Kāshāni replaced the more tolerant General Abbās Izadpanāh in 1972, and even sought to sabotage the performances Sha'bān was responsible for during the ceremonies for the shah's birthday.[54]

In Sha'bān's memoirs, recorded by Homa Sarshar, there is a passage that reveals the origin of this brutal opposition. In addition to quarrels over funding, General Hojjat Kāshāni considered that Sha'bān had no place within the STB and, above all, that *pahlavāni* wrestling, which was historically linked to the world of the zurkhāneh, should come under the authority of the STB alone, and thus the IWF. Sha'bān did not agree, and is said to have declared to the General's face "I am *pahlavāni* wrestling!" in the style of an absolute monarch.[55]

As the relevant archives remain unfortunately inaccessible, it is not possible to verify these allegations; we must simply observe the facts and consider the hypotheses. In 1976 a sociocultural study of the zurkhānehs of Tehran, published by the High Council for Arts and Culture (Showrā-ye Āli-e Farhang va Honar) conducted a census of the number of zurkhānehs. It had remained the same, as there had been no progression.[56]

As Vieille and Mohseni reveal, there is also an opposition between the construction of sporting infrastructures in the north (including gymnasiums and swimming pools) and in the south (where they remain primarily zurkhāneh). The authors provide an analysis of this opposition, which independently of the strength of tradition, is quite astute:

52. Tehrānchi 1985, 271.
53. Vieille and Mohseni 1969, particularly 331–35.
54. Interview with Sha'bān Ja'fari by Houchang Chehabi. Santa Monica, 15 May and 2 June 1997. See also Chehabi 2008, 366–67.
55. Sarshār 2002, 242–44. The author, who recorded the confidences of Sha'bān four years before his death, accomplished a work that is indeed worthy of praise. However, Sha'bān, cunning as ever, found a way to say only what he wanted to say. Thus, his statement that he had nothing to do with Tayyeb, and the descriptions of the relations between them (p. 246), will bring a gentle smile to anyone familiar with these figures. It is also very revealing that he does not refer to Seyyed Ahmad Mir-Ashraf at all.
56. Showrā-ye Āli-e Farhang va Honar 1976.

It has a more general meaning, to do with the opposition of traditional organizations based on small groups of members connected by personal links to the leader, and modern organizations which tend to include a large number of people; the populations of the old city are more resistant to these new forms of social relations than those in zones of recent urban expansion.[57]

The world of the zurkhāneh would pay dearly for this isolationism in the 1970s, when Iranian society discovered the attraction of new combat sports and martial arts. Moreover, soccer was eclipsing wrestling as the most popular spectator sport. It was broadcast on television, while zurkhāneh sports were not. This made it even more difficult to attract younger men, and thus the proportion of thirty- and forty-year old athletes grew. Iran had changed its tastes and preferences without the world of the zurkhāneh, which had no serious institutional representation, realizing what was happening.

Possibly in response to pressure from the STB, there was, however, an attempt by Sha'bān in the 1970s to, as he put it, "organize all that a bit."[58] In 1971 he became the head of the Committee for Traditional Sport (*komiteh-ye varzesh-e bāstāni*) with Habibollāh Bolur[59] and the famous wrestler Abbās Zandi as well-known partners. The committee was designed as a sort of embryonic association with vague statutes, loosely associated with the STB but created by *farmān* (royal decree). The personal connection was still emphasized to the detriment of administrative institutionalization carried out in due form. These initiatives were used essentially for the organization of two competitions of *pahlavāni* wrestling in 1973 and 1975, which saw Rezā Sukhtehsarā'i become the last champion of traditional wrestling of the Pahlavi era.

Even as the field of modern Iranian sports saw an increase in infrastructure and associations, along with the institutions to administer and develop them (particularly the creation of the School of Sport in 1972), the athletic tradition of the zurkhāneh continued to content itself with its place among the relics of Iran's glorious past.[60] This is why they were included in the inaugural performances of the athletic demonstrations for the traditional birthday celebrations of the shah, on 4 Ābān (October 26), or when Iran hosted the Asian Games in 1974.[61]

This desire for isolation can best be understood by consulting veterans. According to them, the creation of a formal federation for zurkhāneh disciplines would beget a system of rankings that would not be an accurate indicator of who was worthy of special respect. From their point of view, the fact that the presidents of federations can change periodically poses a problem of continuity in a world where the stability of networks

   57. Vieille and Mohseni 1969, 336.
   58. Chehabi interview with Sha'bān Ja'fari.
   59. It is important to add that Bolur was the author of an excellent book on wrestling technique, Bolur 1976. Bolur knew a lot about the techniques of antique sport; his father was a *morshed* and taught him the art of the *zarb*.
   60. One of the publications that is representative of this period is Barzegar 1971.
   61. On this event see Huebner 2016.

is highly valued. What outside observers might consider as a good thing is not seen that way by those who reason in terms of networks of relationships and protection. Although the traditional system lacked dynamism, the omnipresence of a figure like Shaʿbān insured comfortable revenue and a stability in allegiances, and that was enough.

And yet, Shaʿbān was responsible for several initiatives. He created a Museum of the Traditional Zurkhāneh and Pahlavāni Wrestling, which housed the leather armband worn by the great Yazdi Bozorg, another champion of the time of Nāser al-Din Shah in the second half of the nineteenth century. Unfortunately, we do not know what became of the objects in this museum after the revolution. Shaʿbān also tried to introduce American-style professional wrestling and had it taught for two years. However, Iranian professional wrestlers did not accept the theatrical side of the sport, did not know how to act, and refused the staging and artifice in which some had to accept to voluntarily lose. When the athletes he trained got involved in too many physical fights, the experiment was stopped.[62]

Shaʿbān's protection allowed the world of the zurkhāneh to continue its trajectory and remain on the fringes of sporting institutions as such, without having to worry about the future. The zurkhāneh maintained a kind of functioning in which patronage and professional connections remained the essential basis for recognition and in which, once the formal authority of Shaʿbān was accepted, each had substantial autonomy. This is how those who did not like being forced to proclaim the official *salavāt* in honor of the shah (Beh salāmati-e Shāhanshāh Aryāmehr salavāt-e boland khatm konid!) were able to still meet in zurkhānehs that still benefited from the generosity of Shaʿbān without being overzealous in support of the regime – a simple matter of tact for those used to being attentive to appearances. But history would do away with this status quo.

The end of a system

October 1975 was the last time everything was "like before" in the world of the zurkhāneh. Shaʿbān was as usual able to bring together the 1800 athletes required for the traditional exercises in the Shāhanshāhi stadium (today the Āzādi [Freedom] stadium) on the shah's birthday. These athletes were generally recruited in the zurkhānehs of national businesses or public transport companies.

An "anticorruption" campaign initiated a few months earlier, in August 1975, by the government of Prime Minister Jamshid Amuzegār primarily targeted industrialists and the big bazaar merchants but broadly avoided court circles, thus turning the major traders, and all their networks, into opponents of the shah. The substantial inflation of 1973 had become catastrophic by 1976. The oil wealth had led to an explosion in prices, rent in Tehran had increased by 300% in five years, and food prices had followed the same upwards curve.

The arrest of Habib Elqāniān and Rasul Vahābzādeh, among the major traders and

62. Chehabi interview with Shaʿbān Jaʿfari.

industrialists mentioned above, was the signal for the largest sources of Iranian capital that they should invest elsewhere. As Ervand Abrahamian states, capital had left Iran well before the businessmen themselves did. Trials of corporations were started in the same year and this led the authorities to imprison 8,000 shopkeepers and merchants and to force 23,000 others into exile from their native city. Overall, 430,000 other merchants were investigated by the justice system, and 250,000 of them were sentenced to fines.[63] To ensure prices were respected, the authorities constituted teams of inspectors who could barely be controlled and who took a cut of the fines, and thereby harassed the shopkeepers all the more. In Tehran and in the provinces there were hardly any bazaaris who had not had a family member imprisoned, fined, or investigated by authorities.

This stigmatization and generalized attack against the bazaaris unleashed an unprecedented reaction. The large bazaaris started to pay their religious tithes (*khoms* and *zakāt*) to the dissenting ayatollahs, who would soon be followed by all of the bazaar and local retailers. In the eyes of those who discussed this with me, Shaʻbān effectively lost control of the world of the zurkhāneh during this period, aside from a limited group who remained loyal. The whole sphere around traditional sport, which is an inherent part of the bazaar and small merchants in general, suffered from these operations and distanced themselves from the regime. Those who did not paid dearly after the revolution, while others who were slow in switching their allegiances had difficulty escaping the reputation of the sport and the anger it provoked among some. Through its anonymous denunciations, the revolution provided opportunities to settle old scores in a particularly sordid way, but this threat also gave the athletes a reason to mobilize together for the first time.

Shaʻbān fled first to Israel and from there to the United States (he died in Santa Monica in 2006) in the middle of the summary arrests and executions, and it was at this point that the *pishkesvat*s of the zurkhāneh decided to join Iran's STB and form a genuine sporting association. At its head was the most irreproachable man available, Pahlavān Hājj Seyyed Mostafā Tusi (Figure 26). Remarkably, the athletes also sealed this alliance with the Islamic Revolution in the only way that seemed legitimate, by going to Qom to solemnly swear an oath of allegiance to Ayatollah Khomeini (Figure 27). They still needed the direct connection with the incarnation of power. This official alliance in dramatic circumstances was above all an eminently political act; the "strong men" tacitly promised to dedicate themselves exclusively to physical activity.

Motivated primarily by self-preservation and initially unaware of the long-term implications of this new way of operating, the world of the zurkhāneh would rapidly discover that nothing would ever be the same. It was the end of the personal connections that allowed them to circumvent any type of bureaucracy. The hierarchical legitimacy of the old social model had been weakened considerably. The Shiite clergy did not have the same consideration for the world of sport in general and the zurkhāneh in particular

---

63. Abrahamian 1989, 28–29. See also Denoeux 1993, 135–148.

What the World of the Zurkhāneh Remembers　　　　　　　　　　　　　　　　71

Figure 26. The founders of the VBKP Association, in 1979. From right to left: Habibollāh Bolur, Mostafā Tusi (first president of the Association) and Ahmad Vafādār. ('Abbāsi, 1995).

that the monarchy had. Its connection with sport was late coming, much as it was in Europe, and remained partial in spite of official declarations. When the clergy intervened in the world of sport, it was always to talk about Islam, national honor, and morality.

There was now an association to run, competitions to organize by age group at the national and regional levels, a president appointed by the STB, to which he was accountable, a budget to be drawn up and rules to respect – other than simply those of the usual social background. The second major turning point in Iranian traditional sport and the world of the zurkhāneh since the birth of the IWF in 1939 had just occurred. The era of Mir-Ashraf's zurkhāneh was long past.

"But why Create a Federation?! We Had Everything to Lose!"

For Ezzat Karimi, since the birth of the VBKP Federation, the days have been bleak. He remains perplexed about its usefulness and bitterly observes that everything seems to be upside down:

> We did not need this federation. This association is worthless for the zurkhāneh, we cannot trust something that is managed by the state (*dowlat*). We

Figure 27. The *zurkhānehkārān* swearing allegiance, to the Revolution and to Khomeini in 1979 (photo from the journal *Rokhsat Pahlavān*, 31 May 1997).

cannot give them money, they just put it in their pocket and in the meantime the zurkhānehs are closing.[64]

The idea of the prevaricating or corrupt state (*dowlat*), remained a common assumption in Iran after the 1979 revolution. Saying this does not amount to denunciation. In this instance, the newly elected president, Seyyed Abdollāh Sajjādi, was not accused of anything in particular, but this statement was clearly self-evident in talking about a state institution. In Karimi's words:

> At the time of Ghafuri-Fard and Mohammad Khoshjān [former presidents of the STB and the VBKP Federation, respectively] things were still alright. They were part of the "family," we knew them, but not this president [Sajjādi].[65]

64. Personal interview, 5 November 1997.
65. Ibid.

MELLAT HEMMAT-E VĀLĀST, NAH FARD!
"The people are a noble ambition not the individual!"

In 1997 Ezzat Karimi founded the first real newspaper dedicated to the world of the zurkhāneh. It was published regularly and discussed all sorts of themes to do with the sport and its traditions. Born in 1928, Karimi began by making a living as a baker, but he felt irresistibly attracted to journalism and at the first available opportunity joined the newspaper *Keyhān*. He smiled as he thought about that period, "I made a better living at the bakery, but what passion!" He began on the lowest rung of the ladder and slowly climbed upward. He fulfilled all the different roles within the newspaper and specialized in the "arts and sports" pages. He also worked for Atā Behmanesh, Iran's most eminent sports journalist.

Alongside his career as a journalist, Karimi has practiced traditional sport since 1956. He began in the zurkhāneh of Karim Siyāh (Karim the black). Around this time he was able to approach several of the celebrities in the sport, including Tayyeb, of whom he has several photos surrounded by his lieutenants. Sha'bān Ja'fari, he said, "was not *bi mokh* [brainless] as his opponents called him; on the contrary, he was very crafty! Lots of athletes owed their first jobs to him!" He had a particular affection for Mostafā Tusi, the grand pahlavān of Iran and the first president of the VBKP Federation in 1979. According to him, Tusi had been the living honor of the sport (*eftekhār-e zurkhāneh*): "that was our mistake, we thought all presidents would be like him." When Karimi reached retirement age, he did absolutely not consider giving up his profession. After a number of projects, he began the newspaper and the obstacle course of obtaining administrative authorizations and subsidies for publication, in particular supplies of paper at subsidized prices, which is a necessary condition for the viability of a newspaper in Iran. His greatest pleasure was receiving thank-you letters from readers who lived on the island of Qeshm in the Persian Golf: "Even over there!" His readership now covered all of Iran and related all the traditional sporting activities around the country.

"I created this newspaper so that the spirit of this sport would not die, to perpetuate the tradition that comes from the culture of the people (*farhang-e mellat*)." Among other things, the newspaper covers both the history of the zurkhāneh over time, allegedly from the Achaemenids to today, as well as the biographies of famous *pishkesvat*s and *morshed*s, and provides long explanations about the traditions of the zurkhāneh.

Yet the name of Seyyed Abdollāh Sajjādi was not entirely unfamiliar in this world; his father had been a *miyāndār* and a *pishkesvat* in the Bank-e Melli zurkhāneh. His son inherited his father's passion. He had great ambitions for the sport and, to the detriment of his family life, spent large amounts of time managing the federation and pushing forward the reforms that he considered essential to ensure the longevity of a sport whose members were aging without the prospect of replacement. According to Ezzat Karimi, he had lacked tact in the early stages; he carried out his reforms in a way that was considered too authoritarian and too personal, and he had ruffled the feathers of the veterans. He was criticized for not having sufficiently solicited the *pishkesvat*s, of not having sufficiently consulted local authorities and other important men. Sajjādi had rectified this somewhat but too late, the rancor had risen and was cleverly maintained and amplified by the former leadership of the federation, who did not appreciate having been ousted.

For Sajjādi and his team, there was too much talk about zurkhāneh and not enough action. The reforms had to be enacted quickly. The veterans complained that he was disrupting their customs without prior consultation. Moreover, the team and its president were seen as lacking solidarity with the athletes. As Karimi explained:

> When you love this sport, which is a world in itself, you have to participate in its life. You have to be generous and not hesitate to write a recommendation letter for a young man who arrives in Tehran, or if someone needs a place to sleep, find him a roof. The protector of this world, who has the means, must accept such responsibilities. They are incumbent upon him.[66]

And the world of the zurkhāneh could indeed provide this assistance.

Rumor had it – the origins of the rumor remain a mystery – that the then leadership of the federation had refused to help beggars who had arrived at the Fahmideh zurkhāneh, the headquarters of the federation, and that Sajjādi had refused to write letters of recommendation for certain people who needed to find work. These accusations, which are unproven and which in any event would have to be considered in context – something no one was interested in doing – sounded like the traditional attacks on the reputation of a person concealing the resentment among former clienteles who had been sidelined. They had lost a president from their own ranks, and in so doing had lost all or part of their influence. Everyone knew that the two former presidents of the federation at the national level and for Tehran were not friendly with the members of the current administrative team.

The fundamental problem was that Sajjādi was passionate, but also a rational manager who could clearly see where the problem was – the need for an image change – and who detested the principle of the *pārtibāzi*, cronyism, and cliques. Realistically, he also wanted the sport to rise to the level of the reputation it officially had, which had been

---

66. Ibid.

affirmed in the more or less scholarly historiography on the subject since the Second World War. In other words, depending on one's perspective, he was either a pioneer or an extra-terrestrial.

Sajjādi was implicitly criticized for not having shared the same lifestyle as those who, whether simple athletes or notables, made up the usual clientele of the zurkhāneh. Vice-president of the VBKP Federation in 1985–86, under the presidency of Mehdi Shirgir, Seyyed Abdollāh Sajjādi returned to head the federation in 1993 at the same time as the team of Hāshemi Tabā.[67] He had a number of university degrees, and in addition to managing his personal fortune, had taught journalism at the University of Tehran. His cultural references were clearly not those of the athletes, nor were his attitudes. He did not participate in the daily life of sporting clubs in Tehran's zurkhānehs: he neither entered the *gowd* with the athletes, nor did he eat *kalleh pācheh* or *ābgusht* with them afterwards. They did not speak the same language and they made him feel it. Sajjādi replied that "grabbing people by the sleeve off the street and encouraging them to go into the zurkhāneh" was not enough to save the sport. It had to be overhauled from top to bottom; old habits had to be got rid of. It had to be daring, and above all it had to attract people who had different ambitions than their elders. He was not wrong at all, for the recruitment crisis was real and severe.

All of those involved in the zurkhāneh, both traditionalists and reformers, were undoubtedly attached to this world, but their languages and behavior differed. The specific experiences they had of the world and of Iranian society reflected a contradictory image of today's Iran. On the one hand, some still had the image of connections that demanded solidarity of the community united by a certain number of social practices and cultural references. On the other, there were those who now saw this as a form of individual fulfilment and expression in which everyone should be able to find what interested them without necessarily having to swear allegiance to anyone.

The questions that are the foundation for these diverging considerations are thus the same as those implicitly asked in 1934, when the world of the zurkhāneh saw the permanent creation of a new, modern sporting organization. Who are we? What do our traditions mean? How can we live with our era? However, a sign of the times perhaps, these questions were only asked by a small group of leaders and intellectuals in the 1930s and 40s, but by the late 1990s they had spread to the community of athletes as a whole. To pursue this investigation further, I had to go back to the time of these first questions.

67. Vice president of the Islamic Republic of Iran and head of the STB from 1993 to 2001, very close to former President Ali Akbar Hāshemi Rafsanjāni.

Chapter Two
Identity Matters

THE DEVELOPMENT OF MODERN DISCOURSES ON THE ZURKHĀNEH

The period of reform and initial questionings: 1915–1934, the birth of modern sport in Iran

During the period of modernization launched by Reza Shah (r. 1926–1941), the emerging role of sport was not something that seemed self-evident, in view of the customs and traditions of Iranian society. However, the decisions that were part of this modernization only served to bring coherence to a movement timidly kindled in 1915 by those whom traditionalists called *mostafrang*, a pejorative term used at the time to refer to Iranians who returned from the West and adopted Western customs out of snobbery.[1]

Contrary to what a later critic of Westernization claimed, namely that "everything began with the ball," it was in fact gymnastics that paved the way for the era of reform in sports and physical activity in Iran, through the (multiple) modernizing effects of the army and its European-trained officers. It was from this perspective – both in terms of military preparation and patriotic melting pot – that physical education, sports, and scouting, were introduced and conceptualized during the reign of Reza Shah. Football arrived in Iran in 1872,[2] but back then it was reserved for the British, and a handful of European or American schools (particularly the American high school, later renamed Alborz) that were established in the late nineteenth century and which played a non-negligible role in spreading the practice of sport among the Iranian elite.[3] The Iranian pioneers of physical education often had their first jobs in these schools, like Mir-Mehdi Varzandeh (1880–1982) who was one of the key figures in the development of sport and physical education in Iran. As is often the case in non-Western countries, the army was one of the primary vectors for the transmission of Western practices. Varzandeh had become familiar with gymnastics in Belgium while he was posted there as

---

1. Shafi'i Sarvestāni 1376/1997–98. See also Chehabi 2002b. For the additional information concerning the birth of modern sport in Iran, I would like to thank Houchang Chehabi for providing a series of sources and documents of the utmost importance. His own analysis of this material has since been published in Chehabi 2002a; Chehabi 2006..
2. Bromberger 1998, especially 106.
3. For an excellent historical synthesis and insightful anthropological analysis of this worldwide process see Darbon 2008; Mangan 2011; and Holt 1989.

a young officer, and then in Istanbul where he trained in fencing, before teaching in various private and international schools, and eventually continuing his career within the national Iranian sporting institutions.[4]

In 1915, a German-trained Iranian officer named Gerānmāyeh, introduced gymnastic sports into the Iranian army. These sports were developed in Berlin by Friedrich Ludwig Jahn (1778–1852) at the beginning of the nineteenth century.[5] The Turnverein was a gymnastics movement that helped to nourish and develop the political current that wanted to see a union between German-speaking states following the Napoleonic war and Prussian defeat in 1806. This political approach led to the Zollverein, the German customs union, in 1833 and then the proclamation of the German Empire under Chancellor Bismarck in 1870, after the fall of Napoleon III and the Second French Empire. It is not surprising to see that the German Turnverein model was imported so quickly to Iran, and we might expect this nationalistic and militaristic model to have become dominant, but that was not the case. In 1919, the minister for education, Ahmad Bader (Nasir al-Dowleh), instead adopted the method of Swedish gymnastics created by Per Henrik Ling (1776–1839). Swedish gymnastics is more focused on medicine and orthopedics than its German cousin, and also requires less equipment. It had a significant influence on the physical education program in many European countries where issues to do with public hygiene had become a priority. Sweden was also a neutral state that the Iranian authorities had successfully entrusted with the role of training the first gendarmerie. These education reforms needed a media outlet. This was provided in 1924 with the creation of the journal *Ta'lim va tarbiyat*. It was also in 1924 that the first *olampik-e Irān* competitions, associating Iranians athletes and athletes from other embassies, were held at the *Meydān-e mashq-e Tehrān*.[6] These events were held in reference to the Paris Olympic Games and their founder Baron Pierre de Coubertin. The rise in the symbolic importance of the international sporting scene was also one of the driving

---

4. Chehabi 2014.

5. Seyyed Hasan Taqizādeh, a major figure in the Iranian constitutionalist movement, wrote three short texts on physical education. One was on sport in Germany, in which he rejoiced at the fact that sports were practiced in every German village, while stipulating that "sports" referred to leisure activities like "snow sports, swimming, or horse riding." For him this should not be confused with the meaning of the word *varzesh* in Iran which only refers to the gymnastic activities of the zurkhāneh. Another text evokes the creation of a "sports space (*mahfel*)" in Shiraz, which he saw as proof "that in this time of despair, hope clearly blows in from Fars" and that "if those who play King leave the provinces in peace, the rebirth of Persian civilization will begin there, as has always been the case." Finally, he presents *varzesh- e bāstāni* in Iran in a comment on Xenophon where he expressed his anger against the Sufi and Dervishes who he sees as having broken the "Zoroastrian traditions of physical training and developing moral and physical will" and introducing a kind of fatalism, whereas the Mu'tazilites and the Shiites had, in his view, preserved the idea of an individual with free will. See Sayyed Hasan Taqizādeh, "Khiyālāt," *Kāveh* 2:6 (8th June 1921), reproduced in *Kāveh* (Tehran: Vis, 1997), 1–4. I thank Tim Epkenhans for having brought these articles to my attention. For more on Taqizādeh and *Kāveh*, see Epkenhans 2000.

6. Shafi'i Sarvestāni 1376/1997–98, 32–37.

forces in Iran's sporting policy, as it was for all the nation-states who had joined the then very new League of Nations. In 1925 the scouting movement created by Baden Powell (1857–1941) in 1908 also began to slowly develop in Iran.[7] On 6 July 1926, the High Commission for Education created the Dār al-moʻallemin-e varzesh, the training school for sport teachers, under the tutelage of the minister for war, General Afkhami. On 5 September 1927 (14 Shahrivar 1306), the Iranian parliament passed a bill calling for the ministry for education (Vezārat-e Maʻāref) to introduce physical education into all new Iranian state schools.[8] The bill provided for the application of the law in all provincial prefectures within eighteen months and remaining towns within three years. The application of this law encountered numerous obstacles, however.

These reforms remained symbolic and their impact was limited because the funding in the provinces was difficult. The Iranian authorities demanded that local councils spend 0.5% of their budget on implementing these reforms, but councils did not all have sufficient revenue to comply.[9] Moreover, those proposing these reforms encountered significant opposition from the Shiite clergy, which considered gymnastic exercises to be like dance, something that encouraged bodily passions, and was therefore frivolous and morally condemnable. They also came up against resistance from provincial authorities, who did not understand the usefulness of these new "gesticulatory" activities, which they saw as contrary to the gravity and decorum of honest Iranian men. The social model that Iran inherited was an aristocratic one, as it was in Europe; frantic running around is something that servants and other subalterns did. Iranian aristocrats traditionally pursued sports like hunting or equestrian activities such as *chowgān* (polo) or *jerid* (horseback javelin throwing).[10] Wrestling, however, was a performance that was widely appreciated but sociologically marked by a genuine professional corporation in which the athletes were all from poor and lowly backgrounds. There were certain aristocrats who practiced the sport in private, but needless to say they did not make a living from it. However, like traditional athletic exercises, modern Western sports came up against the problem of exhibiting the bodies of young athletes (both male and female) in the public space. As one veteran of the STB remembers, "back then horse-drawn tramways ran through central Tehran, everyone was veiled, no one was brave enough to wear shorts!"[11] The population did not like the idea of its children – and especially the honor of its young women, who were then also encouraged to do physical exercises – exposed to the four winds in total opposition to the teachings of Islam. Those who defended sport tried unsuccessfully to moderate the clergy's fundamental opposition by showing that physical exercise had been recommended back in the time of Avicen-

7. For an in-depth analysis of scouting in Iran, Daghigh-Nia 1968–69, quoted by Chehabi 2002a, 279.
8. *Taʻlim va tarbiyat* 3:7–8 (Mehr-Ābān 1306 /October-November 1927), no page number.
9. See Yaldaï 1965, 31.
10. Chehabi and Guttmann 2002.
11. Rahim Safavi, quoted by Shafiʻi Sarvestāni 1376/1997–98, 32–37.

na.[12] In many respects the development of these new physical practices in Iran came up against the same socio-religious hurdles that were present in many Catholic countries in the nineteenth century.

The new momentum, more durable this time, was the result of new governmental measures that were part of the wave of reforms that took place in the second half of the 1930s, and which caused profound changes in Iranian society.[13] It was based on the creation of the Sāzmān-e Tarbiyat-e Badani (Organization of Physical Education) on 17 April 1934 under the patronage Crown Prince Mohammad Reza Pahlavi,[14] and also the ministry of education, where many of the reformists of the previous period had ended up.

In the same year 1934, the STB called on the services of Thomas R. Gibson, an American graduate of Columbia University, to assist with the organization of sports and scouting that had lain idle since 1925. He remained in Iran until 1938, and organized football competitions with the logistical support of high schools. He managed to create twenty-four teams.[15] In 1936, after the *kashf-e hejāb* decree "unveiling" women,[16] the central authorities sent emissaries to the provinces to supervise the implementation of the new measures. They also had to supervise the application of the decrees on sport, (*towse'eh-ye varzesh-e modern* the spread of modern sport), the establishment of spaces set up for sports (funded by the municipality) and women's sports. One of these emissaries, Shamsoddin Shāyesteh, reported that his mission to Tabriz came up not only against those he calls *kohneh-parast*, conservatives, but also a categorical refusal from the local representative of the ministry of education, which logically should have been responsible for implementing the two government directives.[17] As far as the obligation to encourage the practice of football, the latter said, "*Futbāl?! Digeh chi?!* (Football?! What next!?). The only way Shāyesteh could impose this practice was by relating the attitude of the local officials to his hierarchy in Tehran, who took on the task of writing to persuade the recalcitrant office to let him supervise the "literal" application of the two imperial *farmān*s.

To attract young women to these new sporting practices, Shāyesteh got around their initial reticence by asking them to simply play "the same little games that they ordinarily played at the time."[18] But to do this, he organized teams, and then put up "family photos" of these teams in the girls' schools. When they saw these photos, the other girls

12. *Ta'lim va tarbiyat* 2:6 (Sharivar 1305/August-September 1926): 313–19.
13. For an an overview of the fundamental reforms implemented during this period see Jean-Digard, Hourcade, and Richard 1996, 63–95; Banani 1961 and Chehabi 2014.
14. This is the date that is currently considered the official beginning of the sporting organization in Iran, and not the law of 1927.
15. *Ta'lim va tarbiyat*, 4:2 (April-May 1928) and 5:9–10 (November-December and January-February 1929). Page number unavailable.
16. On which see Chehabi 2003.
17. See Shāyesteh 1346/1967), 653–54; quoted by Shafi'i Sarvestāni 1376/1997–98, 34.
18. Ibid.

wanted to enroll in the teams to be able to take part in the photos. The same issues came up all around the provinces and revealed how slowly the reforms spread throughout society, and the difficult work done by "sporting emissaries."

Apart from the zurkhānehs, private clubs were rare. It was the administration, state companies, and the army that funded and hosted the first activities. The construction of the Amjadieh stadium in 1939 in Tehran remains an isolated example, well below the needs of the period. The lack of infrastructure was a problem until the early 1960s, when Prime Minister Ali Amini launched the famous five-year plan that gave Iran (among other projects) its first major sporting infrastructure at the national level.

Many local leaders could therefore hide behind arguments to do with the lack of means, and the persistent dearth of qualified staff in the 1930s, to try to slow the application of measures that were in tension with both the municipal budgets and the dominant morals of the period. To try and improve the training and recruitment of staff, the Iranian government created Dāneshsarā-ye Moqaddamāti-e Tarbiyat-e Badani (the National School for Physical Education) in 1939, four years after the first teacher training schools. This situation is something we observe in all countries where these practices are imposed "top-down" and do not necessarily have the support of the population and local elites. These reforms to the world of sports did not suffer from the fall of Reza Shah in 1941, when the Soviets and the British forced him to abdicate in favor of his son, Mohammed Reza Pahlavi.

1928–1942: The Transition Years for the Zurkhāneh

We can see that all these reforms focused solely on modern sports and left the zurkhānehs quite out of the picture. We can imagine that the latter were identified with the recent past that the Pahlavi regime sought to erase from memory, at least initially. The zurkhānehs were considered potential supporters of Qajars, whose position can be guessed at if we follow Willem Floor's discussion of the *luti*s in Tehran, who supported Mohammad Ali Shah against the constitutionalists in 1908.[19] The exceptions were the *luti*s in Tabriz who supported Sattār Khān and Bāqer Khān, the two heroes of the constitutionalist struggle against despotism, but they were just that: an exception. The men of the zurkhāneh were always linked to their local protectors, the notables of the bazaar and above all the clergy. These were all potential adversaries for Reza Shah's new administration and were watched closely between 1925 and 1934.

Another reason for the fact that the zurkhānehs were not always included in these

---

19. Floor 1979; and Floor 1971. On this question of social banditry, the author agrees with Anton Blok's analysis; see Blok 1972. These two authors provide a welcome critical perspective on the overly generous thesis expounded by Eric Hobsbawm; see Hobsbawm 1969. This latter book, however, inspired very much the article written by Asghar Fathi; see Fathi 1979. Despite the immense respect I have for Hobsbawm's work, my observations of the supposedly "socially positive" effects of banditry lead me to nevertheless fully support the criticisms of W. Floor and A. Blok.

Identity Matters

reforms, which can be seen in the comments by certain sports reformers, is simply that the zurkhāneh athletes did not feel concerned by the emergence of new sports and new forms of sporting organizations.[20]

Figure 28. Jashn-e Ferdowsi, the celebrations for the thousand year anniversary of Ferdowsi, 23 May 1934; first official appearance of VBKP athletes, directed by pahlavān Razzāz ('Abbāsi, 1995).

The first official reappearance of zurkhāneh athletes occurred on 23 May 1934, during the commemorative celebration for the thousand-year anniversary of the poet Ferdowsi (ca. 329–411 h.q./941–1020) (Figure 28), author of the *Shāhnāmeh*, Iran's national epic. The symbolic date chosen and the way in which the athletes appeared were in more than one respect the result of the breakdown that had occurred over the decade and the new interpretation of the athletic tradition of the zurkhāneh. This was the work of a small group of enthusiasts involved in an association, *Jam'iyat-e gordān-e Irān* (The "Iranian Heroes Society), created in 1924 by one Mirzā Mahmud Sharif Jurābchi Qomi. The goal of Jurābchi and his friends was to promote traditional Iranian athletic practices and bring them into line with the new regime's expectations regarding health, politics, and morals. The group's activities barely extended beyond Tehran and the small group of volunteers, but they were an early sign of the general direction the world of

20. Shafi'i Sarvestāni 1376/1997–98, 36–37

Figure 29. Traditional hair and mustache; Pahlavān Razzāz (standing, second from the right) and other *pahlavān*s in Tehran in the 1910-1920s, the last years of Qājār traditional style ('Abbāsi, 1995).

the zurkhāneh would soon take under pressure from the Pahlavi administration. They also suggest a modest but courageous attempt to lobby the new cultural and sporting authorities. In the photos from the period, we can see that the physical appearance of the athletes had changed. Between ten and twenty years earlier, zurkhāneh wrestlers had sported the traditional partially shaved head (from the middle to the front) (Figure 29), but by 1934 they no longer did so. When they attended ceremonies, these wrestlers were then directed by the most famous *pahlavān*s and *pishkesvat*s of the period, Pahlavān Hājj Seyyed Hasan Shojā'at (d. 1946), known as "Razzāz " ("Rice Seller," a reference to his primary profession), who was known for his victory against the great Indian wrestler Tākhutā (Figures 30 and 31). These practitioners of "old sports" (*varzeshhā-ye qadim*) by comparison with the new "modern sports" – to use the still vague terminology of the time – performed a demonstration of (*sic*) "*pahlavāni* practices" (*namāyesh-e amaliyāt-e pahlavāni*), and "antique wrestling" *koshti-e bāstāni* in a parade before the actual sporting competitions.[21] These were performed before a giant podium, the *sardam*, where the *morshed* provided the rhythm for the open-air exercises.[22]

    21. *Ta'lim va tarbiyat* 10:3 (Khordād 1314/May-june1934): 151.
    22. See Abbāsi 1375/1995, vol. 1, 295–318.

Identity Matters 83

Figure 30. Pahlavān Hāj Seyyed Hasan Shojā'at, called "Razzāz" ('Abbāsi, 1995).

During the whole reign of the Pahlavis, the *varzesh-e bāstāni* of the zurkhāneh was stuck with this role, parade demonstrations. The terms "antique" or "old" sports refer to a distant past and evoke the *Shāhnāmeh*, which tells the story of mythical sovereigns of pre-Islamic Iran. This book was the key symbol of the new regime.[23] We will return to this new national discourse, which hastened the promotion of the country's pre-Islamic past further.

To better identify the ways the zurkhāneh changed during this period, it is necessary to understand the context. The hygienist discourse, already present under the Qajar dynasty, had become dominant,[24] which in terms of physical education meant Swedish

23. Marashi 2009.
24. See Schayegh 2002. See also Shehābi [Houchang Chehabi] 1387/2008. See in particular all of the physiological and social critiques of the zurkhāneh athletes' exercises made by Iranian or foreign observers during the whole interwar period, which reveal with even more weight than in

Figure 31. Pahlavān Sa'id Tākhutā ('Abbāsi, 1995).

gymnastics. The work of Pier Henryk Ling was well known and translated into Persian.[25] Within the new state organizations there was a reflection on what "good" development

---

my own analysis, the violence of the social changes occurring in Iran at that time. Far from attesting a decline in the world of the zurkhāneh, it shows above all a radical shift in paradigm driving new modernised Iranian elites. The argument about decadence is a ploy that should be considered with the utmost mistrust. The violence and sexual practices denounced by observers of the period demonstrate above all the shift in the perspective of the new authority and the new social elites of Iran, with regards to the mores that pre-existed the new social model in Iran. The new discourses in the zurkhāneh were not a return to respectability, but an alignment of the zurkhāneh with the new goals of recently created Iranian sporting institutions. The same phenomenon can be seen in Japan in the late nineteenth century, and between the two world wars, when the country was struggling with the same socio-political shifts and the establishment of a new public morality.
25. M.T.T. 1319/1940, 15–16 and 58.

Identity Matters

Figure 32. Zurkhāneh in the 1930s; new body building tools alongside old ones; the zurkhāneh are still considered a weight training space in their own right ('Abbāsi, 1995).

of the human body should be, which also included the physical exercises of the zurkhāneh. The appearance of new bodybuilding techniques and tools in the zurkhāneh did not necessarily date back to this period, for the photographs from the end of the Qajar period already show athletes using other tools (weights and dumbbells in particular[26]) alongside traditional tools like the *sang, mil,* and *kabbādeh* (Figures 32 and 33).[27] However, by the late 1930s it was no longer a matter of improving the physical exercise program, but rather of introducing total reform, beginning with wrestling.

When the newly founded IWF organized the first national freestyle wrestling championships in 1939, the rules were those of international competitions as codified

---

26. Some of these weightlifting tools are illustrated in the excellent film *The wrestler and the clown*, a Soviet film by Boris Barnet and Kostantin Yudin from 1957. It shows the difficulties in the career of a wrestler in czarist Russia in the early twentieth century.

27. See the numerous illustrations in Partow-Beyzā'i Kāshāni 1337 /1958), and in the works of Mehdi Abbāsi.

Figure 33. A zurkhāneh in Tabriz, 1936; weights for the back and neck, carried in the same way as the *sang-e na'l* ('Abbāsi, 1995).

by FILA. These regulations concerned dress codes (singlets), weight categories, time limits, calculation of points, and the first qualifying regional competitions. In the years that followed, these reforms, particularly those linked to attire, weights, and thus appearance, led to a few tragicomic dramas. In 1946, for example, the local branch of the IWF of Kermanshah had classified its wrestler in the new weight category "featherweight" for the Tehran finals, but the car carrying the athlete to the competition was stopped and the poor man was beaten up by wrestlers from the zurkhāneh, angry that they would be dishonored by "everyone thinking that a-52 kg child in shorts with braces is worthy to represent the *pahlavān* community [of Kermanshah]" (Figures 34 and 35).[28] In another incident, wrestlers from the town of Rey refused to wear the new official singlets for ten years and saw themselves eliminated from the first competitions as

28. Abbāsi 1374/1995, vol. 2, 373–74.

Identity Matters 87

Figure 34. Mostafā Tusi and the first competitions of *pahlavāni* wrestling after the 1979 revolution, with traditional breeches ('Abbāsi, 1995).

a result.[29] The testimonies collected by Mehdi Abbāsi illustrate the progression during this period of a new model of wrestling from the capital to the provinces. A new type of wrestling was officially introduced into Iran in 1939, but had arrived in the city from as early as 1926–1928; it only began to spread permanently into the provinces from around 1946–48, at the time when Iran was preparing to participate in its first Olympic Games, in London in 1948.

The introduction of international standards of wrestling meant that tradition-

29. Abbāsi 1374/1995, vol. 2, 116.

al Persian wrestling, which was heavier and more static, was essentially downgraded. New age and weight categories meant wrestling could spread more easily among young people and provide new opportunities for a whole range of lighter, younger athletes. The desire to be able to test oneself successfully against other athletes on the national and international stage was also a powerful driving force. In the world of wrestling, the paths to glory and international renown would no longer pass through the zurkhāneh. The *pahlavān*s Mostafā Tusi and Habibollāh Bolur were the last winners of the 1939 championships to have been trained and educated in traditional gymnasiums. The freestyle wrestling champions who came after them, like Gholām-Rezā Takhti, were familiar with zurkhāneh practices, and attended the spaces, but essentially trained in the new gymnasiums.

Figure 35. The singlets with of freestyle wrestling (comparison with the style in figure 33 explains the reaction of the *pahlavān*s in Kermānshāh in 1946!) ('Abbāsi, 1995).

The first official move to promote the zurkhāneh came under the patronage of Mohammad Reza Shah in 1941. He approved the reforms to the STB which was divided into two departments, one responsible for clubs, and the other for physical education in schools. The new sovereign enjoyed sports very much and had avidly played football when he studied in Switzerland. Unlike his father, he considered sports a leisure activity, not an accessory to military service. Under his reign, physical and sport education, along with scouting, broke away from this martial vision that was the legacy of the dynasty's founder.

Identity Matters

Published sources tend to consider the shah as the founding father of many things, but the discourse of Hoseyn Alā, general director of the STB in Tehran, on 26 October 1941, is unequivocal. The "interest" for the zurkhāneh did not come from the authorities, or from the new world of modern sports, but from certain people within the intellectual and cultural sphere who sought to attract attention to this institution as a valuable part of Iranian history.[30]

On 18 August 1942, during the Iranian sports championships, of which the finals were held on the Shah's birthday on October 26, a circular from Hoseyn Alā asked all regional directors to add a new sport to the qualifying events in the Iranian championships, namely "ancient *pahlavāni* sports," consisting of spinning, juggling with small *mil*s, the wooden shields, *kabbādeh*, and *bāstāni* wrestling. The author of this circular felt obliged to specify that *bāstāni* wrestling was performed in traditional *pahlavāni* breeches (*tonekeh-ye pahlavāni*), to avoid any confusion, which implies that the leaders of the STB were not familiar with the world of the zurkhāneh. Two circulars written at the time for the province of Isfahan can be studied more closely. Information in these two documents from the Isfahan branch of the STB allows us to see for the first time how these first competitions of 1942 were decided and organized in very concrete terms, and the problems that the organizers faced. The first circular, dated 30 August 1942, was signed by Kamāl Hedāyat, the governor general of Isfahan province, who was also the director of the province's STB. He simply relayed the orders received from Tehran. The second circular, dated the same day, was signed by the director of the Department of Physical Education, Hoseyn Ali Ehsāni. The circular gave the necessary instructions and implied that Varzandeh himself, who had become technical director of the STB (*modir-e fanni-e tarbiyat-e badani-e Irān*), had been appointed to oversee the innovative inclusion of zurkhāneh sports in the 1942 events. This document sheds very clear light on how this process was carried out. It seems the order came through just when the budget was being prepared (a handwritten note was added in the margins to that effect). It stipulates that all athletes who wished to participate had to be given authorization and the means to do so. Therefore, notices advertising the competition had to be published in newspapers and prospectuses had to be distributed in administrations and public spaces, including zurkhānehs. However, neither the sports facilities of the STB nor the physical education teachers who trained at the Bāgh-e Homāyun in Isfahan (a royal garden that had been transformed into a training ground) had the exercise tools required for zurkhāneh exercises. Ehsāni thus ordered that either the exercise tools be bought in sufficient number, or that "an agreement be reached with the director of a zurkhāneh in the town so that the athletes who wish to might train there at specific times." A note added by hand indicates that the latter option was chosen. This document provides important detail. It reveals a situation that was unprecedented since the beginning of the sports reforms, in which new and old athletes could find themselves either in the same

---

30. *Āmuzesh va parvaresh* 12:5–6-7 (1321/1942): *vāv*.

competition, or in the same training spaces. The author of the document felt obliged to find a solution, implying that it would be impossible for veterans of the zurkhāneh to be asked to come and train the athletes themselves in the Bāgh-e Homāyun, and if the athletes had to train in the zurkhāneh then it would have to be "at specific times." Why not at the same time? So that the athletes who were not used to being in the zurkhāneh could avoid mixing with traditional athletes? This perhaps reflects a barrier between the STB and the zurkhāneh. Or was it a barrier between practices or social groups that did not mix?

In the meantime, there was very little time for organizing the qualifying rounds in zurkhāneh exercises, "new" disciplines that had not yet emerged at the national level. There were barely two months between the first instructions and the date of the finals. These were held as planned, and on that occasion, the shah himself awarded an armband to the champion in traditional wrestling. However, there were no medals for the other exercises in traditional sports. The journal *Āmuzesh va parvaresh*, which was covering the events, announced a "sporting demonstration by Iranian athletes with a new competition of "antique" Iranian wrestling and *farangi* (Greco-Roman) wrestling"; and that was all. A little later, it was mentioned that the zurkhānehs in Tehran and the provinces would be "reformed to develop and revive them."[31] Thus the first attempt to organize specific competitions for the various zurkhāneh exercises was reduced to a simple parade, similar to the one held for the 1934 thousand-year anniversary of Ferdowsi, inaugurating the competitions in the various disciplines. In subsequent years, the STB organized competitions in what came to be called *varzesh-e bāstāni* (ancient sport); as we saw earlier, Shaʿbān Jaʿfari became *kabbādeh* champion in 1946. But these occasional competitions remained opportunities for sporadic recognition within a limited circle of athletes, rather than competitions involving all those who practiced *varzesh-e bāstāni* in Iran.

The reforms of the zurkhāneh and the "sports of ancient Iran" mentioned by Hoseyn Alā in the article of *Āmuzesh va parvaresh* were significant in that they determined the direction taken between 1941 and 1967. The zurkhānehs were referred to as *varzeshkhāneh* and placed under the auspices of the STB that recorded them "if the owners of the zurkhāneh so desired," along with the names of their major *pishkesvat* or *miyāndār*.[32] This non-compulsory registration allowed them to access funding from the organization as part of the register of sporting infrastructures (and not as an ensemble of infrastructure and practices). The zurkhāneh was just considered an old gymnasium that ought to be modernized in response to new public hygiene norms, with bigger rooms, more light and aeration, changing rooms, and if possible, showers (which supposes access to running water, which Tehran did not have at the time). In 1944, a new zurkhāneh in this vein was inaugurated, that of the Bank Melli, for which the bank's director at the time, Abolhasan Ebtehāj, was hotly criticized by a member of parlia-

31. *Āmuzesh va parvaresh* 12:5–6-7 (1321/1942): *alef, be, he*.
32. Partow-Beyzāʾi Kāshāni 1337/1958, 223.

ment who argued that it did not behoove a bank director to sponsor a zurkhāneh.[33] This became the model for new zurkhānehs that aimed at respecting modern standards of hygiene, including that of Shaʿbān Jaʿfari, built in 1954.

Several innovations occurred in the world of the zurkhāneh during this period. There were moves to reorganize the training program to intensify warmup exercises in response to criticism the athletes themselves had been expressing since 1939.[34] A radio program was also broadcast at five o'clock in the morning, which allowed athletes to do their exercises at home (on the new Radio-Tehran, inaugurated on 24 August 1940). This was the first time that a program of "standard" zurkhāneh exercises was proposed, and it still exists today. It is difficult, however, to measure the regional impact of this. In 1941, there were still lots of people who did not have radios, but this program was very successful and many of the athletes I spoke to in the zurkhāneh recorded the best episodes onto cassettes, particularly those by Jaʿfar Shir-e khodā, who was the virtuoso and highly respected *morshed* of the Bank Melli zurkhāneh.

The two most important innovations were firstly the emergence of an attempt to organize the weightlifting and gymnastic exercises of the zurkhāneh into competitive disciplines in 1942, and secondly the move to question the practices, instruments, and exercises of the zurkhāneh. It bears repeating that these questions did not come from the authorities or sporting institutions but from certain Iranians intellectuals who felt the need to reconstruct the heritage of this athletic tradition so that it could take pride of place in the new national historiography.

1934–1979 Different Ways of Interpreting a Tradition

The year 1934 saw a revival in national fervor with the festivities honoring the birth of Ferdowsi. It was also the year the founding stone of Tehran University was laid and the Academy of Persian language was inaugurated (*Farhangestān-e zabān*). Among other things, this academy was responsible for finding Persian equivalents for Arabic and European loanwords. By 1941 the university already had over 2000 students. The cultural effervescence of the period was directed at the rediscovery of the country's pre-Islamic past. The archaeological digs – largely directed by the French between 1894 and 1927 – were perfectly timed to reveal Iran's exceptionally rich archaeological heritage. This rediscovery occurred at the very point when the new Pahlavi authorities were trying to obscure the memory of the former Qajar dynasty, by holding them responsible for all of the country's woes. The revalorization of Iran's pre-Islamic past and the denigration of the Qajars went together, but one was not necessarily the consequence of the other. The period of questioning began well before Reza Shah; he simply knew how to use this, and successfully imposed what the Qajars had never managed to.[35]

33. Partow-Beyzā'i Kāshāni 1337/1958, 224.
34. Partow-Beyzā'i Kāshāni 1337/1958, Introduction.
35. This paragraph is broadly inspired by Digard, Hourcade, and Richard 1996, 63–95 and 341–79.

Iranian reformist scholars have been exploring the history of mediaeval and pre-Islamic Iran since the late nineteenth century. Benedict Anderson observed that this was a universal tendency among states that had to redefine their identity during the progressive establishment of the nation-state model around the world.[36] Indeed, as the authors of *Iran in the 20th Century*, note:

> The political exaltation of the national past did have a positive consequence- in the emergence of a pointed interest in historical and philological research and in Iranology (*Irānshenāsi*) among Iranian intellectuals, which were no longer the exclusive domain of foreigners. A new generation of scholars, like Ebrāhim Purdāvud (1885–1968), Mohammad Qazvini (1877–1949), and Abbās Eqbāl (1896–1955) participated in intellectual renewal and creation of the Iranian academic sphere in which the admiration for antiquity and the Middle Ages went hand-in-hand with a certain militant patriotism.[37]

However, the first significant analysis of the zurkhāneh produced in Iran came from Iranian Marxists. In 1947, Hasan Gusheh, who was for a time vice-principal of the famous Alborz school, published the text of a talk he gave at the Center for Irano-Soviet relations, in the journal of that same Institute.[38] This article was, to my knowledge, the first ethnographic study by an Iranian author about the zurkhāneh. The fact that he was a Communist is not unrelated. Indeed, it was the Communists who were the first to conduct sociological studies on contemporary Iranian society. Gusheh's work provides a precise description of what authors would later seek to conceal, that is, a rather crude depiction of the zurkhāneh as they existed in Tehran in the 1940s. He went into the old zurkhāneh and interviewed the athletes and the *pishkesvats*[39] and received help from Shamsoddin Shāyesteh, who, as we saw, was trying to spread the sport in Tabriz in the 1930s and who was *mo'āven-e edāreh-ye tarbiyat-e badani*, vice president of the STB in 1947.

As Gusheh noted, there were no sources available in Persian on the zurkhāneh and VBKP sports. However, there were "many books on *javānmardi, mardānegi, ayyāri, ayyārpishegi, luti* and *lutigari*," particularly those written by Mohammad Taqi Bahār, *Malek al-sho'arā*, Iran's last Poet Laureate. Gusheh declared that Bahār's work was useful but only briefly mentioned the zurkhānehs themselves. Among other things, Bahār

36. Anderson 1991.
37. Digard, Hourcade, and Richard 1996, 351. Our translation.
38. Gusheh 1947.
39. This is a highly unusual approach that is rarely observed afterwards. The main sociological study on zurkhānehs in 1976 by the High Council for Culture (Showrā-ye Āli-e Farhang va Honar) is merely a gigantic mass of more or less relevant statistical data (systematic measurement of the depth of the *gowd*, mostly around 79–80 cm but falling in a broader range between 50 and 100 cm etc.) combined with fieldwork techniques that are more like a national census questionnaire than anything else. There is also a short but very informative article by A. Reza Arasteh (see Arasteh 1961), which makes original use of the information contained in Hoseyn Partow-Beyzā'i's book.

published the *Tārikh-e Sistān*, which tells the story of the Saffarid dynasty in the eighth century, and its founder Ya'qub-e Leys, a humbly-born coppersmith (*saffār*) who joined and came to lead a mercenary-style military group common in Persia, the *ayyār*s, with whom he managed to break away from the caliph in Baghdad. In the twentieth century, the events recounted in this work were interpreted as a Persian reaction against the Arab conquest. It is therefore not surprising that Gusheh presented the story of the zurkhāneh as a military institution born out of a reaction against the Arab invasion. "Pure and valiant men of Iran" (rādmardān-e pāk-e Irān) decided to educate young people and prepare them "for widespread movements of revolt." Without further explanation, his account then jumps to the thirteenth century and he uses the same explanation for the reaction against the Mongol invasion and describes the zurkhāneh as "special organizations, very well structured with bases distributed throughout the country (*ayālāt-o velāyāt*)," in each town and village, in each neighborhood, under the direction of a chief appointed by the "apparatus," *tashkilāt* [a clearly Marxist vocabulary!] to bring young people together and communicate the "organizational directives" of the "apparatus." These young people had a special weapon (the author does not say what that weapon was or what it was used for, the zurkhānehs having never taught fighting with weapons), came together in sporting houses (*varzeshkhāneh*, the equivalent of zurkhāneh), and had a *pātoq*, a favorite place to meet. This is how the zurkhānehs in working class neighborhoods were exalted as a veritable network for national resistance against invaders. Marxist interpretations aside, we can see the first appearance of an interpretive framework that would reappear later in all the variants of the history of the zurkhāneh. These were the consequences of Bahār's interpretive work, and the first major historical summaries published at the beginning of the Pahlavi era.[40]

Nevertheless, Gusheh was one of the only, perhaps the only, scholar to have closely analyzed the social relations within the zurkhāneh in his time. He correctly noted that far from being a space of humility, the zurkhāneh was a space for personal promotion within the group. A place where men "from villages could shine, gain recognition, and find work" before the most illustrious *rish sefid*s (the "white beards," the wise old men, but also local notables) of the neighborhood, who, he noted, were also the protectors and constructors of the zurkhāneh. Gusheh had perfectly understood one of the unspoken but essential functions of the institution. He also noted the architectural resemblance between certain zurkhānehs and the old *hammām*s, and the fact that they were both found in little side streets in the oldest neighborhoods of the city. The rooms were small, and the exercise pits could hold no more than sixteen people, eight or ten being the ideal to be able to perform the exercises correctly.

As a good representative of the proletarian avant-garde, Gusheh tried to note the benefits and disadvantages of the institution and provide constructive solutions. He noted that this sport could be a useful means of drawing young people away from the

---

40. On the nationalism of Iranian historiography in this period, see Zia-Ebrahimi 2016); and Ansari 2012.

attraction of drugs and of reinforcing religious practice.[41] It created brotherhood and unity among athletes and developed the values of *javānmardi* and *pahlavāni* (moral values in the most positive sense of the term). Nevertheless, he bemoaned the fact that these exercises were "lacking in the educational benefits of modern sports" such as the *pās dādan* ("to pass," a term borrowed from football), a symbol of an action that leads to "participation, together, in collective victory." The zurkhāneh exercises and wrestling were sports for individual success that pushed the institution to produce athletes who were often "too proud and arrogant, and who have not understood the deep meaning of this sport and the [moral] position of the athlete, and who have committed reprehensible acts that have done harm to the sporting world as a whole."[42]

An internal memorandum within the STB, dating from 1955 and written by its director general, General Izadpanāh, sheds light on what Gusheh implies. The memo reminds all directors of gymnastic clubs (*bāshgāh*) and zurkhānehs (*varzeshkhāneh*) that "they must ensure that groups of young athletes do not attack women and young boys and do not bring shame on their *nāmus* (honor) when leaving the training rooms, as has been reported in several incidents."[43]

In terms of hygiene and physical education, Gusheh describes the old zurkhāneh as follows:

> dark and humid, where never a ray of light enters, and where athletes progress in an atmosphere that is burdened and poisoned by the smell of the coal in the braziers of the music master (the *morshed*), or the smell from the toilets, the petrol lamps, and the smoke from the spectators' pipes (*chopoq*), as well as the smell from the *long* (the exercise towel that is knotted around the waist and between the legs, over the traditional pajama pants), which are rarely washed, and the rugs that are rarely cleaned.[44]

He reiterates the criticisms raised by new athletes about the old gymnasiums and their exercises. These herald a complaint that would become more and more peremptory in spite of the changes made, specifically the lack of stretching and warmup exercises (*narmesh*), the fact that they are tedious and sometimes dangerous and performed without regard to the weight and strength of the athletes. Yet older sources show that there were warmup exercises well before this period. Was this critique therefore unjustified, then, or had the zurkhānehs in the 1940s neglected them? It is impossible to know. Gusheh also argued that the development of the body was inharmonious. The lower body was abandoned, according to him, while the exercises strengthening the top part

---

41. Gusheh 1947, 54. I must admit that I was surprised to find this remark in a list of positive points laid out by a member of the Iranian Communist party, in the context of Stalinism.

42. Gusheh 1947, 54

43. Many thanks again to Houchang Chehabi for having given me the photocopy of this document, which is unfortunately unreferenced. The archives of the STB were inaccessible to me, as they are to many researchers, until the very end of my stay in Iran (April 1998).

44. Gusheh 1947, 49.

Identity Matters

Figure 36. The *pahlavān*'s body is now considered too fat; on the left, the famous *pahlavān* Bolurforush (Partow-Beyzā›i, 1958).

of the body were overly emphasized, giving too much mass to that part. The body was then too heavy and the stomach too fat (Figure 36). However, he notes, "the worst is on the inside!" According to him, after a few years of these routines, the intestines and lungs are affected and the heart becomes too big and therefore weak, while the body becomes dry and stiff (*khoshki-e badan*). Asthma develops, along with sluggish nerves, general fatigue, and eye troubles.[45]

45. An exploration of this kind of questioning can be found in Jozani 1994.

This is a somewhat contradictory description – a body that is described as fleshy and humid, and then later dry – seems to correspond to a chaotic vision of the generalized imbalance in humors in the pure tradition of Galenic medicine, well-known in Iran thanks in particular to Ibn Sina (Avicenna), and here used as part of a radical critique of the bodies of traditional wrestlers. Fatigue, sluggish nerves, sore eyes are all results of an excess of heat and dry, and thus yellow bile (*zardāb* or *safrā*), the lightest humor in the Galenic system. An excess of flesh results from too much humidity, resulting from the strong presence of earth and water, which favors black bile (*sowdā*). The imbalance in these humors corresponds to the above description of the zurkhānehs, with their persistent smell and the air poisoned by heat from wood, charcoal, and tobacco, humid and impure because of the toilets and the floor of the training pits, washed down for the exercises.[46] In passing, we can note the once again negative judgement of the athletes' bodies, in contrast with the traditionally accepted view that a strong body with a fat stomach was a sign of prosperity, harmony of the humors, and, in India, a good circulation of breath.[47]

For Gusheh, all these shortcomings were due to the "athlete's lack of attention to his own needs," making the mistake of wanting to "imitate others out of jealousy and rivalry" (*cheshm-o hamcheshmi*). This has the additional consequence of adding an emotional burden. Indeed, new trainers insist too much on the fact that athletes must not be *keneft* (literally ashamed, shamefaced). The term has a strong moral connotation and transforms sporting failure into a shameful defeat. Gusheh deplores this because he sees it as nonconstructive, a source of violence and discouragement for young people, which as a result weakens many *pahlavān* ("who had to eat dirt one hundred times before being *pahlavān*," in other words they had to be beaten).[48] He documented a constant decline in the number of *pahlavān*s between the 1930s and the time of his writing, 1947. This of course can be interpreted as the impact of new infrastructures and the consequence of a profound change in Iranian society, which we will come back to.

By way of conclusion, we can note that, unsurprisingly, in 1947 Hasan Gusheh's suggested changes were identical to those promoted in 1939 by officialdom. It was by no means an accident that the photos of the zurkhāneh he published were those of the Bank Melli zurkhāneh. These were clearly a counterexample to the uninviting descrip-

---

46. The use of arguments inspired by the canons of traditional medicine to justify this radical change of opinion is fascinating because it demonstrates the overlapping interpretive frames that are produced when a new cultural situation arises with its processes of appropriation and adaptation. It deserves more in-depth analysis but is beyond the scope of this book. See Ebrahimnejad 2004a; and for the later period Schayegh 2002; and Schayeg 2009. See also Chehabi 2019a; and Chehabi 2018. Also of interest is Ebrahimnejad 2014b.
47. I would like to thank the late Professor Françoise Aubin (1932–2017) for having enlightened me as to the traditional signification of having a fat belly in India and China, which also sheds light on its representation in Iran.
48. Gusheh 1947, 54.

Identity Matters 97

tions of the zurkhāneh then commonly found in Tehran and in the provinces, and an illustration of what should be promoted henceforth.[49]

Gusheh's article summarized all the issues at stake for the zurkhāneh at the time. Unfortunately, his observations did not lead to any further studies in the years that followed and, given his openly Marxist political position, were not quoted or reused afterwards. The only researcher who used Gusheh's work was Sadreddin Elāhi, whom we will discuss in more detail below. However, aside from the fact that Gusheh provided a poignant perspective on the zurkhāneh and the reforms needed, he was already quoting Bahār and his work on the Iranian *ayyār*. There was therefore a similarity between his analysis and the one we observe today: the idea of an institution based on military history and a symbol of resistance to invasion. That the techniques taught there were inefficient in "military" terms clearly did not seem to bother anyone.

The first book truly dedicated to the institution of the zurkhāneh was published in 1357 (1958/59) and promoted a reading that was much closer to the official line during the reign of Mohammad Reza Shah. Yet to a certain extent it is complementary to the article by Gusheh. It was written by a poet and intellectual, Hoseyn Partow-Beyzā'i Kāshāni,[50] who frequented the zurkhāneh at a certain period. The protector that made his work possible financially was none other than Teymur Bakhtiyār, deputy prime minister and founder in 1957 of the new political police of the imperial regime, Sāzmān-e Ettelā'āt va Amniyyat-e Keshvar, which would become famously known by its Persian acronym SAVAK.

Partow-Beyzā'i was concerned with three major issues: the need to lay the foundation stones for a history of the zurkhāneh, to record for posterity the recent past of an institution that was only preserved in the memory of older athletes, and to document recent changes. He notes that the world of the zurkhāneh had changed profoundly since the 1930s. In his book, he set about documenting the ancient traditions and anecdotes collected from old athletes, and above all, collecting and publishing the rare written sources available. He published two documents specifically mentioning zurkhāneh exercises, both from the late Safavid dynasty, which are essential for the argument presented in this book: the *Tumār-e afsāneh-ye Poryā-ye Vali*, which he discovered thanks to one of his friends, and the other, previously published in the 1920s but since difficult to find and then republished, the poem of *Gol-e koshti* by Mir-Nejāt Qomi, known as Esfahāni. These two texts are treated in more detail in chapter three.

Partow-Beyzā'i was the first author who seriously tried to provide an outline of the origins of the zurkhāneh as an institution. Alongside the tradition of the *ayyār*, which

49. We should also bear in mind that his comments should be considered nuanced because his descriptions were perhaps a deliberate exaggeration to support his argument, or the response to a brutal contrast between the social world he was used to and the world of the zurkhāneh he discovered.

50. Partow-Beyzā'i Kāshāni 1338/1958.

had carved out the lion's share for itself in its historiography, there was also the mystic tradition that could be traced back to Puryā-ye Vali, the patron saint of wrestlers. Beyzā'i conducted an initial analysis of written sources, followed by a comparative study that attracted the attention of Angelo Piemontese, who was the first – and to my knowledge the only – scholar after Beyzā'i to use the information contained in the *Tumār*.[51] In his work on Puryā-ye Vali, Partow-Beyzā'i concluded that at a date prior to the sixteenth century (Puryā-ye Vali lived between the thirteenth and fourteenth centuries) wrestling was framed within a mystic and Sufi interpretation. He considers the term *morshed* proof of this. This title refers to the music master of the zurkhāneh but it is also the title given to a Sufi spiritual guide, having replaced the older term *kohneh-savār*, which literally means "old horseman."[52] For Beyzā'i, the fact that it is the *morshed* who plays the *zarb* rather than a simple *motreb* (musician), bespeaks the decline of the zurkhāneh tradition. It seems, however, that this has more to do with the fact that the roles of the *motreb* and that of the *kohneh-savār* fused and then arrogated to themselves a title that was initially reserved only for Sufi masters. By the end of the nineteenth century, the fusion between the three roles (*morshed*, *motreb*, *kohneh-savār*) was complete.[53]

Beyzā'i is also critical of the spinning exercises, which he believes to echo a Sufi ritual, suggesting that Sufism, although not the essence of the zurkhāneh, finds an eloquent and original expression there. From there, he makes a parallel between the architecture of the zurkhāneh and that of the Sufi meeting places, the *khāneqāh*s.[54] We will see below to what an extent this comparison is appropriate. Unlike the *khāneqāh*s, zurkhānehs did not offer accommodation to their adepts. However, *zekr* ceremonies, prayers in which phrases are repeatedly chanted in order to remember God, could be held in both.

Finally, Beyzā'i's work identifies the composite aspect of the sports program, showing that the exercises derive from different professional activities, including those practiced by the *shāter* corporation, who were both messengers and guards of honor required for the ceremonial protocols of Iranian sovereigns and nobles in general.[55] He also signals the existence of other more specialized exercise schools, such as *āmājkhāneh* in Isfahan which was a space for archery training on moving targets set on wheels (*charkh-e kamān*). Although he overlooked the fact that *shāterkhāneh*s and *lutikhāneh*s[56]

---

51. Piemontese 1965a; Piemontese 1965b; Piemontese 1966; Piemontese 1967.

52. Partow-Beyzā'i Kāshāni 1337/1958, 18. See also Tehrānchi 1364/1985, which presents the *kohneh-savār* as the ancestor of the *morshed*. The old title has nothing to do with the equestrian arts but simply refers to one of the favorite positions in traditional wrestling, connoting a man person's status as a responsible individual.

53. I would like to thank the ethnomusicologist Jean During for having suggested this eminently plausible explanation.

54. Before being conveniently and explicitly identified as a "second mosque" after the 1979 revolution. Personal observation.

55. Partow-Beyzā'i Kāshāni 1337/1958, 66–68. The term *shāter* refers to the members of a professional corporation of messengers and bodyguards who frequented the zurkhāneh..

56. Aubin 1908, 234.

existed alongside the zurkhānehs, he wanted to identify the space himself and establish coherent comparisons. For a long time, he remained the only one who did so.

Partow-Beyzā'i reiterated the hypothesis of the birth of the zurkhāneh in reaction to resistance against an invader, and cautiously noted that there was no evidence concerning the pre-Islamic period apart from the terms *kohneh-savār*, *pahlavān* (and *jahān pahlavān*), and *nowkhāsteh*, which were perhaps, according to him, military titles of the pre-Islamic period that found their way to the zurkhāneh. According to Beyzā'i, these terms could suggest a filiation for the transmission of titles and the value attached to these words.[57] Although he advanced his hypotheses in a tentative way, admitting that they required further research, unfortunately thereafter they fed into a number of fantasies. He also suggested that the first occurrences of the name of the institution in Iranian sources appeared under the term *varzeshkhāneh* in Mir-Nejāt's *Gol-e koshti* in 1700. He was also familiar with the narratives of the French traveler Jean-Baptiste Tavernier in the seventeenth century, which describe a *shāter* inauguration ceremony in Isfahan.

With Gusheh and Beyzā'i, we have the key elements of the first historiography of the zurkhāneh: an institution allegedly forged in resistance against an invader and a place where warriors and corporations could train. *Pahlavān*s and *shāter*s are seen as heirs to idealized and marginalized social groups (*ayyār*s) who incarnated a particular moral value (*javānmardi*) and mysticism (Sufism), and the zurkhānehs were places that played an important role in integrating young people from the countryside into urban life. Both authors evoke the pre-Islamic period but remain very cautious for want of evidence. After these initial studies, which in spite of their limitations remain by far the best available, an official discourse would emerge from the 1960s to the beginning of the 1980s. This discourse that would become dominant is essentially a work of four authors, Kāzem Kāzemeyni, Gholām-Rezā Ensāfpur, Mostafā Sediq-Imāni, and Mehrdād Bahār.

The first three authors provide the same information, repeating hypotheses as if they were certitudes, unlike Partow-Beyzā'i, who had presented them cautiously, clearly emphasizing the need for further evidence. The most original contribution comes from Gholām-Rezā Ensāfpur, who published an ethnographic study in 1974 with a glossary of expressions that provide additional testimonies and documents on the zurkhāneh during the period of the Constitutional Revolution. He reveals the predominantly lower-class membership of this institution through a study of the names of the *pahlavān*s of the time. A half-concealed Marxist interpretation emerges here, one that could not be as openly expressed as Hasan Gusheh's had been in his time.[58]

Kāzem Kāzemeyni, deserves particular attention because he seems not to have written the books he claims to have authored. Between 1952 and 1979, Kāzemeyni was the director of the Bank Melli sports club mentioned above. In the mid-1950s,

57. Partow-Beyzā'i Kāshāni 1337/1958, 3.
58. Sediq-Imāni seems essentially to have revisited the work of Gholām-Rezā Ensāfpur. See Sadiq 1353/1974–75); Sadiq 1343/1964; and Sedigh-Imāni 1981). See also Ensāfpur 1974); and above all, Showrā-ye Āli-e Farhang va honar 2535sh/1977.

this zurkhāneh was part of the official circuit for the court, and remained so until the 1979 revolution, when it was closed because of its overt association with the Shah's regime.[59] In 1964, Kāzemeyni published a book entitled *Naqsh-e pahlavāni, nehzat-e ayyāri dar tārikh-e ejtemā'i va hayāt-e siyāsi-e mellat-e Irān. Ta'rif-e zurkhāneh va tahlil-e varzesh-e bāstāni*[60] (The Role of the *pahlavāni* and the Ayyāri Movement in the Social History and Political Movements of the Iranian People. Description of the Zurkhāneh and Analysis of *varzesh-e bāstāni*). After several good descriptive chapters focused on the practices of the zurkhāneh, Kāzemeyni resuscitated all the previous hypotheses and sang the praises of the *ayyār* and *shāter* in the most flowery language, as though they were white knights, trained secretly in the zurkhāneh to defend the Persian people against the cruel Arab, Turkish, and Mongol rulers. In this, he also drew on certain fundamental elements of Abdolhoseyn Zarrinkub's book, *Do qarn sokut* (Two Centuries of Silence, referring to the silencing of Iran's spirit by the Arab invasion and subsequent occupation of Iran) which was published after Hasan Gusheh's work and is widely read in Iran.[61] Kāzemeyni's publications would not be worthy of any further attention if it were not for the fact that he is currently the most well-known author among the zurkhāneh athletes themselves, who still refer to his publications. He is still sometimes also quoted as the only reference on zurkhānehs by academic texts of genuine scholarly importance (Figure 37).

The vision of the zurkhāneh as a space for military and chivalrous training intensified during the 1960s and 1970s. This thesis has to be seen in a broader research context begun by Mohammad Taqi Bahār on *javānmardi* in the 1940s, and then developed by Parviz Nātel Khānlari, Mohammad Ja'far Mahjub, Morteza Sarrāf, and Henry Corbin (to mention only the most significant studies), whose academic works also inspired the historiography of the zurkhāneh.[62] Zurkhāneh practices and *javānmardi* are systematically compared, and all the training tools and movements are interpreted to correspond as much as possible to this new image, at the great risk of unfortunate slippages between

59. A sign of the times, this zurkhāneh was reopened in 1996 and is once again an essential destination for the guests of the current government.

60. His ghost writer was none other than Gholām-Rezā Ensāfpur, who wrote in his own name ten years later. Indeed, in the later book Ensāfpur declared that he had written a book about the zurkhāneh under a different name several years earlier. I strongly suspect this book to be the *Zurkhāneh* co-authored by Kāzemeyni and a certain Babayan, some 160 pages published the same year as *Naqsh-e pahlavāni* quoted above; Kāzemeyni and Bābāyān 1343/1964). This book strongly resembles Ensāfpur's writing. However, Kāzemeyni ensured the longevity of his works, publishing a shorter version (119 pages) of his *Naqsh-e pahlavāni* with help from a researcher Térésa Battesti, who co-authored both the book and the summary article that appeared in 1968. See Battesti and Kazemaini 1968.

61. Zarrinkub 1951.

62. See Khānlari 348/1969; Mahjub 2000. See also Vā'ez-e Kāshefi Sabzevāri 1350/1971. For this edition of *Fotovvatnāmeh-ye soltāni* see the very interesting study and commentary by Jean-Claude Vadet (Vadet1978). See also Sarrāf and Corbin 1973; and Corbin 1983. Corbin and Vadet's approaches show how the same kind of documents can inspire vastly different reflections. For a rejoinder to Vadet's article, see Rochard and Jallat 2018, 251 note 51.

Identity Matters

Figure 37. Extract from the portrait gallery in the zurkhāneh of the Melli Bank. The French Prime Minister Georges Pompidou and the Minister for Foreign Affairs Couve de Murville in 1967 (Kāzemeyni, 1968).

the larger-than-life claims (a breeding ground for heroes) and everyday reality (performance artists who shared the stage with *luti*-acrobats). This version was once again dominant in the 1990s, even though it had distanced itself from the "Mithraic" theories of the 1970s, to which we can now turn.[63]

The Questionable Theory of Mithraic Origins of Today's Zurkhāneh

The alleged connections between the actual zurkhāneh and Mithraism can be traced back at least to Mehrdād Bahār, a respected academic and the son of Mohammad Taqi Bahār. Sadreddin Elāhi recounts the emergence of this new hypothesis in a critical article on the different historical theories associated with the zurkhāneh.[64] Elāhi had brought together a number of people to discuss the future of sport in Iran, and it was here that Bahār, a renowned philologist and specialist in the philosophy and religion of ancient Iran, presented the hypothesis that certain zurkhāneh practices were inspired by elements of rituals associated with Mithraism. Among other things, Bahār focused on the strong hierarchy within the Mithraic initiations which, according to him, evoked the hierarchy within the zurkhāneh between *nowkhᵛāsteh, pishkhiz, pahlavān,* and *kohneh-savār*. From this perspective, wrestling was seen as the symbol of the eternal struggle

63. Tehrānchi 1985,13–36.
64. Elāhi 1373/1994, 726–727.

between the forces of light and darkness, and the fact that the zurkhāneh were often built slightly underground was seen as an extension of the Mithraic custom of holding its ceremonies in caves, grottos, and other underground spaces. The fact that some of the oldest zurkhānehs – in Kashan for example – were built near to the city's reservoirs or *qanāt* – as in Malāyer – was, for him, evocative of the importance of water in Mithraism and therefore a throw-back to ancient customs. Bahār declared that these hypotheses ought to be closely examined because "like all ancestral traditions, their origins are lost in the dust of history [...] We have no precise formal documents to prove the origin of these rituals. In truth, we have found nothing, we are reconstructing [the past]."[65] Elāhi, who was a friend of Bahār, had his doubts. Even Bahār himself later admitted doubting his first hypotheses and set aside his reflections on this matter. However, these hypotheses emerged at a time that was highly favorable to rapid ideological recuperation.

In 1971, the shah held a lavish celebration of the 2500th anniversary of the birth of the Persian Empire.[66] The same year, Farāmarz Barzegar wrote a "History of Iranian Sports," printed by the STB, then led by General Parviz Khosravāni, which emphasized the pre-Islamic period.[67] This book is not uninteresting and demonstrates the dominant sporting ideology in Iran at the time – as an age-old tradition that brought forth a nation of warriors, an era overshadowed by the decay of the Qajars, and fortunately destined for a glorious future thanks to the strength of the new dynasty. After the personality cult of the emperor intensified and existing political parties were dissolved in 1975 to be replaced by the single *Rastākhiz* (Resurrection) party, Iran on 21 March 1976 shifted from the age-old solar hijri calendar to the new imperial calendar based on the founding of the Persian Empire: the new year was 2535 rather than 1355. This was presented as one step in the march toward a "great civilization." In this unusual context, a few months after the calendar was changed, a team of researchers from the Showrā-ye Āli-e Fahrang va Honar (High Council for Arts and Culture) published a "Cultural and Social Study of the Zurkhāneh in Tehran" which compiled statistics and, by way of an introduction, the article by Mehrdād Bahār.[68] The Mithraic thesis had initially been presented as a series of hypotheses that were to be confirmed or not confirmed by later research, but through the force of institutions, it became irrefutable official dogma. And yet, most of the elements put forward by Bahār are debatable.

The hierarchy within the zurkhāneh

The succession of titles and ranks in the zurkhāneh may be misleading for contemporary observers if one does not pay close attention to their history and the functions to which they refer. According to the available literature,[69] between the sixteenth and nineteenth

---

65. Bahār 1376/1997, 5.
66. Steele 2020.
67. Barzegar 1350/1971.
68. M. Bahār 1376/1997, 5–39.
69. *Gol-e koshti*, *Tumār*, and *Ganjineh-ye koshti*, discussed in detail in chapter three.

centuries, a community of wrestlers within a zurkhāneh was ideally made up of the following figures: a head wrestler, the *pahlavān*, who fights and teaches; his most advanced student (his successor if everything goes well), the *pishkhiz* (literally, "he who stands first"), who teaches the youngest students, the *nowkhᵛāsteh*s. There is nothing unusual about that so far. There was also an elder *pahlavān*, the *kohneh-savār*, a term that, as we have already seen, did not mean "old horseman" but rather a veteran who no longer participates in wrestling matches. This veteran is the owner or manager of the zurkhāneh, but he also oversees the matches of a *pahlavān* who has a contract with him for a season. He does this for wrestlers who do not have a contract directly with a chief *pahlavān*, a *pahlavānbāshi*, who manages a team of wrestlers for a powerful protector. There may therefore be a delicate relationship between this *pahlavān* and the *kohneh-savār*. One of the documents written during the Safavid period and edited by Partow-Beyzā'i, the *Tumār*, reveals that they were paid the same amounts, which seems to be a source of conflict between these two figures who vied for dominance. The *pahlavān*s who made a living from their wrestling and were not contracted to a powerful aristocrat did not stay in the same zurkhāneh, but moved regularly from town to town with their main students and anyone else they were supervising or who wanted to follow them. This was done very explicitly to renew clients and spectators. Finally, the zurkhānehs were also home to local musicians, the *motreb*s, paid for the essential music and rhythmic accompaniment, as well as a masseur, the *moshtomālchi*, who was recruited by the *morshed* and also performed minor menial tasks.

Outside this community, in the zurkhāneh, we also find a local clientele including occasional wrestlers who had a day job elsewhere, and the *rish sefid*s (white beards), who were the elders and also very often local financial backers of the zurkhāneh, mostly linked to the bazaar. They attended the training sessions and sometimes participated. They also came to look for future employees or men who would support their cause, whatever it was.

The titles of *pishkesvat* (which means "he who wears the Sufi cloak, who has embraced the path"), and *morshed* (guide) are links to the Sufi brotherhood. Sufis and non-Sufis could train together in the *gowd* or be spectators. It was possible to be a *kohneh-savār* without being a genuine mystic follower, a Sufi *pishkesvat* or a Sufi *morshed*. Today, the only titles that remain are *pishkesvat* and *morshed*. It is easy to understand the process that led to the situation in the twentieth century: in constant search for legitimacy and social ascendency, the groups of athletes and regulars of the zurkhāneh assigned the most prestigious titles to themselves, all the veterans becoming *pishkesvat*s whether they were linked to a Sufi brotherhood or not, and the *kohneh-savār*s, taking on the title of *morshed* (whether or not they were Sufi), started to play the *zarb* themselves. *Motreb*s were no longer hired, but some of them who specialized in zurkhāneh music took on the title of *morshed*. The iconographic sources available seem to suggest that the last third of the nineteenth century was when this transformation took place.[70] This was

---

70. Partow-Beyzā'i Kāshāni 1337/1958, 19.

by no means a sign of decadence but simply a socio-economic evolution. Moreover, in the hierarchy of wrestlers there were never more than three or maybe four different "statuses," of which two (*pahlavān* and *kohneh-savār*) were indeed distinguished by age and rank, but in practice had the same importance because they shared the profits equally. Finally, and this point is crucial, there was no initiation ritual to establish individuals within these statuses, except of course the *pahlavān* ceremony. This is a far cry from the seven levels of initiation and grades documented in Roman Mithraism. Moreover, the latter were based on sociological distinctions and roles that made it impossible for most members to aspire to the higher grades. The zurkhāneh was therefore a simple professional organization in the Muslim world, with its specific roles and connections linked to certain Sufi congregation models.

Let us now consider the argument about the proximity with water.

Mithraism and the zurkhāneh's proximity to water

Mehrdād Bahār argued that the fact that the old zurkhānehs were found near water sources was a hint that there was a link with Mithraism, but there is a simpler explanation. An Iranian treatise written in 1875 about zurkhānehs and their weightlifting exercises (the analysis of which will be presented in chapter 3) describes the preparation of the exercise pit and thus demonstrates the need to be near a good water source, before modern water facilities became available:

> The ground is dug out to a depth of one *zar'* and a half,[71] three quarters of this are then filled with twigs. After spreading them out, the twigs are covered with *ney-ye buriyā* (a screen made of reeds) and two knots of *shefteh* (mortar made from a mix of lime and sand) and on top *khāk-e ros* (clay) is added. Every day this clay is wetted down so that it is soft underfoot.[72]

It was imperative to water down the ground of the *gowd* every day, sometimes several times a day, during the hot dry days (regions around the Caspian Sea excepted). So, the proximity to a source of water was crucial for obvious technical and practical reasons. Once filled with the materials enumerated above, the exercise pit was less deep than it is today (25 to 40 cm, compared to around 80 cm today). Thanks to the matting of twigs and reeds, it had a soft flexible floor that was also robust and resistant. The earth was loose, and the athletes would sink a little, which explains the various boards used for the exercises (*takht-e shenā*, *takht-e shelang*) which in fact more than anything provide athletes with adequate stability. The exercise pits constructed in this style (which take up almost the whole room and are quite different from the *hammām*-style architectural model also found in the nineteenth century) completely disappeared around the 1950s.

---

71. A *zar'* is equal to 1.04 meter. A knot (*gereh*) is equal to 6.5 cm.
72. Kāshāni 1875–76, folios 2–3.

Identity Matters

This soon allowed the zurkhāneh to put an end to the expensive and time-consuming maintenance of the traditional exercise pits, and the need to water down the training surface. However, the oldest zurkhānehs can still be found in traditional neighborhoods, close to the old cisterns and public fountains.

Iranian wrestlers, at least from the Muslim period, did not attach any crucial symbolic signification to the use of earth and water, and they moved away from that practice quite easily once a new and more economical solution was found. By contrast, South Asian *akhara*s preserved their soft earth training surfaces, because earth is seen as a sacred element with healing powers and linked with many uses and significations.[73] This is another important element: Islam, unlike Zoroastrianism or polytheistic religions, accords much less place in its liturgy and ritual practices to the physical elements (earth, air, fire, water), with the exception of ablutions before prayer. The *pahlavāni* initiation ritual involves little more than a cup of water mixed with salt (the only absorbable mineral the elders would take for its purifying virtues), specific clothing (wrestling breeches), a spatial orientation (Mecca), and, above all, ritual prayers.

When *pahlavāni* wrestling moved out of the exercise pit between the 1930s and 50s, the only things that remained were the individual or collective athletic and weight-lifting exercises, which were performed on a much harder surface, such as floorboards, or cement covered with linoleum. Moreover, the end of the traditional *gowd* in Iran was associated with the new social hygiene discourse; we saw how Hasan Gusheh criticized the old zurkhānehs, specifically for their excessive humidity. As was the case for the supposed internal hierarchy, the presence of water is therefore not a decisive factor in establishing a genuine association with Mithraism.

Mithraism, the zurkhāneh architecture, and the shape of the exercise pit

Another element in this alleged connection between the zurkhāneh and Mithraism is the general architecture of these spaces. Mithraic sanctuaries, *mithraeum*s in ancient Rome, were generally characterized by a semi-underground room with a small door leading into it, which is seen as similar to the zurkhāneh. But what does a study of the architectural models of the zurkhāneh really tell us? In 1875, the architecture of Iranian zurkhānehs followed one of two styles: the older and most suited to wrestling training had a large rectangular pit as described in the *Ganjineh-ye koshti*, and can still be seen in Bam,[74] but it could also resemble the relaxation room in a *hammām* (Figure 38).[75] There

---

73. Alter 1992, 156–61.
74. There is also a description in the second volume of Niebuhr 1799. See also Jourdain 1814, vol. 4, 240.
75. Piemontese 1966, 219 and 220 note 54 is unequivocal. This resemblance is also noted by Minorsky, "zurkhāna," *Encyclopaedia Islamica*, 2nd ed, vol. 4: 1242–43; by Dubeux (1841); by Jamalzadeh (1983, 59–60); and by Mostowfi (1944), 413. All these references show that at the time the connection was also present in the minds of those who frequented these two places of relaxation, the zurkhāneh and the *hammām*. Kashan and Tabriz have seen *hammām*s transformed into zurkhāneh

was a lower room with a *gowd* in the shape of a *howz*, a large reservoir (filled with water when it was a *hammām*), at the bottom of which could undoubtedly be placed the same preparation of reeds and clay when used for wrestling. The ceiling was vaulted, with an open pinnacle letting in air and light.

Figure 38. "*Hammām* de Khosrow āqā in Isfahan." Note the *sardam* in the back and the *howz*, that, if it were larger, would make an excellent *gowd* (Mohammad 'Alidust, Me'māri-ye Irāni az negāh-e tasvir, Sāzmān-e Chāp va Enteshārāt-e Vezārat-e Farhang va Ershād-e Eslāmi, 1996).

There are a number of pragmatic reasons for these architectural decisions. First, rather than a reference to a particular sacred architecture, these were simply the designs and techniques with which the Iranian builders of the period were familiar. For zurkhānehs inspired by *hammām*s, the architects to whom I spoke were unanimous: when a *hammām* changed its purpose, if it was large enough it could be converted into a zurkhāneh, and when a new zurkhāneh was built, the builders (who were not genuine architects) were recruited from among those who built *hammām*s and similar buildings. There are also crucial advantages both in terms of insulation and practicality in this architecture. These are not specific to the zurkhāneh and can be found in all the tra-

---

over the last century. See also Texier 1852, 52; the illustration reprinted here (Figure 38), "The *hammām* of Khosrow āqā in Esfahān" in the work of Mohammad Alidust (1996, 13), which is a republication of the drawings by Pascal Coste and Jean Flandin (1839–41). I would like to thank my colleague Christoph Werner for having drawn my attention to an article published in the Tehran daily newspaper *Hamshahri* 941, 4th year (18 April 1996 / 20 Farvardin 1375), 14, which suggested once again that the ancient *hammām*s of Tabriz were being transformed into zurkhāneh, in 1996.

ditional Iranians houses with a *zirzamin* (basement).[76] Second, in terms of insulation, an underground room remains at a constant temperature, warm or cool, which is clearly beneficial for a space that is open to certain comings and goings and in which men do not wear much clothing. Third, there is also a practical advantage, because by digging into the ground (relatively easy in Iran because of the general quality of the earth, which is almost never flooded by groundwater), architects avoid having to build what is known as a blind wall, with no large windows.

We can now see that certain characteristics of this architecture were maintained even as traditional Persian houses disappeared from urban zones over the course of the twentieth century. This continuity attracted attention and generated a recent interpretive tradition (one that was not documented in sources prior to the second half of the twentieth century), leading to interpretations such as that entrance doors are deliberately small to oblige wrestlers to bow and show humility. This peculiar tradition, which was indeed invented and which was not recorded in ancient sources, is, however, perfectly suited to the promotion of *forutani*, humility, a quality highly valued by the world of the zurkhāneh. If the athletes choose to see the size of this door as an opportunity to demonstrate humility, we must respect that. Traditions belong to those who enact them and those who perpetuate them are free to transform them. Nevertheless, that does not mean we must also accept the historical constructions associated with them. In any event, it is impossible to affirm that an underground room close to a source of water is proof of a link to Mithraism. If that were so, it would apply to all the *hammām*s and pre-twentieth century Iranian urbanism.[77]

Why Mithraism?

This desire for a connection between Mithraism and the zurkhāneh is genuinely intriguing. There are clearly no signs of an association with the main elements of that religion: nothing about the killing of the cosmic bull or any reference to the seven planets and luminaries and their very precise links to the Mithraic hierarchy; none of these are present in the zurkhāneh or in the most ancient treatises studied. Aside from a few unoriginal metaphors there is no real and serious connection to the stars as the final destination for the souls of those who followed Mithras – none of this appears in the zurkhāneh. Finally, given the lack of genuine proof, the sociological objectives of this religion in Roman society cannot be projected as such onto the objectives of the religion in the Persian Empire and in Central Asia, its original birthplace.[78]

76. This is an underground room that allows the family to escape from extreme temperatures. In wealthy households there is often a fountain or running water to cool the air in hot periods. This same idea of a space that is built into the ground (or a hillside) to maintain a constant temperature is also found in other parts of the world.

77. Adle and Hourcade 1992; particularly Habibi 1992, 199–206, esp. 204; and Scarce 1992, 73–94.

78. For a new approach to studies on Mithraism see Gordon 1972, 92–121; Gordon 2017a, 93–130; Gordon 2017a, 279–315; Gordon 2014. For Mithraism in Central Asia, its various forms

What seems to mislead researchers working on this hypothesis is an erroneous analogy. The fact that there was a close link between the army and Mithraism in the Roman Empire is seen as echoing the supposed military function of the zurkhāneh. This feeds into an assumption about an identical structure in the Persian Empire. Once that parallel has been made, this "military" religion is pinned onto the zurkhānehs, which are claimed to be fundamentally, or even exclusively, reserved for military training. I take issue with this point. The wrestling and weightlifting exercises of the zurkhāneh constitute physical practices that have a variety of social functions. Naturally, bodybuilding is very useful for all professions involving strength, including soldiers, but above all for professionals working in wrestling games and performances. All the testimonies from the past that I have been able to study converge on the idea of a community of individuals dedicated to combat technique without any lethal content, who live off teaching their knowledge and performing their skills. The world of the zurkhāneh – like all performative combat sports – also lives off betting (an element that is crucial and never openly addressed) as is documented in the sources concerning the court of Akbar the Great at the turn of the sixteenth century in India. Indeed, at the time these fights, either between animals or men, were the object of bets that were so large that a very specific legislation was introduced to oversee them and regulate the maximum amounts involved, in order to avoid sudden ruin and the risk of conflict between the "Grand" courtiers.[79]

The Iranian zurkhānehs I attended over the years are heirs to this particular past and mode of operation: a former school for performing arts, wrestling and juggling. So why does this "desire for Mithras" still emerge in certain books and articles on the zurkhāneh? There are probably two reasons for this. In addition to the ideological weight of the Pahlavi era, with its emphasis on Iran's pre-Islamic past, transmitted by a renowned author perhaps in spite of himself, there is the general idea that the more ancient a practice is, the more prestigious it is. I see this as a desire to project a purely pre-Islamic and military origin that glorifies a certain type of national virility, a project that is more attractive than a simple civil origin. Although it cannot be said openly, a religious (Islamic) origin is mostly rejected, all the more strongly because of the politization of religion since the 1979 Islamic revolution.

And yet, if there is a pre-Islamic heritage here, it is to be found in certain rituals that bear the mark of *fotovvat* and the professional guilds (particularly in terms of dress: the breeches, the belt...). But these are not widely emphasized in common contemporary reinterpretations. Perhaps we should see this as the natural inclination of the historiography studied above, to want to consider the zurkhāneh ancestry as an exclusive space for military institutions and to neglect – or even deny (with the exception of

---

and transformations, and particularly the disinterest for the Sasanian power in regards to this god, see Grenet 2001.

79. See Abu al-Fazl ibn Mubarak 1949, vol. 1, book 1, 218; and vol. 1, book 2, 253.

Partow-Beyzā'i) – the importance of mystic-professional references to an institution combining *fotovvat* and Sufism. Another pre-Islamic possibility to explore could be the influence of periods prior to the Sasanian era.[80]

How should we approach the problem of origins?

From the outset this question of origins was an important obstacle to the study of the history of the zurkhāneh. The political weight of the evocation of ancient Persia is so poignant in Iranian historiography that it is important to specify a certain number of things here that the specialists of antiquity, possibly interested in the history of wrestling and the bodily traditions associated with the zurkhāneh, cannot avoid. Indeed, if we were to establish the foundations for a global history of traditional wrestling, as it appears in Turkey as well as in the Indian sub-continent, as well as in the Caucasus, Iran and Central Asia, it might be called, perhaps, the history of "Khorasanian wrestling" after the name given to it by certain Muslim intellectuals in sixteenth-century Mughal India,[81] to differentiate it from the Indian physical traditions belonging to the cultural spheres of Hinduism and of Buddhism. By the sixteenth century, the region of Khorasan had long been the heart of the culture that was at its height at the end of the Timurid era, bringing together people of different languages and cultures, Turkish, Persian, and many others, all inextricably intertwined. The region must therefore be understood here in its largest possible geographical form, covering *also* Central Asia with all its major cities, such as Khiva, Urgench, Samarkand, Bukhara, Merv, Herat, and Kabul.

But this form of wrestling would have itself been a legacy of the synthesis between Greek/Byzantine, Persian, and Indian traditions because it seems that its tutelar figures in the sixth century, at the heart of the ancient Gandhara region (nonetheless influenced by Sasanian culture), were still Heracles, Balarama and Krishna (and to the best of my knowledge, not Mithra).[82] However, physical practice adapts to changes in religious paradigms, as we can see in India, where the Hindu deities venerated by wrestlers changed over time. Indeed, wrestling is now associated with the monkey-god Hanuman (beginning apparently around the eighteenth century). It is difficult to say why there was a shift from Krishna to Hanuman. However, we are clearly faced, as in Iran and elsewhere, with a realignment of ancient frames of references with new expectations of contemporary practitioners. When we consider the weightlifting program of the zurkhāneh and its tools, we can see that it constitutes a corpus which had already experienced many syntheses combining the Persian, Hellenic, and Indian worlds during the

---

80. For an exploration of the mention of wrestling during the Parthian/Arsacid period and the signification of the word *koshti* (belt) and *pahlavān* (Parthian) see Chehabi 2018.
81. Flatt 2010.
82. Di Castro 2007, particularly 369; Di Castro 2003. Finally, for a fascinating text, see Di Castro 2005.

Seleucid, Parthian, and Sasanian empires, well before the coming of Islam.[83] This was a world of wrestling and physical exercises in a multicultural Persian empire that was necessarily in contact with the Greco-Roman empire to the west, later Byzantium, and with the kingdoms of northern India to the east. This was the intersection of three major cultures. However, this initial all-encompassing physical culture of the Mediterranean and Middle East was rapidly associated with a fourth actor that would contribute to the transformation, including the processes of diffusion. This was the Turco-Mongolian nomadic peoples and cultures of the Siberian steppes. The influence of this fourth actor was felt first in Khorasan during the Sasanian era, and then everywhere else. Its impact on the Near East and Middle East is well-known, but it extended beyond this area from Siberia to the Caucasus and India, from Cairo, Tunis and Algiers, three cities where wrestlers were overwhelmingly Turks, thanks to the Ottoman Empire.[84]

There is no single starting point for the history of wrestling and its institutions. It has multiple origins that can be traced back to time immemorial. Its origins are neither entirely Greek, nor Persian, nor Indian, nor Turco-Mongol. Coming out of neolithic and bronze ages, in the cultural area we are looking at, this wrestling tradition is indeed a combination of these three, then four, influences, in varying proportions at different times, with spiritual and institutional frameworks that change over the course of the major socio-cultural transformations.

THE ZURKHĀNEH, MARTIAL ARTS, AND THE *SHĀHNĀMEH*

The Shāhnāmeh *as proof of the military origins of zurkhāneh pahlavāni wrestling?*

Before moving on to the heart of the question, it is important to reiterate certain elements. As we have seen, the reason why the zurkhānehs were imagined to be connected

---

83. On this particular subject, the Hellenistic period is vastly underestimated in Iranian historiography overall. The only well-known institution that included wrestling in an educational and military program for its citizens was the Greek city and its gymnasiums. Greek gymnasiums were well established in the former Achaemenid territories under control of Hellenistic rulers. See the presentation by Aikaterini Samara for Ptolemaic Egypt (Samara 2017). The author emphasizes that in peacetime this institution, which developed in response to rich Greek or Macedonian settlers, was reserved for this Greek minority to meet among themselves (men only) but in wartime it was opened to young soldiers from the local populations, who followed "Greek-style" training there. In an army where infantry (peltasts and phalanx) was the heart of the matter, this made more sense than the projection of this institution into the heart of Persian military culture based on mass equestrian fighting. However, there were necessarily long-term cultural interactions that influenced local cultures in the zones occupied by Greek colonizers between the 4th and the 1st centuries BCE. See the enlightening synthesis of Laurianne Martinez-Sève (Martinez Sève 2012, which on page 383 mentions a certain Nicolaos, a Greek gymnasiarch working in territories controlled by Parthian rulers.

84. Canard 1932, especially 135–45.

Identity Matters 111

to Mithraism comes from the fact that traditional *pahlavāni* wrestling was often presented as directly linked to ancient Persia's military arts, or, like its Turkish and Indian cousins, even defined first and foremost *as a martial art in itself*. In the eyes of those who believed in this idea, it was confirmed through the inclusion of wrestling contests in the pages of the *Shāhnāmeh*, the Book of Kings, written in the tenth century CE by the great poet Ferdowsi, which tells of the deeds of the kings and knights of pre-Islamic Persia.[85] The reasoning is as follows: if warriors engage in wrestling, and open-handed wrestling is mentioned in the *Shāhnāmeh*, this wrestling would be a military technique and the zurkhāneh a direct descendent of a military academy.

However, these considerations overlook a central and serious issue: not only is open-handed wrestling not a martial art,[86] but in addition, even though wrestling is enjoyed by all social classes, the social status of professional wrestlers is historically very low in Mediterranean and Middle Eastern societies. Naturally, a powerful lord who practices wrestling is of high social rank, but his trainer is a simple servant, as are the wrestlers called in to perform at his banquets. As far as we can tell from extant written and pictorial documents, the zurkhānehs of the late twentieth century were indeed the heirs to the wrestling academies that made good money from performing before powerful figures. These wrestlers could even earn up to ten times as much money when they let themselves be beaten by nobles who wanted to shine in front of their friends, by staging a bout in the arena.[87] Ultimately, the fact that soldiers and aristocrats enjoyed wrestling did not mean that the wrestlers who made their living from their art were considered their equals or even true soldiers. Once again, understanding the social status of professional wrestlers, those who create and teach the best techniques to apprentices, and who are the heart of the life of the traditional zurkhāneh, is *the key question* in understanding the real history and identity of this institution.

Both in the Mediterranean and in the Middle East, with the possible exception of the Greek hoplites and the legions of the Roman republic (sixth to first centuries BCE), professional wrestlers from late antiquity up to the modern period had a particular social status, and were clearly *inferior* to the military and, of course, aristocratic classes.[88] As far as military arts are concerned, for soldiers in general and aristocrats in particular, open handed wrestling was a thrilling game (especially if betting was involved), a fascinating performance, or a useful physical exercise, but it was not lethal enough to be an effective fighting technique and clearly not central to their status or profession, unlike the martial arts practiced by Japanese warriors for example.[89] A zurkhāneh master does

85. See Chehabi 2018.
86. For more on this debate see Rochard and Jallat 2018, 239–42.
87. See the observations by Gaspard Drouville 1819, 58.
88. See Rochard and Bast 2023.
89. For example, in Renaissance Italy of the *condottieri*, in the sixteenth century, Baldassar Castiglione wrote in his famous "Il Libro del Cortegiano" (Book One, Chapter XXI), in reaction to the fashion among languid courtiers who "pluck their eyebrows," has one of his characters express a

not teach his students how to kill, there is no teaching about the vulnerable nerve points of the body. Wrestlers never train with any kind of weapons in Iranian, Turkish, or Indian open-handed wrestling schools, not only today but also as far back as the practice can be traced. Even the most violent expression of Persian open-handed wrestling, known as *khasmāneh*, hostile wrestling, which once allowed biting and blows to the eyes or strangulation,[90] must be considered in the context of ancient performances that accepted higher levels of violence and which progressively diminished, apparently following a form of euphemization of violence well analyzed by the sociologist Norbert Elias.[91] Professional wrestlers were there to provide a performance that fell within established rules and provides the opportunity for gambling before an audience familiar with the game. *Pahlavān*s were neither soldiers, nor gladiators, nor boxers; there was absolutely no vocation to fight to the death or to kill, whether out of necessity or to entertain the crowd. Open-handed wrestling from the pre-modern period is a very rough combat sport: participants may be gravely wounded and even die from their injuries. However, this is unusual, accidental, and constitutes a fault rather than an objective explicitly envisaged, cultivated by appropriate teaching and precise anatomical knowledge as is the case, for example, in Indian *Kalarippayattu*, Chinese *kung fu*, or Japanese *jujitsu*. In Iran, as far back as can be reasonably traced, genuinely lethal military techniques were learned elsewhere, and often on horseback.

Thus, the fact that open-handed wrestling is often the ultimate stage in duels between the heroes of the *Shāhnāmeh* is merely the artifice of the storyteller bringing the tale to its climax thanks to the description of a combat performance well known to all, and in so doing, promoting the intrinsic value of the fighters, which is the only thing that sets them apart. The storyteller always ensures that it is "innate skill" and "experience" that triumph against the pure technical mastery of weapons, in a moral conclusion that expresses the idea that a warrior's value lies not in technical knowledge but in sheer bodily strength and cunning. It is difficult to imagine any other interpretation of these legendary fights because, from both a historical and military perspective, none of the fights depicted in the epics are actually realistic. To the best of my knowledge, anyone observing these practices and traditions closely – whether in Asia or in Europe – would see duels between champions preceding a battle, but never plain open-handed wrestling.

One example is not the basis for a conclusion, of course, but even in the example I managed to find, in which the hero of a military duel (a historically documented duel, not a fictional one) is a professional wrestler, the situation does not support the theory of specific military training, equality of rank, or teaching of lethal open-handed techniques, even in the sixth century CE.

---

positive opinion on wrestling, which he considers a favorable *accompaniment* (this is an important nuance) to fighting with weapons when on foot.
90. Kāshāni 1875/76, passim.
91. Elias and Dunning 1986.

Identity Matters 113

Procopius of Caesarea (d. 565 CE) was a famous historian of the Byzantine Empire who, as the personal secretary of General Belisarius, wrote a history of the Justinian wars in the sixth century. In this history he presents the case of a professional wrestler and Greek hero in two duels during the war against the Sasanians. The text suggests that this wrestler, known as Andreas "with a vigorous body," was able to arm himself and managed to slip into the ranks of the Byzantine soldiers without permission. He attacked a young Persian opponent from horseback with a lance, mortally wounding him and then finishing him off with his dagger on the ground (there was no wrestling as such). He then disobeyed a direct order from the commanding officer of the troop and attacked a second Persian champion who had come to defend the honor of the Sasanian army by avenging the first fallen champion. After the initial and very violent shock threw the riders to the ground (the Mongols would invent stirrups some time later), he overcame his opponent, who was trying to get up but was still kneeling, by getting up faster than him and striking him first with his blade. Procopius attributes this speed to his physical training as a wrestler. However, he also described Andreas like this: "He was not a soldier, he had never been in a war. He was a simple gymnastics teacher who presided over a wrestling school in Byzantium. He was in the army as the bath boy of Buzes [a general in the Byzantine army]."[92]

It seems that Andreas was not more than the private masseur of a superior officer. This is explained by the fact that the art of massage always accompanied wrestling, although perhaps the fact that Andreas was shown such indulgence from his master may indicate that he was more than just a masseur. It is most likely that his position as Buzes's attendant (voluntary or not) facilitated Andreas's infiltration among the Byzantine cavalry. Reading this passage, we have the impression that Andreas would never have been able to do what he did if he had not been protected by Buzes. However, clearly Andreas is not in his rightful place and did not have the status of a soldier. Similarly, it was not wrestling techniques that bought him victory in the second fight, but his physical condition, which was a result of his wrestling training. There was no open-handed fighting, no typical wrestling holds, just an ability to get up quickly and strike an opponent described as older than the first Persian soldier. Finally, and this is the key point, his status, his profession, and his result are so astonishing (compared with those of "real" soldiers) that Procopius considers the anecdote worthy of a place in his official chronicles.

The conclusion is that wrestling is useful as a form of physical preparation, but even among the Byzantines – who had become Christian but remained influenced by the classical Greco-Roman culture and its traditional athletic institutions – a professional wrestler, director of his own school in Byzantium, was not seen as a true soldier, but rather as a civilian responsible for looking after his superior officer's body, who had to

---

92. Chaliand 1990, 213–14. These elements are taken from Procopius, *The Persian War*, Book I, chap. XIII and XIV; in Cameron 1967.

be cunning and disobey in order to show his martial quality. It is worth thinking about this in light of the possible situation of Persian professional wrestlers and the status of wrestling in Persia during the Parthian and, in our example, the Sasanian era. Byzantium in the sixth century clearly did not share the importance awarded to the gymnasium and palaestra of Pericles' Athens, or even Ptolemaic Egypt.

The difference of status between wrestlers and soldiers was also clearly marked in other cultures, particularly in Japan. Over the course of Japanese history, the authorities and the samurai showed little consideration toward *sumo* and *sumotori*s, up until the end of the nineteenth century. This tradition was then entirely re-configured, and largely reinvented, to preserve its public image and integrate the new Japanese national institutions that oversaw martial arts from the 1890s.[93]

This was also true of the bare-handed wrestlers of the Indian courts during the Mughal era (sixteenth to the nineteenth centuries). In the great administrative treatises of this period, such as the *Akbarnāmeh*, and more specifically in the *Ā'in-e Akbari*, a shorter extract of the *Akbarnāmeh*, we can see the *pahlavān*s listed at the very end of the "infantry" section.[94] Despite its title, this section in fact covers all the servants of the sovereign Akbar Shah, both civilian and military, in decreasing order of importance and salary (the *pahlavān*s at the end of the list were thus among the least well paid). This list puts the *pahlavān*s below those who duel with weapons, who are themselves below all military troops, as well as spies.

Famous wrestlers could bring prestige and money to their protectors, who in return paid them lavishly, providing them a shortcut to higher levels of the social hierarchy that would provide the possibility of benefiting further from the generosity and comfort of the powerful. But this situation at the top was extremely precarious. Any disgrace sent the wrestlers back to their lowly origins, or worse. Above all, this social proximity cannot obscure the fact that even at the peak of their glory these professional wrestlers remained socially inferior if they did not find a way to transform this ephemeral glory into long-term resources and higher social status.

Zurkhāneh athletes were outsiders in subaltern positions performing for the rich and powerful, but they were also respected, feared, and sometimes despised by the general population who had had no choice but to live and come to terms with these local strongmen and what they stood for – whether protection or predation. This "in between" social status also deserves further reflection. Wrestling in pre-modern Iran was

93. The temples of Japanese sumo wrestlers organized competitions for religious festivals and to attract pilgrims. This was also a street spectacle for the lower classes, often repressed by Japanese authorities before being "ennobled" in the seventeenth century and accepted in the court of the Tokugawa shogunate. It was given a sacred dimension in the late nineteenth century to allow this very lucrative professional sport to be seen as a genuine martial art, alongside kyudo (archery) or kendo (sword-fighting), and therefore make it more attractive to spectators. For more details, see Guttmann and Thompson 2001, 13–26 and 108–15. See also Gaudin 2009.

94. Abu al-Fazl ibn Mubarak 1949, vol. 1, book 1, chapter 84, p. 218; and vol. 1, book 2, chapter 6, p. 253.

a key male social practice but mastering it at the highest level was something associated with a group of professionals competing with each other, and a lifestyle that de facto situated them on the margins of respectable society. Let us now turn to another affirmation that also sadly seems improbable.

The Shāhnāmeh, *once the sole poetry source chanted by the* morshed *in zurkhāneh?*

Many of the people I interviewed, younger athletes as well as notables and *pishkesvat*s hardened by forty years of practice, all of them pious Shiites, often used swear words when talking about the *mollā* and the *ākhund*, that is, clerics. They assured me that these religious figures had nothing to do with the original *pahlavān* and zurkhāneh, and that "before" (an affirmation pronounced in solemn tones and often accentuated by an index finger pointed towards the sky) *only* the *Shāhnāmeh* was recited by the *morshed* in the zurkhāneh. This was something I often heard repeated both inside and outside the world of the zurkhāneh. Interestingly, the older people who claimed the existence of this reputedly abandoned tradition must not have been more than twenty years old in the 1940s – a period that was already marked by the historical reinterpretation of the zurkhāneh by the new Pahlavi regime. However, in reality this claim is not credible at all; there are no real eye-witnesses, no old tape recordings or real first-hand reports, no mention in ancient texts, and no direct proof for the centrality of the *Shāhnāmeh*.

Although certain historical sources clearly mention the heroes of the *Shāhnāmeh*, they do not mention the recital of chants using the *Shāhnāmeh*. The very specific *pahlavān* initiation ritual described in the *Tumār* makes no mention of chants from the *Shāhnāmeh*, even though it lists all the phrases that have to be pronounced. This treatise also openly expresses the connections to the major Sufi brotherhoods and the *fotovvat*.

Finally, and this is the most important point, the Iranian musicians and *zarb* players I spoke to all affirmed that the prosodic rules for the epic poetry of the *Shāhnāmeh* are such that reciting it would require the *morshed* to produce a musical tempo totally unsuited to the exercises. Jean During, a renowned ethno-musicologist specializing in the study of Middle Eastern musical traditions confirmed this: only a virtuoso would be able to adapt certain rhythms or extend pronunciations to make Ferdowsi's verse fit into a line of music fitted for the zurkhāneh training chants.[95] This would be a genuine musical prowess that is clearly not within the reach of the average *morshed*, either sixty years ago or today. Finally, it is important to remember that daily training is a question of routine, which has no time for this kind of virtuosity. Out of preference, simplicity, and above all feasibility, *morshed*s logically and almost exclusively resort to classical Persian poetry, whose prosody lends itself to accompanying zurkhāneh exercises with musical rhythms. Hafez (1325–1390), Sa'di Shirāzi (1210–1296) or Rumi (1207–1273), to

---

95. Personal communication. See also the recent work of Spinetti 2021.

only mention the most famous, therefore provide the accompaniment for the athletes' exertions.[96] All the *morshed*s and *pishkesvat*s know this and an examination of their music books, where possible, confirms this choice. However, many people continue to proclaim that the recitation of the *Shāhnāmeh* has been shamefully abandoned. Sincere believers, they are nevertheless expressing their perspective on the current regime and revealing an opinion that is deeply connected to the identity aspect which they see as more important – military Iranian identity stripped of any religious aspects.

Since 1997, the VBKP Federation has tried to revive this invented tradition by insisting that before the final of the *pahlavāni* wrestling championships, a dramatic and famous passage of the *Shāhnāmeh* is read in which the hero Rostam confronts and kills the young warrior Sohrāb, without knowing that he is murdering his own son.[97] However, the coaches of the wrestlers in the competition asked that this recitation be removed because it is very long, and the competitors (who have warmed up just before the final) get cold waiting for the end of the chant and lose concentration. Beyond the evocation of legendary figures, the *Shāhnāmeh* and the zurkhāneh do not seem to fit well together at all.

In spite of this, it is true that the book itself remains an important reference in today's zurkhāneh. Each time that it was mentioned by middle-aged interviewees and veterans, it was clear that along with the Koran, the work of the poet Hafez, and the writings of Imam Ali, it was the only book considered as really being necessary for Iranians to read and know in order to understand who they are and how they should behave in life. It is important to note that the Koran and Hafez's *Divān* are still used every day as part of bibliomancy (*estekhāreh*). This practice is not encouraged by religious authorities but remains – like reading tea leaves (or coffee grounds in Iran) – very common.[98]

Beyond being a national symbol, the *Shāhnāmeh* is often quoted by many veterans as an inspiration for those who consider they do not need anyone to tell them how to run their lives and who simply address God directly when the need arises, without going through his earthly servants. It therefore symbolizes honor, courage, determination, and above all a mistrust of authority. As before the revolution, official power, its symbols, and its institutions – whether civilian, revolutionary, police, or religious – remain a syn-

---

96. The choice of poetry has become a sign of distinction for the best *morshed*s. One of them (frowned on by many) does not hesitate to recite the fierce and sulphurous verses of the poet Forough Farrokhzād.
97. The episode is summarized in Chehabi 2018, 244–248.
98. I was the involuntary beneficiary of this tradition towards the end of my four-year stay in Iran, in 1998. A specialist in air freight, who had initially flatly refused to assist with my move from Tehran to Marseille, called me back the next day to tell me enthusiastically that he accepted my case and, what is more, for a lower rate than the one he had refused me the day before. I was as surprised as I was happy. When I came to his office that evening to thank him and fill in the papers, he explained to me, with a photocopy as proof, that on the evening he had refused, he had performed an *estekhāreh* about me using Hafez's poetry. The response, he told me, had flabbergasted him. The poem indicated by the *estekhāreh* was a strong and explicit reminder, for those who truly loved God, of the sin in not helping those who traveled and who are far from home. My deepest thanks therefore to this generous man, and to the spirit of Hafez!

onym of an arbitrariness and a danger that can be courted, and which must be contended with, but which must be mistrusted above all.[99]

In hindsight, the analysis of some of the discourses of both *pishkesvat*s and younger interviewees take on additional meaning. They did not simply express a favorable or unfavorable opinion about the power holders of the Islamic Republic, although (outside of very politically militant spheres that support the current regime) the international reputation and economic prosperity of the time of the shah provoked immense nostalgia. Rather, they are the expression of a generally pessimistic vision of the way of the world that derives more often than not from painful everyday experience. As I noticed on many occasions, this pessimistic vision of the world gave rise to a penchant for conspiracy theories.[100]

What historic discourse does that ultimately produce?

The analysis of discourses on the history and origins of the zurkhāneh in the late 1990s shows that they were inspired by the whole range of elements previously mentioned. During the first years of the Islamic Revolution of 1979, the new VBKP Federation tried to make its connection to religion and spirituality clear – the zurkhāneh found itself reinvented, with the status as a "secondary mosque." In 1993, President Ali Akbar Hāshemi Rafsanjāni, declared that the "highest spiritual aspirations" were expressed within this institution.[101] However, the role of Sufism was constantly denied or swept under the carpet by almost all my interviewees, whether private individuals or institutions. I discovered that, as far as the private individuals were concerned, this was a very understandable precaution. The current regime favors a vision of the zurkhāneh in which the only spiritual aspect of *javānmardi* that is recognized is that which is an expression of a Shiite faith devoid of any connection with Sufism. More generally, Twelver Shiite religious orthodoxy in the mosques benefits from its omnipotence, to settle its score with its old rival, the *khāneqāh*.

However, the re-election of President Rafsanjāni in 1993 also marked a period of rehabilitation of a discourse that was clearly and simply nationalist. The reappearance of the pre-revolutionary theses was clearly compatible with the official declarations of the president about the zurkhāneh. The old and new discourses simply overlapped without erasing each other. Henceforth they constituted a whole, a reservoir of symbols, legends, and myths on which my respondents could draw as they pleased, adding elements of their own invention to construct the discourse that seemed the most appropriate to them – a discourse that of course took into account the situation and audience. How-

99. Due to the authoritarian state, this mistrust generated a strong culture of rumor, linked to "ways of talking about politics, and particularly one of its cousins, conspiracy paranoia." To understand the complete structure of the phenomenon of the rumor, see Aldrin 1992.

100. For conspiracy theories in Iran see Chehabi 2009.

101. A quote from the speech Rafsanjāni gave in the zurkhāneh Bank-e Melli published in the newspaper *Puryā-ye Vali*, 18 *Āzar* 1372 / December 9 1993. This was given in honor of the first international competition of *pahlavāni* wrestling.

ever, even when my interviewees were not forced to take into account the possible audience of their opinions, their discourses suggested several levels of belief, unwaveringly accepting the coexistence of theses that, although they seemed contradictory, all shared the fact that they did not question the dogma of *javānmardi*, nor its roots in the oldest, purest Iranian identity and tradition.

What can we see in the different historical constructions studied in this section? Not a serious and documented historical account, but ideologies upheld by different authors. These accounts do not engage with the actual lived history of the zurkhāneh and read like a paraphrase of the history of political ideas in Iran. They may be romantic, martial, pan-Iranist, gnostic, Marxist, or modernist, but they always bespeak an ultimately chauvinistic mindset. This is an interpretative bias that I have observed in all of the historical narratives of various national "physical" and "martial" traditions the world over.

Perhaps unsurprisingly, the official discourse does not explore the equally terrible reputation that the zurkhāneh has had in the same society, other than to explain it, as Gholām-Rezā Ensāfpur did, by positing a supposedly decadent period during the Qajar dynasty. This old catch-all notion has never explained anything. However, it has often served to erase the paradoxes – which are too obvious to be denied – that arise from the confrontation of an idealized past with a very concrete reality in periods where there are many eyewitness accounts. Thus, in light of the accounts from contemporaries in the nineteenth century, there was a surprising shift in situation, whereby a place that was once the birthplace of heroes became a dirty hovel filled with lowlifes, rapists, and pederasts, "vile and despicable types" in people's eyes, as the *Ganjineh* put it.[102] It became a place for sinister individuals who put fear into the streets, and into "pure souls," particularly given that the latter never entered the zurkhāneh to verify such accusations. In both cases, these are simply stereotypical generalizations and far from everyday reality. Whether as a prestigious symbol or infamous space, the zurkhāneh has always had its place in the received ideas of Iranian intellectuals. Celebrating it was the opportunity to express nostalgia for a lost golden age, the virtue of the ancestors, admiration of purity and nobility of soul and the incarnation of bravery and heroism to which people like to imagine themselves the heirs. Others denounced it as a place of ill repute, frequented by dangerous marginals whom they saw as indulging in all imaginable social vices.

However, a certain number of questions remain unaddressed. How did athletes practice wrestling on an everyday level? Where did the physical movements come from? Who were their employers, sponsors, protectors? How did wrestlers organize their profession? What were their everyday interactions with the populations and authorities of the time? Moreover, research has its "noble and important" subjects and its "superfluous" ones. Yet, behind what might seem humble and superfluous are fundamental, but often neglected, social mechanisms. Behind the explicit functions of social facts

102. Kāshāni 1875-76, folio 2.

are their latent functions.[103] Attaining and understanding them is one of the primary objectives of the social sciences.

Notwithstanding the pioneering approach of Hasan Gusheh, the major Persian-language study worthy of admiration on these issues remains undoubtedly that of Partow-Beyzā'i. He was both erudite and a former zurkhāneh athlete, and that is undoubtedly the reason for the value of his work. He did not study the zurkhāneh as a pretext through which to support an ideology, but as a genuine object of research. He was a passionate pioneer, concerned with saving and compiling everything he could find, without fitting the data he accumulated into an imperative and selective ideological mold. Therefore, although he accepted the chivalrous pre-Islamic theses, he did not exclude the documents and information that proposed alternative hypotheses. He provided his readers with the best available synthesis on this institution, and suggested numerous avenues for future research, in response to questions that were then not yet formulated. It matters little that certain aspects of his analysis and his questioning are partially dated now, or false;[104] like all social and human sciences, he was marked by his time. This present book would not have been possible without his research, especially because his book includes two Safavid-era texts that allow us to attempt a reconstruction of the actual history of the zurkhāneh bereft of ideological embellishments.

103. On this question, see Digard 2003. The author reiterates the importance of these sociological concepts developed by Robert Merton among others.

104. For example, he did not see that one of the documents he published, the *Tumār-e afsāneh-ye Poryā-ye Vali*, was a genuine *fotovvatnāmeh* and not simply a *morshed*'s notes.

Chapter Three
History of a Professional Practice

WHEN THE FIRST ATTEMPTS WERE MADE in the twentieth century to write the history of the zurkhāneh, there was some real confusion as to the identity of the men who frequented the institution, especially of those who made a living from their physical aptitudes. To shed light on this question, we have only three known Persian documents that deal in length both with wrestling *and*, rarely mentioned elsewhere, the other athletic exercises performed in zurkhāneh. Two date from late Safavid times, one from the late nineteenth century.

PAHLAVĀNS, LUTIS, AND SHĀTERS

What we learn from the two Safavid sources

The first of these texts is the *Gol-e koshti* (Rose of Wrestling) written in 1700 by Mir-Nejāt Qomi (also known as Esfahāni), a poet and the chief librarian of the royal library in Isfahan. It is a long *masnavi* (a genre usually associated with didactic and romantic themes) that playfully evokes the world of wrestlers and *luti*s, the movements and instruments they train with, and the names of the holds and throws they use in their bouts. This document is remarkable because it confirms that the spinning exercises of the zurkhāneh are in fact a form of *zekr*, in this case discreetly dedicated to the patron saint of wrestlers, Puryā-ye Vali.[1] Moreover, throughout the text we find glimpses of how male same-sex desire and love could be expressed in terms that were socially acceptable at the time.

The second document is a *fotovvatnāmeh*, that is, a type of treatise for a professional activity. Titled *Tumār-e afsāneh-ye Poryā-ye Vali* (Scroll of the Legend of Porya Vali), it is the oldest extant Persian-language professional treatise on wrestling, and was probably written by a public writer for a *kohneh-savār* living in Tabriz.[2] This *kohneh-savār* has a one-year contract with a wrestler in his prime, the *pahlavān*, who trains aspiring young athletes in the art of wrestling.

The surviving document is incomplete, but the extant chapters contain the usual rubrics of a professional treatise needed by a local magistrate (*kalāntar*) to authorize a

---

1. Rediscovered by Adib al-Molk Farahani, this document is reproduced and analyzed by Partow-Beyzā'i Kāshāni 1337/1958, 379–419. Puryā-ye Vali is mentioned only discreetly (399) because by this time the Safavid state pursued anti-Sufi policies.

2. The document, whose original is lost, is reproduced in Partow-Beyzā'i Kāshāni 1337/1958, 350–64. More in-depth analyses of the *Tumār* can be found in Rochard 2002; and Rochard and Jallat 2018.

professional activity, in this case that of the *kohneh-savār*, by enumerating the duties, rules, and traditions that govern it. In the case of the *Tumār*, these are the traditions pertaining to the official patron saint of wrestlers, Puryā-ye Vali; the customs and rituals of the profession that need to be rigorously enforced; the moral rules demanded of the wrestlers, particularly the ones pertaining to the training and treatment of novices/apprentices by the *kohneh-savār* and the *pahlavān*; and regulations about salaries that avoid abuses and too large fluctuations. Reading between the lines, one senses a somewhat tense situation concerning the distribution of profits between the *kohneh-savār* and the *pahlavān*.

The analysis of these texts together with the secondary sources presented earlier in chapter two, led me to conclude that today's zurkhānehs are the heirs to the physical practices of three ancient professions, that is, wrestlers, *luti*s, and *shāter*s, that had nothing to do with military training but rather played essential roles in three main areas: performance, state ceremonies, and court society. The practices of the royal court were imitated at lower levels of society until the gradual demise of the ancien regime in the first three decades of the twentieth century brought about new social forms and new representations of power.

The first two professions, wrestlers and *luti*s, often trained together in the zurkhāneh, which was reserved for physical training, and the *lutikhāneh*, which was a professional space bringing together primarily members of the *luti* corporation consisting of public entertainers such as acrobats, jugglers, puppeteers, magicians, and specialists in bawdy comedy.[3] Both wrestlers and *luti*s belonged to the category of performers and collaborated very closely, to the point of constituting homogeneous groups of performers documented in the early twentieth century.[4]

The *luti*-acrobats and showmen were the incarnation of laughter, as much for the people as for the shah, seen as both frivolous and essential. But what were they laughing about? It would be worth exploring at length the subject of humor in Iran, but it is impossible to do so here. Suffice it to say that the *luti*s were regularly condemned in the name of morality. The clergy never liked them, nor did the enlightened nationalist elites – and the revolutionaries of 1978 still less. They objected to their implicit challenge to the appropriate order in the name of the holy duties of solemnity and atonement, tight-lipped desires for elevation, and the deadly seriousness of all the revolutionary messages on re-education and reformation. The sad fate of Iranian comic theatre, the Siyāh Bāzi, and its central figure, the buffoon who pokes fun at the powerful, is ample proof of this.

The third profession was that of the *shāter*, a courier or bodyguard in the private and personal service of the realm's elites. In addition, *shāter*s played important ceremonial and security roles in state functions, including official travels of the shah, the

3. Aubin 1908, 234.
4. Ibid. See also the description of the performances associated with acrobats and wrestlers in Eastwick 1864, 112–13. Eastwick provides a superb description of a wrestling match, probably by the great Pahlavān Yazdi Bozorg, who was then at the peak of his career.

Figures 39 and 40. Shāter; Nāser al-Din Shah Qajar era, ca. 1890 (Kāzemeyni, 1964).

comings and goings of state officials, princes, and powerful figures of the kingdom, as well as foreign consuls, ambassadors and the like. *Shāter*s were also involved to a lesser extent in the third area, court society, concerned with establishing the smallest details of protocol and rules of honor and distinction for those in the ruler's entourage (Figures 39 and 40).[5] These *shāter*s required, above all, immense endurance because they had to run *on foot* alongside people traveling on horseback, or in the nineteenth century, in carriages (Figures 41 and 42). The corporation of runners also had its own *shāterkhāneh*, although they also frequented the *zurkhāneh* (less regularly, probably to build muscle tone).[6]

As a public or private courier, but also as an element in the state ceremonies and court societies, the *shāter* was also important in the security protocols of traditional circles of power, acting as vigilant guardian over the roads that his masters took. He cleared the road before them, yelling "Khabardār!" (Attention!), and thus protected their dignity, because a true source of power was only accessible if it consented to be accessed. Since no being or obstacle could be imposed upon the prince's gaze, the *shāter* was there to make sure there were no unwelcome opportunists. Armed with a long and formidable stick with a solid silver head, he represented this same vigilant attention when his masters sent him to accompany guests. His presence was as useful as it was

---

5. To understand the complexity of the notion of rank and hierarchy in court society, see especially Cosandey 2016; and Giesey 1987b.

6. See the detailed presentation of the *shāter* in Rochard 2002, 327–31.

History of a Professional Practice 123

Figure 41. *Shāter* accompanying an ambassador, Mohammad Shah Qajar era (1834-1848) (Kāzemeyni, 1964).

symbolic. It signified that the person whom he accompanied was under the protection of the *shāter*'s master. The powerful could also use the services of the *shāter* to punish those who had incurred their anger. The *shāter*s were often feared by those who crossed their paths in the bazaar.

Kings were not the only ones to use their services. Governors, royal administrations (such as the customs department, for example), and all notables of importance had *shāter*s around them. This popular figure and its corporation only disappeared when it was eventually replaced by new forms of communication and security that rendered them unnecessary and the protocol they embodied was considered obsolete by the new Pahlavi regime. Probably those who were forced into other professions found work in the new public services, like the postal system or the police force. Yet their prodigious physical endurance left no lasting legacy in sport, even though they could have become internationally renowned long-distance runners. Iran may have deprived itself of many Olympic gold medals because it abandoned this traditional physical activity. But the *shāter*s' endurance was a means, not an end in itself, and so the *shāter*, as both a runner and as a bodyguard, disappeared from Iranian collective memory.

The *luti* had a better fate in collective memory. True, Iranian society rapidly forgot the entertainers, the tellers of bawdy stories, the acrobats and jugglers who were concealed behind the profession of *luti*. But in an interplay between denigration and valorization of the faults and qualities attributed to certain types of men from working-class backgrounds who had made the street their way of life, the figure of the *luti* was intimately connected to and identified with the world of the *jāhel*, evoking a "good boy" or "bad boy" of the streets, depending on the context. Seen in a positive light, the

Figure 42. *Shāters* accompanying a young prince, Qajar era (Kāzemeyni, 1964).

term came to evoke agility, cleverness, bravery, and vivacity, associated with a certain sense of honor towards one's friends, the poor, or the value of one's given word, a kind of "likeable thug."[7] From a negative perspective, this same sense of honor could be seen as tyrannical or shady, and associated with misconduct, cynicism, and a reprobate life (which might be secretly envied) combining all forbidden pleasures – drinking alcohol, gambling, pigeon fancying, frequenting prostitutes, abusing minors, a strong tendency for heavy racketeering, and from time to time serving as hired thugs for those who were able to pay. With increases in police power and the end of the neighborhood cultures of preindustrial time, the term became little more than a figure of style, associated with a genre, "*jāheli*sm," which was magnified in Iranian literature and cinema before the Islamic Revolution, and then censored or moralized afterwards.[8] Thus, of the three professions that once rubbed shoulders in the zurkhāneh only wrestling remains. As we have seen, it has been entirely renewed following the radical sociocultural transformations between the two world wars and the advent of the Pahlavi era.

The analysis of these three professions led me to an investigation into the socio-historical discourse produced around the zurkhāneh in Iran between 1940 and 1990, as presented earlier in chapter two. These ideas still largely shape the dominant discourse on the zurkhāneh both inside and outside the country today. However, what our sources tell us is that wrestlers and *luti*s lived on the revenue generated from their performances, although there were also part-time wrestlers who held additional jobs in the bazaar. There is much that could be said about these three professions, but here I will limit myself to three central points related to the zurkhāneh.

7. For a fascinating account of this issue in a Pakistani context, see Rollier 2021. See also Frembgen and Rollier 2014..
8. Breyley and Fatemi 2016.

First, a ruler's attitude to his *pahlavān*s, his *shāter*s, and the other men of his entourage confirms that they were an extension of his own identity and power.[9] A *shāter* sent before a visitor incarnated his employer's power of protection and distinction. The strength of the *pahlavān* was an adrenaline-rich distraction, but also a symbol of his patron's physical power. In victory or defeat they symbolized the victories and losses of the prince. Given their tendency to gamble on all kinds of fighting, a good wrestler could win or lose *a lot* of money for the prince. This could bring fortune and glory to the winners, and more or less serious disgrace for the losers. We can imagine the permanent fear of defeat in which wrestlers must have lived during this time, particularly when we observe how unscrupulously some competitors eliminated adversaries whom they considered too dangerous. Our sources are full of these accounts.[10] Far from being signs of the institution's decadence, these reports bespeak the consequences of the symbolic and material stakes inherent in this intensely competitive sphere. This is a far cry from the ethos of the *javānmardi*. By the same token, those who refused to succumb to the general trend were all the more admirable.

Second, wrestlers, who necessarily had a rather short career at the peak of their strength, could hope to win prosperity and social recognition in two ways, either through the importance and wealth of their protectors, or the recognition of a lifestyle considered legitimate for its spiritual ambitions. Angelo Piemontese's works in particular, and the documents studied over the course of my research, suggest strong parallels between, on the one hand, the world of traditional wrestling during the Timurid, Safavid, and Mughal eras, and on the other, the world of craft- and tradespeople who were organically connected to various Sufi brotherhoods and provided the main membership of the communal solidarity organizations known as *fotovvat* and *akhilik*.[11] The legend constructed around the mythical teachings of Pahlavān Mahmud Kh^vārazmi, known as Puryā-ye Vali,, who died in Khiva in 1322 CE, are ample proof of these connections.

9. For the case of Mughal India see Alter 1992, 70–89; for Central Asia and Iran, see Piemontese 1966.

10. For one example among many, see the accounts of Pahlavān Akbar Khorāsāni in Ensāfpur 1974, 143 and Abbāsi 1374/1995, vol. 2, 25–30.

11. For the most complete synthesis on this theme available to date, again see Ridgeon 2018b. Also of great interest is Keyvani 1982. It appears that the crystallization of professional associations out of the more inchoate world of crafts and trades took shape when the *akhilik* and *fotovvat* welfare and support associations were weakening or even disappearing towards the end of the fifteenth century in the Middle East. See Yıldırım 2018, 94; and Asceric-Todd 2018, 163–64. For the Persian realm, Wilhelm Floor writes that "... Ebn Baṭṭūṭa in A.D. 1392 gives the earliest information on the existence of guilds in Isfahan and Shiraz, where 'the members of each craft appoint one of their members as headman over them, whom they call kolū." The same author related that these guilds were taxed as a corporate body and that they had a vivid social life (Ebn Baṭṭūṭa, tr. Gibb, II, p. 310) ... More substantial information on guilds becomes available after 1600. During the Safavid period each trade or craft formed a guild headed by a headman elected by at least two-thirds (four dāngs) of the guild's masters." Willem Floor, "AṢNĀF," in *Encyclopaedia Iranica Online*, http://dx.doi.org/10.1163/2330-4804_EIRO_COM_5959. Consulted online on 18 October 2023.

Who was Puryā-ye Vali? According to Angelo Piemontese, who wrote the most complete studies of this famous patron saint of wrestlers, he was born in Urgench, in today's Uzbekistan. It seems that he held the post of leader of the troupe stable of wrestlers at the court of the governor of Khiva. At that time Khiva came under the authority of the khanate of the Golden Horde, making the city a multi-religious space with the presence of Islam, Shamanism, and Buddhism, and allowing all manner of influencing, borrowing, and adapting across the different traditions. According to legend, he became a Sufi saint after a spiritual revelation he obtained while fighting against a young Indian wrestler whom he allowed to win – against all the odds – because of the tears of his opponent's mother. A little while later, he saved his sovereign's life under dramatic circumstances using his superhuman strength. When his ruler, taken aback by such physical prowess, asked how a man like him could have been beaten by a young Indian wrestler, Puryā-ye Vali is said to have pronounced a famous quatrain that sums up his spiritual awakening and constitutes the core of his preaching:

> Gar bar sar-e nafs-e khod amiri, mardi
> Var bar digari nokteh nagiri, mardi
> Mardi nabovad fetādeh rā pāy zadan
> Gar dast-e fetādeh rā begiri, mardi

> If you can dominate your own self, you're a man
> If you don't find fault with others, you're a man,
> It is not manly to kick one who's down,
> If you take the hand of the one who is down, you're a man.[12]

After that, Puryā-ye Vali went out into the world and started to teach, although we do not have any written source about his teachings prior to the sixteenth century.[13]

Whether this key episode in the life of this wrestler saint is true or legend matters little, because it casts the pinnacle of the art of wrestling as a question of spiritual illumination in which the greatest victory is the one achieved over oneself. This transcends the usual reliance on physical force for achieving a man's goals and constitutes an admirable life philosophy. These ideals pervaded all social spheres within the area of cultural Islam beginning in the late fifteenth and early sixteenth century – and perhaps before that as well. According to this philosophy, a man is only a man when he helps his neighbor in need, even at the cost of his own ego and his own interest. Very early on, Muslim mystics saw wrestling as a metaphor for the struggles the human soul must face.[14]

The links to this mystic dimension were also reinforced by the fact that each profession had to prove its professional and spiritual legitimacy to the legal authorities of

---

12. Rochard 2002, 333.
13. See ibid and and Rochard and Bast 2023 for a more comprehensive presentation and comparative analysis of the legend of Puryā-ye Vali based on Piemontese 1965.
14. See Piemontese 1966.

the time, through professional treatises (supervision of apprentices, initiation rituals for new masters, distribution of revenue, and other fundamental elements of the profession), as exemplified by the Safavid-era *Tumār* presented earlier.[15] These treatises provided an opportunity to put forward professional demands and to alter existing traditions in order to serve current interests.

Indeed, the founding myth of Puryā-ye Vali has been constantly reworked and adapted to new periods in light of the different objectives of those commissioning the *fotovvatnāmeh* treatises. The contrast between Puryā-ye Vali, proclaimed founder of the spiritual tradition of wrestling, who died in 1322 CE but was celebrated beginning in the early sixteenth century throughout Central Asia, Persia and the Ottoman Empire, and the Puryā who appears in the *Tumār-e afsāneh-ye Poryā-ye Vali* in the late Safavid period is a splendid proof of this type of adaptation. In the text of the *Tumār*, it is the old *kohneh-savār*, named Shirdel, who, contrary to previous traditions in which he does not appear, teaches Puryā-ye Vali the traditions and techniques of wrestling and associated exercises. He asks for gifts to reflect the respect due to his status, an equal share of the revenue with the *pahlavān*, and the privilege of dividing this revenue between himself, the *pahlavān*, and the young apprentice wrestlers. In the oldest sources, however, it was Puryā who, having received the first wrestling breeches, brought to him on the horns of a deer that emerged from the desert as a messenger of God, who was the original source of both mystical and technical knowledge. But in the *Tumār*, the commissioning *kohneh-savār* transformed the tradition so that he would be considered at least equal, perhaps even superior, to the *pahlavān*, in order to protect his authority and financial revenues. In sum, the impresario (*kohneh-savār*) won out over the artist (*pahlavān*), in whom he had only limited trust. Thus traditions are transformed.

In spite of their proximity to the world of the court and to the dervishes, in other words, to power, wealth, and spiritual illumination, the wrestlers and their training spaces remained marginal in their societies and were regarded with suspicion. These spaces were sometimes feared or despised, sometimes appreciated or respected by the rest of society, but never formally prohibited by the authorities. However, their marginality was more due to the specificities of the professions that trained there than to an exceptional moral shortcoming. It is worth restating that zurkhānehs, for better or worse, reflected both the good and the bad attitudes common in Iranian society at one time or another.

Finally, an important element of the wrestlers' physical training program had a much more diverse background than it might at first appear. My original research showed that the spinning and weightlifting exercises had connections with various cultures from Central Asia and northern India. The spinning exercises and the *mil* have connections to Central Asia, its shamanist and perhaps Buddhist traditions, while northern India in particular showed that contact sports as varied as Turko-Persian bare-

---

15. Rochard 2002, 334–38.

and open-handed wrestling, and the techniques of the Gujarati *Jyesthimalla*, although they use weapons, involve very similar training exercises.[16] This comparison throws into question the most common hypotheses, which are based on Muslim invasions of India in the medieval period, and suggest that we need to go back to the pre-Islamic period to understand transregional contacts. Although it is true that under the Mughal and Bahmani empires (thirteenth to nineteenth centuries) the physical traditions of Muslim and Hindu cultural areas coexisted, it is worth noting that their techniques for physical preparation and training seem to have coexisted long before.

All of this suggests that the evolution of these fighting techniques, and the physical training they involve were not purely national and immutable, as the nationalist historical narratives observed in this cultural area (and others) have long claimed. These exercises, tools, traditions, and those who practice them have been subject to influences and borrowings from other cultures; they have synthesized and reinterpreted these practices, both in the past and in the modern era. However, there is a clear hiatus between these traditional practices and those that are documented in the first studies by Iranian authors in the 1940s and 50s. Fortunately, we have a manuscript that fills this gap. It was written in 1875 by a member of the Dār al-Fonun in Tehran for the Iranian Minister of Public Instruction, Commerce and Mining, and provides a veritable archaeology of the specific practices of the zurkhāneh from the time of writing to today.

The Ganjineh-ye koshti

The *Ganjineh-ye koshti* (Treasure of Wrestling), of which the only extant copy is kept at the National Library of France (BNF), was the first attempt to compile a manual of physical education based exclusively on the athletic tradition of the zurkhāneh.[17] It was written in 1875 by Ali Akbar ibn Mehdi al-Kāshāni, a secretary at the Dār al-Fonun, Iran's first modern school, on instruction from the director, Prince Ali-Qoli Mirzā E'tezād al-Saltaneh, who was also minister of science and education. This richly illustrated treatise set out to explore the possibility of using zurkhāneh exercises for hygienist and patriotic goals that are reminiscent of the reforms of the French education system and medicine in the late nineteenth century.[18] It constitutes a kind of link between the Safavid and the Pahlavi eras.

The description of the history of the zurkhāneh and wrestling that Kāshāni gave in the introduction to the *Ganjineh* suggested that in Iran, as in other countries, the history of athletic practices became associated with an interpretation of physical culture

16. Rochard and Bast 2023.
17. For a more detailed analysis of this treatise, see Rochard and Jallat 2018, 253–58.
18. These left their mark on the *Ganjineh*, for it was owned by the French personal physician of the shah, Joseph Désiré Tholozan, who left handwritten notes in the margins on the process of the writing of this manuscript.

as a patriotic and hygienist social duty. It was also a way to strengthen the population in the face of the terrible epidemics ravaging the country in the late nineteenth century.[19]

The Qajar administration attempted to base its hygienic approach – as far as sport was concerned in any case – on the traditions and practices that already existed in Iran, rather than on the adoption of the new nascent European sports and physical education programs. This turned out to be a failure, as the *Ganjineh* never became an official manual. Why? Aside from the contingencies of often unfulfilled political projects during the Qajar period, we can see that physical exercise in Iran in 1875 was not a general practice that could be envisioned to be shared by all; rather it was life choice that was only valued by some. Collective representations of traditional sporting practices were very distinctive, whether positive or pejorative, and it would have been impossible to imagine this kind of lifestyle for society as a whole. This was already clear in 1875, but it was made even more so after the divisions that occurred in Iranian society in the 1930s, with the progressive emergence of new social classes and practices resulting from the modernization of Iran. Faced with a choice between the newly-arrived foreign athletic disciplines a local sporting tradition that had marginal or negative connotations, the new Iranian middle class, even in the most nationalist spheres, chose the foreign sport. This choice has also been observed elsewhere, in India for example. The practice of zurkhāneh sports was no longer a simple path within Iranian society, but rather was a character trait of a *certain kind* of society.

While the attempt in 1875 to build a modern national physical education system based on the zurkhāneh was a non-starter, the institution did not fade away. It did, however, undergo several major transformations in subsequent years.

Post-1875 transformations

Between 1900 and 1940 new weightlifting tools were introduced, including dumbbells, pairs of cast-iron weights that replaced the old *sang-e na'l*, which were stones carved into a horseshoe shape and worn around the neck during certain exercises.[20] These new tools and instruments progressively disappeared from the zurkhāneh with the spread of modern weightlifting gyms between the end of the 1930s, when the STB and the IWF were established, and the early 1950s, which saw Iran's participation in the 1952 Olympic Games. Within the zurkhāneh, however, certain tools and exercises (*sang* and *kabbādeh*) were standardized, and exercises became more complex. The *sang* exercises (which originally used two big stones, as in India, but which have been performed with heavy wooden shields since at least the eighteenth century) were still performed with one leg on the ground lying on a cushion in 1875, but are now done lying down with legs in the air, to work the abdominal muscles more. A longer-term observation, from

19. Afkhami 1999, 122–36.
20. See figures 32 and 33, previously mentioned.

Figure 43. A *soffeh* without a *sardam*, the *kohneh-savār* with musicians on either side (Niehbur, 1778).

Figure 44. The *soffeh-ye sardam* with the *kohneh-savār* and *motreb*, behind, playing the *zarb*, Fath-'Ali Shah Qajar era, ca. 1830 (H. Partow-Beyzā'i, 1958).

the eighteenth century to the late twentieth century, shows the considerable evolution of the *sardam* (Figures 43, 44, 45, 46) which has adapted to modern architecture.

Exercise categories changed slightly over the years and they also changed names, for example the warmup, known as *narmesh*, which in 1939 replaced the older term *kham-giri*. When the *luti*-acrobat and juggler corporations died out in the 1920s, all the *shirinkāri* warmup exercises described in the *Ganjineh* but criticized by the author as "useless" lost their professional purpose. They were progressively abandoned and what remained of them was simplified.[21] They were no longer performed with the *sang* and the *kabbādeh*. The *shirjeh* exercises – literally a dive – which involve jumping forwards and backwards, landing and walking on one's hands were abandoned, as were the *shelang* boards and exercises, which are said to have come from the *shāter* exercise program, and which were also used to stabilize all of the *shirjeh* exercises (handstands and variations thereof).

As wrestling was gradually abandoned in the zurkhāneh, there was no longer any need for covering the bottom of the *gowd* with clay and reed. A harder floor was less costly to maintain, and had the advantage of suppressing the humidity criticized by hy-

---

21. They made a comeback in the 1990s, as we shall see.

gienists. This led to a transformation of certain tools and exercises, particularly for the *takht-e shenā*, the "swimming board." This wooden board ensured that the athletes were stable when they performed the different kinds of push-ups on the uneven and unstable floor of the *gowd*. It progressively became shorter and narrower, and now it always has two small feet to raise it up off the ground (which is now stable, hard, and smooth) and make it easier to hold.

Figure 45. The *soffeh-ye sardam* in 1875, now with a *morshed* who plays alone (Ganjineh-ye koshti, 1875).

The transformations that took place between the writing of the *Ganjineh* in 1875 and the first competitions in 1942 went hand-in-hand, as we saw earlier in chapter two, with the rise in the hygienics and modernist discourses that no longer wanted physical exercise to be reserved for the groups whose strength was a way of making a living or self-expression: wrestlers, *shāter*s, *luti*s, or anyone adopting a certain image of strength in society. Instead, physical exercise was to be an educational tool for mental and bodily training used by society as a whole. This discourse (already present in 1875 but implicitly focused only on men) became dominant during the Pahlavi era both in the spheres of power as well as among the regime's opponents. It was extended to women through the modernizing discourse of the Pahlavi regime.[22] Under the influence of new sporting bodies, traditional gymnastics and its weightlifting techniques were revised and the

22. Koyagi 2009.

Figure 46. The *sardam* is now the object of all the *morshed*'s attentions (zurkhāneh, Isfahan, 1996; photo Philippe Rochard).

discourses around them changed. The zurkhāneh were adapted to the new demands of public health (larger room, more light and aeration, less humidity). The emerging sporting discourse was constructed by Iran's modernizing and secularizing elites. This discourse is associated with a breakaway from the old models of legitimacy that rely on Sufi tutelary figures such as Qotboddin Heydar or Puryā-ye Vali, even though Sufis still have an important place within the zurkhāneh, although they remain discreet, because of the persecution of which they have been a victim since the Islamic Revolution.

In addition to its discussion of physical exercises, the *Ganjineh* also contains valuable information about the economics of the zurkhāneh world, a matter already touched upon for the first time in the *Tumār*. In the absence of any reliable statistical data, the following section cannot aspire to be more than a sketch.

Outline of an Economy of the Zurkhāneh

Model of ownership, management, and staffing of the zurkhāneh in 1875

The author of the *Ganjineh* explained that "once the zurkhānehs were built, they were rented to a *morshed*. Others were private, so that athletes could take care of themselves, but they were nevertheless open to the public."[23] The *morshed*s in this kind of rented zurkhāneh managed the premises. According to Kāshāni, they employed a *moshtomālchi*, a masseur, who opened the doors of the zurkhāneh early in the morning, swept and watered down the floor, prepared what was needed for the *qalyān* pipe, and made sure that there was enough hot water for tea and other purposes. He also gave athletes (here called *varzeshkonān*) a pair of training breeches (*tonekeh*) made of leather or strong fabric, a towel of red cotton (*long*), and a wicker basket for their clothes (*zanbil*). The *moshtomālchi* massaged the athletes when they finished their exercises and looked after the beginners. For the distribution of earnings, the *morshed*s came to an agreement with the visiting *pahlavān*s who came to teach for a season. On this issue, the *Ganjineh* provided more detail: it specified that "The *morshed* and the *pahlavān* must come to an agreement (*tāleb va matlub*) as to the distribution of earnings collected after each session (or demonstration)."[24] But it is the *morshed* who manages the room. This was a change from eighteenth-century practice, for the *Tumār* laid out the portions: four for the *pahlavān* who serves himself first, four for the *morshed*, and two for the young wrestlers still learning. It is clear that the portions each received were subject to constant challenges and could be disputed. It seems that the *pahlavān*s tended to demand more, but thanks to the *Ganjineh* we can see that in 1875 the *morshed*'s moral and financial superiority over the *pahlavān* was clear and strong.[25]

The *Ganjineh* specifies: "For each tool of the zurkhāneh that is worn out, repaired,

---

23. *Hefz-e sehhat-e kh^vish*. (to look after themselves, literally "to maintain their health"). This is an interesting expression, elliptically evoking the existence of zurkhānehs of ill repute. This co-optation thus allows the zurkhāneh to filter and eliminate undesirable elements from among the athletes.

24. Kāshāni 1875–76, folio 5.

25. There is a source prior to the *Ganjineh* that reveals the potential financial stakes in this battle between the *kohneh-savār/morshed* and the *pahlavān*. In 1812 and 1813, a French cavalry colonel serving in the Russian army recorded his observations of wrestling contests in Iran: "[a wrestler who wins a match] receives all the compliments made to him with gravity, but these are of little matter because as he is obliged to accept to fight the other athletes, it often happens that he is beaten in turn, and it is only ever the final winner who receives the praise and the money, which is proportional to the number of wrestlers he has beaten. If he was the first in the ring and beat all the others, then he is fêted, held as victorious, and often receives considerable gifts such as horses, clothes, cloth, and money. These cases are excessively rare, but I did see one day a Turk who knocked down twenty-four other wrestlers. The gifts that he received on that occasion were worth more than 2000 *tomans*." Drouville 1819, vol. 2, 57–58. This amount of money is enormous and the *morshed/kohneh-savār* who organized the fights could reasonably claim half of it.

or destroyed, the costs are shared between the *kārkonān* (the users), each according to their means. Repairs within the zurkhāneh itself are the responsibility of the owner, unlike the floor of the *gowd*, where the costs are shared among the athletes. The *morshed* must pay the *Moshtomālchi*'s salary, the rent, and any associated costs." The money is to be collected at the end of the exercises and after the *miyāndār*, that is, the *pahlavān* leading the exercises in the center of the pit, recites the *do'ā*, the invocation. Kāshāni's text also adds that "In reality, the *morshed* is the trainer of the *miyāndār*. The *miyāndār* and the *nowcheh* must respect the *morshed* and give him garments of honor or recompense him in one form or another (*khal'at va jāyezeh*)."[26] Thus, between the late Safavid period and the year 1875, the former *kohneh-savār*, the old wrestler, the veteran, now called the *morshed*, took precedence over the *pahlavān*, even at the height of his prowess.

Summarizing what we now know, we can thus see several ways professional wrestlers could manage their career. They could move from town to town with a contract with the local *kohneh-savār/morshed*. They could also join up with groups of *luti*-acrobats and perform together. If they were among the best, they could find a rich protector, such as the king or a powerful lord who had a private zurkhāneh for his friends and acquaintances managed by a *pahlavānbāshi*. This chief *pahlavān* drew up the contracts with wrestlers and thus established the prince's "stable."[27] A wrestler could also benefit from income from the bets placed on his bouts, and those linked with his victories (pity the fighter who disappointed his patron!). Then fighters who had reached the age of the *kohneh-savār/morshed* would in turn move on to managing a zurkhāneh. Perhaps in the meantime, they might have found favor with one of the rich notables, who might offer them one of their richly endowed daughters, ensuring a stable revenue and a place among the local notable. Some of the more forward-thinking wrestlers might have used their winnings to invest in property, buy shops to rent, or build zurkhānehs, and would then live off the revenue of these rents and, again, join the ranks of the local notables. That is the best a wrestler could hope for. At the other end of the social scale, serious injury, poverty, or violent gangs were also potential fates for unfortunate zurkhāneh *pahlavān*s.

Today, wrestling, whether modern freestyle and Greco-Roman or traditional *pahlavāni*, is no longer systematically taught in traditional zurkhānehs. The *miyāndār* no longer calls on people to pay after the training and no longer receives a salary, while the audience and the athletes directly pay their offerings into the *morshed*'s cup. The

26. Kāshāni 1875–76, folio 5.
27. In Iran, the most famous *pahlavānbāshi* of the nineteenth century was Hājj Hasan Badoft, who in 1266 h.q.(March 1850) recruited, on behalf of Nāser al-Din Shah, the *pahlavān* Ebrāhim Yazdi, later nicknamed Yazdi Bozorg, the penultimate great champion of the Qajar era. See Partow-Beyzā'i Kāshāni 1337/1958, 144–46. Yazdi Bozorg was born in Yazd in 1245 h.q./ 1829, and died at the turn of the 1900s. He was known for his weight of 61 *man*, some 183 kilograms, and for the *sang* of 18 *man* (108 kilograms each) that he used for his daily exercises. See also Kolāhi 1358/1979, 57–86. Generally, in addition to the aforementioned works by Kolāhi and Abbāsi, a lot of biographical (but often redundant) information can be found on the key figures of *pahlavāni* wrestling in nineteenth- and twentieth-century Iran. See Kamandi 1984; Kāzeruni 1376/1997; and Mir'i 1349/1970–71.

morshed is often (but not always) the owner or co-owner of the zurkhāneh where he practices his art (whereas he was a tenant in 1875). But it can also happen that he renders his part- or full-time services for a fee. Zurkhānehs now belong to either individuals (legal persons), private companies, or institutions (corporate entities, the army, etc.) and they are managed very differently depending on this. Let us look more closely at this point.

Individually owned zurkhānehs since World War II

Zurkhānehs are sometimes jointly owned by several people. The possession of all or some of the six parts (the *dāng*s) that traditionally divide all property in Iran sets the rules for the distribution of profits made during the year. The employees, those who are responsible for offering tea and cake to the audience and distributing the training towels and the *long*s (which was essentially the role of the masseur in 1875, a role that has now disappeared), are paid set but low salaries. These are rounded out by tips or presents for *Nowruz* and religious ceremonies given to them by their employers and those who frequent the zurkhāneh. Such an arrangement is not unusual: this is how it works in most low-level professions, taxi agencies, print shops, cleaning services, and the *ābdārchi*s who prepare tea for everyone in the offices. However, the *morshed*s are now obliged by the VBKP Federation to have another source of income, aside from their activity in the *zurkhāneh*. For the federation "a *morshed* must not be a *morshed* out of self-interest, but out of love of his art."[28] They nevertheless receive a certain amount from the federation, which is not considered a salary but rather a compensation, discreetly given and received. The amount is rarely considered sufficient, and some prefer to forgo it altogether so as not to be beholden to the federation. Since *morshed*s are not employees of the VBKP Federation, they are ineligible for social security benefits, although some regularly demand that they be made eligible.

Other types of subsidies can be obtained from the federation and local or national authorities so long as certain conditions are met. For example, owners of new gymnasiums and fitness rooms have been able to avoid paying local taxes by setting up a space for zurkhāneh and VBKP sports in their clubs. This type of local relations with municipal authorities is particularly valuable, and many *salavāt*s are dedicated to the latter's representatives during major public athletic performances in a zurkhāneh. It is also worth adding that many discussions and quarrels are related to financial assistance that is supposed to be received and is not.

In theory, zurkhānehs are open to all, but in reality people always attend in groups, which implies a system of co-optation. The membership fee today (and probably, also back in 1875) is dependent on what "honor dictates." As we have seen, young people who are not yet employed, or athletes who are struggling financially, are exempt from paying. Notables generally pay much more. Thus, in May 1996, 50 *tumān* per session was a minimum for non-members (membership being between 500 and 700 *tumān* per

---
28. Interview with VBKP officials, May 1996.

month), 200 was an average, and between 600 and 1000 *tumān* a maximum, paid only by notables, as a particular sign of support and friendship toward the zurkhāneh that they came to visit. Of course, as we will see, some periods of the year are more important than others and provide the opportunity for zurkhānehs to double their annual revenue.

Zurkhānehs attached to public institutions

Aside from the zurkhāneh of the Dār al-Fonun, the first zurkhāneh to have been managed by a major public institution in the twentieth century was that of the Bank Melli in 1944. But this was, in fact, not a modern phenomenon. As far back as we have been able to go, the zurkhāneh and wrestling were above all the expression of the king's pleasure and entertainment (and that of other aristocrats'), who possessed a "stable" of wrestlers and acrobats in addition to their other assets. Indian or Timurid sources devote significant attention to the wrestler and his patron. Wrestling, as we said above, is also the symbolic connection between the master of the house and his wrestler, between true power and the image of power. A member of parliament who denounced the creation of the Bank Melli's zurkhāneh in 1944 did not understand why these external traditional signs of personal power should be the prerogative of a bank.[29] Yet it was a perfect symbol of the structural transformations of the expression of power, that went from being royal and personal under the Qajars to the new financial and administrative centers of power created in the course of the state-building of the Pahlavi era. The fact that it was the Bank Melli, an institution that had by definition financial means, was a pioneer in this area was quite emblematic.

Yet we cannot conclude that there was a simple shift in organization, functioning, and social representation of the zurkhāneh. Instead, high-level employees of private and state-owned enterprises who have been given responsibility for a zurkhāneh (or a sports club in a different discipline) sponsored by the enterprise end up functioning in a traditional mode exercising personal power as men embodying and thus possessing part of the state. On numerous occasions I observed that once they had been appointed, certain senior public servants seemed to consider themselves the owner of the thing for which they had acquired responsibility. This leads to a problem with the delegation of power in Iran that can be seen at all levels of society. Indeed, in 1944 – as in 1997 – the zurkhānehs created in companies or, more recently, companies that sponsor VBKP sports teams, were the expression of the desire of a particular individual, CEO or senior public servant, who was in a position of power within the institution but not accountable to it. In theory, the senior public servant must keep accounts in case of a possible investigation, but this happened rarely. It seems clear that the management of public assets is still largely modeled on a patrimonial system. Changes in this area, as Fariba Adelkhah very rightly noted in her book, are relatively recent.[30] The genuine birth of "public goods" in Iran is perhaps happening before our eyes, but at this stage it is still far from being the norm.

29. Partow Beyzā'i Kāshāni 1337/1958, 224.
30. Adelkhah 2004, 249–54.

Of course, zurkhānehs supported by institutions benefit from networks of patrons of a much higher social and financial level than those most private owners can turn to, and therefore receive more substantial assistance from the authorities. They may be open to the public or, on the contrary in some instances, very much closed. For example, in the early 2000s, the Iranian Air Force possessed twenty-three zurkhānehs in Iran, set up in the military bases. Some sessions included up to 140 young athletes from the military – in the children and adolescent categories – participating in exercises. In these instances, the training took place in grand sports halls, and the trainers were themselves members of the air force who volunteered their time. Attendance was exclusively reserved to members of the military and their families.

The NIOC functions slightly differently. It opened several zurkhānehs in the towns where it was active, such as Sanandaj, Hamadan, Kashan, and Mashhad. For Mashhad and its surroundings alone, the combined subsidies from the Ministry of Culture and Islamic Guidance, from the Āstān-e Qods-e Razavi (the shrine of Imam Reza, which controls a very powerful agricultural conglomerate and charitable trust in Khorasan province), and from the municipality of Mashhad represented 40,000,000 *tumān*,[31] in addition to what the oil company provided (amount unknown). This means that the oil company was responsible only for the annual costs, with the tax exemptions and payments of the costs associated with constructing the zurkhānehs paid by the Ershād, the Āstān-e Qods, and the city council. It is important to note that the money from these institutions benefited several zurkhānehs. The NIOC also funded freestyle wrestling and bāstānikārān teams, all of which wore its logo in different competitions. There was no obligation for the teams' members to be employed by the company or to be members of an employee's family. Membership was set at 600 *tumān* per month, but the NIOC generously exempted anyone who did not have the means, as well as members of the families of martyrs of the Iran-Iraq war, disabled people, war wounded, champions, and veterans.

Many state institutions have their own zurkhānehs. This was also the case before the revolution, but according to the VBKP Federation managers, the people I interviewed, and my own observations, it is widespread now. This situation seems to confirm the comments by the head of the VBKP Federation, who refused to give me its exact budget but did confirm that 75% of the overall budget came from external sources, with the remaining 25% coming from the annual contribution of the STB.

The disparity in income within the world of the zurkhāneh

Generally speaking, having a position of responsibility within the VBKP Federation means being financially very comfortable, for only those who are very well off have sufficient free time and are able to put forward capital from their own pockets for the institution. Some of the important leaders of the federation have been shareholders

---

31. In 1996–97 this represented a relatively large amount of money, around $ 30,000. In 2020, it was no more than $1,300.

in pharmaceutical companies, for example. One referee of *pahlavāni* wrestling, who was also a freestyle wrestling coach, owned several shops, whose rents he claimed were his only income. Another zurkhāneh owner possessed warehouses in the bazaar that brought in substantial rent, which allowed him to run his club for the exclusive use of his circle of friends and clients. It goes without saying that this club was not supervised by the VBKP Federation.

Most of the athletes who came to train in the zurkhānehs had revenues that varied between modest and comfortable, which meant they did not suffer serious financial hardship. In 1996, these included taxi drivers (who earned between 50,000 and 200,000 *tumān* per month), low-level public servants (between 20,000 and 30,000 *tumān* per month), shop workers (between 15,000 and 20,000 *tumān*), or retirees who combined their pension with another profession. Having several jobs and constantly looking for more is a way of making ends meet, and a common practice for many of those who attend the zurkhāneh.

Thus, through this simple overview of the general economy of the zurkhāneh, we can see the great disparity in both organization and in revenue among those who frequent this world. Wealthy individuals mingle there with the less privileged, everybody carefully respecting certain rules of interaction as we saw in the first chapter. Their prime motivations can be cultural, spiritual, esthetic, focused on social recognition and networking (private or professional), fitness and well-being, or sheer spirit of competition and adrenaline high, as we will see in part two.

PART TWO

Social and Symbolic
Aspects of the Zurkhāneh

As we have seen, after the 1930s–40s, zurkhānehs were no longer a means of forging a path within Iranian society, but rather a subcurrent within traditional society, for which the socio-economic modernization of the country created upheaval in its references and customs. Whether they liked it or not, these social groups had their cultural references transformed.

Thus, searching for the identity traits specific to the world of the zurkhāneh in the early twenty-first century is not as easy as it might seem. It amounts to trying to draw out the specific sub-culture of this milieu, the culture that emerges from its particular social and physical practices; the culture that is linked to what Sébastien Darbon calls "the formal properties of practice."[1] Yet the world of the zurkhāneh is closely linked both to the world of modern sport and to a much broader traditional popular culture, which it would be impossible to present exhaustively in all its social and temporal complexity here. Each of the aspects of this culture would require a study in its own right (all the festivals, *Āshurā*, *hey'at-e azādāri*, and so forth). In spite of this, I have tried to construct a systematic account of this cultural sphere.

In chapter 4 I set out to sketch the spaces and times in which the values of the world of the zurkhāneh are the most clearly expressed. I particularly focus on the sense of sharing and solidarity which is the greatest concern within this community. Of course, these values are not exclusively reserved for athletes. However, the sense of solidarity (and its constraints) is expressed here in a way that is specific to the world of the zurkhāneh (for example, the *golrizān*). Other social values are glorified every day in the *gowd*: filial piety, religious duty, but also duties of protection, gratitude, humility, forgiveness, sincerity, a duty to defend the good, glorify elders, and pay tribute to the departed. These values are demanding, even overwhelming, when they are confronted with the modernization of Iranian society and everyday experience. I have tried to document the symbolism, values, and social reality of this milieu in the spirit of Clifford Geertz's anthropological approach.

However, and this is a warning, between simplistic interpretations (either romantic or sordid) and social reality, some academics studying Iran and this athletic tradition have tended to be overly complacent about clichés and popular thinking. Above all, they have not sufficiently questioned the historical reinterpretations of this institution and its culture. When one experiences the zurkhāneh on an everyday level, and the groups of athletes that frequent it, a certain number of myths disintegrate. The modern reinterpretations studied in part one were partly responsible for the 1994–1996 transformations in this athletic tradition. Yet when an institution changes the rules of the game to try and conform to the image of a tradition and a reputation that were in fact very much *reinvented*, surprising things can happen.[2]

To account for this socio-cultural reality and its transformations, I chose – from the midst of my four years of fieldwork – to relate and analyze three significant moments that serve as reference points for a whole range of experiences and observations.

More detail will be given in the chapters that follow about the methodological motivations for this. "The night of 15/16 January 1998" is covered mainly in chapter 5 and serves as a leitmotif. The month of Ramadan is its general theme, and it presents both the chronology of the important dates and significant actors in this world, and provides a framework for the description and analysis of the major celebrations of solidarity in the fourth chapter, entitled "the *golrizān* of the *gardan koloft* in the north." This theme carries over to the fifth chapter with the description and analysis of the internal functioning of a group of athletes in the zurkhāneh.

Over the course of the chapter 5 it will become clear that the social practices that I observed follow complex strategies and rules of interaction, which have become unavoidable both by the nature and the weight of group expectations. Analyzing them will pave the way for the sixth and final chapter. Focusing on a third grand event described as a "somewhat rowdy closing ceremony," this will serve as a way to identify the quasi-existential issues at stake in the world of Iranian zurkhāneh during this key period of its evolution. It will allow us to take stock in chapter 6 of the ongoing transformations and their symbolic significations, and ultimately the future of the zurkhāneh and the only sport it is for all intents and purposes home to, the *varzesh-e bāstāni*.

Chapter Four
The Time Frames of the Zurkhāneh and *Varzesh-e Bāstāni*

IN ESTABLISHING THE CALENDAR OF THE ACTIVITIES in the world of the zurkhāneh, with a view to detecting the key moments – those ideal and memorable events so sought after by anthropologists to nourish and consolidate their analytic and interpretive activity – the choice of events that have had the greatest heuristic impact is clearly delicate. Should we concentrate on the events directly created by the VBKP Federation, such as the sporting competitions with their ability to mobilize different kinds of energies, some toward the organizational competition, and others towards the thirst for victory? Or should we instead choose events that regularly and directly affect all of Iran's zurkhānehs and those who share its culture? Let us first identify these moments.

THE TIME FRAMES OF *VARZESH-E BĀSTĀNI*

The competition calendar

Iran's climatic diversity and the generosity of provincial bodies mean that regardless of the season, there is always a region in which the VBKP Federation can hold its national competitions. In winter the athletes go south, and in summer to cooler areas, to seek, for example, the fresh air of Sanandaj in the mountains of Kurdistan.[1] Spring and autumn allow for more options; athletes fondly remember the 1996 championships that provided the opportunity to briefly taste the sweetness of life in Isfahan. Equally hospitable were the athletes in the holy city of Mashhad, because their delegation had been well

---

1. For more information on the zurkhānehs of Sanandaj and Kermanshah, or the arrival of *pahlavāni* wrestling in Kurdistan, see Ayāzi 1371/1992; Nikitine 1922; Kāzeruni 1376/1997; and Kamandi 1984. Kurdistan has a Sunni majority but is very structured around its Sufi brotherhoods, which recognize the primacy of Imam Ali. The historic Iranian provinces of Azarbayjan, Lorestan, Gilan, Mazandaran, and Khorasan, as well as the areas of the Iranian Plateau around Tehran, Kashan, Isfahan, Yazd, Shiraz, and Kerman are all famous for their age-old wrestling traditions, unlike the southern provinces of Iran where local Sunni elites, particularly Arab and Baluch, seem disinterested in the zurkhāneh athletic tradition. In the 1990s, the only criticisms I heard of the world of the zurkhāneh because of their heritage being seen as too closely connected to Shiite Islam and Imam Ali came from people who were originally from these regions. The local branches of the VBKP Federation are small there and essentially made up of Iranians from the Central Plateau region who have moved to Ahvaz, Bushehr, Bandar Abbas, or Sarāvān for professional reasons.

received in Isfahan, and they now had a duty to reciprocate.[2] When different officials from the federation in Tehran and the provinces pay courtesy visits to each other, it is understood that they will be hosted in their hosts's homes, and when athletes travel, the locals are encouraged, depending on their means, to host one or more visiting athletes for a night or two. Major officials are expected to be ready for the (sometimes genuinely impromptu) arrival of fifteen or twenty athletes who may have to be housed and fed for several days. Iranian hospitality is renowned and the world of the zurkhāneh is careful to honor this reputation.

The calendar of competitions within this sport fluctuated somewhat during the years of my fieldwork. This was not due to a lack of enthusiasm or organization by the VBKP Federation. On the contrary, even its most fervent detractors admitted that the federation, because of its energetic president, had never organized so many competitions. All age groups now had annual tournaments both at the regional and national level, which provided an additional justification for weekly training sessions for aspiring competitors. This had not always been the case, particularly for the youngest categories, the *now javānān* (young adolescents), aged 11 to 14, and the *javānān,* aged 15 to 18. The zurkhānehs were traditionally spaces reserved for young adults and mature men. This is no longer the case. Yet how could the calendar with its frequent competitions be observed when the subsidies from the public budgets were sometimes four, five, or six months late? Competitions were therefore often dependent on the generosity of certain federation officials, the president above all, who put forward considerable sums of their own money that would be reimbursed only much later.

There are many other kinds of external assistance. Provincial administrative authorities host national competitions, and municipalities, major local businesses, or state companies often make contributions to the amounts required to organize these competitions. Luckily there are many volunteers, but these also have professional constraints. Thus, the dates selected for competitions are often dependent on the fragile conjuncture bringing together the financial means and the free time of all participants. The possibility of complying with this calendar is always balanced on a knife's edge and any success is a credit to the VBKP Federation, its patrons, and its volunteers.

Other important dates: the religious and political calendars

Alongside this sporting calendar, other major events in the life of the athletes of the zurkhāneh take place during the religious festivals that punctuate the Lunar Hijri calendar. This includes the entire month of Ramadan and the first seven days of the ten-day period of intense mourning at the beginning of the month of Muharram, days that commemorate the martyrdom of Imam Hoseyn. It also includes all the days that precede

---

2. The occasion was the first *pahlavāni* wrestling championship in 1998, under the name of *Jām-e Ayyārān*. It did not include *varzesh-e bāstāni* competitions, an ominous sign of the progressive rift between these two sporting disciplines.

religious festivals in general and the anniversaries of the deaths of imams in particular, because it is forbidden to practice this sport on the day of mourning itself.

Throughout this period, groups of athletes go from zurkhāneh to zurkhāneh, according to their affinities or the people to whom they owe some gratitude. But they also attend, like everybody else, memorial services (*khatm*) on the third, seventh, and fortieth day after a person's passing. In addition, they participate in *dowreh*s, *rowzeh*s, *and hey'at*s. These terms need more explanation because they form the basis of an intense social life in Iran, particularly in the social milieu to which most zurkhāneh athletes traditionally belonged.

When I did my fieldwork, the world of the zurkhāneh was aging. Mourning deceased athletes was frequent and since each passing was experienced as a serious loss, the athletes' community showed its solidarity. After a death, the third, seventh and fortieth days are key moments of mourning, and for an outstanding person the death may be commemorated on these days even for a second year. During the first three days, the mourning ceremonies take place at the mosque, on the seventh at the house of the deceased's family, and on the fortieth day the deceased's family (at least those who have the means to do so) hosts a great feast for anyone and everyone known to the person who died. For this a room is reserved in a restaurant, or a hall is used with a meal served by a caterer. Anyone is welcome, as long as they present their condolences to the family members as they enter. Each death within the group of athletes gives rise to an exercise session in the late man's zurkhāneh specifically organized in memory of the deceased. In four years of fieldwork, I cannot count the number of sessions I observed that were dedicated to "recently departed" veterans. The concern expressed by veterans and the federation's president about the ageing population of the athletes was sadly based on a harsh reality.

The term *dowreh* simply refers to informal friendship groups, while *rowzeh* denotes a lamentation session where the martyrdom of Shiite saints is recited. *Rowzeh*s may be performed informally in *dowreh*s, or more formally within a *hey'at-e azādāri*, on which occasions a religious figure might be invited to recite the martyrdom of an Imam. The most well known of these of course is that of Imam Hoseyn and his father, Imam Ali ibn Abu Tāleb, but the recitation can evoke other Shiite martyrs. *Hey'at-e azādāri* (literally, "mourning association") refers to a neighborhood group that gets together to organize ten day-long mourning rituals during Muharram in memory of the martyrdom of Imam Hoseyn and his family and followers massacred at Karbala. The celebrations culminate during the ninth and tenth days (Tāsu'ā and Āshurā),[3] and, as is too often forgotten, on the third day after *āshurā*, knowns as *ruz-e sevvom-e Emām*. This day in particular should not be overlooked because it brings together tens of thousands of people. It represents the third day of the commemorative mourning for Imam Hoseyn and brings the ceremonies to a close. In Tehran it involves a gathering of all of the *alam*s of the city

---

3. See also the excellent analysis by Vivier-Muresan 2020.

along Sirus Avenue. The *alam*s, also called *towq*, are beautiful and intricately decorated metal standards carried in the processions of self-flagellating mourners. The most remarkable of these standards is also the heaviest and since the 1950s it has always been the last in the procession: it is the standard that belonged to the *hey'at* of Tayyeb Hājj Rezā'i, whom we encountered earlier.

Independently of permanent institutions dedicated to celebrating Imam Hoseyn, *hoseyniyyeh*s and *hey'at.hā-ye azādāri* are often temporarily created at the initiative of one or several pious figures and generous patrons in a particular neighborhood, who provide the necessary space, the *tekkiyeh* (an informal synonym for *hoseyniyyeh*) for the organization of meetings and meals in a courtyard or a large room in a commercial space. For example, a car dealer might empty the showroom to provide a space for religious activities. Neighbors and friends get together and share the cost of the meal and the preparation of the *alam*. These *alam*s are rallying points for the *dasteh*s, the groups of self-flagellating mourners who parade through the surrounding streets. They are made up of young men for whom this is an opportunity to fulfil their duty as sons, men, and believers, but also a chance to be noticed by the young women who are actively encouraged by religious authorities to watch the procession. This unexpected social interaction is also a factor in the success of the celebrations, and when evening comes, it often transforms these processions into a space for the discreet but intense exchanges of telephone numbers. This exchange goes some way to explaining the surprise expressed by the middle-aged people with whom I watched the procession, who noted that the mourners were remarkably well-dressed and well-groomed for people supposed to be covering their heads in mud and ash or flagellating their backs with chains. Given the widespread sexual constraints on young people imposed by the economic and social situation in Iran, a spoiled T-shirt seems a small price to pay for a certain kind of hope.

When I participated in a procession that included several athletes from a zurkhāneh, my companions explained that there had always been clear specializations among the mourners. Although there were those who genuinely planned to make their bodies an object of penance, using mud and ash (now that blood is officially forbidden), and were suitably prepared, the majority of the other self-flagellators contented themselves with a symbolic gesture in which real violence, pain, and serious damage to clothing were excluded. I was shown the wrist technique that could transform a harsh whip on the shoulders into a benign caress and I began an initiation worthy of the *catenaccii* of my mother's native Corsica.[4] The flagellators do suffer a little however, because over the last five nights the processions go from *tekkiyeh* to *tekkiyeh* to visit all the nearby *hey'at*s. This leads to numerous welcoming ceremonies. Being a stopping place for a procession may be a great honor for the *tekkiyeh* that welcomes them, depending on the identity of the master of the *dasteh*. This results in a great honorific assault, in which the flagellators who had lessened their blows as they hurried towards the *tekkiyeh* to

4. On whom see Bertoncini 2013; and Bartolini 2004.

be honored, accelerate their rhythm over the last hundred meters, chanting the hymns and landing their blows all the more forcefully in front of their hosts. This ardor is in response to the warmth of the reception, which is also a marker of the importance of such a visit. The highest honor is the sacrifice of a sheep before the *alam*; a sheep that would be prepared the following day for the great votive meals to come, and whose blood might even be used to bless the forehead of the man carrying the *alam*. It sometimes happens that being regularly "forgotten" by certain *dasteh*s has immediate and serious significations. Another kind of message is sent and another organization of social networks in the neighborhood emerges, which gives a glimpse of how urban identities and rivalries were once expressed – much more violently. The zurkhānehs naturally have a certain role in these rivalries.

One venerable *pishkesvat* related an anecdote that shows how the *dasteh*s are both powerful identity markers in the neighborhood and an impressive way of giving or acquiring prestige. This elderly member of a *hey'at* explained to me how in the 1950s the *dasteh*s could also be redirected to the advantage of crafty and daring individuals who knew how to manipulate social codes and neutralize the risk of reprisals:

> In the *hey'at* in my neighborhood, when I was young there was a *luti* who had begun attending our meetings a few months before the Muharram celebrations and he gave us a magnificent *ālam*. It was a splendid gift. However, he politely insisted we deviate from our ordinary parade path. We understood it was so we could walk by his house and so he would impress those in his neighborhood. It wasn't traditional to parade through that neighborhood, but the *alam* was truly magnificent so it was worth the favor. So we did as he wanted and on the day of *āshurā* his neighbors knew that this man had considerable backing because there was a huge number of us and our *dasteh* was really very impressive. Two weeks later, a truck came to pick up the *alam* and the driver handed over the bill for the rental! The elders sulked but they paid without saying a word. Needless to say, the *luti* did not come to the *hey'at* anymore – he had got what he wanted.

I asked why he had not immediately denounced the man in his neighborhood and why they had not made him pay (in other ways). He immediately responded: "And let the whole town know that we'd been tricked?! Certainly not! It wasn't worth it. He'd been more crafty than us, that's all." So it was preferable to remain silent and pay up rather than see the *hey'at* and all the neighborhood publicly ridiculed. The cheeky fellow had cleverly manipulated his unfortunate victims' sense of honor and reputation. He had won on two accounts: he succeeded in making people in his neighborhood believe he was powerful, and he showed he was crafty and daring. Power, cleverness, and audacity were clearly the key characteristics for a "good" reputation as a *luti*.

Of course, with the modernization of society, changes in social fabric, and an urban sprawl that diluted the cohesiveness of traditional neighborhoods, this kind of stunning trickery lost some of its attractiveness. Nevertheless, the generosity of the neighborhoods did not decrease. A *hey'at* I attended in 1995, which was quite small compared to others, still distributed more than 100 kilos of rice and 100 kilos of meat each night in meals for people in the neighborhood. Those who had the means to pay their share did so, in money or in kind, and the rest was paid by the major donors. There are *tekkiyeh*s reserved for women, but where I was, women and men ate in the same place, although separately. The men ate first, grouped by age cohorts. Either they came straight after they arrived from the first procession of self-flagellators, who left early in the evening, or they were preparing to parade later in the night. Then the women and children could relax and stay longer, or they could take the remaining meals to those who had been unable to attend: the elderly or the needy who were ashamed to show it. In any event, people did not linger, because they had to make room for others and ensure everyone could eat their fill.

As mentioned above, certain *hey'at*s and *tekkiyeh*s are formed only for the mourning of Muharram and are subsequently dissolved, but most remain active throughout the year. They are organized either around a *hoseyniyyeh* or around a mosque, or around the shrine of a saint, an *emāmzādeh*. One well-reputed *hey'at*, made up exclusively of athletes from a social group bringing together some of Tehran's zurkhānehs, meet every Thursday evening at the Emāmzādeh Zeyd, a famous shrine in the heart of Tehran's bazaar. Here, the athletes circumambulate the saint's tomb, weeping abundantly and beating their breasts, and then go on to share a meal and discuss the latest news. Being invited to this ritual is a rare honor, particularly for those who are identified as having been too close to the faction governing the VBKP Federation between 1994 and 1999. The *hey'at* of this *emāmzādeh*, opposed to the federation at the time, was managed by the former leader of VBKP Federation in Tehran. This was a fifty year-old bazaari, an excellent athlete, who had grown wealthy from rents from warehouses, who managed his own religious and charitable institutions, and who was constantly accompanied by an entourage of friends and acolytes.

Another calendar is superposed over this religious one. The important dates of this calendar are the key dates of the Islamic Revolution, such as the *daheh-ye fajr* (from 12 to 22 *Bahman* / 1–11 February), the "ten-days of dawn" between the date Khomeini returned to Iran and the date of the overthrow of the Bakhtiyār government. These dates replaced those of the imperial period, which were focused on the anniversaries associated with the reigning dynasty. This calendar also marks the key dates of the Iran-Iraq war. The anniversaries of the liberation of the city of Khorramshahr in particular, which was a turning point in the war, are opportunities for special competitions in which speeches and the presence of athletes and spectators is a sign of the importance of this celebration. Indeed, many of those who participated had lost one or several family members in the ferocious battles that took place between 1981 and 1983, the most deadly years of the war.

Thus, as we can see, the athletes' schedule of events is extremely busy. In this annual cycle, I have focused on the month of Ramadan, which will serve as a leitmotif for the following analysis. This is not because I consider this period to be intrinsically more significant than other key moments in the religious calendar; Muharram celebrations are more intense and involve the athletes just as much in the community of believers. However, Ramadan, by its very length, is considered by the athletes themselves as the most important period of the year for the world of the zurkhāneh. It is indeed the period in which the zurkhāneh owners make half of their annual revenue.

In addition to the fact that the athletes would more willingly sacrifice a year of competitions than they would the nocturnal activities during Ramadan, this month of fasting also provides anthropologists, such as myself, the opportunity for a long period of observation during which a broader social panel and more diverse situations may be studied. It is a period that sheds light on the values and culture that guide the community of athletes, and which are clearly expressed during this month in a traditional ceremony, the *golrizān*. These values structure the identity discourse within the community of athletes, and those who feel close to them. The next section takes a closer look at the modalities through which this culture is expressed, the attitudes that it involves, and what it leaves unsaid.

Dāvud and His Family

Many Iranian readers will not discover anything new in the following lines, but they do provide an external perspective on an apposite case study, that of Dāvud and his family. They show the articulation between the domestic space and the social obligations of the world of the zurkhāneh today. They are also in keeping with the framework of observations related by Fariba Adelkhah in regards to the social transformations in the traditionally educated Iranian middle-class.[5] Why Dāvud? Any number of other portraits would have been possible; in four years of fieldwork I met many people. To choose my case studies in the contemporary world of the zurkhāneh, I was drawn to the intensity and extent of each person's engagement, and the reasons they had for accepting the heavy and time-consuming responsibilities associated with volunteering. However, at the core of this research I did not forget my primary question – what was the real motivation for the athletes in the zurkhāneh? The VBKP Federation had generously opened its doors to me, but no association, whatever the amount of information I could obtain from its officials, could give me what I was looking for. Focusing on this institution would have been an easier approach, but it would have been closer to a sociology of organizations, which was not my objective, even though the classics in this discipline, such as Crozier and Friedberg and their disciples, remain instructive.[6] Distributing questionnaires would provide little information other than an overview of infrastructures. This

---

5. Adelkhah 2004.
6. Crozier and Friedberg 1980.

was clearly seen in the study conducted by the Supreme Council for Arts and Culture, *Showrā-ye āli-e farhang va honar*, in the 1970s. It quickly became obvious that simply meeting people and asking questions would bring little more than consensual answers. Gaining any depth would be impossible and there was a risk of skewing the analysis. The perspective I wanted could only be obtained by immersing myself in this passion and regularly sharing the everyday rhythms and key moments of a team of athletes. Following a group closely would reveal what one might call its "human and psychological geography," its territories, its obstacles and miracles, the sum of individual ambitions and motivations, and its unspoken forms of organization. By taking this group as a reference point, I could observe the similarities and differences with other groups of athletes in Tehran and in the provinces. I could hope to reach a degree of understanding that can only be attained through long-term anthropological fieldwork over several years, which sheds light on all that remains invisible to a historian.

Dāvud, a certain vision of varzesh-e bāstāni

Dāvud was a well-known *miyāndār* in Tehran's zurkhānehs, married, with a son and a daughter. I use the term *miyāndār* on purpose because it is what is most often used in the zurkhāneh today, rather than the title of *pahlavān*. He had begun practicing *varzesh-e bāstāni* seriously in 1339 (1960) when he was seventeen years old, in an army zurkhāneh in Nārmak (in the east of Tehran). It was his paternal uncle, his *amu*, who introduced him into the world of this sport and gave him his first taste of the *gowd*. In so doing he had given him a way out of a family environment that, suffice to say, had left Dāvud with a visceral hatred of both opium and domestic violence. As a young man, outside his working hours, he had lived as a *mashdi* and a *luti*, in Hamadan as well as Tehran, and had seen much blood flow through the streets, although he had never spilled it himself.

He first made a living as a taxi driver, after spending a few years in the air force, where he had become friends with the man who would become his great partner, his *rafiq*, Jamshid. Then one day, shortly after the revolution, due to a serious accident resulting from the excesses he indulged in at the time, everything changed. To use his own words, God took pity on him and offered him a second chance. He fell in love with and eventually married a "visiting lady" whom he had met at the beginning of his convalescence in hospital and who had convinced him to change his life. She was a volunteer who visited the sick, a strong woman with a traditional education and from a much higher social background than him; she was pious, earnest, and humorous. He was instantly attracted to her altruism. She was so different, he said, from all the women he had seen until then, women who only "thought about getting more money off their husbands for shopping" (an age-old reproach of the *pater familias*). He used to say with a smile, "I have married a woman who is as marvelous as she is formidable."[7]

Dāvud's wife was responsible for the *sanduq-e sadaqeh*, the solidarity collection in

---

7. Dāvud never revealed the first name of his wife in my presence.

the neighborhood, an obvious sign of trust based on an infallible morality and integrity. She managed the funds in this collection with wisdom and discretion, which reinforced the general respect for her and gave her great influence in other families in the neighborhood. Anyone behaving badly was forewarned: financial assistance was conditioned on the moral reputation of potential recipients. However, in spite of this, she herself had once been a woman in danger; divorced, and physically threatened by a violent ex-husband who refused to allow her to make a new life. The police and the justice system could not take preventative action, so Dāvud, with his fiancée's blessing, had intervened. In this instance, he explained to me, the job had to be done properly, since a peaceful solution was impossible.

He had arranged a meeting with the ex-husband, man-to-man, officially to talk and try and find common ground. However, the "ex" had turned up with three other men in an obvious attempt to intimidate him, or even to beat him up. Dāvud had been expecting this. The ex-husband, surrounded by his bodyguards, was already giving himself an air of superiority, when at a signal from Dāvud sixteen zurkhāneh athletes piled out of four cars parked further down the street. They were led by his friend Jamshid, whose smile, I myself once observed, could go from friendly to murderous in an instant. The "discussion" instantly took a new turn and was ultimately quite short. Keeping his voice low, Dāvud simply explained to the ex-husband, who was now pale and silent, that certain things were going to change in his life if he meddled in any way in the life of the new couple. There was no shouting, no violence, simply the unavoidable acceptance of a new power relation, and the implication that it could lead to radical measures. This was something I observed several times during my study. The most dangerous potential violence is never ostentatious, never loud. Yelling and insults may result from a desire to dissuade, but when people start to speak quietly or when there is silence after an unresolved dispute, you best beware.

Finally rid of this threat, the couple was married and all the athletes from the zurkhāneh were invited to the celebrations. In addition to a great love story, his wife brought him respectability, the financial means to own their home and his own taxi agency, and bore him two beautiful children. His son, Ali Reza, became his father's pride and joy in the zurkhāneh which he had attended since he was five years old (in 1986, the same year that children were allowed and encouraged to begin training in the zurkhāneh). Before he was seventeen, Ali Reza had already won several championship titles, first in Tehran and then at the national level, in the spinning movements and juggling with *mil*. His career was already laid out for him, he would take over the management of the taxi agency but, before that, he would finish his studies, for in addition to his schooling and sports training he was taking a course in computer science. Dāvud's daughter, Sāmāneh, received a religious education as well as her schooling so that she could follow in her mother's footsteps. She already accompanied her mother to the *jaleseh*s, the women's associations and religious education classes for women where her mother taught.[8] This distribution of the children with each parent suited everyone.

Dāvud had an ambiguous attitude toward the first period of his life. By his own account he had been *divāneh*, completely unreasonable. He considered that it was thanks to the teaching of the *varzesh-e bāstāni* that he had "resisted" and avoided falling into a more dangerous life. He smiled and shook his head at the bombastic posturing and misdemeanors of his friend Jamshid, who had in many respects remained the likeable thug he had been at the beginning of their friendship. Unlike his friend who, like all fraudsters, was a perpetual chatterbox, Dāvud was a man of few words, and generally ironic. Only once did he discuss with me what wanting to be a *javānmard* meant for him in his life and his work: "this word should never be spoken lightly! It reverts to something that is noble and holy." Yet he heard it far too often from people in the zurkhāneh. "*Javānmardi* is to be practiced discreetly, it must not be boasted about, it is not a subject for public conversation." As for Hasan, whom we encountered in the first chapter of the book, this value involved honesty, generosity, and protection. According to Dāvud, if a taxi driver wanted to behave like a *javānmard*, he would have to always be true to his word, never steal from his clients, and always deserve his tips. He had worked for a long time as a driver of collective taxis and therefore had had the opportunity to protect female clients and passers-by from unacceptable comments, demands, and violence from other men. Violence against women struck a deep chord with him and brought out a cold, pitiless anger, which had its source way back in his past, well before the events preceding his marriage.

Dāvud was an autodidact, he liked mystic poetry and enjoyed discussions with the Sufis, who also appreciated his openness of mind, invited him to share their meals, and attend their healing ceremonies. *Javānmardi* was for him a collection of practical values that had to be applied in silence and in humility – the long perorations of certain athletes frustrated him to no end. One day he even interrupted one of them who was annoying everyone with a long patronizing speech on accepted principles, laconically quipping, "Great! You can start tomorrow…" This brought discreet smiles to the other athletes, except for Jamshid who, of course, immediately burst out in thunderous laughter, which left the would-be giver of lessons in even greater embarrassment. Jamshid had no qualms in telling me later, unsolicited, all the personality defects of the man who had been thus put back in his place.

Dāvud was always ready to spend time with novice athletes. He wanted to give them a taste for this sport and used these sessions to also encourage them never to indulge in opium and tobacco. He would say, "The zurkhāneh is a place that protects, where young people can find work, it must help them fight bad habits."

---

8. This is the female equivalent of the male *dowreh* and *hey'at*. For more information on this kind of group, see Adelkhah 1991, 135–53.

When we met, Dāvud had risen to the rank of inspector for the taxi agency union, responsible for overseeing that rates were respected. He had an excellent reputation in the corporation. He also explained his links with the VBKP Federation. After the revolution, he had received a letter from the then leaders of the federation, to be presented at the STB, recommending that he be admitted. A direct consequence of the post-revolutionary purge, the background of the leaders of the young federation, like others politically associated with the former regime, were subject to particularly strict control by the STB. I was told that Shaʿbān Jaʿfari's shadow still fell over this sport and many people had been struck off the list in Tehran and in the provinces: zurkhāneh owners who had been too close to the former regime and had their space confiscated, or gone to prison, or even – and this in a whisper even though we were alone – simply been executed.

This essential recommendation letter, along with his personal reputation in the zurkhāneh, had meant that Dāvud could be listed as a volunteer in the federation. His workdays spent volunteering during competitions were, luckily, subject to financial compensation. He was asked to be a referee and trainer, and soon became the captain of his own team, still accompanied by the inseparable Jamshid. This team of amateur athletes was a mix of men who had been friends for twenty or thirty years, along with more recent recruits and young novices. They were happy to come when he called for competitions and demonstrations of the sport. At the time, the group did not have their own zurkhāneh, nor any patrons, and up until 1994 they trained in the four or five zurkhānehs that were available and, on Fridays, in the zurkhāneh that invited them, so as to have a high-quality session. Everything changed in that year because they won the competitions organized for the fourteenth anniversary of the liberation of the city of Khorramshahr. The competition was held in the grand Shahid Fahmideh zurkhāneh – Shaʿbān Jaʿfari's old club, and the current seat of the VBKP Federation. There Dāvud's team had drawn the attention of a powerful patron, whom we will encounter in more detail later on.

Celebrating Ramadan with Dāvud's family

I followed the group that Dāvud led, from January 1995 to April 1998. I became friends with him, his son, and his family, and his sudden early departure from this world remains a blow for me.

One might think that Ramadan is a difficult month to go through for a nonpracticing observer, and that to do so might even be a little hypocritical. It might seem like a month in which life slows down during the day – and where some people sneak off to eat secretly at lunchtime and others travel the 22 kilometers required to call themselves "travelers" and thus be exempt from the fast. Of course, Ramadan is also a month of genuine physical and mental asceticism prescribed for a whole community, and is particularly difficult to bear when it is falls during the long months of torrid summer where the days stretch out interminably. It is a time when the community of believers must come together, to examine and purify itself. From the outside, it might seem like a month that is arduous and demanding.

Yet when I expressed this kind of sentiment about the difficulty of respecting the fast, the response was inevitably the same: "Oh no, not at all, it is just a question of habit." Even the children who followed the little *kalleh gonjeshki* (little sparrows head) Ramadan, which allows them to eat certain foods during the day, loudly interrupted to tell me just how wrong I was. They told me this month was "totally great."

In certain respects the community's self-reflection also took place at the family level, at least among those observing Ramadan. During winter this period is much like an extended Christmas Eve, during which the asceticism is transformed into a delicious opportunity to come together with family, to pray without ostentation, sing, listen to family members telling stories and jokes and, and for any lucky guests like myself, experiencing the most charming forms of hospitality as one's cup of tea and plate of fruits are constantly filled. This is a time where children have the great pleasure of staying up late to play with their cousins and indulging in the sweets that are a particular pleasure of this period.

Ramadan clearly inverts the habitual rhythm of daily life. The "day" begins with sunset and ends with the first rays of dawn. At five o'clock in the afternoon (luckily for me, during this fieldwork Ramadan fell in January when, days were short), my friend Dāvud and his family picked me up in their car and we all went to his sister-in-law's house to break the fast (*eftār*). Then followed one of the many all-night Ramadan celebrations essential for those who belong to the world of the zurkhāneh.

For others in the street, fast breaking was more immediate. For those who still had to work, or who could not wait to get home to eat, restaurants were ready to sell a large bowl of hearty noodle soup, *āsh reshteh*, and beetroot and broad bean sellers encouraged people to stop and have a warm snack before they joined the groups waiting for the "collective taxis."[9]

"Without ta'ārof*"*

After arriving at our destination and brief greetings all round, we were soon seated cross-legged on a thick mat around the *sofreh*, the fabric tablecloth, placed over another rectangular wax tablecloth to protect the carpet beneath. The hostess was the maternal aunt of Dāvud's son Ali Rezā, his *khāleh*. She wore a *chādor* and sat at the far end of the *sofreh*, close to the kitchen door. Those who had not yet finished prayers came to join us a little later, wearing loose-fitting traditional trousers. One of the nephews had the flu and spent the evening watching television under blankets in an overheated room, while outside the frost was biting cold. Dāvud's daughters and nieces brought us *halvā* as an

---

9. These taxis took four or five passengers at a time going in the same direction, who each got out at their respective destinations. It was an alternative to the buses and minibuses that were more tiresome to take.

appetizer, a sweetmeat made of flour, rosewater, cardamom, and sugar fried in saffron oil, along with butter, cheese, dates, and *sangak* (bread baked over hot stones, which was increasingly difficult to find in Tehran), and of course as much tea as we liked. The two sisters were coming and going to the kitchen, the rest of the family came and sat around us in no particular order, except that the younger members stayed together and the women sat close to the kitchen. We were brought saffron rice, yoghurt, and chicken with celery. Contrary to ordinary custom, it was not necessary to get up to greet new arrivals: "*beh khodā* Philippe, sit down! For *eftār* we don't do *ta'ārof*!" There were several reasons for this: first, because this was a family gathering, and second, as the expression says "out of respect for the *sofreh*" and the meal served on it. Once the food is served, even ordinarily but particularly for *eftār*, it must be eaten immediately. Woe on him who leaves the table in the middle of the meal or takes too long sitting down (the meal cannot start until everyone is seated).

And then, once everybody had finished their typical fried Ramadan dessert, consisting of *bāmiyeh*, *gush-e fil*, and *zulbiyā* and always accompanied by a glass of tea, the girls (one of whom did not wear a headscarf, unlike the other women and girls in the family), helped their mother and aunts clear the *sofreh* and do the washing up, chatting all the while. The men went into the room next door to watch the football match on television, at which Tehran's Piruzi club wiped the floor with the team from Shiraz.

Dāvud's sister-in-law entered the television room discreetly to take the Koran, kept in a large drawer, and then joined her sister to read and pray. Once that duty had been piously fulfilled, they chatted – I learnt later – about the news they had received of their third sister, a 50-year-old woman with a strong character who had gone alone to visit her daughter in America, which provoked much laughter and admiration from the others. Apparently the third sister had told the others on the telephone, laughing, how American women stared at her when she walked around Washington wearing her *rupush*, the islamic cloak, her *rusari*, the scarf worn over their hair, and the *chādor*, the all-covering cloak worn over the head.

The young men of the family, brothers and cousins, had removed themselves to a bedroom to talk and listen to Iranian music from Los Angeles, as they waited for their mothers to call them for a second dessert. The older men talked about a drop in investment rates on bank deposits, a recurring theme in conversations in Iran, where soaring inflation forced families to be on the constant lookout for the best way of preserving their savings. All was well, and now that this family gathering had been agreeably concluded, Dāvud and I were free to either stay or leave to visit other friends, which would cause no offence. It was nine o'clock, the night was just beginning. Dāvud's wife felt that his role in the zurkhāneh meant he was too often absent during this period that was so important for the social life of the family; but given his personal history and his commitment to the young athletes, she looked on the social price of this passion with a great deal of benevolence. Before delving into my visit to a zurkhāneh in the month of Ramadan, however, a discussion of the significance of Ramadan for the athletes is in order. The following section is based on my observations with Dāvud and other athletes who allowed me to accompany them.

Ramadan with the Athletes of the Zurkhāneh

Remembrance, presence, solidarity

For the *bāstānikārān*,[10] the nights of Ramadan are particularly sleepless. The zurkhāneh-hs are open all night and only close at six o'clock in the morning. Where an ordinary session would rarely attract more than ten or twenty athletes a night – and frequently fewer – easily one hundred attend nightly during this month. On Thursday nights there can be two hundred or more, including spectators. This forces the *morshed*s to plan several sessions in a row.

During this period, an intense social activity takes over this world, which uses this time to honor, remember, commemorate, and strengthen social links. Each person spends one, two, or three hours, depending on how close they are to the host and what the general context of the visit is. They cannot be allowed to leave without having given the host a chance to offer them *āsh reshteh* for *eftār* or tea at least twice. A few hours later, in a different zurkhāneh or at the *dowreh* of a famous athlete or patron, they will eat cakes. They might even be offered a second dinner if there is a commemorative meal organized by the family of a deceased member, or a *nazri*, a meal offered to mark a wish that has been fulfilled during this period, which is favorable to all kinds of religious ceremonies. The most important thing is to be there and be seen to display solidarity and friendship. Some particularly crafty people use this as an opportunity to stuff their stomachs with the generosity of Ramadan. Jamshid, for example gave a sly wink as he told me unashamedly that he never spent a cent on meals during this holy month.

In a zurkhāneh, the visiting athletes cannot refuse the invitation to go down into the *gowd* to perform a few exercises in the company of friends and acquaintances. It is not rare, therefore, that a group of athletes perform two or three series of exercises in a night in different zurkhānehs, before being invited to share a third and final meal before dawn and the new fast it brings. Rest will come then, after the morning prayers (*namāz-e sobh*). Work, at the office, business, or shop, will have to wait. To a certain extent, the nights of Ramadan are for friends and networks of acquaintances what the days of Nowruz, the Iranian new year, are for families and the ten days of Muharram for neighborhood relations. Each person must show that they are part of the group,

---

10. This is the name often given to athletes who practice the zurkhāneh exercises but not wrestling. They used to be called simply *zurkhānehkār*, but with the help of athletic specializations and the fact that traditional wrestling has moving away from the zurkhāneh, *bāstānikār* was increasingly used. Since 2010, the word *zurkhānehkār* is again used officially.

that they think of and are bound to the others in solidarity. The events of the year and the vagaries of life will serve to prove whether they have convinced the members of the group or not.

The generosity of the golrizān *festival*

Ramadan is truly the month of generosity, gifts, and counter gifts, a month favorable to the organization of celebrations of solidarity. Within the zurkhāneh, this takes the shape of *golrizān* (literally "flower throwing"), a ceremony that involves the financial contribution of patrons. While it can be organized at any point in the year, it is mostly held during Ramadan. The word "flower" evokes favors and blessings while glossing over the financial nature of the assistance. An act of solidarity between friends needs to be dematerialized in this way; euphemism avoids this situation being uncomfortable or embarrassing for the receiver. However, the use of this term is also most likely linked to the contraction of the expression *gol-e sar sabad* ("the flower on top of the basket"), which refers to the best part or the best element of something. In the zurkhāneh, in addition to the *golrizān*, we have already mentioned the *morshed*'s head covering (which comes from Sufism), the *gol-e tāj*, which translates as "rose of crowns" (meaning "the best of all crowns"), but there is also the poetry of the *gol-e koshti*, "rose of wrestling" and the *gol-e charkh* "rose of spinning," which is the name given to the best twirling movements in the *gowd*.

Without wishing to question the genuineness of the patrons' generosity, it is also important to note that their donations maintain their social networks and reputations in this milieu, vis-à-vis both their peers and other notables and those who are the beneficiaries of their patronage. Such gestures can make all sorts of other things easier for the patrons over the course of the year.

The *golrizān* traditionally serves to collect funds for an individual in need, often elderly athletes or *morsheds* who are respected in the milieu and whom local patrons of the zurkhāneh have decided to honor. However, this assistance may also be used for other projects, for example struggling small businesses or charitable institutions. On the nights where a substantial *golrizān* is organized, an average-sized zurkhāneh might see up to 600 visitors in the course of one night, 100 of whom might be athletes who perform exercises in the *gowd*, usually in groups of twenty athletes. That means around five or six consecutive programs of muscle training, each lasting an hour, broken up with lots of rhetoric and public speaking, to the rhythm of the percussions provided by several *morsheds* taking turns throughout the night.

The contemporary oral explanation of this tradition stubbornly assures us that previously the beneficiary used to remain perfectly anonymous to preserve his honor. The zurkhāneh veterans and the *morshed* acted as guarantors for the authenticity of the recipient's need and discreetly transferred the money collected to the person in question.

Nevertheless, in such a small community, where everybody knows everyone else's business, how is it possible to conceal the name of an athlete who is appreciated by all and in a sufficiently vulnerable state to benefit from this collective assistance? Anonymity was undoubtedly more a matter of convention.

For example, a man in his fifties whose grandfather had been mayor of the town of Shahrud, told me he had seen many *golrizān*s in his native area, where his father and grandfather, as local notables, had often made donations. He assured me that everybody always knew who was receiving this particular assistance. A *long* was spread out on the floor of the *gowd*, and the *miyāndār* asked the attendees, "how many flowers must there be for the light not to go out?" And, in response, the notables gave amounts of money (opinions seemed to differ as to whether the amounts were known to all or kept secret). The *miyāndār* collected the donations and then knotted the four corners of the *long* and gave the parcel to the *morshed* or *pishkesvat*, to give to the person in need. The ceremony then concluded with a prayer to Imam Ali.

Some might be tempted to use this occasion as an opportunity to indulge in a little racket, known as *pardākht* (literally: "payment"). The term refers to a scam consisting in colluding with the first person to donate, who therefore gives an ostensibly large amount to force the others (who do not want to appear miserly) to give at least as much. Needless to say, the person who receives the money then reimburses the extra amount to the first donor. It is exactly this kind of practice that has led to an obligation to discreetly establish the amount of the donation in advance.

The alleged decline of the traditional anonymity that supposedly attached to the ritual of *golrizān* is blamed on the fact that it is no longer possible to trust anyone. However, did this trust ever exist, particularly when talking about money in Iran? Today the size of the donation is established in advance, but everybody officially gives what they like and, miraculously, the exact amount appears in the basket on the night. Unfortunately, sometimes this celebration is denounced as a genuine form of extortion to the benefit of people who in reality have no need of it. In light of this, an observer cannot help wondering what the *golrizān* of former times might have looked like in zurkhānehs linked to the *luti*s' mafia, and just how free shopkeepers were to participate or not.

Apparently in response to a number of scams, and seeking to reserve the exclusive right to organize the ceremonies, in 1995 the VBKP Federation tried to prohibit this ceremony which it considered as too often corrupting the disinterested solidarity it is supposed to represent. Having presented the zurkhāneh as a school for – or even the incarnation of – *javānmardi*, the community of athletes was suddenly obliged to measure up to the reputation assigned to it over the last half century in a certain historiography. As the VBKP Federation took the official discourse about the zurkhāneh and *javānmardi* that was based on this historiography seriously, it sought to reserve the *golrizān* ceremony for situations recognized as being of public interest (such as raising money for victims of the earthquake that struck Khorasan province in 1997, for example), or to honor people who met the federation's new criteria for respectability – an issue to which we will come back. It was difficult to openly counter the arguments put forward by the federation, but, after a moment of collective disbelief, the discomfort and resentment created by this announcement became clear. However, the federation is not all-powerful and cannot really impose such a rule on the zurkhānehs that are not under its direct – or indirect, via financial support – influence. As we saw above, only 25% of the federation's budget comes from the state, via the STB; the rest is made up of private donations and other institutional support that fluctuate, more or less depending on circumstances. This limits the amount of financial assistance that is available each year and thus potential retaliatory measures, because those running the zurkhānehs are constantly trying to diversify their sources of income and can try to break away from the yoke of the federation if it became overly constraining.

The appointment of the new president of the VBKP Federation in 1993 went badly; those who were unhappy with the result still had the possibility of saying they were following the advice of "their" president. The former president, who lost his place also ran a zurkhāneh and took sly pleasure in constantly breaking rules that were not his own, and making sure everybody knew about it. Strengthened by this demonstration of lingering authority in spite of his change in status, he maintained the cohesion of his former clienteles and inner circle of athletes.

Quite aside from these quarrels, many athletes resented this decision to prohibit *golrizān* as an unbelievable and incomprehensible abuse of power, an attack on a tradition that might one day be of benefit to all. Thus certain *pishkesvat*s who did not want to quarrel with the federation organized this ceremony directly with the support of a circle of friends and generous donors, without the support of the federation. That is how it was that during Ramadan of 1997, a *golrizān* was held in honor of the old *morshed* Rahbar, which brought him 400,000 *tumān*. For a man whose pension was 20,000 a month, this was a lot of money. In that year, the federation had not organized any *golrizān* to help individuals, and it was consequently considered most ungenerous.

The golrizān *among the brothers of the north*

One year earlier, at the end of Ramadan in 1996, a large *golrizān* had been organized by the *morshed* (and owner) of the zurkhāneh of Farahzād, an old village on the edge of the Alborz mountains in the north of Tehran, now swallowed up in the sprawling northwestern suburbs of Tehran. It was thus in a freezing cold mountain winter that I observed a *golrizān* that was both traditional and unusual. The *morshed* had just finished extensive renovations and restorations of his club and had been assured of financial support from both the networks of the zurkhānehs in the generally more prosperous northern parts of the city and those in the more popular southern parts, which was unusual since these two networks maintained only relatively distant relations.

Making the most of the fortieth day of mourning for a local notable who had died and whose memorial service would be organized in the zurkhāneh, the *morshed* scheduled a *golrizān* for himself at the same time. There was no false modesty here, because the beneficiary himself was guiding the session from the *sardam*. The guests included leaders of the four other zurkhānehs from the north of the city (Chizar, Farmāniyyeh, Niyāvarān and Vanak) as well as delegations from the south of Tehran, local notables, and well-known athletes (including two footballers from Piruzi, then one of the major teams in Tehran). Also present were district officials, representatives of the police and the army (including a colonel in active service), officials from the national radio and television and the STB, as well as public contractors who were known for being generous towards *varzesh-e bāstāni*. All had answered the call for assistance a month earlier. In spite of the cold and the snow, we made our greetings at the door to the garden of the zurkhāneh, and then hurried to enter it in search of a place to sit that was not already reserved for someone.

A *golrizān* of a certain size implies a well-timed ceremony. Certain zurkhānehs from the north were particularly careful about staging their entry. Just when it seemed that the room could not hold any more people, the *zarb* and the bells announced the entrance of men from the Zurkhāneh-ye Tāleqāni in the Chizar neighborhood. The simple presence of this group would ensure the *morshed* of Farahzād that there were generous and influential local protectors in attendance.

The Chizaris were feared and wooed in more than one aspect. After the revolution, a number of upwardly mobile people from the south of Tehran who embodied a certain religious and pro-revolutionary conservatism had moved to this already quite conservative but wealthy neighborhood, long known for its religious school which, led by Mohammad Mofatteh, was one of the first to protest against the shah. The men from the Zurkhāneh-e Tāleqāni, which was built in 1980, represented a bridge between the world of the *varzesh-e bāstāni* and the dense webs of more or less legal activities surrounding the parastatal (often paramilitary) associations created after the revolution, such as the Basij and the Ansār-e Hezbollāh. These connections, and the influence they were thought to have, gave them an unparalleled feeling of independence among the zurkhānehs of Tehran, to the extent that they famously provoked the ire of the VBKP Federation by organizing a *golrizān* for a member of their group who had recently been released from prison. The federation had asked for what reason the man had been imprisoned and had publicly denounced the ceremony, restating the obligation to ensure the integrity of the people benefiting. The Chizaris had not deigned to respond. They were never seen in the competitions organized by the federation anyway.

The origin of this rift lay in early post-revolutionary times. When the new VBKP Federation was set up it was not given oversight over military zurkhānehs, which were given a separate administration. On one hand there were the civilian zurkhānehs, which at the time of this study were led by Seyyed Abdollāh Sajjādi, and on the other hand there were the zurkhānehs of the army and security forces, then led by General Mohammad Nejāt of the *Niru-ye entezāmi* (police force). This was an inevitable division due to the fact that the army and security force zurkhānehs were located in zones that were forbidden to civilians. However, the zurkhānehs of the military forces had adopted the same objectives and reforms as the civilian federation. General Nejāt is considered responsible for the construction of more than one hundred zurkhānehs in the country, including eight in Tehran. This is far fewer than the number of civilian zurkhānehs but provides a very strong basis for athletes in their prime. The air force, for example, had twenty-three zurkhānehs in its different bases, and the army many more (exactly how many is not known). This communal practice gave rise to a community life and inter-army competitions that naturally excluded civilians – and anthropologists! But thanks to connections and arrangements between good friends I was able to observe a few sessions and I noticed that there were not many significant differences. The circle of friends and the rituals associated with friendship and protection that could be observed in civilian zurkhānehs seemed identical among soldiers, officers, non-commissioned officers, and senior public servants.

Thus, between the two major networks of zurkhānehs, the Chizaris had chosen their side and cultivated connections with the zurkhānehs of the Revolutionary Guards and the police force. For the moment, in view of later organizing a *golrizān*, demonstrating solidarity with the civilian sphere seemed like a good idea. Their presence ensured that representatives of the police, the army, and high-ranking officers of the Revolutionary Guards attended the ceremony in Farahzād. The Zurkhāneh-ye Tāleqāni of Chizar was also one of the favorite houses of strength of Hādi Khāmene'i, the Supreme Leader's younger brother who was an athlete and fine connoisseur of the different symbolic aspects of the art. He was familiar with the zurkhānehs in the south of Tehran and their tumultuous past, but he explained, during our short interview at the Zurkhāneh-ye Tāleqāni, that this art form had a very particular spiritual signification for him. He added that he attended the zurkhānehs in the north of Tehran essentially to avoid the growing pollution in Tehran, and that regardless of what had happened in the past, forgiveness and understanding were also cardinal values that must apply, with full clarity, to all those who had paid their debt and sought honorable redemption. Regarding these people, who may have in the past had reason for reproach, it was particularly important to be forgiving.

The connections made through shared sporting practice sometimes create surprising shortcuts in social hierarchy or political loyalties. Thus, Hādi, whose opposition to his powerful older brother was known to all, is said to have used his influence in the VBKP spheres to set up teams to put up posters in support of his political preferences. That is how the very conservative members of the Zurkhāneh-ye Tāleqāni and the network of athletes linked to the former faction of the VBKP Federation at war with M. Sajjādi's team were said to be putting up posters for Mohammad Khātami during the presidential election of 1997, despite the fact that they were generally considered very close to the political positions of the Supreme Leader and conservatives. It is important to add immediately that the representatives of other circles of athletes, who were individually quite close to the reformists, admitted having shown zealous support for the conservative candidate in this election, Ali Akbar Nāteq Nuri, because their personal network of acquaintances were more closely connected to those of Nāteq Nuri. This did not prevent them from individually voting for Khātami. Having political opinions is good, but not engendering awkwardness in the networks one depends on is more important. The Colonel – who was presented in chapter 1 – had crudely reminded me of this in regards to the coup of 1953.[11]

With support in such high places, it is easy to understand why the Chizaris considered themselves important. This self-satisfaction could be seen in their meticulously staged entrance in the Farahzād zurkhāneh. They had been careful to reserve one of the most sought-after places, next to the *morshed*'s *sardam* and facing the room. One Chizari, with a video camera on his wrist, had set up a full ten minutes earlier opposite the entrance, in order to film the entrance. It was thus with the deafening sounds of the bell and drum, amplified by the thunderous sound system, as well as the powerful *salavāt*s called in their honor three times by almost two hundred people, that ten true *pahlavān*s, all wrestlers in their prime, solemnly entered the room, surrounding their chief, looking around the room somewhat scornfully before taking their places on the podium, where they would be in full view of everyone. These athletes, one of whom seemed to be cultivating his resemblance with *pahlavān* Takhti, showed off their impressive muscles in tight sleeveless black T-shirts somewhat uncomfortably reminiscent of paramilitary attire. Given the dearth of young men in the traditional zurkhānehs of Tehran's south, athletes in their twenties surrounding their forty-year-old leader had become quite an atypical sight in the world of civilian zurkhānehs. Far from the problems of generational renewal that affected the elderly groups in the south of Tehran and Iranians civilian zurkhānehs in general, the Chizaris seemed to have managed to maintain, or indeed inspire, interest among young men looking for good networks of influence. One day, a veteran bitterly remarked: "Today when young men want to join a mafia, they don't become *jāhel*s. They just simply join the Ansār-e Hezbollāh or the Basij," two well-known revolutionary para-military organizations.

But the Chizaris were not the only ones to pay attention to the image they projected. The other delegations of athletes present that evening did too, and soon there were several video cameras and many photographers in the room. The arrival of the representatives of the southern zurkhānehs was the object of a series of ovations that expressed pleasure in this presence, proving to all that this was an important moment and that the organizer of the *golrizān* was able to mobilize support widely. With the drum rolls of the *zarb*, those from the north welcomed their brothers from the south with respect and pleasure. The traditional geographical opposition had disappeared (those from the

---

11. See above, page 52.

south traditionally considered themselves the only true *mashdi*s in Tehran, which generally gave rise to muffled taunts on both sides). The large room was full to overflowing, and some of the younger spectators were even asked to give up their places for the guests now arriving. My place was safe, as I was a photographer and cameraman attached to one of the groups from the south.

The *gowd* and its edges were soon the object of the most formidable display of *ta'ārof* I ever had the opportunity to see in a zurkhāneh. As positions in the pit were limited, it was impossible for all athletes (many of whom had the rank of *miyāndār* in their respective zurkhānehs) to have a place. The problem was resolved by a strict application of the rule of seniority, assuring that almost each veteran present in the *gowd* had a chance to speak, respecting the rule of precedence for athletes and veterans with the title of *seyyed*.

There was no lack of *ta'ārof* among the spectators either. One guest, a former Piruzi footballer whose leg was in plaster, refused to remain seated while *pishkesvat*s thirty years his senior were standing. Seeing that he ran the risk of not being allowed to give up his chair, the man unceremoniously threw himself to the ground to put an end to the humiliating situation. This was for nothing, because he was quickly lifted and forcibly sat on another chair. Later he was saluted by the *miyāndār* of the *gowd* in these words: "We know you, and your father before you. You are much like him. I remember the time when I kissed your father's shoulder." Another *pishkesvat* close to the footballer added, "Your father taught me what I know of the *gowd*" and lent to kiss him. Embarrassed, the young man tried to lift himself up on his crutches to kiss the veteran's shoulder as a sign of deference, but the *pishkesvat* prevented him because his tribute was directed at the young man's father, who had been his elder. There was therefore no reason for the young man to feel embarrassed by this unusual mark of respect from a veteran to a much younger man.

The *morshed* made sure that all the important people had spoken and sharply chastised the lower-ranking athletes who dared have a private conversation during the speeches of the *miyāndār*s, who took turns in the center of the pit. In fact, there was more talk than exercise (but the exercises were performed magnificently, particularly the spinning) and, unusually, appropriate political declarations – the liberation of Jerusalem and the cursing of Israel – were skillfully presented before the representatives of civilian and military institutions. Ezzat Karimi, owner of the newspaper *Rokhsat pahlavān*, whom we encountered in chapter 1,[12] mentioned the 2500 years of history claimed by this sport, from Cyrus to Khomeini.

It was half past two in the morning, and we were leaving together with the delegations of the other southern zurkhānehs, when I observed discreet discussions occurring. It turned out they were subtly ensuring that everyone had given the amount agreed on. Generally speaking, the donors were separated into three groups: the delegations, which

---

12. See above, page 71.

each gave an envelope in the name of their zurkhāneh or group of friends; the local notables, who gave in their own name; and the others, who contributed smaller personal donations. There were also a few people who had come for the ceremony of the fortieth day of mourning and had only discovered once they were seated that a *golrizān* was organized that night. Honor forced them to also take out their wallets, although their gaze was heavy with disillusionment and unspoken reproach. The *morshed*, who had noticed these looks, assured them, by way of apology and consolation, that he was simply the depository of this money; in spending it on the zurkhāneh, he was in fact dedicating it to Imam Ali, protector of the site and VBKP sport. Three million *tuman*s were collected, and the *morshed* of Farahzād was now under obligation to all. I was later told that in return he had assured the Chizaris of his presence and financial participation in their own *golrizān*. Thus revolves the generosity of the zurkhāneh during Ramadan, in a series of gifts and counter gifts that would not have gainsaid Marcel Mauss.

However, a year later, the *morshed* of Farahzād once again called on his friends and colleagues, but this time the matter was far more serious. There was a project to construct a highway exit to the *Yādegār-e Emām* (Memory of the Imam, a reference to Khomeini's son Ahmad) highway, right through his zurkhāneh. The project was subsequently modified and the exit built elsewhere. It is not far-fetched to suspect that the zurkhāneh benefited from the fraternity of the athletes and protectors who had been present in Ramadan 1996. It may have helped that Tehran's city council was facing problems at the time.[13] Nevertheless, independently of fate, the brothers of the zurkhānehs in the north of the city had proved that solidarity and friendship were not empty words. Through the practice of *golrizān* they genuinely sought to cultivate the memory of these values.

13. These "problems" refer to the imprisonment of the mayor of Tehran and some of his pro-Khātami deputies, on the pretext of the usual accusations of embezzlement and misuse of public funds.

Chapter Five
Big Brother and Little Brothers: Privileges and Constraints of Fraternity

It is clear that the dimensions of solidarity that we have discussed so far involve close ties resulting from both fraternity and a shared network of friendship and influence. The concrete expression of this solidarity supposes a mode of relations and operational rules intertwined with a system of values, which we will look at in more detail in this chapter. On this subject there are existing studies that have considerable theoretical breadth and which are useful because of the insights they provide. However, they are difficult to synthesize succinctly. I prefer to refer to them only where necessary, because it would be pretentious and dangerous to summarize an entire society into a series of definitions and schemas. Yet I also want to show how these general theoretical elements help us understand crucial points. I therefore chose to allow the descriptions of the practices I observed to provoke the necessary theoretical explanations in and of themselves. When it seems possible to include these theoretical points in the text I have done so, but when they required too great a digression I have added them separately, in the form of text boxes, which allow the reader to either finish the descriptive chapters and return to read them later, or to momentarily pause in the general reading to explore the theory in more detail.

The Night of 15 January 1998:
When a powerful patron goes to Qazvin

On the night of 15 January, there was no *golrizān* planned, and there was no work the next day, as it was a weekend during Ramadan, when professional activity is considerably reduced in general. Having taken leave of his family, Dāvud and I went to wait for the NIOC bus at an appointed place. It picked us up an hour later on Āzādi Avenue. Dāvud's team and his powerful patron Mehdi Tarkhāq were going to visit the *bāstānikārān* in Qazvin. The session was initially planned to go from eleven o'clock at night to two o'clock in the morning, but ended up going on until four.

Beginning in 1995, Dāvud and his team had found a rich and powerful patron in Mehdi Tarkhāq. This man (whose real first name was Soltān-Ali) had been a cofounder of the Islamic Association of the ministry of oil, and by 1995 he had become director general of the administrative and social services of that ministry. In that capacity, he had been tasked with reorganizing the sport sponsoring activities of the ministry.[1] Tarkhāq had undertaken to build a grand zurkhāneh in the capital on behalf of the company in one of their complexes near the Tehran railway station. The oil company, as we have seen on previous occasions, is generous.

Figure 47. Zurkhāneh Sherkat-e naft. The experienced athletes (on the left) show young novices (on the right) how to swing the mil. Note the very young members of audience at the back. (1995 - Photo Philippe Rochard).

Tarkhāq had noticed Dāvud's group of athletes in the 1994 competitions and had encouraged them to take residence in the company's zurkhāneh, which was inaugurated during the month of Muharram in 1995. This meant being able to train in peace, to train novices (Figures 47, 48, and 49), and more generally to organize the life of the new zurkhāneh that had adopted his group. After 1944, many companies had been funding zurkhānehs, but Mehdi Tarkhāq did not limit himself to simply doing that. He also made sure the athletes had the means to travel, covered their fees during national competitions, and took athletes with him when he traveled to the provinces on official oil business, so that they could perform in the local zurkhānehs. He also offered them free meals after the meetings at his own *hey'at-e azādāri*, which now met in the newly constructed grand zurkhāneh. In exchange, the team agreed to compete under the name "Tim-e Naft-e Tehrān" (Oil Team of Tehran). As a busy man, Mehdi Tarkhāq had entrusted one of his close associates, Mr. Shir-Mohammadi, to oversee the opera-

1. "Soltān-Ali Tarkhāq mehmān-e Rādio Varzesh," 21 Mordād 1396 (12 August 2017). http://radiovarzesh.ir/NewsDetails/. Accessed on 24 February 2023.

Figure 48. Inaugurated during Muharram 1374/1995, the zurkhāneh did not yet have many photos of athletes, but the portraits of the Imam 'Ali and Āyatollāh Khomeini; the banner on the wall reads: "The secret to life is the blood of Hoseyn, that is all." (1995; Photo Philippe Rochard).

Figure 49. The line of athletes and *pishkesvat*s. Behind them is a space for teaching freestyle wrestling (1996; photo Philippe Rochard).

tions. This kind of comprehensive sponsorship was a "first" at the time in the world of the zurkhāneh, but it quickly gained popularity. This is how the best VBKP sports team in the town of Arāk came to be sponsored by a major company in the region, Āluminiyomsāzi (Aluminium Works), for the national championships.

In accepting this proposition, Dāvud and his friends were in fact very much aware that they had become dependent on a figure who was acting out of a genuine love for the art, out of faith, out of dedication to an ideal, but who would also now be accompanied by a large retinue in all his prestigious visits. Whether intentional or not, it is clearly impressive being accompanied by ten or fifteen men at all times.

During the trip to Qazvin, Tarkhāq himself recited a prayer in honor of Imam Ali Tāleb and then had someone chant the martyrdom of his two sons, Imam Hasan, whose birthday it would be a few days later, and Imam Hoseyn. There was much weeping in the bus, mostly near where Tarkhāq was seated. Mehdi Tarkhāq had not become a sponsor of this sport by accident. In the early 1980s, he was the president of the most prestigious sport federation in Iran, the renamed Islamic Republic of Iran Wrestling Federation (IRIWF). While a connoisseur of wrestling, he had also always had a deep admiration for *varzesh-e bāstāni* and everything it stood for. He saw it as the mother of all sports, dedicated to Imam Ali and the physical expression of a spiritual truth that all must try to follow and understand in order to be a man in the true sense of the word. In other words, it shed light on the distinction between good and evil. He told me that, "The zurkhāneh is the tradition of Iran's warriors, of Imam Ali, of God's Lion. Every Iranian has a duty to remember this."

Anxious to promote the practice of this sport and aware of prevailing mentalities, he had had the idea – on International Women's Day (which in Iran is renamed the Day of Fatima, the Prophet's daughter) – to organize a demonstration of *varzesh-e bāstāni* before a mixed audience of men and women, to take place in the buildings of the NIOC on Tāleqāni avenue. The idea was that the ladies would discover that the sport no longer had any connection to the heritage of Sha'bān Ja'fari and the negative reputation it had in the past, after which they would perhaps be more willing to allow their sons to train there. In this respect Mehdi Tarkhāq was close to the president of the federation, who was also working towards the same goal. Of course, in front of women, the rules of modesty meant that the athletes wore long-sleeved shirts for the occasion, but if there was to be a younger generation at the zurkhānehs, then mothers would have to be convinced that their sons had nothing to fear.

When Tarkhāq spoke to the audience, as the *miyāndār* or as leader of his *hey'at*, he often began with a thunderous *Barādarān*! (Brothers!). Of course this is common in the spheres that are now called the conservative circles of the revolution, but Tarkhāq genuinely acted as a big brother. As we saw above, he was a *sofrehdār*, and regularly held meals for his little brothers. He looked after them and tried to help them, while being careful to ensure they did not confuse generosity and weakness; giving is an art that requires a certain agility.

The art of refusing to give ever more

In the first chapter we saw how local notables are solicited by those who believe that they have become close enough to them to ask for recommendations or money, and how the notables are able to manage these situations – for example by using the prerogative of their selective gaze. However, how can they refuse when a person of recognized status lowers himself to ask for financial assistance? They must try to avoid the insult of a direct refusal, but also manage to make themselves understood.

The director of the Tehran district branch of the VBKP Federation, Mr. Mellati, was clearly envious of the assistance given to Dāvud and his team, and thought he was in a position to obtain the same favors. During a meal in honor of Tarkhāq, hosted by the NIOC in the city of Sanandaj, and in the presence of the whole team supported by Tarkhāq, Mellati complained regretfully that the VBKP Federation did not give him enough money, that its president, Sajjādi, only gave him a budget of 800,000 *tumāns*. Such a statement in front of the whole team and other guests could have forced Tarkhāq to accept the thinly-veiled request for fear of losing his status as a protector. Dāvud, who was not expecting this unfortunate initiative, did not move – only his eyes revealed a quick and sudden attention. Was Mellati taking the risk of having all assistance withdrawn from their group by leading Tarkhāq to think that Dāvud was party to his sudden request? Mehdi Tarkhāq stared closely at Dāvud for two very long seconds, which only amplified the latter's discomfort – and he admitted to me later, his fear. Then Tarkhāq, without looking once at Mellati, replied offhandedly that that was the same amount he gave to a freestyle wrestling team that he sponsored and that the wrestlers were quite happy with it.

Mellati then committed the unpardonable sin of continuing to complain – and thus to demand assistance. Once again Tarkhāq did not respond directly to him, but turned towards those close to him and told the following story. A few years ago, he had decided to help an amateur football team. The players had initially been extremely grateful, but then they became arrogant: the next year they declared that they would only play if they were paid five times as much as he had given the first year, some five million *tumān*. They were told that they would no longer be sponsored. The captain tried to make amends honorably, accepting the initial sum – all in vain. Tarkhāq concluded, surrounded by deadly silence, on the unbelievable audacity of these football players, the rottenness of money, and the fact that *varzesh-e bāstāni* and *pahlavāni* wrestling were clearly above all that because of the noble modesty of that tradition. The subject was changed, some managed to suppress a smile, and Mellati sheepishly remained silent for the rest of the evening.

Once we left, Dāvud's team spoke constantly of this affair for nearly a week afterwards, guffawing with laughter. Nevertheless, Dāvud had had a nasty scare and would never forgive Mellati for the way he had risked the unwritten agreement between him and Tarkhāq with his inopportune demands. Mellati's reputation suffered a lot from this unfortunate attempt, and he rapidly became highly unpopular in the world of traditional sport.

High status, low status, taʿārof

Mellati had tried to use the noblesse oblige inferred from Tarkhāq's status to his own advantage. As William Beeman notes,

> hierarchical differentiation seems to be a nearly universal feature of human life, but in some societies, such as India ... or Japan .... hierarchy takes on special symbolic significance. There are few societies that take the obligations of status [resulting from this hierarchy] as seriously as does Iranian society."[2]

Beeman also specifies that an individual in a position of superiority must also be equal to that rank and fulfil their obligations toward those who are beneath them in status to ensure the latter's support. Conversely, those below must also fulfil their obligations. The person above must be a source of abundance and the person below must be generous with their time and services and provide unwavering support for their generous patron in all situations that demand their presence. This hierarchical status is verbally and somatically formalized in *taʿārof*, as we have seen – this cannot be understood as simple "politeness" but is closer to the "rules of etiquette." There would never be a a lot of *taʿārof* between individuals who are close and of equal status, unless it was performed ironically or playfully. True intimacy can only exist between equals, therefore services cannot be rendered in the absence of a preexisting friendship. Although *taʿārof* is the sign of a true attention to the other, it is also ultimately an ensemble of expressions of politeness designed to manage the unequal relationships that may exist on an everyday level, and to identify marks of respect that it might be desirable to express to another person.[3]

The consequences of unequal relationships between a "patron" and those "indebted" to him can in extreme cases theoretically lead the person in the superior position to their ruin, and the person in the inferior position to sacrifice their life. Luckily, these extreme cases are now rarely an option and the inferior position provides real advantages, to the point where an avalanche of *taʿārof* consists in positioning oneself "below" the other, both out of modesty and precaution. In this "inferior" position nothing can be asked of you, nor can you be obliged to undertake risky maneuvers, because all movement (and even a simple recommendation letter can be a risky move because it is a commitment) involves symbolic, financial, or social risk to some degree. Thus, anyone who

---

2. Beeman 1986, 12, quoting Dumont 1970; and Lebra 1976.
3. It would be impossible to provide a list of these here, but we can refer to some of the expressions we have already seen in the first part of this book, and also to the examples given in Beeman 1986, 132–201.

finds themself publicly set on a pedestal in a zurkhāneh by someone else best beware, because the person so acclaimed may have to return this favor at some stage by opening either his check book or his network of contacts.

Nowcheh *and* hāmi: *the art of choosing a good protector*

But let us return to the night of 15 January 1998. Those sitting around Mehdi Tarkhāq in the bus driving to Qazvin would have liked to see him become the president of the VBKP Federation. He had the reputation and the attitude of a leader that they would have been happy to follow. He was reserved, imposing both in size and in his actions, generous, educated but not pedantic, powerful yet approachable, influential, and rich in friends who were equally rich and well-connected. He was also appreciated for the fact that he shared some of his precious time with a group of people with whom he shared a passion, social customs, clothing, and taste in food. Tarkhāq was an accessible man.

If he had become president of the VBKP Federation, Tarkhāq would have given new status to the members of the group of athletes around him. They would have been in the inner circle of the president, his *nowcheh*s, his devotees, necessary intermediaries for anyone who wanted to approach him. This would have been a big improvement in their status within the world of the VBKP. Through their team being attached to a man of the reach and influence of Mehdi Tarkhāq, they would have been able to indirectly benefit from possible *pārtibāzi* (exchange of services) between important figures.

> **PĀRTIBĀZI AND EGALITARIAN RELATIONSHIPS**[4]
>
> *Pārtibāzi* operates as a kind of personal-interests lobby that can be mobilized in the interests of each of its members. Its efficiency comes from the feeling of equality within the group, and from the ability to make a complaint or demand made possible by the complicity of a familial or amicable connection. This feeling of equality must be consolidated on several occasions. Members must participate financially, demonstrate the same cultural references, and in the case of zurkhāneh notables, for example, manifest the same external signs of power and recognition that are obtained from good style, knowledge of the practice, and genuine generosity. In this circle, friendship is always associated with the same birthplace (a town, childhood friends in the neighborhood), the same professional activity or hobbies, or past experiences (three years military service for example, or VBKP wrestling, or pigeon fancying). This system operates at all levels of Iranian society, from the socio-political and economic elites to the neighborhood *hey'at*s and *dowreh*s.
>
> The members of this lobby constitute an informal association. The term

---

4. The text box is inspired by the chapter on "Relations of equality: *dowreh* and *partibazi*" in Beeman 1986, 44 and following.

used to describe this varies depending on the occasion for the meeting and the social environment in which it takes place. In so-called traditional spheres, where the religious calendar and its various festive occasions (the sacred ten-day period during the month of Muharram, the first month of the lunar year which is the opportunity for believers to pay their legal tithes to religious authorities), are scrupulously respected, the term *hey'at* is generally used, as we have seen elsewhere in the study. In other more bourgeois circles, the term *dowreh* is used. This generally refers to a more informal group that meets regularly in the home of a different member each time. It is in these meetings that useful information circulates and opinions are formed. The broader family also constitutes a *dowreh*, but each person is responsible for diversifying it. This explains the importance, both in Iran and elsewhere, of strategies relating to friendship, partnership, and marriage. Being genuinely accepted in different *dowreh*s or *hey'at*s broadens one's scope of action and possibilities for intervention.

Of course, for certain members of the group who did not hesitate to "have a drink" in secret, Tarkhāq's unwavering religious faith was somewhat frustrating. He was known to be close to the conservative faction of the Supreme Leader, and he had many friends in the clergy. In the name of the art of wrestling and the lifestyle that connected them, Tarkhāq had become their *hāmi,* their patron, protector of men who were light years away from his social status. In other words, it was impossible to sing bawdy locker-room songs, as in a previous trip to Sanandaj.[5] However, in all, Mehdi Tarkhāq was a good person and praying for the Imams Ali, Hasan, and Hoseyn during this month of Ramadan was very honorable. So the mood of the trip stayed serious.

It was the same bus that we had taken to go to Isfahan. The seats in the middle of the bus had been taken out to create a space where we could spread out our rug, sit in a circle, and chat. On very long trips, those who wished to could remove their trousers and adopt the more comfortable traditional pajama trousers, sit on blankets, drink cinnamon tea, and eat while chatting, joking, praying, singing, and reciting poetry, all while the two drivers took turns driving and monitoring the mechanics. This time the trip was not long and we stayed seated.

We arrived in Qazvin an hour and a half late and were welcomed by representatives of the local branch of the STB. The night was brutally cold, and the wind, snow, and sleet barely truncated the traditional rounds of *ta'ārof* outside the gates of the sporting complex. The only exception to the rule this time was that once the salutations had finished, we jogged off towards the entrance to the zurkhāneh where ordinarily, in more pleasant weather, we would have borne ourselves with more dignity.

The zurkhāneh and its exercise pit were large. There were five such spaces in Qazvin. Sixty to seventy people were already present, with around twenty athletes in the

---

5. See above, page 142.

gowd around their *miyandār* Mahmud Farhangdust, the leader of *varzesh-e bāstāni* in Qazvin. This zurkhāneh was recent. It had been built in 1987 inside the STB sports center, and over the last three months had begun to host classes for young people under the impetus of the VBKP Federation and its president, Abdollāh Sajjādi. There was already a group of fifty teenagers who assiduously attended classes in *varzesh-e bāstāni*. In just three months, this was a great success. The general recruitment policy undertaken in all regions of Iran was beginning to show results.

A true sense of responsibility

His comfort and family tradition meant that it was natural that Farhangdust should be the leader of *varzesh-e bāstāni* in Qazvin. His father had been a well-known athlete and his uncle had been one of the best wrestlers in Iran. He himself was a wrestler. During the Iraqi invasion, he had answered his nation's call and enrolled voluntarily in the Revolutionary Guards. He eventually received an honorable discharge following the death of his two brothers in combat, after being wounded three times and left partially deaf. He then followed in his late father's footsteps and, while continuing to manage his business in the Qazvin bazaar, had naturally accepted the honor and responsibility of taking on the management of *varzesh-e bāstāni* in his home city. Like all those who had seen war up close, he did not talk about it much. However, he was particularly attentive to the *jānbāzān* (wounded veterans), who always had their place in the *gowd*. One of them, who was present when I was there, had come in second in the spinning exercises category at the national championships for disabled athletes organized in August 1997. He had had one of his arms amputated, which made it even more difficult to control the rotations, and the other athletes therefore took care of and admired him. No one around me used the word *javānmard* to refer to Mr. Farhangdust, yet he was humble, generous, with a sense of responsibility and sacrifice, and protected those in need – all the criteria that the *pishkesvat* had given me to describe one. But, because all of this was sincerely felt and believed, he would probably be called a *javānmard*, beginning with his funeral eulogy.

When we entered the zurkhāneh, we were met with the *salavāt*, along with the sound of the bell and the drum rolls. We instantly knew where the positions of honor were: along the wall with the best lighting, closest to the *sardam* and the *morshed*, facing the Qazvinis, who were all standing to salute us on the other side of the *gowd*. There was already a *mollā* sitting on the bench of honor, a professor at a private religious university in Qazvin. Mehdi Tarkhāq obviously sat to his right. On the wall facing us, next to the portrait of Khomeini, there was a banner in honor of Tarkhāq and his *hey'at*. The *hey'at* was us, the NIOC's Tim-e Naft-e Tehrān. The portrait of *pahlavān* Takhti stared down at us, near the ceremonial cups and certificates brought back by the athletes of Qazvin. The two *morshed*s leading the session were brothers. The elder, Ali Akbar Valiyān, had been the *morshed* for Tehran's team during the zurkhāne'i competitions in Sanandaj.

Dāvud, who was now the official trainer of the NIOC team, was exasperated by the overwhelming mediocrity of the young *morshed* appointed to the NIOC zurkhāneh in Tehran. For certain reasons, which I was led to believe were associated with the rank of the young *morshed*'s father, no one could officially complain about his abysmal mediocrity; he only knew how to bellow without being able to push his *zarb* beyond the most basic elementary rhythms. And so Dāvud had asked Valiyān to come with us to the zurkhāneh'i championships, which was against the rules since each zurkhāneh team was supposed to come with its own *morshed*. Dāvud did not like cheating, but here he was caught between a rock and a hard place. Either he discreetly bent the rules a little, or he would lose face in front of the whole national sporting community.

Eight months earlier, after the Sanandaj competitions, Valiyān had invited us to visit him in Qazvin. It had been planned back in October and announced several times a week in advance, and then on the day before pushed back "until later" because Mehdi Tarkhāq was overbooked, and as it was out of the question to make such a visit without him, the NIOC bus had remained unavailable until this particular night in January.

The delicate matter of forutani, *social modesty*

The athletes from Qazvin had begun a series of exercises while they were waiting for us, so it was only after midnight that it was the turn of the athletes from Tehran. When he descended into the *gowd* to the *zang-o zarb* rhythm of honor, Tarkhāq went directly to the place of honor on the edge of the *gowd* closest to be *sardam*, with a view to curtailing the politeness rituals. However, it still took several long minutes to resolve the problem of the hierarchical order in the exercise pit. Plunged into *ta'ārof*, the Qazvinis and Tehranis competed for who could be the most polite. The hosts had to give up their places to the guests, and the latter, out of modesty and *forutani*, had to refuse this honor to show they were not arrogant or presumptuous (*por-ru*). Whether hypocritical or sincere, *forutani* (social modesty) is the primordial value and it is directly opposed to a general trend toward increasing valorization of the individual. It stems from a time in which society attempted to channel the excesses of those with power and strength in any way possible, to prevent displays of hubris, a cardinal social sin. Like vice paying homage to virtue, even the most arrogant of people must – ordinarily – demonstrate this humility for a certain length of time in order to be seen as honorable. Therefore, at the end of a reasonable amount of time refusing, the athletes from Tehran eventually took their position in the places of honor. A strange diagonal line thus formed in the hexagonal pit, which was much larger than usual, with the nine senior athletes from Tehran on the side closest to the *sardam* and on the opposite size, forming two ranks, a group of twenty athletes made up of all those from Qazvin along with the four youngest athletes from Tehran. Salutations and official responses followed.

But the problem of precedence had not yet been resolved. Tarkhāq had willingly accepted to lead the *shenā* exercise (although he did not fail to ask others to take his place as honor dictated), and he also had to designate the athletes who would kneel to his left and right, facing the *sardam*. However, out of modesty, *everyone* refused the honor of sitting on either side of him. All this took place while the veteran of the Qazvin wrestlers, Mr. Yazdi, recited the prayer; as he was seventy-seven years old, this responsibility was his.[6] Like Tarkhāq, Yazdi bore the permanent mark of the prayer stone on his forehead. He was nearly finished with his prayer and the problem had to be resolved.

Tarkhāq brought the one-armed Qazvini athlete to be on his right, and finally decided on Jamshid the taxi driver on his left. Jamshid was visibly happy to be able to accept this honor without losing face, as Tarkhāq forced him to take this place. There is always a risk when a very high-status athlete invites a "brother" of lower rank to be temporarily "close," in spite of the immense difference in status that separates them in everyday life. The contrast can be humiliating, even in the *gowd*, which is supposed to expunge social differences and allow for a temporary perfect order in which, except for a connection to the prophet (for the *seyyed*), the chance of fate and birth are officially not taken into account.

The rest of the session took place without incident, and around 3 o'clock in the morning we found ourselves sharing a great *kalleh pācheh* with our hosts, sustenance for tired bodies in preparation for the fast the following day. Along with ābgusht, it is one of the favorite restorative foods of *varzesh-e-bāstāni* athletes.

Ru dādan, *or the inconvenience of familiarity*

Like any good *hey'at* leader, Tarkhāq made sure everyone was seated and had a full plate before allowing himself to sit with his host. This meal provided the true lesson of the evening for me. Several of us were surprised at the direct and silently furious gaze that Tarkhāq leveled at Jamshid, who dared to ask for a second helping before everyone had been served. He had been honored in the *gowd* and now he dared to do this, in front of the guests, in a most obvious and vulgar way. These are the risks involved in liberating someone from the rules of *forutani*. When someone is temporarily given extra status (*ru dādan*), they may forget they are not actually close to those in power. Because Tarkhāq had momentarily honored him, Jamshid now forgot his place and thought he could behave as he wished. One of his friends, observing that he had turned his back on the sponsor and therefore could not see the threat that was building up, casually approached him and whispered something to him. Without anything else being said, and without having turned his head toward the friend who had warned him, without any hasty gesture that might drawn more attention, but in a desperate attempt to save face, he quickly sat back down without turning around, and remained rooted to the

---

6. His happiest memory was the mark of honor and esteem that the federation's president had shown him by paying for his trip to Isfahan, where the championships in 1996 had taken place, to give him his official diploma honoring him as a *pishkesvat* of the federation. This was an official recognition and reward for sixty years of experience and service.

spot, with Tarkhāq still staring at him. I learned later that Jamshid had come very close to being banished from activities the group shared with Tarkhāq, if not forever, at least for a certain time. There would have been no more restaurants, no more *hey'at*s, travels, honors, advantages, or *pārtibāzi*; it would have resulted in total social degradation and perhaps permanent exclusion for having made the guest of honor lose face, because he was responsible for the group's behavior and it would necessarily reflect badly on him (Figure 50).

Figure 50. The image of a social shortcut. The back line, from right to left: the trainer of the junior national freestyle wrestling team of Iran, Mr. Jahāniyān; the team's patron and sponsor Mehdi Tarkhāq; an unknown person; my friend Dāvud, the team leader; and the *morshed* of the zurkhāneh Shahid Fahmideh. In the front and middle lines: some athletes from Tim-e naft-e Tehrān (who work as taxi drivers, shopkeepers, car sellers and employees) (zurkhāneh Shahid Fahmideh, 1997; photo Philippe Rochard).

Different Circles and Levels of Friendship

Jamshid the rafiq-e zerang *(cunning accomplice)*

This misbehavior had made Dāvud very angry too because he was the head of the team and Jamshid's impropriety also reflected on him. Jamshid was used to this and generally seemed to be completely indifferent to it, except for that evening with Tarkhāq. He was the clown of the group, a good athlete, a womanizer, a braggart, and a drinker, but he made up for his more questionable qualities in his unwavering commitment to Dāvud. At any hour of the day or night, Dāvud could ask him to come, and he came, except if he was in the middle of a bibulous *viski-miski pārti*.

The term *miski* is simply a play on whiskey.[7] It does not mean anything, but it might be understood as a kind of generic "et cetera" for the other things that might be involved in a whiskey party. A *viski-miski* involves renting an apartment for a day or an afternoon from an accommodating owner and friend and stocking it well with alcohol. Close friends come with their current ladies or mistresses, and a good afternoon is discreetly had by all. Then everybody leaves, with their *chādor*s and their three-day old stubble, back to official life. If the young women on Vanak Square wearing sunglasses or jeans under their Islamic dress are arrested by the police for letting a lock of peroxided hair escape from their headscarf it is because they are displaying the external signs of supposed freedom of mores. Not so for the happy bunch from the so-called traditional neighborhoods in the south of Tehran. They know the rules of the game and how to play with them, while remaining perfectly invisible.

Dāvud had tried to tell him to better his behavior, but Jamshid had no intention of changing his ways. Every group of athletes has their clown, apparently straight out of the Siyāh Bāzi, Iranian comedy theater, with the same rich repertoire of rude mimics and jokes.[8] The person in this position is not the most esteemed member of the group. Jamshid seemed to have definitively abandoned all the external markers of *vaqār*, the self-mastery and gravitas that is generally the mark of self-respecting men who give value to their *ru*, their "face." A person like Jamshid is nevertheless accepted and even sought after, because in a certain way, he provides his friends with the performance of a kind of freedom of expression that only the male intimacy of the group can tolerate. Within a limited space, this person channels and provides a field of expression, allusions, and jokes that are generally described as being below the belt, *band-e tonbāni* (literally "boxer drawstring" jokes). This character therefore means everyone can laugh while preserving the dignity of those who do not want to engage in that kind of register themselves. In this respect he is the direct descendent of the professional *luti* of the nineteenth century, who was also an entertainer and teller of bawdy stories.

But the buffoon knows his prerogatives too and necessarily has a sense of caricature and repartee. He also has an ability to make remarks that are met with immediate laughter and that no one dare express disapproval of for fear of being the object of similarly biting ridicule in turn. The designated joker, in other athletic zurkhāneh communities, might not hesitate to remove his dentures with his tongue, while rolling his eyes around to make his complacent public laugh, or to caricature the *miyāndār* behind his back during the exercises. Happily, Jamshid still had all his teeth and his favorite pastime was dancing like a belly dancer while singing pornographic songs with mixed-up Turkish and Persian. This gave rise to thunderous laughter from the *kabbādeh* champion in the

---

7. The linguistic term is "reduplication," a better-known example of which is the Yiddish shm-reduplication. See Feinsilver 1961. I thank Houchang Chehabi for this reference.

8. To understand to what extent this connection with the professional corporation of *luti*s, as public entertainers and acrobats, is obvious, see the enlightening paper by Yeganeh Tabrizi and Rayani 2005. As regards the tradition of itinerant acrobat-entertainers and the links with India, see Rao 1988.

group – a man of 1.90m and 115 kg – and a slight head movement, half laughing, half embarrassed, from Dāvud, who raised his eyebrows at me as a way of saying nothing could be done about him. Luckily for the team's *āb-e ru*, he more or less managed to control himself in the presence of people from outside, and saved his most questionable poetry for the athletes' dormitory.

But often all of this went together. During the competitions in Isfahan, the team was supposed to sleep in the dormitory but Jamshid had heard that one of the federation's guests was not using his allocated hotel room – so he had the nerve to go and ask for it. Moreover, he made up a story about the guest having agreed he could use it, which was not the case. He was caught by the president of the federation red-handed usurping the room and had to return to the dormitory, after being chastised by Dāvud. When he wanted to obtain some advantage (going to the front of a queue, having a second helping, being in front of the cameras, etc.) he would declare that he was doing it to as a favor to someone else, after which he would try to be compensated by that person for his effort. If he was caught, either by his friend Dāvud or by the person who realized he was using their name to get his ends, he would break out in wild laughter, striking his right hand on the back of his left hand in a sign that he recognized he had been caught, and began grand declarations of friendship and respect for the *zerangi* of his friend, his clever mind and perspicacity. Jamshid was a great comedian but he was often at the extreme limits of what was honest and socially correct. However, the art of the cunning person, *ādam-e zerang*, is precisely understanding – better and faster than others – the general context of a social interaction, guessing what others want while concealing one's own objectives, drawing advantages to the extreme limits without breaking ties. He was a great strategist of speech and staging, and he knew how to use external signs of light-hearted behavior to disarm the impact of his words or his gestures which otherwise would have been highly insulting. It is not possible to be angry with someone who never seems to think about what they are saying and who knows how to ask for forgiveness so cleverly. The *zerang* is therefore a man who is both a manipulator and a concealer, the incarnation of the *luti* and *jāhel* in his most "swindling" form. When I asked the *pishkesvat*, it seemed that the older zurkhānehs, even the most famous ones, always had some men like Jamshid.

However, what remained a mystery in the eyes of many was the nature of the friendship between Dāvud and Jamshid. They seemed like polar opposites, and the respect that the others had for Jamshid was largely due to Dāvud's presence. Several times I was told, by way of explanation, that "he is his *rafiq*" accompanied with a knowing smile and a hand gesture linking the two index fingers, like an unbreakable link between two men. This term is not used as a simple synonym for *dust* (friend). Nor does it have a sexual connotation. Of course, homosexual relationships can exist between *dust*s or between *rafiq*s, but in this instance, Jamshid and Dāvud's relationship was exclusively one of friendship. A *rafiq* is neither a *dust* (friend), nor a *dādāsh*, in the sense of a friend so close they are referred to as blood brothers. Before seeking to understand what this refers to, let us explore the vocabulary of Iranian friendship, as these terms are very present in the zurkhāneh and cover different aspects of affinity.[9]

Dādāsh, dust, rafiq

In the world of the zurkhāneh, we can identify three terms that refer to the male relationships that occur there and that are distinct from simple *āshenā'i* (acquaintance). The following considerations must not be seen as strict or exclusive rules, rather as tendencies or trends, which demonstrate their operational force through usage.

As we saw in part one, *dādāsh* is a word of Turkish origin that means elder brother. The feminine equivalent is *ābji*, "elder sister." Ideally, one only has one *dādāsh*. In the strict sense of the term, it is used in families to refer to the brother one feels closest to, the great confidant, the chosen twin, with whom one shares all ones' secrets. The term expresses a sense of solidarity, a response to the question, "In whom can I confide?" It can also be used between *pesar-khāleh*s (maternal cousins who are traditionally complicit) or between two people linked affectively in the same way and with the same intensity. However, brothers or not, they all share the fact that they are childhood friends, linked before they reach the age of thirteen or fourteen. This is a life-or-death relationship, perfectly equal and with complete trust. Each would give everything, without reservation, for the other. Beyond that age, new friendships are understood differently. They become connections of instrumental solidarity, responses to questions like "upon whom can I rely? What can I expect from this?" More or less consciously these relationships involve a sort of internal accounting of services rendered and repaid over time. As Degenne and Forsé, as well as Allan show, this type of friendship seeks to maintain a balanced account in order to ensure longevity. Even if this is denied, it must be recognized that when the balance is lost, eventually so is the friendship.

In Persian, adding the auxiliary verb "to have" to the word friend (*dust*) forms the composite verb "to love." *Dust*s form the second and broader circle of friends and the *āshenā*s, simple acquaintances, form the third, final and larger circle. *Dust* is the word most frequently used to translate "friend." However, misunderstandings often arise between an Iranian and European, for example, on the issues of the dividing line between expressive solidarity and instrumental solidarity; this is perhaps more clearly marked in Iran than in Europe. Schematically we could say that most of the expressive and affective solidarity is reserved from the relationship between *dādāsh* or childhood friends and the proportion of instrumental solidarity is very present in the standard understanding

---

9. I use the term "affinity" employed by Degenne and Forsé and the analysis that follows is inspired by this work: Degenne and Forsé 1994, 39 and following; Graham 1989, 18–19 and following; see also Goitein 1971; and Beeman 1986. Beeman is himself inspired by Erving Goffman's work on social interactions, which was also used for the study of this chapter, in particular Goffman (1967) 1982 and Goffman 1959. To complement the study of Persian *ta'ārof* with its place in rural Iran, see Vivier-Muresan 2006a, 292–304; and Vivier-Muresan 2006b.

of the term *dust* in Iran. "Becoming friends" (*dusti kardan*) is a necessary pre-requisite to extend the power for action of this new connection into one's own network of influence. This does not mean that disinterested friendship cannot develop, or that genuine appreciation is impossible, or that this approach is understood as a hypocrisy seeking to obtain favors without returning them. Instrumental solidarity is an exchange in which proof must be offered before one can expect the same in return, but misunderstandings do happen, in spite of everything. Sometimes there is a mutual incomprehension between an Iranian who considers their European *dust* completely ungrateful, and the European who considers that their Iranian *dust* is decidedly too self-interested. Before going further, let us explore the concept of affinity as Degenne and Forsé have described it in their work on social networks.

Affinities

According to Degenne and Forsé, friendship is experienced as an egalitarian relationship, reciprocal and freely consented to without constraint or coercion. It is incompatible with hierarchy or authority but not with influence. This seems to be the current state of understanding.

According to Robert Brain, in rural societies friendship is almost as institutionalized as marriage, sealed by an ensemble of rituals. Indeed, in the European high Middle Ages friendships were sanctioned by the church. The priest said a blessing and prayed aloud, reminding would-be friends of their duties toward their blood brothers, for example. Or when a blood pact was weakened, the priest would use baptism to establish links between godparents and the parents of the baptized child.[10]

Thus, and here I quote Degenne and Forsé:

> Just as marriage primarily functions to establish an alliance between two kinship groups who exchange women, friendship functions to establish solidarity between two people or two groups these people belong to [...] In our contemporary industrial societies, some elements of these representations remain. When we talk about a "best friend," is that not precisely to differentiate this friendship from others we accept may be less durable? This distinction is the sign of the weakening of traditional affinity connections."[11]

The authors conclude that there is a discrepancy between ideal friendship, which is still close to its traditional understanding, and practices that are actually observed, particularly the fact that in Europe friendships are increasingly made and unmade depending

---

10. Brain 1976, 91. Brain also mentions the *compadrazgo*. "Compadrazgo or co-godparenthood is the relationship between the parents and godparents of a child christened in church ... Having replaced the 'pagan' institution of blood brotherhood, compadrazgo became common all over Europe and still exists in parts of Greece, Spain, Italy, Serbia, and Russia." Ibid.
11. Degenne and Forsé 1994, 41.

on professional or geographic mobility, for example. This is absolutely not the case in Iran. Distance is by no means an excuse to forget one's friends. A *dowreh* of old friends who grew up together in the same town, or the same neighborhood, or were in the same year at school, will get together at least once a year regardless of the distance that now separates them from each other.

Our understanding of friendship is therefore perhaps partly based on this ideal of chosen twins who irresistibly attract each other, a fusional image that is also strongly implanted in Iran, where mystic poetry has emphasized the romantic attachment of the lover and the beloved. However, the values of this ideal, although they remain strong, focus above all on tried and true childhood friendships, or on love at first sight. Given that the latter is relatively rare, the effectiveness and value of these connections and solidarity are evaluated over time, based on the observation of the everyday reality of this friendship. For example, among the zurkhāneh athletes, men called "new arrivals" (*tāzeh āmadeh*) may have lived in the city or neighborhood for ten years already. Friendship within the group is divided between one's *dādāsh*, a synonym of fusion, equality, and no accounting, and then the others. Friendship with the other members of the group often gives rise – in spite of of the constant and very vocal affirmations to the contrary – to a strict, meticulous, even niggling accounts of services rendered, which emerges rapidly whenever there is a real or supposed oversight.

In these friendship relations, the link between the two *rafiq*s is of a different nature. These are people who, although they are not childhood friends, have an intimate connection to one other. It is possible to be friends with a *dust*, and then see this friendship wane and disappear without too many social consequences. A *rafiq*, through the knowledge that they have of a certain aspects of your private life, or events they have experienced with you, can become a mortal enemy if there is a falling out. Nothing is worse for friendship and a man's honor than the *rafiq-e do ru*, a two-faced friend, a hypocrite. This type of person is regularly condemned during the *miyāndār*'s speeches in the *gowd*. We were even told on one occasion that drinking alcohol was a less serious offence than being a *rafiq-e do ru*, because the first vice is candid but the *rafiq-e do ru* is an unpardonable and essentially incurable crook, that is concealed and only identified later. Ultimately it is impossible to separate from a *rafiq* without taking a major social risk. This was how it was for Jamshid and Dāvud, who had lived nine years together in the same military base in Hamadan when they were barely twenty years old. What they knew about one another, and what they had been through together, bound them together forever. Dāvud's youth had perhaps been more tumultuous than he admitted to me.

The term *rafiq* is not understood in the same way in the different social spheres that use it. In the middle classes, it is largely disparaged and considered as being below the word *dust*, which only reinforces the morally ambiguous connotations of complicity, "friends for better or worse." By comparison, *dust* appears magnified, as the symbol of generous, disinterested friendship (in discourse at least, if not in fact).

Big Brother and Little Brothers: Privileges and Constraints of Fraternity   181

It is therefore not surprising to hear and see *ādam-e zerang*, a person who is clever, crafty and sly, invent strategies to associate themselves with people whom they expect something of, and use all sorts of plots and tricks to incur their debt, through an exaggerated use of the vocabulary of friendship and conviviality. This is how it was that I found myself in the following situation: a man who had gravitated around the world of Iranian wrestling, and whose name I will not mention, used me shamelessly at the beginning of my stay to obtain invitations from members of the IRIWF by claiming to be my best friend. He tried to pay for everything for me, by force, only to declare later to his wife, in front of me, that we were now best friends and that I would get them visas for France. It was just as the Iranian general secretary of our host institution had warned us "do not trust those who immediately declare themselves to be your friends (*dust*)! The true friend stands in the shadows, behind the one who speaks, and is silent, he observes you and will reveal himself to you in time." (Figures 51, 52, 53, 54, 55 and 56).

Figure 51. – On the right two *dādāsh* and on the left their *rafiq* (Āshurā 1996; photo Philippe Rochard).

Zāher *and* bāten[12]

The risk of indiscretion associated with a *rafiq* cannot properly be understood without immediately explaining that in Iran the nature of social interaction involves a major division between *bāten and zāher*, the intimate sphere and the rest of the world, the out-

12. For more information about these notions and their consequences see Bateson et al. 1977; and Thaiss 1978. Of interest, the chapter on "womens clothing" in Adelkhah 1991; and Hillman 1981.

Figure 52. Āshurā, *hey'at* of Mamad Siyāh surrounded by his childhood friends, those close to him, and his son (Tehran, 1996; photo Philippe Rochard).

Figure 53. The president of the VBKP association, Seyyed 'Abdollāh Sajjādi visiting the *hey'at* of Mamad Siyāh (Tehran, 1996; photo Philippe Rochard).

Big Brother and Little Brothers: Privileges and Constraints of Fraternity 183

Figure 54. The next generation of friends, *rafiq* and *dādāsh*. (1997, photo Philippe Rochard).

Figure 55. "In life and in death"; a young athlete and his *pesar khāleh*, his maternal cousin. (1997, photo Philippe Rochard).

Figure 56. New blood in the zurkhāneh and friends forever. On the right, a group that is already solid, in which we can perhaps guess who is the leader (1997, photo Philippe Rochard)

side. These two fields are delimited by a dividing line consecrated by Islam and Shiism but not invented by it. This division crystallizes opposing values that find their expression in behavior, expectations or well-known verbal expressions.

Bāten is the deepest personality, hidden intimacy, the most precious part of the self, which will be defended and concealed tooth and nail behind the ru_s the "face." As Goffman puts it:

> The term *face* may be defined as the positive social value a person effectively claims for himself by the line others assume he has taken during a particular contact. Face is an image of self-delineated in terms of approved social attributes – albeit an image that others may share, as when a person makes a good showing for his profession or religion by making a good showing for himself. [...] A person may be said to *have,* or *be in,* or *maintain* face when the line he effectively takes presents an image of him that is internally consistent, that is supported by judgments and evidence conveyed by other participants, and that is confirmed by evidence conveyed through impersonal agencies in the situation. At such times the person's face clearly is something that is not lodged in or on his body, but rather something that is diffusely located in the flow of events in the encounter and becomes manifest only when these events are read and interpreted for the appraisals expressed in them.[...] A

person may be said to *be in wrong face* when information is brought forth in some way about his social worth which cannot be integrated, even with effort, into the line that is being sustained for him. A person may be said to *be out of face* when he participates in a contact with others without having ready a line of the kind participants in such situations are expected to take.[13]

By contrast, the *bāten* is as much the space for internal conflicts, torments of the heart (*oqdeh-ye del*), as it is as the space for bursting joy and mystical illumination. If *bāten* were to have an equivalent in social space, it would be the *andarun* of the house, this space where women can take off the outer clothing (*chādor*, *rupush*, etc.) protecting their *nāmus* (this value that refers to family virtue, the main component in honor) because they know that only *mahram* men enter here.[14] The *nāmahram* (those who are not close family) are received in a room that does not connect to this space. Protecting the family *andarun* and *nāmus* is the responsibility of the men's *gheyrat*, their self-respect. Thus, describing a man as *bi-gheyrat*, without self-respect, or *bi-nāmus*, without honor, particularly in public, is essentially a declaration of war that requires an immediate violent response. In both affective and ideal terms, the family *andarun* space is characterized by a certitude of love and affection, and socially by a freedom of language. It is a space that, ideally, should be peaceful, and ensure stillness of the soul and rest for the spirit, and that must be protected at all costs from disruptions from the outside, just as one's personal *bāten* must be protected from one's *zāher*, the vector of corruption. It is also where the worst disagreements happen of course, but they immediately cease if there is a risk they spill out beyond the space into the outside, or that the outside impinges upon this private space.

As a counterpoint, the *zāher* represents all that is unpredictable about the outside world. It is what is inevitably required for life, which is not very prestigious or valued in moral terms. When faced with this world, in which we expect always the worst, Shiism allows *ketmān* (mental dissimulation) by lying to protect one's values, a historic legacy of a faith long persecuted by Sunni political and religious powers. The *zāher* always presents a risk of corruption and hypocrisiy in the context of the outside world. As Jean During rightly pointed out in a discussion about a fruitful observation made by Beeman,[15] in Iran, when the *zāher* is too present, to the point where you feel soiled by it, when you are tired of lying to keep face, depending on your personality, you go into the mountains to purify yourself by reading a few immortal lines by the poet Hafez in a

13. For more details about this notion, see the work by Erving Goffman, from which these extracts are taken, particularly chapter 1 in Goffman (1967) 1982, 5–22, here pages 5–8. See Joule and Beauvois 1987.
14. This term refers to close family members, those with whom marriage is forbidden, father, brother, son etc.
15. We were discussing his chapter, "*Partibazi* and *Ta'ārof*: Some Final Comparisons," from Beeman 1986 (60–63).

peaceful landscape, or by playing music, or reciting a piece of poetry, or meditating on the Koran in a mosque.

The *zāher* is therefore a space where you have to be on your guard; you have to maintain perfect control over yourself; you have to to show a social appearance that is the best possible ("zāher-rā hefz kon!" keep up appearences!), and which surrounds a *bāten* that must be protected from other people's gazes, manipulations, and cunning (*zerangi*). Others are always suspected of being *fozul*, potentially indiscreet. In this respect, it is necessary to present smooth courses of actions that give rise to no remarks. As Goffman shows, public life is a risky space, in which people try to provide others with a coherent and valorizing image of themselves, and therefore particularly accentuate the respect of social norms. In the case of Iran, we can also add that people particularly avoid any critique that might have a direct or indirect impact on the *bāten*. "Face" is the major symbolic expression of this self-image, and it is fueled by a range of attitudes:

> By entering a situation in which he is given a face to maintain, a person takes on the responsibility of standing guard over the flow of events as they pass before him. He must ensure that a particular *expressive order* is sustained – an order that regulates the flow of events, large or small, so that anything that appears to be expressed by them will be consistent with his face. When a person manifests these compunctions primarily from duty to himself, one speaks in our society of **pride**; when he does so because of duty to wider social units, and receives support from these units in doing so, one speaks of **honor**. When these compunctions have to do with postural things, with expressive events derived from the way in which the person handles his body, his emotions, and the things with which he has physical contact, one speaks of **dignity** [...] In any case, while his social face can be his most personal possession and the center of his security and pleasure, it is only on loan to him from society; it will be withdrawn unless he conducts himself in a way that is worthy of it [...] this is a fundamental social constraint...[16]

This fundamental social constraint, to use Goffman terms, is the symbolic means by which to put pressure on the group, where certain individuals within the group will use it to ensure the relative conformity of behavior of each group member. However, as we will see, this is far from systemic Manichaeism; there are as many individual strategies adopted to avoid these constraints as there are techniques for conformity. The goal here is not to establish an exhaustive account of relationships and practices that have been widely studied and theorized elsewhere.[17] However, through several examples, we will see how these theories are concretely materialized in social relations within the zurkhāneh, where this collective aspect is particularly strong.

16. Goffman (1967) 1982, 9–10.
17. See the work of scholars of social psychology such as Michael Argyle, Gerald A. Bayley, Jeremy Boissevin, Nicholas Emler, and Germaine de Montmollin.

THE UNCERTAINTIES OF VERBAL EXCHANGE IN IRAN[18]

The particularly flagrant existence of a hidden world, a face that must be protected at all costs, and necessary composure in all circumstances, makes verbal exchanges and social interaction in Iran both uncertain and often heavy with innuendo. William Beeman shows, based on Jakobson's models of linguistic analysis[19] and an unpublished study by Nico Kielstra, how the logic of message management in this country makes it desirable (or even aesthetically satisfying) to maintain a certain ambiguity in discussions. This is for the following reasons:

1. Always refuse a situation leading to a decisive decision.
2. Avoid any crystallization on a subject that could lead to 1, in order to 3.
3. Avoid having to offend or disappoint someone.

Why is this?

Based on the principle that it is only possible to really know one's own *bāten* (the inner state) and that each *bāten* represents many forbidden spaces, there is nothing to stop us imagining that the values or expectations of person X are diametrically opposed to what is said and imagined by their interlocutor Z.

Person Z knows this and takes their own precautions. Each Iranian interlocutor must therefore manage the uncertainty of the whys and wherefores of the interactions in which they participate. For example: if I want to do business with person X, is he able – as he says he is – to provide what I ask of him? Is he just saying yes simply to not miss an order, or so that I do not go around saying he is unable to provide what I need? Is he going to make me wait under any available pretext? To be sure of this, I would have to know to what extent he himself is at the mercy of his own provider. It would be no good to ask him directly because his *āb-e ru* will prevent him from admitting that he is himself caught in the power of his provider. To try and resolve these issues I will have to try and get information either from him indirectly using my *zerangi*, my cunning, trying to break open his secrets without him recognizing my strategy. For this, I will have to rely on trustworthy intermediaries, because it would be too dangerous to act myself directly. That would reveal my thoughts and be contrary to a certain understanding of dignity.

Caught in social interaction in the world of *zāher*, Iranian interlocutors must be on their guards to defend their *bāten*, while forcing themselves

---

18. For more detail see the chapter "The management of messages," in Beeman 1986, 21–35, which this section draws on, and more particularly the sub-section "Uncertainty and Insecurity in Iranian Life," 22 and following..

19. Jakobson 1960.

to understand other people's. They do this by using *zerangi* to reduce the uncertainties and insecurities in their own exchanges. With the effect of reciprocity, we find ourselves with interlocutors who have a reserved attitude that can be transformed into total mistrust if they feel that the "range" of their *zerangi* is smaller than that of their interlocutor.

"How much can I believe him? What did he mean by that? How close is he to me, does he consider me close to him?" These questions might give nightmares to anyone with a tendency to pessimism. This is one of the reasons for the professions of faith and overt attachment to values opposed to these everyday doubts. It is also the reason for the emphasis on the values of trust, friendship, family, and the value of one's word, and also "the admiration for the soul of the *sufi* and the *luti* who care not for these obligations."[20]

One of the results of this fundamental uncertainty is the near-universal option of relegating all problems and all decisions that need to be made – and in which we do not sufficiently master the whys and wherefores – to a later time. Yet the mastery of these is further made more complex by all the factors already mentioned (concealing each person's *bāten*, uncertainty as to the real goals of the other, lack of knowledge about the networks and contacts of one's interlocuter etc.). Very often this leads to an impasse in which the actors wait to see how the other will react before deciding. It is when, after lengthy discussions, exhausted, sad, exasperated, and increasingly detached, you throw in your towel and begin to move away, signaling that these are your last propositions, that your interlocutors suddenly hold you back and make an agreement. They did not do this out of pleasure. They gave themselves the time necessary to gauge your determination and the value you set on this agreement. Trust is difficult to win in Iran and woe betide anyone who betrays it.

I will leave it up to the reader to imagine the consequences of a *pārtibāzi* and the use of *ta'ārof* in the context of these social strategies. It should be clear that any social actor in Iran will have – from their first experiences in public life – gained the means and opportunities to rapidly develop the skills and abilities of a sophisticated diplomat!

Strategies for conformity within the team

In and of themselves, the elements presented shed light on the ability of traditional zurkhāneh fraternities to exert normative pressure over their individual members. I was able to see the techniques used by the most influential or strategic members to make sure the others toed the line, or to obtain something from someone who had incurred their wrath or their jealousy.

20. Beeman 1986, 62.

One of the athletes in Dāvud's group had irritated him. This athlete, who was a former member of the ground staff in the air force, owned a Toyota dealership, and had once implied (he thought discreetly) that Dāvud helped me with my research for money, which was completely false. However, this allusion proved that some people were wondering about the nature of our relationship, and that it was this athlete, who also demonstrated a certain freedom in his tone and attitude towards Dāvud, who was feeding the rumors. This particular event was added to the list of little instances of being *az khod-rāzi* (self-satisfied), which showed that this particular athlete was, and had been for some time, in complete contravention of the rules of humility and self-effacement, *forutani*. This was the final straw that unleashed a process of retaliatory measures by Dāvud to make him understand he had to fall into line or risk being permanently excluded.

It began with more and more frequent remarks that this athlete "was clearly never on time, and never called to say sorry." Ordinarily this was not something that was particularly criticized, as athletes could often be late for meetings and training sessions. Then it was decided that "clearly" this athlete performed this or that exercise poorly. The sources of the different criticisms changed but the members understood whom they were coming from and what was happening. The spinning exercises performed by this athlete were deemed to be suddenly *bi-namak* (literally, "without salt," listless, without energy). This was explained by his flabby stomach, proof that he ate too much, did not train hard enough, and lacked willpower. Any shortcoming was noted, counted, and shared with the other athletes with a little nod that reinforced the negative opinion constructed of him over the course of these experiences, which little by little, became "unfortunately" evident. At the same time, he was no longer regularly told when the team was training, so he missed a few meetings and training sessions. Then he was less and less counted among athletes who could participate in the competitions.

Thus sidelined, they could now say of him that *digeh tu gowd nist*, he was "no longer in the exercise pit." In other words, he was no longer in the inner circle, no longer party to the right information. This expression used in the zurkhāneh is a variant of another more widespread one, *tu bāgh nisti* ("you are not in the garden") which means the same thing. It is a way of saying, "you are not in the know," you are "off the mark," or simply, "you have no idea what is going on."

A few weeks of this kind of treatment was enough to radically endanger the athlete's status. He understood, or was warned, that his disgrace was becoming every day more serious. He took to running in front of Dāvud and the others, suddenly became contactable day and night, and stopped the little criticisms he used to express and simply sang the praises of everyone. He remained silent when others were talking and merely concurred with other members if he was given the opportunity to do so. Six months later, when I asked Dāvud about this athlete's change in behavior, his only answer was to smile and say, "you noticed that?" The athlete had rejoined the ranks.

Similarly, Mellati, who as we saw above had failed to extract financial assistance from the sponsor of Dāvud's team, saw the reputation of his *bāten* take a beating after that episode. He had put the team at serious risk and apparently his blunders had been accumulating for a while. This fault against Dāvud would be the last. The retaliation was massive and proportionate to the collective terror felt by the the members of the group and their friends, who relayed the incident to the federation's officials, implying that it had been a criticism of the federation itself. Mellati was accused of being an *alaki* (lousy, a hypocrite who played *hezbollāhi* [that is, a person beholden to the regime]) to Tarkhāq even though he was just a drunkard whose wife wore too much make-up and bossed him around, which led to him also being accused of being *bi-gheyrat*. His moral reputation was destroyed, which explained his lack of commitment and the mediocre results of his activity at the head of the Tehran district branch of the VBKP Federation.

These accusations spread rapidly in all circles and seemed to foreshadow his disgrace. Did the others allow themselves to say all these things because they knew he was on the way out, or had he thrown in the towel because he knew what they were saying about him? I never knew. In any event, Mellati withdrew from his role in the federation and we never heard of him again. When I asked about him some time later, I was simply told, "tamām shod!" ("it's over!") accompanied by a sweeping hand movement, as though brushing something away. This was a far cry from settling scores with knives, but they knew how to symbolically liquidate someone when they needed to.

The maneuvres of Morādi

In general, the first rumbles of discontentment were enough to bring any recalcitrants back into line, but what happened if the person did not obey? I scarcely had the opportunity to observe this, except in one incident that was to my own detriment and in spite of myself. It is the heuristic value of this "borderline case" that leads me to relate events that I would not otherwise.

One day, an athlete from the Tim-e Naft-e Tehrān by the name of Morādi, a tailor by trade, decided that he had not yet concretely benefited from my presence in the group and decided that it was time for him to get what he wanted from me. The man, a good *shirinkār*, thin and agile, around forty years old, was known to have a high opinion of himself and to assume that life and other people had been created for him. One night, after having sung my praises in the *gowd*, he immediately asked me as we were leaving the zurkhāneh to bring him something back from France and if possible, a dozen male fashion magazines. He was used to this kind of manipulation.

I always gave Dāvud the photos I took of the group; he then redistributed them to the other team members – more or less. After our return from Isfahan, Morādi decided that I had to give him all the photos that I had taken of the group while we were there. I had already offered them to Dāvud so he could redistribute them and some were already put up on the walls of the recently established NIOC zurkhāneh, which were progressively filling up with photos of the life of its athletes. I knew what Morādi would do if I accepted. He would boast of it to the others who would have all come asking me for them (which would have cost me the repeated developing and printing of at least five hundred photos). It was therefore impossible to accept his request.

Having seen that the complimentary use of *ta'ārof* had come to nothing, as we were getting ready to leave for Sanandaj, Morādi came up to me inquisitorially, with his hand out. He asked me for the photos, in an authoritative tone that was barely concealed by his smile and overt politeness. I explained that I had already given them. He pretended to not have heard and asked again, and again I explained that I had given the photos to Dāvud.

"So you will not give them to me?"

"I do not have them anymore, Dāvud has them. Why do you keep asking me this question?"

"Because you have not put them in my hand!"

"But I did not promise you any!"

One of Dāvud's close friends hearing this discussion and seeing that things were getting heated, replied to Morādi that I had indeed given them to Dāvud and that they were already displayed in the zurkhāneh. Thus caught in flagrant discourtesy, Morādi moved away shooting dark looks in my direction, muttering about the photos that Dāvud had not given him.

From that point he undertook to commit all the misconducts of *ta'ārof* imaginable toward me. If we were exchanging civilities before entering the bus, he would add another layer of *ta'ārof* for the others and then bluntly cut directly in front of me. If a poorly infused cup of tea was being passed around Morādi gave it to me without ceremony other than an ironic smile. If we were sharing bread and Morādi was sitting next to me, he would give me the smallest pieces with the same sly smile. If we were sitting down, he would without ado seat himself comfortably at my expense. He did all this discreetly, making sure not to be directly observed by the others. He made sure that I noticed, however, when he whispered funny remarks to his friend Khalaj while looking mockingly at me to make sure that I understood he was making fun of me.

I told Dāvud that Morādi had not received a photo of the trip to Isfahan and he seemed to blame me for it. Dāvud was surprised, as Morādi had had his group photos along with the others. I explained my dispute jokingly and Dāvud went to talk with Morādi, who protested that there had been a misunderstanding and of course everything was fine.

His hands now tied, Morādi's friend Khalaj took up the cause, having heard the details from Morādi. He used another harassment technique. During the bus trips that we had to make while visiting Sanandaj, Khalaj made sure that he always sat in my field of vision and every time our eyes met he would mime taking a photo and silently mouth the words "aks.hā ku?" (where are the photos?) with a snide smile. After a few hours of this I again told Dāvud, who smiled because he had noticed the little game without initially understanding it, and then taking advantage of an opportune moment I remarked in the presence of six or seven athletes that Khalaj seemed upset to have forgotten his camera because he was constantly pretending to take photos – did he want me to lend him mine? Dāvud and the other athletes, who were not fooled, smiled at Khalaj and asked – "did you hear him?" This game began to amuse everyone. Who would give in first? Khalaj protested that he did not need one. The harassment stopped.

But shortly afterwards, in Tehran, I realized that Khalaj and Morādi had taken things even further. They were attacking my *āb-e ru* with certain veterans by implying – jokingly of course – that Dāvud and I were probably having sexual relations and that I was the passive partner in the couple. In the traditional Iranian heterosexual sphere, it is this passive role that is the genuinely shameful element in homosexual relations; the active partner remains a man. In fact, these innuendos were to Morādi's detriment because the *pishkesvat*s, who were friends of Dāvud's, reprimanded him severely and in front of everyone. As for Khalaj, he just implied that I was ungrateful and never gave anything in return. To the point where, one evening when some veterans were invited to his house, Dāvud showed them the photos I had taken and given him (many of which he kept for himself – which was part of the problem!) and finally distributed them. On another day, Mehdi Tarkhāq in person came to shake hands with me at the zurkhāneh of the NIOC. It was only after this distribution of photos (to everybody except Morādi and Khalaj, because Dāvud intended to punish them for their attitude) and above all this handshake followed by a long and ostentatious discussion with the primary protector of the group, that the bad intentions of these two troublemakers were definitively disarmed. I was untouchable, and from that day I became completely invisible to them and they said nothing to me. They did not dare try anything against me, but I still would not have wanted to find myself in a situation of weakness with them far from the others.

Morādi had successively used all the available forms of pressure against me to obtain something from me – except for physical threats. Firstly he had sung my praises, he had increased my *āb-e ru*, my face, and had used *ta'ārof* to put me in a position that forced me to return a favor that I had not asked for. Then, faced with an insufficient response, he had silently withdrawn my social rank by behaving in a way that was totally *bi-tarbiyat* (ill-mannered). When that was not enough, he included his friend Khalaj in his strategy. The latter had adopted a system of disagreeable, direct, and repeated reminders. When they still did not achieve their ends, they attacked both my reputation and that of Dāvud by spreading rumors of passive homosexuality to force me to make honorable ends or withdraw from the group. Finally, having totally failed, they excluded me from the networks of their personal exchanges by ignoring me totally and decisively.

I was only able to extricate myself from this trap without giving up by calling on witnesses. Then when the rumors emerged, I was "saved" by the support of the other athletes, veterans, and important figures, who defended me against these two slanderers and those who had listened to them. The attack had come from only two people, who had not succeeded in rallying the group to their opinion, and I was not really part of the life of the group. If I had been a full member of the group, or if they had gained the support of a large number of members, I would have indeed been obliged to comply or leave.

In this respect, this experience confirms Goffman's and Beeman's analysis of face, *āb-e ru*, and the reality of a politeness (*taʿārof*), experienced as an expression of a temporary projection of each person's hierarchical status that is dependent on the opinion of others, and which the *zerang* can use to manipulate the general context of interactions. This temporary projection of hierarchical status takes into account the sum of external social markers expressed by each "brother," and first and foremost the "big brothers."

Pārtibāzi is a mobilization of a group of equals that is focused on the benefit of one person, who, having benefited, must now be ready to render services himself. In this respect the initial solicitation of Morādi was not a real *pārtibāzi* but a strategy, a bluff, to take advantage of certain predispositions of group members for a particular type of social relationship. That was his weakness, because as he wanted to *force* me to give in, he was able to recruit only his best friend.

A genuine case of *pārtibāzi* presented itself when the whole group used their influence to extricate me from a hellish situation with Iranian customs regarding expensive video equipment that I needed for my work. They identified an officer in the customs administration and gave me a letter of recommendation for him. When I presented myself, it turned out that the addressee had retired and that I was dealing with his successor. This man, to honor his predecessor, acceded to my friends' request, and allowed me to clear my equipment through customs. The group further proposed to arrange for me to make free and informal use of videocassette recorders at the ministry of culture to assemble my footage, but this time I refused. This level of *pārtibāzi* left me dumbfounded. However, it was also clear to me that when they asked for invitations to the Bastille Day celebration at the French embassy in return, I had to do everything I could to obtain them. I succeeded, and (as I did on many occasions) used my institute's four-wheel-drive to take them to the embassy. They had a good time, but Jamshid and a few others were disappointed that no wine was served that afternoon.

I also made sure that French diplomats who were curious about Iran's native athletic tradition would, in addition to the official Shahid Fahmideh zurkhāneh, also visit a traditional one whose patron my friends wished to honor. In four years, the world of the zurkhāneh taught me well.

Passive resistance

But how is it possible to resist pressure from the group as a whole or from the patron himself? Khalaj and Morādi, who were masters in this business, had inadvertently shown me during the same trip to Sanandaj. The competition took place over several days and a visit of the Tim-e Naft-e Tehrān in the company of Mehdi Tarkhāq was planned in one of the zurkhānehs of Sanandaj. The athletes were already in the *gowd* when the Tehranis realized that Khalaj was not with them. He had not even got undressed. Dāvud and the others called him several times, but he declined the offer by shaking his head and giving the pretext of a sore arm. It was inconceivable that he should not participate, for he was one of the guests, he had accepted to come, and moreover the team was depending on him for the spinning exercises in which he excelled. Then Mehdi Tarkhāq himself asked, in a tone that gave Khalaj no alternative but to accept. He nodded, indicated that they should begin without him, and went to prepare, without giving up on the idea that he would not do the exercises.

I do not think that anyone has ever put on his breeches more slowly. Each preparatory stage was performed with cautious gestures. The choice of the appropriate weight of the *mil*, the bodybuilding clubs, was the object of thorough reflection that allowed him to use up the time of the break between the warmup and pushup exercises and the bodybuilding exercises with the *mil*s. When he had chosen the appropriate ones, he was complacently contrite to see that the *mil* exercises had already begun. He now had to simply wait for the next pause to go down into the *gowd*. In so doing he managed to avoid these exercises and left his two *mil*s, so carefully chosen, where he put them down. However, he saw in the eyes of Dāvud and Tarkhāq that they had had enough and he would not get off free from this little game. So, smiling, he finally descended into the octagonal pit to participate actively both in the break and the statements of gratitude. Then, like an artist, he finally gave in to the demands of his audience and performed a single, unique, and superb rotation exercise.

Generally speaking, the best defenses against the multiple solicitations that arise within the group are either a deaf ear, or a "yes" followed by a pause, that saves time while allowing the person to avoid saying no or, worse still, the ominous "chashm" (at your service), in various ways, all equally weary, signaling that contrary to what is said explicitly, nothing will be done. The hope is that the person asking will eventually become exhausted and turn their attention to someone more responsive. Nevertheless, it is important to ensure there is no feeling of participative imbalance. Thus, the height of the art is to choose the easiest or the most visible tasks to maintain the appearance of an equitable distribution; or to give the impression of being constantly active. Above all it is necessary to avoid demonstrations of bodily inactivity. At one point, when a light bulb had to be changed, calculating attitudes were adopted. Initially everybody pretended not to hear the reminder, and then once the "victim" had been designated by name, six people gathered around the man on the stool to provide advice and warnings – officially on the pretext of participating and helping, but actually to demonstrate their involvement in collective life at the lowest cost possible. However, even the most *zerang* could not completely escape direct orders. Thus, in the bus that took us back from Sanandaj to Tehran that night, Morādi arranged to have the best place lying down on the central space of the bus – rather than choosing a position that would have meant more people could lie down. He pretended not to hear when he was asked by name to change positions, but he reacted very quickly when Dāvud called him by his family name in a different tone. He had gone to the limit of convention, hoping that the others would give in first, but he was forced to comply – and he did.

Although this chapter may not totally shed light on the complex systems of exchanges involved in social interactions in Iran, I hope that it will help the reader understand the reasons why a simple and definitive "No" is almost never heard in Iran, and why "Yes" refers only to a nuanced world of imaginable possibilities. Above all it should reveal that behind the romanticism associated with the forms of behavior that are advised or demanded, the brotherhoods of the zurkhāneh function just like other social groups of this type. Moral rectitude and moral or physical violence are neither more nor less common there than in the rest of Iranian society. What Norbert Elias described as the euphemistic expression of violence is evident.[21] Scores are settled through attacks on reputation, reprisals, and symbolic threats just as they are in the village square, businesses, or universities (which is, of course, also true outside Iran).

Between what you are and what you "say you are" there is a principle of reality to be reaffirmed, which goes for all institutions around the world that consider themselves morally superior, from simple wrestling combat sport to the world of martial arts. All around the world, martial arts have always alternated between glorification and, when faced with uncomfortable realities, the endless excuse of supposed decadence or social deviance. This chapter also sheds light on the complex functioning of the group linked by fraternal friendship, but also by a vast web of services rendered, or expected, by big brothers and little brothers in the world of Iranian traditional sport. This is a circle in which an individual must pay the price – in the form of highly restrictive conformity – for having sometimes received precious assistance. It is a world where respect for one's independence of body and mind is only constructed through one's skill in mastering social interactions or discreetly handling and, where needed, manipulating the group codes. As Ezzat Karimi said, in relation to the traditional doctrine that reigns in the zurkhāneh, Mellat hemmat-e vālāst, na fard! – it is the people [here the group] that is a noble ambition, not the individual!

But these social interaction patterns, like everything else in Iran, are subject to social changes that are deep and powerful, but also contradictory, which are increasingly leaving their mark on Iranian society, and which are discussed in the next and final chapter.

21. Elias 1994.

Chapter Six
At the Crossroads

WE HAVE SEEN that for Iranian society, the late twentieth century was strangely similar to the historic shift that occurred in the 1930s,[1] except of course that instead of the state institutions setting the pace of transformation, it was now civil society. Authoritarian reformism, revolutionary voluntarism, or simple corruption among certain elites now had to contend with the vox populi. Questions were emerging from an increasingly large group of citizens, who rightly considered that they should have their say and be listened to. In other words, the grand men who expected sacrifice and obedience were now chastised in the newspapers, which in Iran, it has to be said, had clearly not always been the case. We might wonder how this (perhaps disconcerting) shift was relevant to the study of the zurkhāneh, a supposed bastion of conservatism. This chapter will answer this question through a study of the closing ceremonies for the VBKP competitions, particularly in the "juvenile" category, which took place in Tehran on 28 and 29 November 1996 in the Haft-e-Tir Hall, and the overall analysis of the innovations incorporated into the world of the zurkhāneh during the late 1990s.

REFORM AND RESISTANCE

A somewhat disrupted closing ceremony

After two days of national VBKP and *pahlavāni* wrestling competitions for the eleven- to fourteen-year-old and fifteen- to eighteen-year-old categories, the leadership of the federation decided to make these ceremonies the symbol of the policy that it had put in place since 1993. This would be an opportunity to reconcile with the veterans that it had neglected.

The VBKP Federation proceeded in two stages. Firstly, it would pay homage to the *pishkesvat*s and then demonstrate the future of the sport through a twenty-minute program performed by young athletes between four and eighteen years old. There would also be a speech in a respectable official Islamic tone but emphasizing the moral inspiration of the zurkhāneh rather than the accepted images of other post-revolutionary institutions. They would honor *mardānegi, javānmardi,* the imams and the most famous *pahlavān*s, like Gholām-Rezā Takhti, or the holy figure of Imam Ali.

One hundred *pishkesvat*s were invited for the occasion and everything was going

1. Of course, I was writing these lines in 1999–2000, and a new hope was emerging. This was before the parliamentary elections of 2004 and the presidential election of 2009, which dashed those hopes.

well. Then they were called up, much to their surprise, to parade one by one under an archway decorated with flowers to receive a gladiolus from the federation's president. They were asked to line up in three rows facing the *sardam*, which was so covered in flowers that it was almost impossible to see the two *morshed*s who had taken turns providing the rhythm for the exercises that morning. The long line of veterans were flanked on either side by the delegations of the fourteen provinces who had wanted or been able to send their teams. This made a rather disparate but joyful line, under the flashes of the photographers and video cameras. As always, the sound system was too loud and the voices echoed and faded out in a constant hubbub, interspersed with various overhead announcements, worthy of a train station.

This had been intended as an act of recognition full of good intentions, a homage paid to those who symbolize the continuity of tradition. They had wanted to honor all the veterans, their years of experience, and their deep knowledge of this art form. Unfortunately, it failed due to the constraints of audiovisual technology and the various divergent understandings of what a public event should look like.

The joyous troop of veterans were surprised and happy to be called on, and they formed groups according to friendship without necessarily making a line or a hierarchy of any kind. However, an overly zealous organizer, an ex-gymnastics teacher, called on the elders gruffly, "You were told to make three lines! Three is not four! (Seh ya'ni chāhār nasheh!) You are adults! The oldest and the *seyyed*s in front!" And he moved forward to physically rectify what displeased him in the order of the line, just like a teacher in a schoolyard. During this time the loudspeakers in the sport hall were broadcasting a monotonous and deeply uninspired voice saying, "flowers in your right hands please." These bland instructions, added to the physical act of being taken by the hand like an unruly school student, unsurprisingly rubbed some of the veterans the wrong way, including the venerable Qorāb. The latter was a legendary figure in the zurkhāneh of the prerevolutionary period. Even after the revolution, which had cost him his zurkhāneh, he still took pride of place under the *sardam*, calling and receiving the most important *salavāt* and speaking last from the *gowd*, to pronounce the final act of glorification, the *do'ā*, the invocation of Imam Ali, the Prophet Mohammad, and God.

Qorāb was always a "stickler for principles" and concerned about his own person, in spite of the trials and tribulations of life. He had not abandoned the habit of wearing a tie for all occasions (which was a clear sign of support for the former regime) nor of saying what he thought, and what he saw on this day displeased him greatly. However, he remained silent like the other *pishkesvat*s whose eyes betrayed their concern, as they felt somewhat lost in all of this bustle. Then the discourse of the president began, which although it paid homage to all the veterans, went on a little long and yet did not manage to overcome the initial discomfort of the veterans. The ceremony was already running nearly an hour late (the car that was supposed to bring the flowers had been blocked in traffic in Tehran) and we had all been standing for at least half an hour when Qorāb decided that all this had gone on long enough and it was time to sit down.

He brutally interrupted the president's speech by calling out – in a voice that clearly conveyed his anger – "be ruh-e pedaresh, be ruh-e pahlavānesh, salavāt-e pahlavāni miferestam!" This salutation was chorused by all the *pishkesvat*s in the first rows. Given the tone and the context, this was extremely embarrassing. Literally speaking, he had called out a salutation for the soul and the *pahlavān*'s dignity of the president's father, but the real meaning of the phrase was clearly "I have had enough of this, he has talked long enough, and this *salavāt* for the father is so I do not have to make one for the son." The president was thus forced out of politeness to call out a *salavāt* in honor of the "great *pishkesvat*," and the speech was concluded without further ado. Having thus taken the situation in hand, Qorāb, ever dignified, took his place at the head of the line of *pishkesvat*s who left the room to the sound of the *morshed*'s *zarb*. They were led by a young child carrying the Koran on a tray and an adult holding a brasier (at arm's length) in which burned the purifying wild rue (*esfand*) seeds.

Changing minds, teams, and rules

The staging of this event had therefore encountered a serious obstacle. This was in fact a good illustration of the situation of the zurkhāneh and *varzesh-e bāstāni* in late 1996. Because of the aging population of the zurkhāneh and the persistent desertion by eighteen- to twenty-four-year-old athletes, the federation's president, Seyyed Abdollāh Sajjādi, appointed in 1993, had carte blanche from the STB to conduct the reforms he had been advocating since 1985–86. In fact, since the re-election of President Rafsanjani in 1993 at the head of the reconstruction movement Hezb-e Sāzandegi (a political trend that was considered the most reformist at the time) there was a general instruction to stir things up in the choice of new nominations. The emphasis was now on the professional abilities of managers rather than simply their ability to show their devotion to the revolution.

In response to the new direction of the STB in general and the choice of leaders for the federations in particular, one of the latter's leaders aptly concluded, "now you have to have at least a bachelor's degree, or the equivalent, to be able to apply for these positions." As far as zurkhānehs were concerned, this policy de facto prevented access for a certain number of people who had already fulfilled these functions in the past but whose profile was clearly associated with old clientelist management styles. Those who had adopted this goal and who were now members of the new administrative team criticized the former team directed by Mohammad Khoshjān (apparently not without reason). First, they criticized them for exacerbated cronyism and a focus on the capital of the country at the expense of the federation's provincial branches; second, for having not put into place the fundamental reforms that were needed to renew the sport; and third, for having launched the organization of international competitions of *pahlavāni* wrestling before the discipline had been renewed at the regional level, an essential stage for the development of the sport at the national and international levels. These strategic errors betrayed a poor long-term vision and inconsistencies due to a lack of ability to act in a rational and coordinated fashion. It was no longer a matter of having money, friends, a good reputation, or knowing the exercises to be able to oversee the sport. To a certain extent, an era of Weberian legal-rational domination had begun, as had the time of modern planning, experts, and strategists. It was no longer possible to be content with simply being former practitioners, or passionate about the sport, and finding rich sponsors. This was a shift that also occurred in other Iranian sports, such as horse riding, handball, volleyball, and taekwondo.

Yet if we look more closely, Khoshjān's team had essentially adopted the ideas that a previous team – directed by Mehdi Shirgir and whose vice-president was none other than Abdollāh Sajjādi – had imagined and begun to organize in 1985–86. There was thus hardly any difference in the objectives except that those behind the projects to renew the federation considered themselves naturally better equipped to implement them. We will see to what extent and for what reasons the opinion of Shirgir and Sajjādi turned out to be well-founded in its analysis but overlooked the fact that the world of the zurkhāneh had many unwritten rules.

However, for Khoshjān and his powerful ally, the head of the Tehran province branch of the VBKP Federation, Āynehchi, being squeezed out in favor of their direct competitors was mortifying enough to justify all kinds of resentment. In addition to this was the humiliation of being permanently pushed aside for reasons that tacitly implied a certain lack of competence. The seeds of the future quarrel were sown, but to begin with they were silent, lying low and waiting for the first signs of unrest.

Good strategies, bad tactics: disruptive reforms and regulations

This unrest did not take long to appear. The new team at the helm of the federation was made up of members from the university sector and the Sports Professions Training Schools. They were committed to intensifying the reforms of the mid-1980s, especially regarding young people, but in the early days of their mandate, they were somewhat offhanded with the remaining *pishkesvat*s, who nevertheless remained the most prestigious men in the zurkhāneh. However, these veterans were important for the financial management of VBKP sports because of the generous sponsors they were able to mobilize, and they had a certain influence among the volunteer athletes who provided much of the manpower in organizing the competitions. The new management team in the federation thought that it could implement its reform programs without wooing the old guard, a tragic mistake. This first error would reveal its consequences a year later, but by then there would also be the consequences of the fact that the rules had changed.

The federation was now rigorously implementing new regulations that had previously only been applied sporadically, depending on convenience. Everyone would follow the established rules, in all situations, and without exoneration – now that was a revolution!

The war of the bells

No exception to the prevailing cronyism, the former team led by Khoshjān and Āynehchi had shared the symbolic and financial advantages associated with their positions in the federation with their whole network of friends and acquaintances in the zurkhāneh world. They had generously distributed the honorific titles of *pishkesvat* and *pahlavān* among their friends, transforming the world of Tehran's zurkhāneh into an army full of colonels but with fewer and fewer foot soldiers. At the beginning of the revolution, the original officials of the federation had tried to clean up this sphere by making the titles of "veteran" and "champion" official titles and making them subject to strict control by the federation (at least on paper). This guaranteed a new moral guidance within the institution and among its members, in the wake of the "Shaʿbān years." The federation had also laid the foundations for a reorganization of the sport along the lines of Asian martial arts. As was the case for sumo wrestling in the late nineteenth century, a more or less artificial codification of practices (such as the bell ringing rules) and dress was introduced, (Figure 57) along with a hierarchy of titles. Even the referees were given a new look, a vest decorated with traditional patterns (Figure 58).

It became necessary to fulfill a certain number of sporting and moral criteria in order officially to obtain the external signs of recognition associated with these statuses, namely the drum rolls and bells. Without going into detail, a system of grades and coefficients provided a number of points which over the course of several years' experience (competitions won, attestations from the Ministry of Culture and Islamic Guidance etc.) would allow an individual to progressively climb the echelons in the hierarchy. The hierarchical order of titles was as follows: *pahlavān*, *pahlavān-e zarb* (champion recognized by a drum roll), *pahlavān-e zang-o-zarb* (champion recognized by the bell, the drum roll, and the *salavāt*), and finally *pishkesvat* (veteran, automatically lauded by the bell, drum, and the *salavāt*). As we saw in the first chapter of this book, the roll of the drums and the ringing of the bell were offered by the *morshed* when he wished to honor people as they entered or left the zurkhāneh.

The new rules established by the federation in the mid-1980s were not applied rigorously in many zurkhānehs.[2] *Pahlavān*s and *pishkesvat*s continued to obtain these titles, and the honors that went with them, simply based on the general recognition of other athletes and *morshed*s. Someone with a good reputation locally would be acclaimed in one zurkhāneh but not have this recognition in another one. Being recognized, and thus acclaimed, in all the zurkhānehs one attended was a genuine mark of the truly great athletes and important *pishkesvat*s recognized by all connoisseurs. This was not based

---

2. Federāsion-e Varzeshhā-ye Bāstāni va Koshti-e Pahlavāni 1365/1986.

At the Crossroads

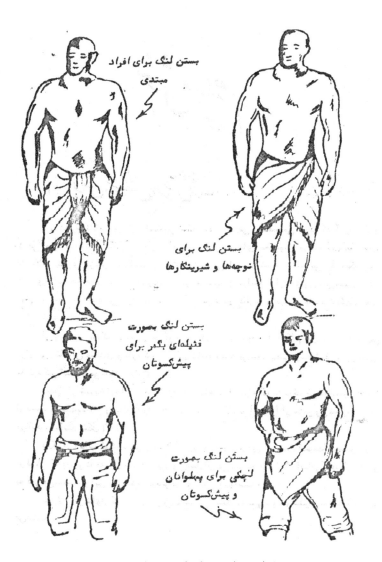

Figure 57. An innovation that was far from adopted. An attempt to organize the various traditional ways of wearing the *long* (cloth) and the *tonbān/tonekeh* (breeches) according to status recognized by the new VBKP association: beginner (upper left), *nowcheh* (novice) and *shirinkār* (upper right), *pishkesvat* (lower left), *pahlavān* and *pishkesvat* (lower right) (Tehrānchi, 1985).

Figure 58. New code dress for referees (11 October 2016. https://www.liputan6.com/bola/read/2623090/atlet-indonesia-juara-dunia-gulat-tradisional-iran).

on a list established by the federation, whose legitimacy in this matter was not self-evident for everyone, but it did correspond to the desire to adopt a more martial-arts type organization.

When Sajjādi returned in 1993, his new team completely reorganized things and discovered that the old team of Khoshjān had substantially increased the number of men who had a right to these honorary salutations. The number for Tehran, for instance, had gone from thirty-seven men to more than 175 in the space of three years. Among them were all the friends of the former federation leaders. The new team carried out a strict cleansing and the list was whittled down to fewer than fifty names – which was severe to say the least. The list was then sent to all the *morshed*s in Tehran with the implicit order no longer to salute those struck off it. The federation leaders considered this fair and necessary to restore these titles to their original value and rarity. This flouted the unwritten rules of the world of the zurkhāneh, which liked to display not only its signs of distinction but also mark ties of friendship and fraternity between those who considered themselves equals.

It is easy to imagine the consequences of this general degradation in a milieu where honor and public face are so important. In addition to the people in question who saw themselves deprived of part of their daily flattery overnight, and let their anger be known, many *morshed*s protested by dismantling the bells so that they did not have to salute anyone. This allowed them to demonstrate their disagreement while not openly disobeying instructions. The war of bells had begun.

The ousted former leaders immediately stirred up discontent, eagerly collecting testimonies from like-minded people. Everyone was talking about the dispute, and this lasted nearly a year. Depending on affinities and antagonisms, the federation's instructions were more or less closely followed, and the zurkhānehs were all visited to see who had dismantled their bell and who had not. The federation put certain people back on the list, but overall stood its ground and put an end to the revolt. There were soothing words on one side and a desire not to burn bridges with the federation on the other, and this reduced the rebels to a handful of diehards associated with the former leaders of the federation. The *morshed*s were above all forced to stop their bells war as soon as they began to be criticized by the athletes themselves. Many *pishkesvat*s considered that the quarrel between those struck off the list and the federation was one thing but insulting all athletes by no longer ringing the bell was quite another. The venerable Qorāb, whom we have already encountered, proclaimed loud and clear before one of his old friends, a *morshed* who had dismantled his bell, "The federation was wrong to do what it did, but a *morshed* who doesn't ring the bell for the important people is not a *morshed*, and a zurkhāneh without a bell is not a zurkhāneh. Say that you disagree but ring the bell anyway when I come in!" The rules of politeness and confidentiality, *āb-e ru*, generally mean that disagreements are rarely discussed openly or before strangers. The very fact that this dispute was mentioned, even during the traditional speeches from the *gowd*, was an indicator of the shock and depth of the resentment.

In this sphere where reputation is essential, where rank and status are the object of discreet but fastidious surveillance, the bell had become a major strategic issue. The reminiscences of the Colonel mentioned in the first chapter are proof of this. In many respects, Iranian society remains a society based on rank in spite of the end of the monarchy and birth of the republic, in which power relations play out through symbols.

A new type of musical education

The federation had also provoked anger from many established *morshed*s when it set up *zarb* classes for young *morshed*s. The aging population in the zurkhāneh also affected traditional instrument players. A zurkhāneh without a *morshed* is unthinkable, and without a *morshed* there could be no exercises. The virtues of the rhythmic chanting, which allows the athletes to push themselves beyond their fatigue, is well known to all. Music with an appropriate rhythm can improve an athlete's resistance to fatigue by up to 25 percent, but the best among the *morshed*s were dying without having trained disciples. The tradition was genuinely in crisis and up until then no one had tried to provide a response.

To remedy this, the federation set up *zarb* classes, just as for modern music, with one *morshed* for twenty students. This was a breakaway from the centuries-old tradition of one master teaching one pupil. It allowed for the training of a new generation, but it also gave rise to a tendency among some young people to answer – in response to the question, "who was your master?" – that they were self-taught. By contrast, the older *morshed*s could recite the *selseleh*, the chain of their own master's teachers, sometimes three generations back. The federation had adopted this collective form of teaching for clear and understandable financial reasons. It only recruited a handful of *morshed*s to give classes at the seat of the federation. Unfortunately, there were many more candidates than there were positions available, and many *morshed*s were bitterly disappointed and resentful that they had not been chosen.

The jealousy crystallized around one of the *morshed*s recruited, Farāmarz Najafi Tehrāni, who was undeniably one of the best *zarb* players in Iran. In 1991, he had published a book on how to learn to play *zarb* in the zurkhāneh, which was something not everyone in this milieu could have done.[3] In it he affirmed that the origins of the musical tradition of the zurkhāneh could be traced back to the great Sufi master Rumi, a claim that is difficult to verify. However, he was a man of excess, he slept during the day and lived the night, and some of his more scrupulous critics frowned on what they considered an overly liberated lifestyle. He was a total nonconformist and proclaimed to whoever would listen that he alone held the key to traditional zurkhāneh music. The leaders of the federation knew all this, but they had decided to recruit "the best" rather than "the friends of." This was a shock to the pride of the other *morshed*s, who intensely resented the fact that such a person should be chosen over them; he was truly brilliant, but he contravened the most fundamental *forutani* (humility). Those who had been struck off the list, some of whom were older than those chosen, refused to come to terms with their lesser status and imagined other reasons to justify this disqualification. They were being made to pay for their friendships with the former officials of the federation, or perhaps there were hidden friendships or shared vices… Yet no one among the leaders was close to Najafi Tehrāni, but no matter, the rumors ran rife anyway. This discontent came on top of the general bad feeling created by the purging of the lists. In the world of the zurkhāneh, everyone was waiting to see what would happen next.

The attempt to control the *golrizān*, which was discussed in chapter four, was part of the same voluntaristic policy to restore prestige to the institution, but it only served to confirm the fears of traditional athletes. They refused to hear the federation's arguments and saw this only as an authoritarian gesture all the more unbearable as it impacted on a source of revenue that everyone could hope to benefit from one day.

The apparent silence and immobility of the veterans suggested that perhaps their influence was waning. Yet, although things were not what they had once been, the *pishkesvat*s remained guardians of the zurkhāneh tradition, along with the *morshed*s. Officially the only responsibility they had was to constitute a council of sages responsible for dealing with contentious decisions during the VBKP competitions if the referee committee could not resolve them. Their decision was then final and acquired the force of law, but opportunities to express themselves in this way did not occur every day. However, their influence went well beyond this official role.

Although no regulation explicitly states this, there had been a tacit agreement in

3. Najafi Tehrāni 1370/1991.

At the Crossroads

place since the beginning of the association between the *pishkesvat*s and its six successive presidents since 1979. The presidents and their teams of officials had always consulted and courted these elders and gained their consent in organizing the major events that regularly marked the world of the zurkhāneh. There was a multifaceted concern to show them respect and ensure additional financial support, which was essential to the organization of competitions.[4] But this tradition was not at all inscribed in texts, and the financial role of the *pishkesvat*s had declined somewhat. The fundamental crisis that affected the world of the zurkhāneh also affected its traditional sources of funding and new sources were needed. The *pishkesvat*s were no longer in a position to make or break federation presidents, but they were nevertheless still a force to be reckoned with.

Given the depth of resentment and dissatisfaction, President Sajjādi had no choice but to change tactics. He admitted his error, which he attributed to wanting to halt the decline of VBKP sports and his unseemly haste to implement necessary reforms. The federation would attempt to obtain the consent of the *pishkesvat*s and pay homage to them through the distribution of honorific qualifications, invitations, and provincial travel at the federation's expense during national competitions. Furthermore, it would continue its policy to rejuvenate the sports leaders, and its attempts to attract young people, which would involve the VBKP entering both the world of competitive sports and the audiovisual sphere. But all this was a bit late: a bad impression had been created and the former federation officials amalgamated everything to create a snowball effect, in the hope of obtaining the intervention of the STB and the resignation of the new federation president.

The means to a new image

To regenerate the practice of VBKP sport, the federation's management knew that it had to work on all fronts. It had to find new sponsors and convince public authorities to act on their grand statements of intention, which had often remained just words. They also had to convince parents, especially mothers, to let young people into the zurkhāneh. Above all, they had to attract young people themselves by offering them recognition and fame through medals and podiums with appropriate media coverage, newspapers, radio, and even, if possible, television. This renewal had to involve the creation of a new brand, a new image, that was young, dynamic, healthy, and morally virtuous. All the images which had long served to stigmatize the zurkhāneh – brutish, potbellied, elderly athletes eating *ābgusht* and even preying on preadolescent boys – had to be fought against.

In 1995, Sajjādi essentially told me that he was ready to change the form and content of the sport in order to save the spirit of the zurkhāneh. For him, the zurkhāneh was the symbol of moral virtue, *javānmardi*, and defended the values of probity and altruism

---

4. The first presidents of the federation were themselves renowned *pishkesvat*s. They considered their position as being simply that of the first among equals. The presidents of the VBKP Federation since 1979 have been: Mostafā Tusi (1979–1980), Qotb (1980–1982), Abbās Hājiyān (1982–1985), Amir Shirgir (1985–1988), Jalālipur (1988–1991), Mohammad Khoshjān (1991–1994) and Abdollāh Sajjādi (1994–2006). Tusi and Qotb died before the end of their mandates.

toward others and toward Iran. Those who practiced the sport had to conform to the system of values; if that was not true for current practitioners, it should be true for future ones. If habits needed to be changed, then they would try to do that. The most important thing for him was to save the values of the *javānmardi* and transmit them to the next generation. This sport should be moral in action. This was said in a tone and with a vision that instinctively brought to mind Charles Kingsley's values of muscular Christianity.[5]

In the meantime, the efforts to save the practice had to go on. In other words, Sajjādi and his friends had to go out into the provinces to convert young people and train them. For this, they needed a budget, which involved soliciting the managing bodies in the STB and their regional representatives to dedicate time and means to this sport as well. The disgruntled members of the zurkhāneh community in Tehran pretended not to see the thankless work done by the president.

This approach received a very encouraging response and meant that Abdollāh Sajjādi had a much better reputation in the provinces than in Tehran. The near totality of provinces – with the notable exception of the coastal provinces in the south, between Khuzistan and Baluchistan – saw their local officials, representatives of the ministry of culture and state businesses sponsor, finance, and facilitate local competitions, and the creation of new zurkhānehs. A serious policy of recruitment among younger people was also launched in these areas. Demonstrations in schools and businesses were organized and all kinds of occasions were used to praise the activity and promote its practice. A shift was taking place.

Sajjādi was thinking about how the identity of the zurkhānehs themselves could be promoted. VBKP sport was more visible now, but the zurkhānehs were not glorified enough. In 1997, the federation introduced an improved version of a type of competition that had existed since 1991. First known as *miyāndāri* between 1991 and 1996 (named after the experienced athlete who leads the exercises in the pit), this competition was first conceived by president Mehdi Shirgir and his vice president Sajjādi, and implemented by President Khoshjān's team. Its goal was to re-establish the spirit of the exercises all the athletes completed in the *gowd* rather than the individual exploits performed in the first type of competition, which had been designed in the 1940s but were organized consistently only after 1979.

In 1997, *miyāndāri* competitions were replaced by *zurkhāneh'i* competitions which, although they maintained the basic idea of a full bodybuilding program, also added the possibility of confrontation between whole teams performing exercises together every day, *in the same zurkhāneh*. For once the idea actually seemed to please everyone. The zurkhāneh teams also had time to prepare an exercise program with long-term goals for the groups of athletes who wished to perform in this new kind of competition. Regional competitions were organized to select the best zurkhāneh and then the regions pitted

---

5. Colloms 1975 and Bloomfield 1994.

their club champions against each other at the national level. This was also a way of promoting the owners of the zurkhāneh and their sponsors. Reorganized in this way, these new competitions managed to bring together the zurkhānehs from fourteen provinces in the town of Sanandaj in Kurdistan in 1997.[6] Then the following year twenty-two provinces out of twenty-six were represented, a sign that this new format was growing more and more popular.

Alongside these competitions, in early 1998, the rich province of Khorasan hosted the first *pahlavāni* wrestling championships distinct from *varzesh-e bāstāni* competitions. This officially consecrated the almost decisive separation of *pahlavāni* wrestling from the other disciplines in this sport. The coexistence of *pahlavāni* wrestling and *varzesh-e bāstāni* in the older competitions perpetuated the fiction of a unity that had long since disappeared. Those who practiced *pahlavāni* wrestling were primarily athletes affiliated with the IRIWF who merely donned the traditional breeches for *pahlavāni* competitions. By comparison, the older competitions of *varzesh-e bāstāni*, which had been reorganized in 1985, took place according to discipline (*kabbādeh*, wooden shields, spinning movements, and juggling *mil*) in all age groups, with teams representing provinces rather than individual zurkhānehs. As we have said, there was no love lost between the VBKP Federation and the IRIWF. The latter's exasperation with *pahlavāni* wrestling, which was accused of complicating the calendar of competitions, even led some of its leaders to suggest that I write (for them) a history of Iranian wrestling in which there would be no mention of zurkhāneh! I was speechless, and of course I refused. It was clear that Sajjādi's battle was far from over.

The audiovisual diktat: to exist, you need to be seen more and heard less

Iranian television launched its third channel in the early 1990s. It was essentially dedicated to sports and football in particular, and had an immediate and total success. Sajjādi, who had a background in information science, which he had taught at Tehran University, approached the programming directors to obtain airtime in the name of the authenticity of the discipline and to attract young people. He hoped to be successful, particularly in view of the official declarations by illustrious figures – such as the then President Rafsanjāni, the speaker of the National Assembly Ali Akbar Nāteq Nuri (who was reputed to have frequented the zurkhāneh in his youth), and the Supreme Leader himself – who had made laudatory declarations about VBKP sport and had called for its development in the name of Islamic values and the tradition of Iranian *javānmardi* (Figures 59 and 60).

It turned out this was not to be. Sajjādi explained to me that the programming managers had objected that VBKP was unsuited to the audiovisual imperatives that reigned over the world of sport. The long and repetitive nature of the athletic program

---

6. They were organized for the first time in 1991 in Shiraz, in 1992 in Yazd, in 1993 in Qazvin, in 1994 again in Shiraz, in 1995 in Mashhad, in 1996 in Malāyer, and in 1997 in Sanandaj.

meant it was not attractive or adaptable to the available airtime slots. *Pahlavāni* wrestling could be covered in the media, but the best wrestlers were absent because they dedicated themselves entirely to national or international competitions in freestyle and Greco-Roman wrestling. There was a long road ahead before *varzesh-e bāstāni* would gain significant airtime.

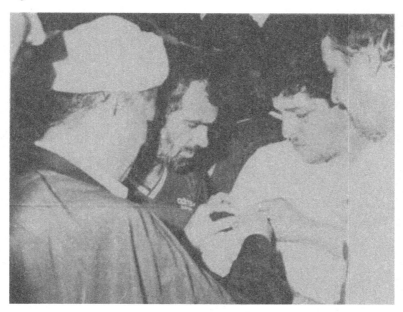

Figure 59. Former President Rafsanjāni awards the *bāzuband*, to the Iranian champion of *pahlavāni* wrestling 1372/1993. He is accompanied by the president of the Office of Physical Education and the President of the VBKP Association of the time, 1993 (newspaper *Puryā-ye Vali*, 9 December 1993).

Sajjādi was well aware that without television there would be no public recognition. Like all the other sporting leaders before him, he decided to make the sporting program of the zurkhāneh more suitable for television. Henceforth, the great tendency within the federation consisted in reducing the length of the exercise program from an hour and a half to just thirty minutes. To manage this, they had to promote the most spectacular exercises to the detriment of the more mundane ones and above all reduce the talking and speeches which took up easily half of the training session. Once again, this was a blow. Delivering a speech from the *gowd* was a distinct honor, which was highly sought after and conferred upon the most illustrious local figures. Asking them to say a bit less and do a bit more was not appreciated by all.

In addition to the motivation discussed above, the federation was operating from a

At the Crossroads 209

Figure 60. January 1998, the separation between VB and KP is growing: *pahlavāni* wrestling has its own competitions separated from *varzesh-e bāstāni*, here in Mashhad, under the name "Jām-e 'Ayyārān" (photo *Keyhān-e varzeshi*, no. 2208, 1997).

purely sporting perspective. It was indeed possible to easily reduce the exercise program to less than forty minutes, but the training sessions in the zurkhāneh were not just about muscles. As we have seen, they involved other values, recognition, pleasure in being seen and heard, coming together with friends, and the opportunity to embark in major or minor social strategies (being seen by an influential man, obtaining assistance, etc.). Talking about reducing the time for speeches in the *gowd* meant messing with all of that. The federation wanted to preserve what it considered essential by strictly reducing the speeches to religious invocations and exaltation of the *javānmardi* spirit. That could fit into fifteen minutes, couldn't it?

The idea of shortening sessions immediately met with hostility from most of the older athletes and especially the veterans. The young participants did not see themselves as concerned because the speeches were exclusively reserved for older members. In general terms, the younger athletes still attending the zurkhāneh considered that they were not given enough space or consideration. Perfectly aware of this often-repeated reproach, the federation officials persisted in its decision to reduce the time allotted to speeches.

The new *zukhāneh'i* competition rules included time limits. Each team's performance now had to last no less than twenty and no more than thirty minutes. Speeches were retained and evaluated but could not exceed ten minutes. This nevertheless represented a third of the total time, but so few points were awarded for it that it actually constituted a handicap, given the missed opportunities for gaining more points for the actual exercises. Therefore the teams only dedicated three or four minutes to it. The thirst for victory is the most powerful of all normative tools; absolutely nothing can stand against it.

Competitive zurkhāneh sport has decisively adopted the logic of competitions where presentations are graded by judges, like gymnastics or figure skating. The goal is a combination of quantitative and qualitative performance. Bad movements do not earn points. Set by the leaders of the federation and by those *pishkesvat*s who support them, the quality of the movements is evaluated according to an ideal model of execution that says much about the aesthetic criteria selected. Compared to the traditional corporal and socio-cultural models it is clear that tastes have changed. By studying these new competitions, it is possible to establish a genuine overview of the changes in the symbolic world of representations that the athletes of this sport can transmit, from their more prestigious characteristics to their more depreciated stereotypes.

The Evolution of the "Perfect Movements" in the World of the Zurkhāneh: The Symbolic Reversal of the Hierarchy of Values

There is an aesthetic dimension of movements performed in the zurkhāneh. They are described as "perfect" if they are both beautiful and correctly executed. These movements are linked to values that express certain physical and corporeal attitudes. Many of these movements were formerly no more than bodybuilding exercises designed to improve wrestlers' strength. In the early 1940s, they suddenly had to compete with other exercises arriving from Europe and America and thus were to a certain extent socially downgraded, along with those who practiced them.

When an action or movement is downgraded in this way there is a genuine loss of meaning. If it is to continue to exist, there is no solution but to become an end in itself through a change in meaning that often involves an aestheticization. From simply being good/effective, it needs to become "beautiful." By transforming the bodybuilding session in the zurkhāneh into a sporting discipline subject to a grading system with significant aesthetic criteria, the reformers of first the 1940s and then 1990s gave these movements a new justification. Now the traditional entertainment movements, the *shirinkāri*, formerly practiced by the *luti*-acrobats, were not the only movements to attract and captivate the audience. Even weightlifting, or movements like the *pā zadan*, the stomping or the push-up exercises with *takht-e shenā*, the swim board, had to respect a certain style and convey emotions. The *zurkhāneh'i* competitions mentioned above represented the peak of these transformations.

As we have seen, usually modern VBKP sport in Iran involves eight types of exercises, all marked by the rhythm of the chanting and percussion of the *morshed*, the music master. These exercises can be divided into two groups, which lead to two kinds of muscle development in the athletes, referred to here as *pahlavān* and *shirinkār*. The *pahlavān* emphasizes static bodily expression while *shirinkār* emphasizes more mobile expression. It is important to emphasize that only the term *pahlavān* "strong man" is used by the athletes themselves, but only for athletes of a certain weight. Those who are lighter are rarely called this, although it does happen sometimes. The word *shirinkār* is significantly less complimentary than *pahlavān*. Partow-Beyza'i used it in 1958 to distinguish these athletes from each other. Sha'bān Ja'fari used it too in his interviews, but in 1875 in the *ganjineh-ye koshti* manuscript, *shirinkāri* was a term used exclusively for the exercises involving both acrobatics and all the movements designed to entertain.

The strong man

The *pahlavān* represents the prototype of the strongly built wrestler, the man of stature (*sangin*), whose neck, shoulders, and chest are a single block. He is said to be *yek tigheh* (a single blade), with legs of marble and fists of steel. He is not afraid of having a big stomach, which is a symbol of the good distribution of breathing and vital energy in the body, as well as a sign that his social and economic comfort provides sufficient food. He aims to be like an unwavering column (*sotun*), before which his adversaries (and adversity in general) bow down. At least, that is how he wants to be seen. Other members of society might call him *dāshmashdi*, *mashdi*, *gardan koloft* (thick-necked), *sibil koloft* (big mustache), *chār shuneh* (broad-shouldered, hefty). His movements are slow and measured, he does not run, he does not stare into people's eyes as if he were soliciting favors. He is often seen as someone who always keeps his promises; his *zāher* is identical to his *bāten*, which means he does not hide his true nature. He is and he does what he says. This also implies that he has the "means" to be so open in society, and thus a certain independence of action. In his category, his opposite is the *pahlavān panbeh*, the "cotton *pahlavān*," who loses his puff whenever he has to act. This figure is known in puppet theaters in Turkey as the "show off" who makes all the children laugh when he farts out of fear, but his negative aspect is also the *qoldor*, the violent brute who uses his strength to get his way.[7]

For this kind of athlete the key exercises in VBKP are the wooden shields, which weigh forty kilos each (the *sang*), the metal bow, which can weigh up to fifteen kilos (the *kabbādeh*), the heaviest clubs (*mil-e sangin*), the slow spinning exercises, the stomping exercises (*pā zadan*), and of course heavyweight *pahlavāni* wrestling. *Pahlavāni* wrestling uses the weight categories of international freestyle wrestling, but beyond ninety kilos it allows athletes to wrestle without any weight limits. On average the wrestlers aiming for the title of *pahlavān-e keshvar* (national champion) way around 110 or 120 kilos.

The cunning man

By contrast, the *shirinkār* has diametrically opposite qualities from those of the *pahlavān*. The *shirinkār* is quick, agile, lively, and has a smaller, lither, more fine-boned build. This was the body of the *luti*, when this term was still used to refer to the corporation of acrobats that Mir-Nejāt Esfahani admired in his *Gol-e koshti* in the early eighteenth century, for their youth, svelte physique, and well-balanced shoulder muscles.

The profession and social background of these *luti*s (public entertainers of lower social standing as we saw earlier) provided all the elements for significant social stigma because the word also became a synonym for sexual debauchery. By extension, the *luti* became a man of dubious morals, known for animal fighting and pigeon fancying, adept at jeers, mockery, and saucy tales. He was also an expert in *matalak*, more or less subtle cat-calls, that were feared but occasionally appreciated by women when they were complimentary and elegantly expressed. The same word was also used to refer to the violent street bosses in traditional neighborhoods (much like Egyptian *baltagi*).[8] These boastful figures easily engaged in *rajazkhāni*, teasing and mockery during night parties of backgammon where insults fly low, bets rain down heavy, and alcohol runs freely. The term evokes a man who is part racketeer and part thief, much feared by the bazaaris. This is a man who is capable of the most brazen lying, or inversely of sacrificing himself for love or friendship (there is a certain overlap with the *javānmardi* here). His *zerangi* (cunning) is legendary, but he can also be described as a little wimp, a *susul*, when faced with a real *pahlavān*.

The favorite exercises of the *shirinkār* are those where he can draw attention to his ability to control his body in a fast movement or demonstrate his agility and flexibility: juggling (*mil bāzi*) with two to four light-weight clubs, spinning at different speeds (*charkh-e motavasset* or *chamani*, and *charkh-e tond*), and free acrobatic movements

---

7. Many thanks to the sorely missed Farrokh Gaffary, founder and former director of the Iranian Film Library, for this information. See also Gaffary 1984. For a reflection on laughter, puppetry, and Turkish shadow theater, Karagöz, see Basch and Chuvin 2007, particularly 249–386.

8. See El Messiri 1977.

called simply *shirinkāri*. He is our Ulysses with a thousand tricks, who seems to travel through time in the form of *ayyār*, *shāter*, *luti*, and *shirinkār*.

Overall, only the swim board exercise, the *takht-e shenā*, which is used for different kinds of push-ups, does not fall into one or other of these two categories of athletes who frequent the zurkhāneh. It is considered well done when the athletes respect the tempo of the *morshed* and good hip movements. The movement must be fluid, and like all the others, must appear to be completely effortless.

The Traditional Hierarchy

The pahlavān *comes first*

The *pahlavān* embodies the type of character and body shape that is traditionally most valued in the zurkhāneh. It suits the strong man's gravitas.

The criteria for a "perfect movement" in this category emphasize the slow movements that conceal the athlete's effort but show off his absolute control of his body. Lifting the wooden shields over his head with straight arms while lying on his back, the athlete must successively lift them without his legs or the shields touching the ground. What is more, he has to do this while moving his legs left and right in synchrony with the shields. We can suppose that this requirement of movement and synchronization is a twentieth-century invention, because late nineteenth-century representations show the athlete lying on a board covered with a cloth with his feet on the ground or his legs crossed.

The metal bow is also maneuvered in a backwards and forwards motion overhead, each movement accompanied by a step forwards or backwards, to show that the athletes' feet leave the floor and thus that his body is totally controlled in spite of the effort. His torso and head must be kept absolutely straight and his face impassive. As the judges constantly say, it is better to have ten "perfect movements" with foot movements perfectly synchronized with the right-wrist left-wrist alternations, than thirty bad hand movements. The national champion of 1996 was able to perform this movement correctly in two series, totaling 134 complete movements of the bow.

Men of this type are usually appreciated more than any other for their supposed humility and quiet strength, and their respect for elders, which shows that they have overcome their notorious pride and acquired the moral strength required to confront the shame of defeat and the dizziness of success. These are the athletes most expected to demonstrate the attitude of the *javānmard* and make noble gestures that ensure the positive use of their strength. While this ideal is close to legend, it does occasionally happen that reality briefly reflects reputation. For example, in the 1996 championships, the athlete representing Tehran in the metal bow exercise won but refused to take the first place on the podium so as not to humiliate his opponent from Isfahan, where the competitions were taking place, having just learned that the local champion was participating in his final championship. The prize-giving ceremony finished after five long minutes (during which all the protocol was in turmoil) when the organizers at long last accepted to pronounce the two athletes equal winners. They took the first place on the podium together, arm in arm, sharing the crown of flowers by putting it around both of their heads. They agreed to jointly perform the prestigious demonstration, which is normally the prerogative of the victor, before a crowd that was wild with joy to see such a display of the difference between *pahlavān* and other sportsmen. The word *javānmardi* was on everyone's lips.

The shirinkār comes after

Lighter, more subtle, and often younger, the athletes in the second category are expected to be seductive, harmonious, energetic, and *bā-namak* (literally, "full of salt"), both in life and in the way they perform their exercises. *Bā-namak* means being humorous, charming, and in this particular case, physically energetic.

The heavier athletes secretly envy them because they are better at the spinning exercises, which are extremely important in the zurkhāneh's program. The spinning is the supreme exercise, the one that sets the best athletes apart. Mastery in this task allows the athlete to gain the esteem of his colleagues, to become a member of the group more quickly, and as a result, to improve his status within the group. The competitions of the 1990s permanently set the rules for this exercise. For the average-speed spinning, the athlete must spin while also moving in a perfect circle within a corridor marked by two concentric circles 5.2 meters and 6 meters in diameter. If he goes over the line twice, he is eliminated. For the full-speed spinning, if he wants to demonstrate his excellence, he must keep as close as possible to the central point and spin so fast that his face becomes blurred. If his arms bend, his head leans, or his steps get heavier, his final mark will suffer, and if this continues, the timer will be stopped.

It is the *shirinkāri* exercises that are favored in the new forms of competition. Today these are seen as a sort of personal improvisation by the athlete, a free movement that can include bodybuilding tools and which is designed to please the audience. This is the time when the more agile athletes can really express themselves. In the eighteenth and nineteenth centuries the acrobat-*luti*s were well versed in the art of *shelang* (jumping forward or backwards), and *chatr* (the peacock wheel), which is also called *shirjeh* (the dive), and which involves walking on your hands with your feet in the air. In the 1940s and 1950s, human pyramids were popular with these athletes. Now it is once again combinations of somersaults, forwards and backwards, and pirouettes that are popular with the public. This reconnects with the art of the late nineteenth-century *luti*s that continually waned in importance within the *zurkhāneh* until the recent renewal, which was facilitated by the increasing importance of spectacle and entertainment in the athletic program. However, as a sign of the times, some of these movements are borrowed from martial arts (particularly taekwondo) that many young *shirinkār*s also practice

At the Crossroads 215

alongside VBKP. However, unlike the zurkhāneh athletes of the nineteenth century, these movements are performed by amateur athletes who have not learned or practiced them in the *gowd*, but elsewhere. In recent times certain athletes have organized short choreographies with two, three, or four people, often brothers or cousins who see themselves often enough outside the sessions to sufficiently rehearse. These *shirinkāri*s take place in the first half of the program, during the warmup and *pā zadan* stamping exercises. Once again, they require precise, coordinated, energetic movements that must be carefully synchronized with the *morshed*'s *zarb* (Figure 61).

Figure 61. An old-style photo, all bare-chested (or almost!) Two physiques are visible, in the back the *pahlavān*, in the front the *shirinkār* (Bāshgāh Sa'id Abu'i, 1997; photo Philippe Rochard).

Reverse values

The *pishkesvat*s and the defenders of the traditional order of values might have accommodated to these innovations and changes in tastes if they had not gone as far as they did. In their opinion, the evolution of the disciplines put too much emphasis on this kind of exercise, and they rendered the demands of television responsible for it. The bow and the shield exercise being static, viewers are very quickly bored. Moreover, in line with its policy to attract young people to the sport, the VBKP Federation promoted a new younger image of itself, in which prepubescent athletes, weighing a maximum of thirty or forty kilos, spun and twirled their way across the screens of the sports channel. The traditional models of the discipline and the hierarchy of "perfect movements" were indeed modified by this.

In addition to this, there were also the new kinds of competition organized by the federation. So far we have only seen the first type, conceived as far back as the 1940s, but readopted and officialized by the young federation in 1979: teams of seven athletes compete in the following five categories: shield, bow, spinning, light club juggling (*mil bāzi*), and *pahlavāni* wrestling (one athlete per *varzesh-e bāstāni* category and three for wrestling). These competitions were accused of begetting a specialization within the sporting program, to the detriment of other exercises, namely, the wooden swim boards or the *pā zadan*, the stamping exercises, and collective swinging of heavy *mil*s. They also lacked the aesthetic pleasure of a genuine session in the zurkhāneh, in which the exercises followed on from each other in an ambience that is constantly marked by the rhythm of the percussion instruments and the poetic chanting of the *morshed*, with the group effect of ten or fifteen athletes all performing the same movements together. As we have seen above, in response to these criticisms, in 1991 the federation introduced *miyāndāri* competitions, renamed *zurkhāneh'i* in 1997.

I was allowed to attend the *zurkhāneh'i* competitions in May 1997 in Sanandaj, the capital of Kurdistan province. Before the media, the cameramen of the sports channel, and the provincial authorities, fourteen teams of ten to twelve athletes, including the *miyāndār*, who acts as captain, and the *morshed*, competed against each other for two days, in a grand modern sports hall fitted out for the occasion. I was thus able to observe that for the purpose of assessment and evaluation, all of the aspects of a traditional session had been taken into account to create a system of codification essentially establishing a sort of ideal session, highlighting the elements that were significant in the eyes of the organizers. Thirty-eight such elements were identified, for a total of 280 fixed points maximum, depending on the number of actions "correctly" performed. Extra points could be gained for executing additional movements bringing, the total to around 800 points. Although theoretically possible, this never happened given the short time available. In this context the "perfect movement," as in figure skating and gymnastics, was a strictly codified element.

Even more revealing is the fact that eighteen of these thirty-eight criteria emphasized the ability of the group to perform its movements and exercises in harmony with its captain, the *miyāndār*, who traditionally leads the exercise. The captain appeared eleven times in the assessment notice. As the coordinator of the team, he had to be in perfect harmony with the *morshed* and the athletes – between 180 and 360 points depended on this. The five criteria that assess the different free movements represent up to 230 points. The *shirinkāri* for the smaller athletes can bring up to 180 points, whereas the "heavyweight" *shirinkāri* using the bow and shields are only worth between thirty and fifty points (Figures 62 and 63). This was no accident; agility and speed were now worth three times as much as pure strength.

But even the criteria that were worth only ten points could be very important in distinguishing between teams of equal value. In this new kind of championship everything was assessed: the virtuosity of the *morshed*, his drum playing, his ability to remain

At the Crossroads

Figure 62. Shirinkār training for future "zurkhāneh'i" competitions. The young athlete is practicing an original and delicate movement that will improve the artistic score for the spinning exercises. (Zurkhāneh Shahid Fahmideh, Tehran, 1997; photo Philippe Rochard).

Figure 63. Sanandāj "Zurkhāneh'i" Competition. The winning team performs the old movement *shirinkāri-ye mil gereftan* (called *gaborgeh neshasteh* in 1875 in the *Ganjineh-ye Koshti*) (photo *Donyā-ye varzesh*, no. 1264, 1997).

synchronized with the captain of the team (twenty points), his voice, and his choice of gnostic poetry, which provided the soundtrack to the exercises and could earn twice fifteen points. This posed a problem for the *morshed*s, who were not clear about what poetry would gain the highest number of points: Hafez, or something more original? Reciting extracts from Mir-Nejāt Esfahāni's *Gol-e koshti* by either the *morshed* or an athlete could be rewarded with ten points. The external harmony of the traditional outfit was also subject to evaluation: did the colors of the T-shirt go with the traditional breeches of the *pahlavān*s? Were these made from leather or just very thick fabric? The athletes' ability to convey their "bravado and knightly nature" during the program with their head high and their chest out could earn the team an extra ten points, as could the proper recitation of the Koran or hadith.

The invocation (*do'ā*) which ended in a salutation to the Prophet and his family (worth fifteen points) sometimes led to unexcepted political dilemmas in training. It was important not to overdo it, because the teams only had twenty to thirty minutes for their whole presentation, which meant having to make strategic choices. Was it better to salute the grand figures of Islam or the leaders of the regime? Do we know the political opinions of the four judges? Are they very religious? Should we cite Abolfazl (the fourth son of Imam Ali, who died in the Battle of Karbala alongside his half-brother Imam Hoseyn), rather than Imam Hasan? Hasan was an Imam and the elder brother, of course, and should take precedence over Abolfazl, but he did not have the same glory in the eyes of the athletes as the heroes of the battle of Karbala. Should we evoke the political slogans so fashionable at Friday prayers ("death to America, death to Israel, tomorrow Jerusalem!")? The choice was generally clearcut: revolutionary slogans gave way to religious invocations.

The complexity of choices and the appeal to each member's sense of aesthetics were all something new. During these same training sessions, the preparation of the actions that would make up the program gave rise to many discussions. For example, for the Tim-e Naft-e Tehrān, Dāvud, the captain, had been obliged to make do with a team that had not been able to meet as often as necessary and in which every single member had a different opinion on what should be done, and did not hesitate to say so. Like any good diplomat, Dāvud had acknowledged everything that had been said and tried to incorporate part of all of these remarks. During the training sessions there was often a tension between two contrasting visions of preparation. When one of his friends asked him to prepare a written list of the transitions between movements, Dāvud flatly refused, telling him that he wanted the athletes to memorize the program by practicing it. A piece of paper, he said, was a false solution that could not replace practice, made memory lazy, and could be a liability in the competition.

Ultimately, the program on the day of the competition involved fourteen gigantic choreographies, staged so that movements planned in the greatest secrecy by each team could be performed before the spectators and TV cameras that replayed extracts the

At the Crossroads

next day. They involved formations in the shape of stars, circles, intertwining lines, or snakes biting their tails. The teams had to be original but not too much, because the more complicated a figure was the more likely it was to end up in confusion and be given poor marks, where a more classical figure would have guaranteed a set number of points.

On this occasion, the team from the town of Birjand, in what was then Khorasan province, wiped the floor with the opposition. Some of the teams with older athletes, or those that were less well prepared to meet the new assessment criteria, were taken aback by the excellence of the teams performing these new movements. So they decided to choose more traditional, *sangin,* "old-style" movements stripped of anything unnecessary, marking the beat with simple arm movements. This enabled them to avoid losing face in front of disappointed sponsors and meant they could then declare that they were not among the winners but at least they were not messing around with those new acrobatics!

There are still *pahlavān*s in the world of the zurkhāneh, but there has been a clear inversion of the symbolic hierarchy of old stereotypes of masculinity. As we have seen, traditionally in Iran, figures of power were impassive, generally silent, and the less powerful rushed around serving them. This is also one of the essential problems affecting the service sector in Iran and elsewhere in the world, as the social consideration of professions in the service sector is astoundingly low. Yet it seems that the world of the zurkhāneh has moved towards the world of new Iranian entrepreneurs. Moving, running, jumping, and twirling are all symbols of dynamism, adaptation, and victory; and they seem to be less and less the external signs of lower social status or obedient servility.

FROM THE CIRCLE OF THE CHOSEN TO THE CIRCLE OF LIFE

Grandfather and grandson

The success of these competitions and the regular appearance of children aged between ten and fifteen in the zurkhāneh confirmed the existence of a new mindset among the practitioners themselves. In the space of two years, I saw the new interpretation and project for the renewal of the sport proposed by the federation adopted by an increasing number of athletes and *pishkesvat*s. The circle of athletes in the *gowd* now included all age groups and formed a symbolic path from childhood to death: *now javānān, javānān, bozorgsālān, pishkesvat, va ba'd az in, Khodā* (child, adolescent, adult, veteran age sixty and over, and after that, God, that is, the passage to paradise). The zurkhāneh was no longer the place where young men could be initiated into the community of adults, but an institution that trained and accompanied men in all stages of life up until they returned to God. There had been a shift from the zurkhāneh as a circle for a chosen few, to a circle of life, with the departure of the elders making way for the young.

Of course, the everyday sessions did not systematically incorporate young people in all zurkhānehs; far from it, but they could be seen more and more often patiently waiting for the right moment to go down into the *gowd* to participate in the only exercises their age allowed them (spinning, running, juggling), in the company of their maternal uncle, their inseparable maternal cousin (*pesar-khāleh*), or their father or grandfather. They were proud to be among the adults, they were serious and tried hard in their spinning and juggling exercises. They were devastated when they failed, and the youngest among them could be difficult to control when they were unable to suppress their laughter during a veteran's speech because a facetious cousin was pulling faces at them (Figure 64).

Figure 64. Father and son. Will he want to be in the gowd in twenty years? (Zurkhāneh Soleymāniyeh, Tehran, 1995; photo Philippe Rochard).

This new vision of the sport, propagated by the federation, would never have been so easily accepted by athletes and *pishkesvat*s if they had not themselves already been predisposed to accept the idea. Looking for the explanation of this acceptance in the awareness of the need for generational renewal and the future of the sport is not sufficient. In addition to the prevalence of new discourses on the role of young people in Iranian society, the aging habitués of the zurkhāneh were now grandfathers, which radically changed their vision of young children. Where for young adults the desire to shine was impeded by the presence of children, veterans were happy to be accompanied by their grandsons. They were their pride and joy, their *eftekhār*. They encouraged them by giving them gifts when they succeeded – a small bag of *tokhmeh*,[9] a soda, a cake, or even a small amount of money if they won. It was also they who consoled the children when

9. This is a popular snack of grilled salted pumpkin, sunflower, or watermelon seeds; a skillful snap of the teeth separates the outer shell from the inner seed.

At the Crossroads

they failed, if they had tried their best. Some *pishkesvat*s did not hide their emotion at seeing children during the official ceremonies wearing traditional breeches made to measure, and asking the audience very seriously for authorization to begin the exercises – the traditional *rokhsat* – before beginning their spinning exercises. "All our hopes are here," one said to me, his eyes red with emotion. It was impossible to tell whether these young children would take up the standard when they became adults, or whether they would turn to ping-pong, football, or martial arts, but they would also be fathers and grandfathers one day.

The management of the federation saw its choices validated by the fact that there were many more young people practicing this sport than before. In the 1980s there had been practically no young people, so this was an easy claim to make, although attempting to put forward accurate data is difficult. The national federation was not able to announce any official figures for 1998 because the regional branches had been unable to furnish the necessary data. However, scattered observations, such as in the city of Qazvin we saw earlier, suggest that the efforts and results were there, but at the end of the 1990s this progress remained fragile, as admitted by federation officials. Would the next president of the VBKP Federation share this goal? Would the current attempts have long-lasting effects? It would only take the federation to decide to discontinue competitions for the youngest participants for the dynamic that has been established to be seriously compromised.

An apparently limited range of expansion

Attracting grandsons and grandfathers is one thing but getting twenty- or twenty-five-year-old athletes into the *gowd* is another. There is almost no need to make an effort to investigate this because it is blatantly obvious to any observer – football is the most popular sport in Iran. The IRIWF had seen its numbers plateau, which it lamented in the press, blaming it on insufficient resources, especially for young wrestlers. By contrast, boxing and especially East Asian martial arts were gaining in popularity. As one twenty-eight-year-old taxi driver, who had gone from wrestling to boxing, said, "Now life is like that. Wrestling is not enough, you have to be able to hit." This seemed to indicate a growing incidence of violence in Iranian society, but a detailed and in-depth analysis of the meanings of this shift and its causes are beyond the scope of this book. However, we can deduce the limitations it imposes on the evolution of *pahlavāni* wrestling and VBKP sports.

The situation of *varzesh-e bāstāni* is slightly more complex. The small world of this sport is progressively moving away from that of wrestling in general and *pahlavāni* wrestling in particular. The social background of its athletes, which was initially the same as that of the wrestlers, is evolving. Of course, there is still much common ground. There are still many garage workers, abattoir workers, low-level public servants, shopkeepers in the bazaar or in the working-class districts in Tehran, bus drivers or taxi drivers, among the practitioners of *varzesh-e bāstāni*. However, the current discourse and the new importance of *shirinkāri* exercises, as we saw above, has attracted other sectors of society. There are families of lower-middle and middle-class shopkeepers, who have enjoyed upward social mobility thanks to the revolution but who continue to respect some of the social practices of their backgrounds even though they now live in more bourgeois neighborhoods.

The new discourse emphasizes the authenticity of this physical and moral tradition, while demonstrating that this sport could be practiced elsewhere than in traditional working-class spheres, and that the new athletes no longer had fat bellies and did not necessarily eat *kalleh pācheh*. The VBKP sessions in high schools and universities had the potential of changing this image, but at the end of the 1990s it was not clear whether these measures would succeed. Young practitioners were still generally linked to the sport by older members of their family. At least the federation managed to convince some children and grandchildren of athletes to participate.

Another salient point is that all of the participants are Muslims. The religious minorities are totally absent from the zurkhāneh. This was not always the case. The Jewish minority that lived in the working-class neighborhoods in Tehran, had its own *luti*s who frequented the zurkhāneh before the revolution, either "friendly" Muslim zurkhānehs, or others run by Jews. The organization of sessions in the Jewish zurkhāneh were in all respects identical to other sessions. They simply replaced the prayer to Imam Ali with a prayer to Moses.[10] The mass exodus of the Iranians Jewish community after the revolution struck a fatal blow to this tradition. The last representatives of this community of athletes now live – with very rare exceptions – in the United States and in Israel. Mehdi Abbāsi noted that there was a Zoroastrian zurkhāneh in the city of Kerman and a Jewish zurkhāneh in Shiraz, but I was never able to find any trace of them when I visited.[11]

New place, new space

All the reforms and transformations documented here have also been accompanied by a transformation of the zurkhāneh itself. In its traditional form, these spaces were massively present in working-class neighborhoods, and they suffered from the declining frequentation resulting from a drop in the number of athletes. The owners were often elderly, and their zurkhāneh alone was no longer a sufficient source of income. They needed other sources, and above all they needed motivated successors. The famous Zurkhāneh-ye Pulād, which was home to Takhti in his early days, is now closed. The son of the late owner preferred to open a space for a modern gym and bodybuilding somewhere else, which brings in much more income. Sometimes there are legal clauses that prevent the destruction or reconversion of the space, which was why the Zurkhāneh-ye Pulād stood empty from the early 1980s on. These zurkhānehs are economically fragile,

10. Chehabi 2001, 7–9.
11. Abbāsi 1377/1998, 2:151 and 348.

At the Crossroads 223

unlike those subsidized by major state institutions and administrations (the army, different components of the security forces, the Bank Melli, the National Oil Company, various other state companies, and so forth) which do not have to worry about funding.[12]

However, and this is perhaps a sign, in the 1990s we were beginning to see spaces for VBKP sports in the sites dedicated to fitness and bodybuilding or multisport places in the more bourgeois neighborhoods of Tehran or in the new suburbs. Now that it was a sport in its own right, *varzesh-e bāstāni* began to break free of the place in which it had been traditionally practiced. It was now possible to enjoy the advantages of a bodybuilding studio, and then practice spinning exercises to the music of a *morshed* without having to change neighborhoods or even rooms. The federation president considered that it should be possible to practice this sport everywhere, beginning with one's own home. This allowed women to perform these exercises at home without contravening social taboos. The only things that had to be preserved, in addition to the instruments, were the sunken exercise pit and the raised podium for the *morshed*. The rest, in particular the "traditional" room of the zurkhāneh, was considered non-essential. Thus, in the spaces I was able to observe, there was often a genuine exercise pit or a simple space marked by a folding wooden barrier, which reproduced the hexagonal shape of the *gowd* while enabling the space to be used for other things outside *varzesh-e bāstāni* training times. However, this new space raised certain problems (Figures 65, 66, 67, 68 and 69).

Very often it was the athletes who practiced VBKP sport as well as another sport (wrestling, weightlifting, etc.) who were behind the creation of these new spaces. In this they were given substantial assistance by the Tehran Municipal Council, which exempted them from paying local tax (in 1995 the managers of the new spaces told me that the sum was equivalent to around 10,000 *tumān* per square meter for one year), in the name of assisting the defense of national athletic traditions. This assistance was the result of another argument put forward by the federation, which was as simple as it was inevitable: "we open our spaces to other Asian martial arts and we leave no room for our own martial arts traditions?!"[13] In the context of a broader struggle against the so-called cultural invasion, the argument convinced the city authorities to make an effort.

This new policy resulted in the introduction of competitive practices. Bodybuilding, freestyle wrestling, and combat sports on one side, and *varzesh-e bāstāni* on the other. Mutual interest, contempt, or indifference – all attitudes have been seen in response to the novelty of having the *morshed's* podium decorated with a portrait of Imam Ali, just alongside a photo of Bruce Lee (Figure 70). However, the financial argument, accompanied by the desire to hear the music and singing of the *morshed*, or perhaps simply the desire to innovate, were enough to convince some directors of sports complexes to

12. See the article in the newspaper *Resālat* on the closing of the zurkhāneh. "Ta'tili-e zurkhānehhā!" 29 August 1999. The article exaggerates. It only counts the closures (the number of which it exaggerates) and fails to count the ones that open. However, But it does convey the genuine difficulty that these zurkhānehs have when they cannot rely on state institutions or companies for financial balance.

13. In the words of the VBKP Federation's officials.

Figure 65. – VBKP sport in a new space – a multi-sport hall (Bāshgāh Sa'id Abu'i, Tehran 1997; photo Philippe Rochard).

Figure 66. Alongside *varzesh-e bāstāni*, the weightlifing space (Bāshgāh Sa'id Abu'i, Tehran 1997; photo Philippe Rochard).

At the Crossroads

Figure 67. A temporary gowd (Bāshgāh Sa'id Abu'i, Tehran 1997; photo Philippe Rochard).

Figure 68. The director of the space, a former athlete of the Melli Bank zurkhāneh (Bāshgāh Sa'id Abu'i, Tehran 1997; photo Philippe Rochard).

include VBKP facilities in their dojos and gymnasiums. Incidentally, this allowed me to attend a session inaugurating a space for VBKP in one of these new sports rooms.

The Amir al-Moʾmenin Gym, a space where both VBKP and karate are taught

In the northwest suburbs of Tehran, after the Hasanābād neighborhood and the Chehel-o-panj metri-e beʿsat Avenue, there is the "Commander of Believers" Gym, named

Figure 69. Behind the *sardam* the Taekwando fighting ring (Bāshgāh-e Saʿid Abuʾi, Tehran 1997; photo Philippe Rochard).

after a title given to Imam Ali ibn Abi Tāleb. It is run by Abbās Nazari, and since 1995 has provided a training space for numerous combat sports (karate, judo, taekwondo), as well as wrestling and now *varzesh-e bāstāni*.

Abbās Nazari, a famous athlete in the world of the zurkhāneh, was 1.9 meters tall and 110 kilos of muscle. He was a veritable iron colossus, with a prominent mustache and a thunderous laugh, who looked like the incarnation of the full *mashdi* ideal. He was born in 1951 and began learning wrestling and VBKP sports at the age of fifteen. When he was twenty, in 1971, he won his first national freestyle wrestling competitions while working in a pasteurized milk factory. He got married the same year and then spent the next ten years establishing his situation as a good breadwinner. It was only after he had settled down and got established that he returned to *varzesh-e bāstāni*. In 1983, he decided to compete in the new competitions organized by the young VBKP Federation. Now aged thirty-two, and having been long out of competitions, he quickly

At the Crossroads 227

understood that he could not compete against the young wrestlers. So, the following year he dedicated himself to one of the four great disciplines of *varzesh-e bāstāni*, the *kabbādeh* (metal bow). The incredible endurance required to maintain the relentless rhythm in this exhausting exercise perfectly suited the stature of the man.

Abbās Nazari remained the unchallenged Iranian champion in this discipline from 1984 to 1994. The following year, he was asked to stop competing so as not to discourage the other athletes. In 1996, he was again allowed to compete, and again won the championship in *kabbādeh*, this time in Isfahan. It was he who, on the same day, in pure *javānmardi* spirit, declared that he would refuse this title unless the champion of the region was declared equal winner and stood with him on the podium, as we saw above.

Figure 70. Imām Ali and Bruce Lee (Bāshgāh-e Sa'id Abu'i, Tehran 1997; photo Philippe Rochard).

This incident shows just how much he valued the idea of the respectability and the importance of this sporting tradition. When I asked him who the most important figures in the zurkhāneh were, he immediately said Imam Ali and Puryā-ye Vali. He also had his own personal interpretation of the meaning of the symbolic objects in the zurkhāneh. The bell was there to salute the honor of the men of the zurkhāneh, "like your church bells" he said, "that rang for Napoleon's victories." The *morshed*'s *zarb* symbolizes war, which is the origin of the tradition according to him.

In 1995, Abbās Nazari sold all of his businesses to build a sports center that rapidly became popular with young people in the suburb where he lived. Helped by his son, who was also an athlete, "shaped" like his father and destined to follow his footsteps in the *kabbādeh* exercise, Abbās decided to dedicate a room to *varzesh-e bāstāni* and installed a *gowd* and a *sardam*. He received an exemption on his local taxes of around three million *tumān*, but it would be wrong to believe that this was his only motivation. This was also about prestige – being declared *sardamdār*, master of the podium where the *morshed* sits, is a mark of respectability – and he also wanted to teach young people the values of the zurkhāneh. Nazari found himself in the role of a missionary. Nobody in these new suburbs practiced this sport and he jokingly told me that apart from his tax exemption (which he conceded was not to be sniffed at) his space for the sport barely brought in enough money to cover its electricity consumption (which is quite cheap in Iran). This is why he dedicated most of his activity to the weightlifting room and the teaching of martial arts which, were more popular with the teens in these suburbs. When I asked some local young men about this, some politely answered that VBKP sports were honorable, of course, but they personally preferred karate. Those who were less polite, when they had moved some distance away from the room, crudely told me that the *varzesh-e bāstāni* was not a real martial art, that it was only good for maintaining "old" bodies. How could you use that to fight in the street?! Even wrestling paled in comparison to real combat techniques. One young man said, "*Javānmardi*?! What *javānmardi*?! It's just idiots! Who does that in this f***ing country?! Here you need to know that the *really* best way to defend yourself is to strike first. You take everything and you run faster than the others!" This brought laughter from his group of friends. It was not the first time I had heard this kind of sentiment, even if that day I did learn a few new strongly worded Persian expressions. These three young people did not seem to be delinquents though, although there were some neighborhoods that were quite tough. Abbās Nazari's exercise room was also frequented by young police officers and was decorated (like in a traditional zurkhāneh) with group photos that showed the strong links between the owner and the police, the Revolutionary Guards, and men in the air force. Abbās had contacts in the zurkhāneh of the police force, which was not generally the case for civilians, but he was famous in this sphere, he was well liked, pious, and a patriot. He also avoided involvement in any kind of politics.

Abbās asked his friends in the zurkhānehs in the south of Tehran to come and conduct his first sessions so that other people would want to come and train there. His friends came and sat on the plush rugs placed in a semi-circle around the *gowd*, echoing the alcoves and podiums where guests generally sit in the zurkhāneh in Tehran's city center. Everyone agreed that the session was of very high quality, both in terms of the exercises and the speeches, which were particularly eloquent.

Yet, when we left the room, the guests made two pitiless comments. This zurkhāneh (as the athletes from the south of Tehran nevertheless called it) was too far away for them to include it in the network of zurkhānehs that they frequented; with all the traffic problems it took nearly an hour to get there and more importantly, the room was much too big (300 square meters). It was even described as ugly and "commercial" by one of the exigent aesthetes of the old neighborhoods. Not everyone agreed though.

Abbās was a friend and he had had the courage to embark upon this adventure. It was good to help him and try other things like this. The debate continued in the car on the way home.

Why such controversy? There were several things that made the experience unsatisfying for some of the attendees. For one, the *gowd* was not in the center of the room and the speeches – which often serve to glorify the group – and the effects of the movements and sound did not fill up the space as they would have done in a traditional zurkhāneh. There was an audience of people curious to see the sport, but they had been seated far enough away from the athletes to allow themselves a few mocking smiles at some particularly grandiloquent speeches. The sense of entering a special space that is found in a traditional zurkhāneh did not obtain here. The bombastic speeches and salutations just seemed ridiculous because of the physical distance afforded by the space. The problem arose several times in rooms with the same characteristics. The traditional space of the zurkhāneh made any spectator a potential actor in the speeches. The salutations filled the whole room and made the space a whole; everyone was "within." These big new rooms seemed to invite athletes to perform their exercises and be quiet. The size and personality of the athletes seemed to be dwarfed by the size of the space, where they would have been magnified in a traditional zurkhāneh. During Friday morning sessions, a traditional space takes on a near-theatrical quality in which informal roles are known and distributed and open to potential improvisation and other happenings. This encourages complicity, and the space is not big enough to allow for the verbal or physical expressions of reprobation that I saw in Mr. Nazari's space – anything similar would have incurred significant social consequences. In a traditional zurkhāneh verbal opposition is as rare as it is serious. An ironic smile or a doubtful pout would have to be very discreet and seen only by those at whom they had been directed – or by anyone who happened to watch you.

In sum, we should avoid imagining that there has been a shift to VBKP as a mass sport and an abandonment of traditional zurkhānehs. The change within the sport will stop where the pleasure of those who practice it stops. From what I saw, it seems that this sport has little chance of developing among young devotees of combat sports. The attractive part of the VBKP program, which draws in younger participants and ensures the sport is televised, is the *shirinkār* exercises. These are at once difficult, and while having an artistic dimension, offer no possibility of combat – except the combat the virtuoso performer wages against himself. As a result, they attract participants who are not necessarily looking for effective combat techniques, unlike the clientele of Mr. Nazari's room. Perhaps this is a new vision of a potential redistribution of tastes and practices resulting from the evolution of the sociological profiles of the new VBKP practitioners. Only a collective and in-depth quantitative sociological study would be able to confirm or nuance these preliminary observations.

It is too soon to say for sure, but perhaps we will one day see young athletes move toward a search for a kind of authenticity, training at home or in these new spaces during the week, and on Friday returning with their friends to exercise in a "real" zurkhāneh. There they can share the pleasure of the speeches, and salutations, the tea and conviviality of the group, and, when it comes time for the spinning exercises, savor the intensity of feeling alive.

Epilogue

WHEN I FINISHED MY MAIN RESEARCH at the turn of the 2000s, Seyyed Abdollāh Sajjādi was still at the head of an association called the "Ancient Sport and Pahlavāni Wrestling Federation" (called VBKP Federation in this book), and official speeches referred to the moral notion of *javānmardi*. Now, in the early 2020s, the association is called "Zurkhāneh Sport and Pahlavāni Wrestling Federation," often abbreviated to "Zurkhāneh and Pahlavāni Federation." Zurkhāneh sports have now reached beyond Iran with the creation of an international association and its inscription on the UNESCO list of intangible heritage. A women's section opened briefly in 2020, and there has been an attempt to highlight the term *pahlavāni* alongside that of *javānmardi* in official speeches. Obviously, all these changes call for an explanation and a commentary by way of an epilogue, which will allows us to consider the role of a major figure in the salvage and renewal of the zurkhāneh tradition, Seyyed Abdollāh Sajjādi.

Sajjādi remained at the helm of the VBKP Federation for a total of fourteen years, from 1993 to 2006, much to the dismay of the old network that had been supplanted in 1993. However, with the progressive repression of the reformist movement led by President Mohammad Khātami (1997–2005) that paved the way for the election of President Mahmoud Ahmadinejad (2005–2013), his days at the head of the federation were numbered. As early as 2003, maneuvers had taken place to remove him from his post: at the time of the elections within the federation, the secretary general of the STB in charge of organizing the election had sent threatening letters to the heads of the provincial branches of the VBKP Federation to dissuade them from renewing their confidence in Sajjādi.[1] This was without counting on the sense of loyalty of the people of this milieu and the fact that Sajjādi had based the renewal of the practice precisely on a very strong policy of listening to and supporting the regional branches, which is indispensable for a successful national sports policy but had clearly been neglected by the previous leadership. When Sajjādi made this move public, the intimidation maneuver was thwarted and he was re-elected for a new mandate. I was not able to talk to him, but I note that the end of his presence at the head of the VBKP Federation in 2006 – an imposed departure – corresponds to the moment when the new Ahmadinejad administration put an end to the autonomy of the sports federations and temporarily reinstated the system of direct appointment of their presidents by the national physical education bureau, to the detriment of the election system set up by the first Khātami administration. There is therefore every reason to believe that it was this decision that allowed Sajjādi's detractors to temporarily win their case. It should be noted that under President Ruhani

---

1. "Doktor Sajjādi: barā-ye defaʿ az varzesh-e bāstāni sokut nakhāham kard," 27 Bahman 1383 (15 February 2005). https://jamejamonline.ir/fa/news/59108. Accessed on 20 February 2023.

(2013–2021), the elective system was reinstated within the sports federations, and it has not yet been abolished by the Ra'isi administration that took power in 2021.

However, Sajjādi continued exerting some influence after 2006. As part of his policy of renewal and rejuvenation of zurkhāneh sports, he participated in 2004 in the creation of the International Zurkhāneh Sports Federation (IZSF) with Seyyed Amir Hosseini, the organization's first secretary general. He even set up the new federation's technical committee,[2] a body that has a key role in defining standards for a sport's content and establishing the format of its competitions. Sajjādi held this position for nine years, from 2004 to 2012, ensuring that his reforms were not undermined. Between 2005 and 2006, he initiated the process of registering the zurkhāneh tradition on the UNESCO list of intangible heritage.[3] The long and tedious process was successfully completed in 2010, just in time to prevent the Republic of Azerbaijan from claiming exclusive ownership of the heritage at the expense of Iran. Indeed, Sajjādi's dismissal in 2006 had been almost fatal to the Iranian cause, as a file can only be submitted to UNESCO for registration once every two years, and his ouster in 2006 had aborted the submission of the file planned for 2008.

Thus, under a political regime that makes it difficult to enjoy the fruits of one's labor without being dispossessed in one way or another by people whose only talent is to have been able to join the right predatory networks or to obtain the right political protection at the right time, Sajjādi's active presence, six years after being removed from the national federal leadership of VBKP, shows how even his opponents could not do without him. At least, as long as there was hard work to be done.

Between 2013 and 2016 Sajjādi no longer figured in the IZSF, but on 2 May 2016 he reappeared as a senior advisor and member of the strategic council of the now renamed Zurkhāneh Sports and Pahlavāni Wrestling, whose vice-president he became soon thereafter.[4] In 2018, the federation achieved a great success by wresting *effective* control of national and international *pahlavāni* wrestling competitions from the Islamic Republic of Iran Wrestling Federation. Until then, international *pahlavāni* wrestling competitions had been in the hands of a World Pahlavāni Wrestling Federation controlled by the powerful IRIWF. It was a long battle and a victory that posed great challenges to the zurkhāneh sports world. Indeed, as Soltān-Ali (Mehdi) Tarkhāq – who, as

2. See the chapter, "Futuwwat in the Modern Era. The Zurkhana between Tradition and Change," in Ridgeon 2010, 183, and passim. Preparations began in 2003 with the creation of a commission under the high patronage of the STB. This international federation now includes a number of countries including Azerbaijan, Afghanistan, Bangladesh, Indonesia, and Tajikistan and has its own website in English and Persian, www.izsf.net.
3. "Ruz-e farhang-e pahlavāni va varzesh-e zurkhāneh'i, goft-o-gu bā Abdollāh Sajjādi pishkesvat-e varzesh-e zurkhāneh'i," 20 Khordād 1399 (9 June 2020). https://varzeshtv.ir/news/172819. Accessed on 24 February 2023.
4. "Abdollāh Sajjādi nāyeb ra'is-e federāsion-e pahlavāni va zurkhāneh'i shod," 2 Dey 1395 (22 December 2016). Retrieved from https://www.borna.news/7/653249. Accessed on 20 February 2023.

we have seen, had been president of the IRIWF in the early 1980s – bluntly stated at the time, the IZSF did not have the means to properly organize *pahlavāni* wrestling championships. The challenge was therefore great and Tarkhāq feared that the IZSF would let *pahlavāni* wrestling decline.[5]

Let us be clear: this was not a fight opposing the historical continuity and respect of the local zurkhāneh tradition and the globalized modernity of freestyle and Greco-Roman wrestling. The struggle was between two modern institutions applying the same rules of development and having identical views on what constitutes good functioning of a sports institution in the twenty-first century. The national and international zurkhāneh federations argued that since they represented Iran's history and identity, they were in a better position to organize international *pahlavāni* wrestling tournaments, which were desirable because a combat sport is more conducive to international recognition than athletic exercises that are specific to one country and culture. For its part, The IRIWF, which had been behind the creation of the World Pahlavāni Wrestling Federation, argued that it worked more efficiently and had greater experience, arguments that hid hegemonic ambitions. It, too, invoked an argument of historical continuity, albeit a more recent one, for all the *pahlavāni* wrestling championships that ever existed had been organized within the IRIWF and its forerunner since the 1940s. From their point of view, the recuperation of *pahlavāni* wrestling tournaments by the national and international zurkhāneh federations was not borne out by the modern history of this combat sport and was motivated by an ideological and historical romanticism that might harm all the actors. The leaders of the IRIWF and the World Pahlavani Wrestling Federation did not come to terms with this change of supervision and it is likely that, in the years to come, the supervision of international *pahlavāni* wrestling tournaments by the IZSF will be challenged by the IRIWF at the first opportunity; all the more so as in recent years the decline of freestyle and Greco-Roman wrestling has been somewhat reversed, and Iranians (most of them from Māzandarān province) regularly gain medals at international competitions.[6]

On the basis of this success, Sajāddi tried, with the support of the president of the national federation, Mojtabā Jowhari, to advance another major project that had been close to his heart for a very long time: the establishment of a women's section

---

5. "Tarkhāq: federāsion-e koshti tafāhomnāmehi rā emzā nakardeh ast/pahlavānhā-ye keshvar hamisheh az beyn-e koshtigirān entekhāb shodehand," 4 Bahman 1397 (24 January 2019). https://www.tasnimnews.com/fa/news/1397/11/04/1929659/. Accessed on 24 February 2023; "Qat'i shodan- e vāgozāri-e koshti-e pahlavāni bā emzā-ye surat jaleseh-ye panj nafareh/Gheybat-e Heydari dar neshast-e enteqāl," 27 Bahman 1397 (16 February 2019). Iran-e Varzeshi. https://old.inn.ir/Newspaper/BlockPrint/180073. Accessed on 24 February 2023, and finally, "Tarkhāq: federāsion-e zurkhāne'i koshti-e pahlavāni rā vāred-e hāshiyeh nakonad/vāgozāri-e in reshteh sehhat nadārad," 28 Bahman 1397 (17 February 2019). https://www.ghatreh.com/news/nn46313983/. Accessed on 24 February 2023.

6. Shamshirian, Halldorsson, and Sigmundson. 2021.

of zurkhāneh sports.[7] As early as 2003 Sajjādi and all those in Iran who defended this idea had argued that if Iranian women could participate in sports, fitness classes, and bodybuilding exercises in modern gymnasiums, they should be allowed to enter a zurkhāneh to practice the national sport of Iran, especially since they were already engaging in zurkhāneh exercises at home.

Women had already been courted by the VBKP Federation when it tried to attract children and adolescents in order to renew and rejuvenate its athletic community. To achieve this, they had to convince mothers that their sons had nothing to fear. What is more, their official participation would be a powerful signal to international sporting bodies, particularly the Asian Games and the Olympic Movement, which in 2007 inserted a provision in its charter that all sports must be open to women and that it would not recognize (and would not provide financial support for) international federations that did not comply with this rule. If India and Japan had braved traditionalist resistance to open their traditional wrestling styles to women, why not Iran?

The Iranian religious authorities, including the Supreme Leader of the Revolution, Ayatollah Ali Khamene'i himself, have confirmed several times in *fatwa*s (religious rulings), that if women respected the Islamic laws in force (separation of the sexes and appropriate clothing) and the spaces frequented were not turned into places of prostitution, then women could practice physical exercises in the *gowd* of the zurkhāneh. The floor of the zurkhāneh and its exercise pit are no more sacred than that of mosques, so the argument went, an argument that those who wanted to keep women out of the *gowd* would be hard pressed to disprove.

The project was strongly supported by women already practicing these exercises as well as the vast majority of national federation executives. For a brief period in 2020 it was successful,[8] but it was finally aborted by the most conservative elements of the ministry of sports, who were themselves under pressure from the Revolutionary Guards, who have seized virtually all the levers of power in Iran since 2016.[9] When Jowhari was replaced by Mehr-Ali Bārāncheshmi after an extremely close election (only one vote dif-

---

7. At first discreetly, Sajjādi first tried to open the debate in 2003, but it was still too early and he was disowned by the authorities of the time. "Doktor Sajjādi dar pāsokh beh enteqādāt-e matrah shodeh: harekāt-e varzesh-e sbāstāni-e bānovān hich man'-e shar'i nadārad. Salāmat-e nimi az jam'iyat-e keshvar ba anjām-e harekāt-e varzesh-e bāstāni ta'min khāhad shod," 5 Ordibehesht 1382 (April 2003). https://www.isna.ir/print/8202–01316. Accessed on 20 February 2023. See also the 2006 survey by Lloyd Ridgeon in Ridgeon 2010, 188. To understand the extent to which zurkhāneh officials were under heavy pressure, see the misadventure of local officials of the Zurkhāneh-ye Vali-e Asr in a suburb of Tehran in June 2020, who were dismissed for having allowed female athletes to enter their zurkhāneh to practice, even though there were no men there and they were dressed according to Islamic codes. See http://varzeshzanan.blogfa.com/post/2278. See also Chehabi 2019b, 412–14.

8. See the excellent article on women-pahlavān, Hojjati 2023, which contains the link to a film made by Rāyeheh Mozaffariān, *Lab-e gowd*, which, in an interview with Fariba Kolāhi and Shahnāz Fada'i, highlights and refutes the arguments against women taking part in this sport.

9. Dudoignon, 2022.

Epilogue 235

ference) in January 2021, the official arguments put forward by his detractors centered on his alleged mismanagement of competitions and budgets, but it is not far-fetched to assume that the real reason was his advocacy of women's participation.[10] Since then, Sajjādi does not seem to have occupied any function either. The IZSF has now been for more than ten years under the leadership of a high-level state functionary, Mohsen Mehralizādeh, which is a clear sign of the symbolic importance given to the world of zurkhāneh by the current authorities.[11]

In 2021 the IZSF joined the International Traditional Sports and Games Association, a non-governmental body linked with UNESCO, which brings together around twenty countries on several continents. The IZSF also joined the World Ethnosport Confederation in 2021. These last two organizations are, in the name of respecting the cultural and ethnic dimensions of local sports, much less scrupulous about women's participation. In line with its general foreign policy orientation, Iranian sports authorities' international initiatives target countries such as Turkey, Nicaragua, and Russia.[12]

In spite of the fact that he no longer has any responsibilities in the two zurkhāneh sports federations, Sajjādi is without doubt the leader who has the most influenced Iran's national athletic tradition since the foundation of the VBKP Federation in 1979, thanks to his persistence in defending very clear objectives and the longevity of his action (nearly forty years) and the results obtained. Developing and implementing his vision of the new zurkhāneh from his first responsibilities within the federation in 1986, Sajjādi overcame almost all local conservatism and demonstrated the accuracy of his diagnosis of the risks of the disappearance of the zurkhāneh world in the 1980s and 1990s, as well as the means to remedy the situation. His impact has been such that even his detractors, when they are in office, hardly ever question the general direction of his reforms, in particular the format of the various competitions and the regional development of competitions or the policy of rejuvenation of the zurkhāneh thanks to the safe inclusion of children and teenagers. In this study, we have seen what he managed to do at the end of the 1990s. The zurkhānehs now offer the possibility of having a physical and sporting activity that is culturally "rooted," original, and offers a complete program for physical fitness that is accessible to all.[13]

10. "Pāyān-e chehār sāl riyāsat-e Jowhari bar federāsion-e zurkhāneh'i," 14 Dey 1399 (3 January 2021). Retrieved from https://www.isna.ir/print/99101410125. Accessed on 23 February 2023.
11. "Mehralizādeh: az varzesh-e zurkhāneh dar Iran hemāyat-e bishtari mikonim," 21 farvardin 1391 (9 April 2012). https://www.asriran.com/fa/news/208620. Accessed on 23 February 2023; for the activities of the international federation also see "Tārikhnāmeh: federāsion-e beynolmelali-e varzeshhā-ye zurkhāneh'i," http://www.izsf.net/fa/post/41. Accessed on 23 February 2023.
12. "Hamid Sajjādi: dar Nikārāgueh zurkhāneh misāzim," 26 Dey 1401 (December 2022). https://iranwire.com/fa/news-1/112684. Accessed on 20 February 2023. Hamid Sajjādi is the minister of sports in Iran. See also "Bāzdid-e vazir-e varzesh Rusiyeh az Zurkhāneh-ye Shahid Fahmideh," 26 Bahman 1401 (15 February 2023). http:// www.izpf.ir/module/news/page-1689/. Accessed on 23 February 2023.
13. "Doktor Sajjādi: varzesh-e bāstāni behtarin badansāzi barā-ye tamām-e reshtehhā-ye varzeshi

Sajjādi also sought to convince the world of the zurkhāneh – and this is, in my opinion, a crucial point – to ask itself the question of its social role within Iranian society today. He defends the idea of a modern, socially useful, morally positive and inclusive world of the zurkhāneh.

My research in the early 2000s ended with a big question mark. The zurkhānehs were then the object of a spatial morphology and a sociological identity in deep mutation: the zurkhāneh had specialized in gymnastic and acrobatic athletics, while *pahlavāni* wrestling had been effectively marginalized. In its competitions, the zurkhāneh adopted an assertive gymnic and aesthetic dimension that was, in fact, quite different from the apprenticeship of wrestling, the world of combat sports, and its usual sociological background. A new sociological profile was emerging. The social identity of practitioners linked to the new practices within the zurkhāneh, and the overall social evolution of Iranian society, seems to follow the trend that I observed at the end of the 1990s. How else can we explain that there was enough demand to embolden the zurkhāneh federation to contemplate establishing a women's section?

The situation reminds us of the Bourdieusian concept of "social distinction" and, especially, the new sociological assessments supplementing and correcting it.[14] Since the 1970s, Bourdieusian sport sociology has highlighted the link between disciplines and the various social groups, using analytic concepts developed in Bourdieu's book, *Distinction*.[15] However, without invalidating Bourdieu's initial approach, new analyses provided by sociologists of cultural practices reveal significant nuances that must be taken into account.[16] These scholars show that social groups are now also distinguished by their eclecticism, the size and the composition of their practice's portfolio, and the sociologically differentiated appropriations of these practices.[17] In line with these new works, sociologists of sport have been able to document this eclecticism, which increases when agents are more endowed culturally and economically.[18] This observation has been made in France, but also in the context of international comparisons, for example between France and Spain, and between Japan and France.[19] In the case of Iran, too, a larger social mixing within zurkhāneh sports and an association of its practice with other sports is the rule today, especially for middle-class athletes, both men and women. This greater eclecticism is the result of the evolution of the larger Iranian society and the reforms undertaken by the VBKP Federation.

In this regard, the change of name of the federation is significant. In the wake of the inscription of the zurkhāneh on the UNESCO list of intangible heritage in 2010,

ast. Gusheh-ye khāneh mitavānad bāshgāh bāshad," 28 Mordād 1398 (19 August 2019). https://www.farsnews.ir/printnews/13980528000610. Accessed on 20 February 2023.
14. I owe the following paragraph to the sociologist Olivier Aubel.
15. Bourdieu 1987.
16. Coulangeon 2011; Coulangeon and Duval 2015.
17. Katz-Gerro and Sullivan 2010; Sullivan and Katz-Gerro 2007.
18. Lefèvre and Ohl 2012.
19. Lefèvre, Routier, and Lopig-Goig 2020. See also, Lefèvre, Nohara, and Nier 2021; Aubel and Lefèvre 2015.

Epilogue

the "Ancient Sport and Pahlavāni Wrestling Federation" became the "Zurkhāneh Sport and Pahlavāni Wrestling Federation," known commonly as "Zurkhāneh and Pahlavāni Federation" in Iran. This change of name has several interesting consequences: first, it removes the reference to the "ancient" period, *bāstāni*. This eliminates a term that is undoubtedly too rooted in the past of a single nation for a sport that has international ambitions. It was also a term that had to be systematically explained to young Iranians, some of whom – as I often observed at the end of the 1990s – did not hesitate to denounce this sport as being old, as old as its name and just good for old people. The change also allows the name of the great absentee of the old title to appear at last: the zurkhāneh itself. We have seen how the federation had introduced a new sports competition entitled "zurkhāneh'i" in 1997 to turn the *group* spirit that exists in the zurkhāneh into a *team* spirit.

The refocusing around the name of the institution, zurkhāneh, has therefore continued and the federation applies a "brand policy" that simplifies its identification at national and international levels. However, as the rules of marketing teach us every day, a good brand needs a good story. All traditional practices around the world that have been brought up to date and wish to achieve international visibility must do so in order to succeed, whatever their real past had been.[20] So what is this story? What is the official history of the zurkhāneh in 2023 Iran?

Apart from the emphasis on its Islamic dimension, there is not much new. The zurkhāneh is always presented as an Iranian plurimillennial institution combining justice, the heritage of martial practices, and a place of mystical and moral education.[21] But perhaps in reaction to the attempt to open up women's sections within the federation, the High Council of the Cultural Revolution started, at the end of June 2020, to highlight the concept of *farhang-e pahlavāni*, "Pahlavāni culture." Since then, a national week has been dedicated to the sports traditions of the zurkhāneh and to "Pahlavāni, Iranian and Islamic culture."[22] As we saw earlier, at the end of the 1990s the government tried to promote the moral concept of *javānmardi* to turn it into a synonym for honesty, courage, sacrifice, and fair play. Now it is the turn of the notion of *pahlavāni* to be instrumen-

20. After the first nationalistic nineteenth- and twentieth-century phase of reinterpretation and reconstruction of athletic and combat traditions, all such practices that wish to achieve a level of international recognition now follow the same way. This adds another layer to the existing interpretations and intensifies the dissemination of narratives attached to, or even disconnected from, historical facts. See the very recent development of "pole yoga" mentioned by McCartney (2023). To understand the building of the Olympic brand, see Chappelet and Kübler-Mabbott 2008; and for study of the invention of tradition in the martial art world, see Moenig and Minho 2016.

21. "Ā'inhā-ye javānmardi va farhang-e pahlavāni dar Irān va jahān-e eslām," 9 Khordād 1401 (30 May 2022). https://www.ricac.ac.ir/meeting/676. Accessed on 26 February 2023.

22. "Namāyandeh-ye vali-e faqih dar Māzandarān: akhlāq pahlavāni dar beyn-e varzeshkārān taqviyat shavad," 1 Khordād 1401 (22 May 2022). http://www.shabestan.ir/TextVersionDetail/1177846. Accessed on 26 February 2023. See also "Ruz-e farhang-e pahlavāni va varzesh-e zurkhāneh'i, goft-o-gu bā Abdollāh Sajjādi pishkesvat-e varzesh-e zurkhāneh'i, 20 Khordād 1399" (9 June 2020) and "Hafteh-ye tarvij-e farhang-e pahlavāni e'lām shod," 2 Khordād 1400 (23 May 2021). https://mehrnews.com/news/5218732. Accessed on 26 February 2023.

talized by Iran's cultural institutions. But what does it mean to be a *pahlavān*, a hero, a strong man, today in Iran? And first of all, does *pahlavāni* and *javānmardi* still attach exclusively to masculine identity?

Pahlavāni is synonymous with the supposedly strong, virile, and courageous way of life of traditional wrestlers. The word *pahlavān*, as we have seen, has also come to mean a hero. In Iran, a simple sport champion is called *qāhramān*. The one and only sport champion who was celebrated in Iran as a *javānmard*, a *qāhramān*, and a *pahlavān* at the same time was Gholām-Rezā Takhti, the greatest Iranian sport legend of modern times; the greatest because he was also the symbol of the incorruptible, humble, loyal, generous, and honest man standing up to the iniquity of the world around him. Given the widespread perception in Iranian society that the current regime is morally, economically, and politically corrupt, its outward promotion of the values Takhti embodied amounts to promoting an insurgency against itself. The day might come, sooner or later, when the zurkhāneh world and all its networks have to ask themselves again, as in 1979, where their loyalties really lie, with the money of the current regime, or with the future of their own children and especially their own daughters.

Interviewed in 2020 by the website *aparat* on the national week dedicated to the sporting traditions of the zurkhāneh and the promotion of *pahlavāni* culture, Sajjādi, a sincere and practicing Muslim who had nothing to do with that initiative, remained true to himself by taking a very clear position.[23] He stated explicitly that *pahlavāni* culture, if it were to have any meaning, must be considered a positive value that everyone, not only athletes, can aspire to. He added that it certainly did not consist in admiring the macho attitudes and virile codes of Iranian masculine society traditionally identified with the world of the zurkhāneh. *Pahlavāni* culture should develop the spirit of honesty, responsibility, solidarity, and altruism in everybody. In his words,

> The concept is simple to understand, if we were all *pahlavān*s, there would be no more crime in this country and the police would be out of work. A civil servant who is a *pahlavān* does not tell you to come back tomorrow, but deals with your problem on the day itself [...] People asking themselves how to behave as a *pahlāvan* must ask themselves, 'how can I be useful to my fellow citizens?'

Although he did not say so in the interview, his approach to *pahlavāni* overlapped almost completely with the notion of *javānmardi* (except for the latter's mystical dimension), representing virtuous moral and social codes extended to the whole population, male and female.[24] Given Sajjādi's willingness to open up the zurkhāneh to women, the

23. See "Puyesh-e Irān pahlavān va payām-e doktor Sajjādi, nāyeb ra'is-e federāsion-e varzeshhā-ye zurkhāne'i," 19 Khordād 1399 (8 June 2020). https://www.aparat.com/v/ri0SK.

24. In 2014 one could still read in the press an association between the two notions of *pahlavāni*

Epilogue

meaning of his words leaves room for a very broad and inclusive interpretation, since the use of *pahlavāni* offers the lexical advantage of no longer referring to a particular gender in its moral and social meaning – contrary to *javānmardi*, whose literal meaning is "young *man*liness." The position taken is courageous and, given the social and political earthquake that occurred in September 2022, very clear-sighted with regard to the aspirations of Iranian society today.[25]

It is true that *pahlavāni* is almost a synonym for *javānmardi*, for anyone wishing to live as a true *pahlavān* must demonstrate all the qualities of a *javānmard*. For that reason I prefer to stick to the notion of *javānmardi* rather than that of *pahlavāni*, while arguing that it needs to be re-evaluated. For today's *javānmard*s are also called Mahsā, Nikā, Sārinā, Hadis, Minou, Sepideh, Nilufar, Narges, Shirin, Parvin, Nasrin. Women, whom the *javānmardi* ethos traditionally considered a category to be protected, deserve to be included in it. Perhaps the term should be paired with the neologism *javānzan* (young woman), for it is the word *javān* that evokes the eternal youth of the virtuous soul; the other word, *mard*, is merely its gendered incarnation inherited from a time that has now definitively passed.[26]

Existing historiographies too often conflate *javānmard* and *luti* figures. Sivan Balslev is right to insist they should be separated.[27] As we have seen, the term *luti* was used to refer to a concrete corporation of performance professionals, acrobat jugglers, bawdy storytellers, magicians, and puppeteers, and was synonymous with an entire urban subculture. This profession often collaborated with wrestlers, and in fact they often trained together in the same spaces. This professional collaboration is almost never mentioned in the official historiography, but it was the secret behind the development of much of the current physical training program in the zurkhāneh. However, *javānmardi*, as recent collective studies demonstrate, was never a profession in itself.[28] In the Middle Ages, between the eleventh and fourteenth centuries, it was the ideological basis for a form of socially organized solidarity, structuring life in many towns and cities of the Middle East with the moral, spiritual backing of the Sufis. Then it came to identify a complete philosophy of life, providing moral criteria for evaluating a man's character. The *javānmard* at his best was, to put it simply, the good and honest man of his time who did things properly in his private, public, and professional lives; a man above perjury and greed, who never boasted about the good he could do; a man who remained true to his moral uprightness without boasting about it regardless of the consequences

and *javānmardi*. See "Ā'in-e pahlavāni va farhang-e javānmardi," 12 Ordibehesht 1393 (2 May 2014). https://www.ettelaat.com/archives/49175. Accessed on 26 February 2023.

25. Khosrokhavar 2023.

26. On this subject see also Rahimi 2018, 27–29 and 292–93; and Seyyed Mas'ud Razavi, "Javānmardi-e zanāneh," in Razavi 2011–2012.

27. Balslev 2019; along with the work of Olmo Gölz, Balslev's work paves the way for new perspectives that will provide substance for future publications. See also Pak-Shiraz 2018, and Rahimi 2018.

28. Ridgeon 2018b.

for himself; a man who was a discreet philanthropist and xenophile who, for the love of God, did not hesitate to put himself at risk to remain true to his beliefs. To a certain extent he represents, in its most uncompromising form, the Sunnite or Shiite equivalent of the Thomas More character in *A Man for All Seasons*.[29] The men who proved themselves *javānmard* could be from very different social backgrounds, from the very poor to the very rich. This is a fact I saw for myself and that was confirmed by the accounts I collected, for there are many ways to be protective and generous even if you have a low income.

However, even if everything I just said about the *javānmard* is still valid now, using the term *javānmard* is quite problematic today, because I never heard or read anything linking it to women. Even the *luti* concept is never linked to them, which is unfair. Fari Siyāh, for example, was described to me as one of the best and bravest members of Tayyeb's criminal organization in the 1950s – a point that the souls of all the men she is said to have stabbed for him would grant, no doubt. Definitely not a *javānmard*, was she a *luti*? Yes, of course. In pre-modern times too, female figures portrayed cleverness, cool headedness, bravery, and cunning, and thus succeeded in overcoming assumptions about gender. In the Iranian countryside, there is a well-known category for women like Fari Siyāh: the *shirzan*s, lionesses, warrior women, horse riders, and weapon users, who show the same daring and cunning qualities as the *jāhel*, the *luti*, or in more distant times, the *ayyār*.

Back in 1994, in order to justify my desire to discover Iranian society and culture, my thesis supervisor gave me the task of shedding light on the past and present practices of the zurkhāneh.[30] This, I hope, is what I have done here, even though my discoveries and conclusions are not necessarily in keeping with what some would have liked. No matter, the results of this anthropological and historical study will take their place alongside the older interpretations without displacing them, because we all know how people react when the legend they wish to believe in is more beautiful than the more complex and uncomfortable reality. In the meantime, zurkhāneh sports will continue to live, adapt, and reach all Iranian society, hopefully including women in the not-too-distant future, on a much more sound, stable, inclusive, and innovative basis. This is all that matters.

29. See the play written by Robert Bolt in 1960, *A Man for All Seasons*, brought to screen by Fred Zinnemann in 1966, about the life and death (1478–1535) of this famous English humanist.
30. And wished me good luck, providing me with a single reference: Popovic 1991.

Bibliography

Abbāsi, Mehdi. 1374/1995–1377/1998. *Tārikh-e koshti-e Irān*. 3 vols. Tehran: Ferdows.
Abrahamian, Ervand. 1985. "The Crowd in Iranian Politics 1905–1953." In *Iran: A Revolution in Turmoil*, edited by Haleh Afshar, 121–48. London: Mc Millan.
Abrahamian, Ervand. 1989. *Radical Islam: The Iranian Mojahedin*. London: I. B. Tauris.
Abu al-Fazl ibn Mubarak. 1897–1904. *The Akbarnāma of Abu-l-Fazl*. Translated from the Persian by Henry Beveridge. Calcutta: Asiatic Society of Bengal.
Abu al-Fazl ibn Mubarak. 1949. *Ā'in-i-Ākbari of Abul Fazl-l-'Allāmī*. vol. 3. Translated by H. S. Jarrett, revised and further annotated by Sir J. Sarkar. Calcutta: Asiatic Society of Bengal.
Adelkhah, Fariba. 1991. *La Révolution sous le voile: Femme islamique d'Iran*. Paris: Kartala.
Adelkhah, Fariba. 2004. *Being Modern in Iran*. New York: Columbia University Press.
Adelkhah, Fariba, Jean-François Bayart, and Olivier Roy. 1993. *Thermidor en Iran*. Brussels: Editions Complexe.
Adle, Charyar and Bernard Hourcade, eds. 1992. *Téhéran capitale bicentenaire*. Paris-Tehran: IFRI.
Afkhami, Amir Arsalan. 1999. "Epidemics and the Emergence of an International Sanitary Policy in Iran." *Comparative Studies of South Asia, Africa, and the Middle East* 19 (1): 22–136.
Aldrin, Philippe. 2005. *Sociologie politique des rumeurs*. Paris: Presses universitaires de France.
Alidust, Mohammad. 1996. *Me'māri-e irāni, az negāh-e tasvir*. Tehran: S.T.E. Vezārat-e Farhang va Ershād-e Eslāmi.
Allan, Graham. *A Sociology of Friendship and Kinship*. London: Allen and Unwin, 1979.
Allan, Graham. 1989. *Friendship, Developing a Sociological Perspective*. London: Harvester Wheatsheaf.
Althabe, Gérard, Daniel Fabre, and Gérard Lenclud, eds. 1992. *Vers une ethnologie du présent*. Paris: Maison des Sciences de l'Homme.
Alter, Joseph. 1992. *The Wrestler's Body: Identity and Ideology in North India*. Berkeley, CA: University of California Press.
Amir Ebrahimi, Masserat. 1992. "L'image socio-géographique de Téhéran en 1986." In *Téhéran capitale bicentenaire*, edited by Charyar Adle and Bernard Hourcade, 267–80. Paris-Tehran: IFRI.

Anderson, Benedict. 1991. *Imagined communities*. London: Verso, Revised Edition.
Ansari, Ali M. 2001. "The Myth of the White Revolution: Mohammad Reza Shah, 'Modernization' and the Consolidation of Power." *Middle Eastern Studies* 37 (3): 1–24.
Ansari, Ali M. 2012. *The Politics of Nationalism in Modern Iran*. Cambridge: Cambridge University Press.
Arasteh, A. Reza. 1961. "The Social Role of the *Zurkhana* (House of Strength) in Iranian Urban Communities during the Nineteenth Century." *Der Islam* 37: 256–59.
Aubel, Olivier and Brice Lefèvre. 2015. "The comparability of quantitative surveys on sport participation in France (1967–2010)." *International Review for the Sociology of Sport* 50 (6): 722–39.
Aubin, Eugène. 1908. *La Perse d'aujourd'hui*. Paris: A. Colin.
Ayāzi, Borhān. 1371/1992. *Āʾineh-ye Sanandaj*. Sanandaj: B. Ayāzi. Abrahamian, Ervand. 1982. *Iran Between Two Revolutions*. New Haven: Yale University Press.
Bahār, Mehrdād. 2535/1375/1977. "Varzesh-e bāstāni-e Irān va rishehhā-ye tārikhi-e ān." In *Barresi-e fahrangi va ejtemāʾi-e zurkhānehā-ye Tehrān*, edited by Showrā-ye Āli-e fahrang va honar, 5–39. Tehran: Showrā-ye Āli-e fahrang va honar. Also available in *Chistā* 1 (October 1981) and reprinted in Mehrdād Bahār, *Az Ostureh tā tārikh*. Tehrān: Nashr-e Cheshmeh, 1376/1997.
Bartolini, Caroline. 2004. "Confréries." *Encyclopedia corsicae*, vol. 2. (Bastia: Editions Dumane), 518–26.
Barzegar, Farāmarz. 1350/1971. *Tārikh-e varzesh-e Irān*. Tehran: Sāzmān-e Tarbiyat-e Badani-e Irān.
Basch, Sophie and Pierre Chuvin, eds. 2007. *Pitres et Pantins. Transformations du masque comique: de l'Antiquité au théâtre d'ombres*. Paris: Presses de l'Université Paris-Sorbonne.
Balslev, Sivan. 2019. *Iranian Masculinities: Gender and Sexuality in Late Qajar and Early Pahlavi Iran* Cambridge: Cambridge University Press.
Banani, Amin. 1961. *The Modernization of Iran 1921–1941*. Stanford: Stanford University Press.
Bateson, Catherine, J. W. Clinton, J. B. M. Kassarjian, H. Safavi, and M. Soray. 1977. "Safa-yi Batin. A Study of the Interrelations of a Set of Iranian Ideal Character Types." In *Psychological Dimensions of Near Eastern Studies*, edited by Carl Brown and Norman Itzkowitz, 257–73. Princeton, NJ: Darwin Press.
Battesti, Térésa and Kazem Kazemaini. 1968. "Le Zour xaneh, gymnase traditionnel persan." *Objets et Mondes* 8:3 (Autumn, 1968): 177–202.
Beeman, William O. 1986. *Language, Status and Power in Iran*. Bloomington: Indiana University Press.
Behmanesh, Atā. 1976. *Man beh mardom taʾzim mikonam*. Tehran: Chāpār.

Behzādi, Ali. 1377/1998. *Shebh-e khāterāt*. Tehran: Zarrin.
Bertoncini, Pierre. 2013. "Corse 2009. Pourquoi le masque? Comment comparer une cérémonie religieuse?." In *Les batailles du patrimoine en Corse*, 131–48. Paris : L'Harmattan.
Blok, Anton. 1972. "The Peasant and the Brigand: Social Banditry Reconsidered." *Comparative Studies in Society and History* 14 (4): 494–503.
Bloomfield, Anne. 1994. "Muscular Christian or Mystic? Charles Kingsley Reappraised." *The International Journal of the History of Sport* 11, no. 2 (August): 172–190.
Brain, Robert. 1976. *Friends and Lovers*. New York: Basic Books.
Bolur, Habibollāh. 1976. *Fann va band-e koshti*. Tehrān: Madreseh-ye Āli-e Varzesh.
Bourdieu, Pierre. 1987. *Distinction. A Social Critique of the Judgement of Taste*. Translated by Richard Nice. Cambridge, MA: Harvard University Press.
Breyley, Gay J. and Sasan Fatemi. 2016. "Contradictory Characters and Marginalization." In *Iranian Music and Popular Entertainment from Motrebi to Losanjelesi and Beyond*, 20–32. London: Routledge.
Bromberger, Christian. 1998. "Le football en Iran." *Sociétés & Représentations* 2 (7): 101–15.
Cameron, Averil. 1967. *Procopius: History of the Wars, Secret history, and Buildings*. Translated, edited, and abridged. New York: Washington Square Press.
Canard, Marius. 1932. "La lutte chez les arabes." In *Le cinquantenaire de la Faculté des lettres d'Alger:1881–1931*, edited by la Société Historique Algérienne, 127–90. Algiers: S. H. A.
Castiglione, Baldassar. 1991. *Le livre du Courtisan*. Presented and translated by Alain Pons from Italian following the version by Gabriel Chappuis (1580) (Paris, Flammarion).
Chaliand, Gérard. 1990. *Anthologie mondiale de la stratégie.* Paris: Robert Laffont.
Chappelet, Jean-Loup and Brenda Kübler-Mabbott. 2008. *The International Olympic Committee and the Olympic System: The Governance of World Sport*. London: Routledge.
Chehabi, Houchang E. 1993. "Staging the Emperor's New Clothes: Dress Codes and Nation-Building under Reza Shah." *Iranian Studies* 36 (3–4): 209–33.
Chehabi, H. E. 1995. "Sports and Politics in Iran: The Legend of Gholamreza Takhti." *International Journal of the History of Sport* 12 (December): 48–60.
Chehabi, H. E. 2001 "Jews and Sport in Modern Iran." In *The History of Contemporary Iranian Jews*, vol. 4, edited by Homa Sarshar and Houman Sarshar, 3–24. Beverly Hills: Center for Iranian Jewish Oral History.
Chehabi, H. E. 2002a. "The Juggernaut of Globalization: Sport and Modernization in Iran." *International Journal of the History of Sport* 19, no. 2–3 (June-September): 276–94.

Chehabi, H. E. 2002b. "A Political History of Football in Iran." *Iranian Studies* 35, no. 4 (Fall): 371–402.

Chehabi, H. E. 2003. *"The Banning of the Veil and Its Consequences."* In *The Making of Modern Iran: State and Society under Riza Shah, 1921–1941*, edited by Stephanie Cronin. London: Curzon, 2003), 193–210.

Chehabi, Houchang E. 2006. "ZUR-ḴĀNA." In Encyclopaedia Iranica Online, © Trustees of Columbia University in the City of New York. Consulted online on 18 November 2023.

Chehabi, H. E. 2008. *"JAʿFARI, ŠAʿBĀN."* Encyclopaedia Iranica Online, © Trustees of Columbia University in the City of New York. Consulted online on 3 December 2023.

Chehabi, Houchang E. 2009. "The Paranoid Style in Iranian Historiography." In *Iran in the 20th Century: Historiography and Political Culture*, edited by Touraj Atabaki, 155–303. London: I.B.Tauris.

Chehabi, H. E. 2014. "Mir Mehdi Varzandeh and the Introduction of Physical Education in Iran." In *Culture and Cultural Politics under Reza Shah: The Pahlavi State, New Bourgeoisie and the Creation of a Modern Society in Iran*, edited by Bianca Devos and Christoph Werner, 55–72. London: Routledge.

Chehabi, H. E. 2018a. *Culture Wars and Dual Society In Iran*. Amsterdam: Farman-Farmaian Family International Institute of Social History.

Chehabi, H. E. 2018b. "Wrestling in the *Shahnameh* and Later Persian Epics." In *The Layered Heart. Essays on Persian Poetry*, edited by Asghar Seyed-Ghorab (Washington DC: Mage, 2018), 237–82.

Chehabi, H. E. 2019a. "The Rise of the Middle Class in Iran before the Second World War." In *The Global Bourgeoisie, The rise of the Middle Class in the Age of Empire*, edited by Christof Dejung, David Motadel, and Jürgen Osterhammel, 43–63. Princeton: Princeton University Press.

Chehabi, H. E. 2019b. "Gender Anxieties in the Iranian Zurkhānah." *International Journal of Middle East Studies* 51 (3): 395–421.

Chehabi, H. E. and Allen Guttmann. 2002. "From Iran to All of Asia: The Origin and Diffusion of Polo." *The International Journal of the History of Sport* 19 (2–3): 384–400.

Colloms, Brenda. 1975. *Charles Kingsley: The Lion of Eversley*. New York: Barnes & Noble.

Corbin, Henry. 1973. "Introduction analytique." In *Rasā'el-e javānmardān / traités des compagnons-chevaliers*, edited by Morteza Sarrāf, 5–108. Tehran-Paris: IFIR.

Corbin, Henry. 1983. *L'homme et son ange: initiation et chevalerie spirituelle*. Paris: Fayard.

Cosandey, Fanny. 2016. *Le rang. Préséances et hiérarchies dans la France d'Ancien Régime*. Paris: Gallimard.

Coulangeon, Philippe. 2011. *Les métamorphoses de la distinction. Inégalités culturelles dans la France d'aujourd'hui*. Paris: Grasset.
Coulangeon, Philippe and Julien Duval, eds. 2015. *Routledge Companion to Bourdieu's Distinction*. London and New York: Routledge.
Crozier, Michel and Erhard Friedberg. 1980. *Actors and Systems: The Politics of Collective Action*. Chicago: The University of Chicago Press.
Daghigh-Nia, Firouz. 1968–1969. *Die Entwicklung des Pfadfindertums im Iran und seine jugendfördernde Bedeutung*. Unpublished Diplomarbeit. Cologne, Deutsche Sporthochschule.
Darbon, Sébastien. 2002. "Pour une anthropologie des pratiques sportives: Propriétés formelles et rapport au corps dans le rugby à XV." *Techniques & Culture* 39:1–27.
Darbon, Sébastien. 2008. *Diffusion des sports et impérialisme anglo-saxon*. Paris: Maison des Sciences de l'Homme.
Das, Veena. 1968. "A Sociological Approach to the Caste Puranas: A Case Study." *Sociological Bulletin, Journal of the Indian Sociological Society* 17, no. 2 (September): 141–64.
Davari, Arash and Naghmeh Sohrabi. 2021. "'A Sky Drowning in Stars': Global '68, the Death of Takhti, and the Birth of the Iranian Revolution." In *Global 1979: Geographies and Histories of the Iranian Revolution*, edited by Arang Keshavarzian and Ali Mirsepassi, 213–44. Cambridge: Cambridge University Press.
Degenne, Alain and Michel Forsé. 1994. *Les réseaux sociaux*. Paris: Armand Colin.
Denoeux, Guilain. 1993. *Urban Unrest in the Middle East: A Comprehensive Study of Informal Networks in Egypt, Iran and Lebanon*. Albany, NY: SUNY Press.
Devictor, Agnès. 2004. *Politique du cinéma iranien: De l'ayatollah Khomeyni au président Khatami*. Paris: CNRS Éditions.
Di Castro, Angelo Andrea. 2003. "A Late Gandharan Wrestlers' Weight." *East and West* 53 (1–4): 257–65.
Di Castro, Angelo Andrea. 2005. "The Barbarisation of Bactria." In *Cultural Interaction in Afghanistan c.300 BCE to 300 CE*, edited by Angelo Andrea Di Castro and Colin A. Hope, 1–18. Melbourne: Monash Asia Institute.
Di Castro, Angelo Andrea. 2007. "Of Handles and Names: Remarks on Wrestlers' Weights." *East and West* 57 (1–4): 367–76.
Digard, Jean-Pierre. 2003. "Pour une ethnologie du 'superflu' en Iran." In *Iran, questions et connaissances vol.3: Cultures et sociétés contemporaines*, edited by Bernard Hourcade, 153–160. Paris: Peeters and Association pour l'Avancement des Etudes Iraniennes.
Digard, Jean-Pierre, Bernard Hourcade, and Yann Richard. 1996. *L'Iran au XXe siècle*. Paris: Fayard.
Drouville, Gaspard. 1819. *Voyage en Perse, pendant les années 1812 et 1813*, vol. 2. Saint Petersburg and Paris: Firmin Didot.

Dubeux, Louis. 1841. *La Perse*. Paris: Firmin Didot.
Duby, Georges. 1990. *The Legend of Bouvines: War, Religion and Culture in the Middle Ages*. Translated by Catherine Tihanyi. Berkeley, CA: University of California Press.
Dudoignon, Stéphane 2022. *Les gardiens de la révolution islamique d'Iran*. Paris: CNRS Editions.
Dumont, Louis. 1970. *Homo Hierarchicu*. Chicago: University of Chicago Press.
During, Jean. 1989. *Musique et mystique dans les traditions de l'Iran*. Tehran: IFRI.
During, Jean. 1994. *Quelque chose se passe*. Paris: Verdier.
Eastwick, Edward B. 1864. *Three Years' Residence in Persia*, vol 2. London: Smith, Elder and Co.
Ebrahimnejad, Hormoz. 2004a. *Medicine, Public Health and the Qajar State: Patterns of Medical Modernization in Nineteenth-Century Iran*. Leiden-Boston: Brill.
Ebrahimnejad, Hormoz. 2004b. "La médecine française, un choix stratégique de l'Iran Qajar." In *Sciences, Techniques et Instruments dans le Monde Iranien: Xe – XIXe siècle*, edited by Nasrollah Pourjavady and Živa Vesel, 281–303. Tehran: IFRI and P.U.I., 2004b.
El Messiri, Sawsan. 1977. "The Changing Role of the Futuwwa in the Social Structure of Cairo." In *Patrons and Clients in Mediterranean Societies*, edited by Ernest Gellner and John Waterbury, 239–253. London: Duckworth.
Elāhi, Sadreddin. 1373/1994. "Negāhi digar be sonnati kohneh: zurkhāneh." *Irānshenāsi* 6 (4): 726–45.
Elias, Norbert. 1994. *The Civilizing Process*. Cambridge, MA: Blackwell.
Elias, Norbert and Eric Dunning. 1986. *Quest for Excitment, Sport and Leisure in the Civilizing Process*. London: Basil Blackwell Ltd.
Ensāfpur, Gholām-Rezā. 1974. *Tārikh va farhang-e zurkhāneh va goruhhā-ye ejtemā'i-e zurkhāneh-row*. Tehran: Vezārat-e Farhang va Honar, Markaz-e Mardomshenāsi-e Irān.
Epkenhans, Tim. 2000. *Die Iranische Moderne im Exil: Bibliographie der Zeitschrift Kave, Berlin 1916–1922*. Berlin: Klaus Schwartz Verlag.
Fathi, Asghar. 1979. "The Role of the 'Rebels' in the Constitutional Movement in Iran." *International of Journal of Middle Eastern Studies* 10 (1): 55–66.
Fathi, Hushang. 1371/1992. *Tārikhcheh va moqarrarāt-e varzeshhā*. Tehran: Enteshārāt-e Madreseh.
Federāsion-e Varzeshhā-ye Bāstāni va Koshti-e Pahlavāni. 1365/1986. *Ā'in-nāmeh va moqarrarāt-e varzeshhā-ye bāstāni va koshti-e pahlavāni*. Tehran: Sāzmān-e Tarbiyat-e Badani-e Jomhuri-e Eslāmi-e Irān.
Feinsilver, Lillian Mermin. 1961. "On Yiddish Shm-," *American Speech* 36:302–3.
Frembgen, Jürgen W. and Paul Rollier. 2014. *Wrestlers, Pigeon Fanciers, and Kite Flyers: Traditional Sports and Pastimes in Lahore*. Karachi: Oxford University Press.

Flatt, Emma. 2010. "Young Manliness: Ethical Culture in the Gymnasiums of the Medieval Deccan." In *Ethical Life in South Asia*, edited by Anand Pandian and Daud Ali, 153–73. Bloomington: Indiana University Press.

Floor, W. M. 1971. "The lūṭīs: A Social Phenomenom in Qājār Persia." *Die Welt des Islam* 13 (1–2): 103–20.

Floor, Willem M. 1979. "The Political Role of the Lūṭīs in Qāǧār Iran." In *Interdisziplinäre Iran-Forschung: Beiträge aus Kulturgeographie, Ethnologie, Soziologie, und neuerer Geschichte*, edited by Günther Schweizer, 179–89. Wiesbaden: Ludwig Reichert.

Floor, Willem. 1981. "The Political Role of the 'Lutis' in Iran." In *Modern Iran: The Dialectics of Continuity and Change*, edited by Michael E. Bonine, and Nikki R. Keddie, 83–95. Albany: State University of New York Press.

Floor, Willem. 1987 (updated 2004). "AṢNĀF." In Encyclopaedia Iranica Online, © Trustees of Columbia University in the City of New York. Consulted online on 19 November 2023 http://dx.doi.org/10.1163/2330-4804_EIRO_COM_5959.

Gaffary, Farrokh. 1984. "Evolution of Rituals and Theater in Iran." *Iranian Studies* 17 (4): 361–89.

Gaillard, Marina. 1987. *Le livre de Samak-e Ayyār: Structure et idéologie du roman persan médiéval*. Paris: CNRS et Association pour l'Avancement des Etudes Iraniennes.

Gaillard, Marina. 2001. "Le champ d'emploi des termes *ayyār* et *javānmard* dans le Dārāb-nāme d'Abu Tāher Tarsusi." *Arabic and Middle Eastern Literatures* 4 (1): 5–18.

Gamson, William A. 1982. *Talking Politics*. Cambridge: Cambridge University Press.

Gaudin, Benoît. 2009. "La codification des pratiques martiales: une approche socio-historique." *Actes de la Recherche en Sciences Sociales* 179 (4): 4–31.

Geertz, Clifford. 1973. *The Interpretation of Cultures: Selected Essays*. New York: Basic Books.

Geertz, Clifford. 1983. *Local Knowledge: Further Essays in Interpretative Anthropology*. New York: Basic Books.

Gilsenan, Michael. 1996. *Lords of the Lebanese Marches: Violence and Narrative in an Arab Society*. Berkeley, CA: University of California Press.

Giesey, Ralph. 1987a. *Cérémonial et puissance souveraine: France XVe – XVIIe siècle*. Paris: Armand Colin.

Giesey, Ralph. 1987b. *Le roi ne meurt jamais*. Paris: Flammarion.

Goffman, Erving. 1959. *Presentation of Self in Everyday Life*. New York: Doubleday and Cie.

Goffman, Erving. (1967)1982. *Interaction Ritual: Essays on Face-to-Face Behavior*. Reprint, New York: Pantheon Books.

Goitein, Shelomo D. 1971. "Formal Friendship in the Medieval Near East." *Proceedings of the American Philosophical Society* 115 (6): 484–89.

Gölz, Olmo. 2018. "Representation of the Hero Tayyeb Haj Reza'i: Sociological Reflections on *javānmardi*." In *Javanmardi: The Ethics and Practice of Persianate Perfection*, edited by Lloyd Ridgeon, 263–80. London: The Gingko Library.

Gölz, Olmo. 2019. "The Dangerous Classes and the 1953 Coup in Iran: On the Decline of 'lutigari' Masculinities." In *Crime, Poverty and Survival in the Middle East and North Africa: The 'Dangerous Classes' since 1800*, edited by Stephanie Cronin, 177–190. London: I. B. Tauris.

Gordon, Richard L. 1972. "Mithraism and Roman Society: Social Factors in the Explanation of the Religious Change in Roman Empire." *Religion* 2 (2): 92–121.

Gordon, Richard L. 2014. "Coming to Terms with the 'Oriental Religions' of the Roman Empire." *Numen* 61:657–72.

Gordon, Richard L. 2017a. "*Persae in spelaeis Solem colunt*: Mithra(s) between Persia and Rome." In *Persianism in Antiquity*, edited by Rolf Strootman and Miguel John Versluys, 279–315. Stuttgart: Franz Steiner.

Gordon, Richard L. 2017b. "Cosmic Order, Nature, and Personal Well-Being in the Roman Cult of Mithras." In *Holy Wealth: Accounting for this World and the Next in Religious Belief and Practice: Festschrift for John R. Hinnells*, edited by Almut Hintze and Alan Williams, 93–130. Wiesbaden: Harrassowitz.

Goushegir, Aladin. 1997. *Le combat du colombophile, jeu aux pigeons et stigmatisation sociale*. Tehran: IFRI.

Grenet, Frantz. 2001. "Mithra dieu iranien: nouvelles données." *Topoi* 11 (1): 35–58.

Gusheh, Hasan. "Varzesh-e bāstāni dar Irān." *Peyām-e now* 3 (6): 47–55.

Guttmann, Allan and Lee Thompson. 2001. *Japanese Sports: A History*. Honolulu: University of Hawai'i Press.

Habibi, Mohsen. 1992. "Réza Chah et le développement de Téhéran (1925–1941)." In *Téhéran capitale bicentenaire*, edited by Charyar Adle and Bernard Hourcade, 199–206. Paris-Tehran: IFRI.

Hershiser, Carl Mehmet. 1998. *Blood honor and money: Turkish oiled wrestling and the commodification of traditional culture*. PhD thesis, University of Texas.

Hillman, Michael. 1981. "Language and Social Distinctions in Iran." In *Modern Iran: The Dialectics of Continuity and Change,* edited by Michael E. Bonine, and Nikki R. Keddie, 327–40. Albany: State University of New York Press.

Hobsbawm, Eric. *Bandits*. 1969. London: Weidenfeld & Nicolson.

Hobsbawm, Eric. 2012. *Nations and Nationalism since 1780: Programme, Myth, Reality*. Cambridge: Cambridge University Press.

Hobsbawm, Eric and Terence Ranger, eds. (1983) 2012. *The Invention of Tradition*. Reprint, Cambridge: Cambridge University Press.

Holt, Richard. 1989. *Sport and the British: A Modern History*. Oxford: Oxford University Press.

Huebner, Stefan. 2016. "Iran and the Indian Ocean Project: The Great Persian Empire, Oil Wealth, and the Seventh Asian Games." In *Pan-Asian Sports and the Emergence of Modern Asia 1913–1974*, 230–260. Singapore: NUS Press.

Jakobson, Roman. 1960. "Concluding Statement: Linguistics and Poetics." In *Style in Language*, edited by Thomas Sebeok, 350–377. Cambridge, MA: MIT Press.

Jamalzadeh, Sayyed Mohammad Ali. 1983. *Isfahan is Half the World: Memories of a Persian Boyhood*. Translated by W. Heston. Princeton: Princeton University Press.

Joule, Robert V. and Jean-Léon Beauvois. 1987. *Petit traité de manipulation à l'usage des honnêtes gens*. Grenoble: P. U. G.

Jourdain, Amable Louis. 1814. *La Perse, ou Tableau de l'histoire du gouvernement, de la religion, de la littérature, etc., de cet Empire*, vol. 4. Paris : Imprimerie de Lebégue.

Jozani, Niloufar. 1994. *La beauté menacée: Anthropologie des maladies de la peau en Iran*. Tehran: IFRI.

Kamandi, Abbās. 1984. *Varzesh va sargozasht-e varzesh-e bāstāni-e Kordestān*. Sanandaj: n.p.

Karamustafa, Ahmet T. 2006. *God's Unruly Friends: Dervish Groups in the Islamic Middle Period 1200–1550*. London: Oneworld Publications.

Kāshāni, Ali-Akbar ibn Mehdi el-. 1875–76. *Ganjineh-ye koshti, Traité de gymnastique et de lutte athlétique*. Copié en l'an 1292 de l'hégire (1875/76). Cent dix-neuf feuillets (quatre-vingt-trois dessins coloriés). Composé sous les auspices du Ministre de l'Instruction Publique, du Commerce et des Mines (vazir-e 'olum va ma'āden va tojjār) [Ali-Qoli Mirza]. Paris: Bibliothèque nationale de France (BnF), MS supplément persan 1169.

Kāshāni, Ali Akbar b. Mehdi al-.1875–76. "Ganjineh-ye koshti." (Manuscript R.C. 8781, Bibliothèque nationale, Paris).

Kāshāni, Ali Akbar b. Mehdi al-. 1875–76. "Ganjineh-ye koshti." Manuscript R.C. 8781, Bibliothèque nationale, Paris. Previously referenced: Kāshāni, Ali-Akbar ibn Mehdi el-. 1875–76. *Ganjineh-ye koshti*, Traité de gymnastique et de lutte athlétique. Paris: Bibliothèque nationale de France (BnF), MS supplément persan 1169.

Katz-Gerro, Tally and Oriel Sullivan. "Voracious Cultural Consumption: The Intertwining of Gender and Social Status." 2010. *Time & Society* 19:2 (July 2010): 193-219.

Kāzemeyni, Kāzem. 1343/1964. *Naqsh-e pahlavān va nehzat-e ayyāri*. Tehrān: Bank Melli, .

Kāzemeyni, Kāzem. 1346/1967 *Dāstānhā-ye shegeft-angiz az tārikh-e pahlavāni-e Irān*. Tehran: Mihan.

Kāzeruni, Ja'far. 1376/1997. *Pahlavānān: tārikh-e pahlavāni dar Kermānshāh dar do qarn-e akhir (1174–1374)* 2 vols. Kermanshah: Tāq-e Bostān.

Keshavarzian, Arang. 2007. *Bazaar and State in Iran: The Politics of the Tehran Marketplace.* New York: Cambridge University Press.

Keyvani, Mehdi. 1982. *Artisans and Guild Life in the later Safavid Period: Contributions to the Social-Economic History of Persia.* Berlin: Klaus Schwarz Verlag.

Khānlari, Parviz Nātel. 1348/1969. "Āi'in-e ayyāri." *Sokhan* 18:1071–77; *Sokhan* 19:19–26, 113–22, 263–67, 477–80.

Khosrokhavar, Farhad. 2023. *Iran: La jeunesse démocratique contre l'état prédateur.* Paris: Fauves Edition.

Kielstra, Nico. n. d. "A Dialectical Model of Attitudes Toward Authority in a Persian Village." Undated manuscript.

Kolāhi, Mohammad Ali. 1358/1979. *Tārikh-e varzesh-e bāstāni-e Yazd.* Tehran: n.p.

Koyagi, Mikiya. 2009. "Moulding Future Soldiers and Mothers of the Iranian Nation: Gender and Physical Education under Reza Shah, 1921–41." *The International Journal of the History of Sport* 26, no. 1 (September): 1668–96.

Krawietz, Birgit. 2013. "Martial Arts Iranian style." In *Sports across Asia: Politics, Cultures and Identities*, edited by Katrin Bromber, Birgit Krawietz, and Joseph Maguire, 158–180. London: Routledge.

Lebra, Takie Sugiyama. 1976. *Japanese Patterns of Behavior.* Honolulu: University Press of Hawai'i.

Lefèvre, Brice and Fabien Ohl. 2012. "Consuming Sports: Distinction, Univorism and Omnivorism." *Sport in Society* 15 (1): 44–63.

Lefèvre, Brice, Guillaume Routier, and Ramon Lopig-Goig. 2020. "Sport participation in France and Spain: an international comparison of vocariousness of sport." *Poetics* 81:101429.

Lefèvre Brice, Hiroatsu Nohara, and Olivier Nier. 2021. "Sports Practice in Japan and France: A Comparative Analysis." *PLOS ONE* 16, no. 6 (June 30): e0253435.

Le Goff, Jacques, ed. 1978. *La Nouvelle Histoire.* Paris: Edition Complexes.

Mahjub, Mohammad Ja'far. 2000. *Ā'in -e javānmardi yā fotovvat.* New York: Bibliotheca Persica Press.

Mangan, James A., ed. 2011. *The Cultural Bond: Sport, Empire, Society.* London: Routledge.

Marashi, Afshin. 2009. "The Nation's Poet: Ferdowsi and the Iranian National Imagination." In Touraj Atabaki, ed., *Iran in the 20th Century: Historiography and Political Culture*, edited by Touraj Atabaki, 93–112 (London: I.B. Tauris, 2009).

Martinez-Sève, Laurianne. 2012. "Les grecs d'Extrême Orient: Communautés grecques d'Asie Centrale et d'Iran." *Pallas* 89:367–91.

Massé, Henri. 1938. *Croyances et coutumes persanes: suivies de contes et chansons populaires* 2 vol. Paris: Librairie Orientale et Américaine.

McCartney, Patrick. 2023. "Poles Apart? From Wrestling and Mallkhāmb to Pole Yoga," *Journal of Yoga Studies* 4:215–70.

Mehdiniā, Jaʿfar. 1373/1994. *Zendegi-e siyāsi-e Abdolhoseyn Hazhir*. Tehran: Pānus.

Minorsky, Vladimir. n d. "Zurkhāna." *Encyclopaedia Islamica*, 2nd ed, vol. 4: 1242–1243.

Mir'i, Hasan. 1349/1970–71. *Āʾineh-ye Pahlavān-nāmeh*. Tehran: Mihan.

Mir-Nejat Qomi (known as Mir-Nejat Esfahāni). 1337/1958. *Gol-e koshti*. Published in *Varzesh-e bāstāni-e Irān: zurkhāneh*, by Hoseyn Partow-Beyzāʾi Kāshāni, 379–419. Tehran: Chāpkhāneh-ye Heydari.

Mirzāʾi, Sinā. 1381/2002 *Tayyeb dar gozar-e lutihā*. Tehran: Media.

Mobasser, Susan. 1985. "Le bazar de Téhéran." *Economie et Humanisme* 286:49–61.

Mobasser, Susan. 1991. "Le bazar: un acteur principal dans le réseau alternatif de relations et de communications sociales et politiques en Iran." In *Modernisation autoritaire en Turquie et en Iran*, edited by Semih Vaner, 55–80. Paris: L'Harmattan.

Moenig, Udo and Kim Minho. 2016. "The invention of Taekwondo Tradition, 1945–1972: When Mythology Becomes 'history.'" *Acta Koreana* 19 (2): 131–64.

Moʿin, Mohammad. 1360/1981. *Farhang-e fārsi*. Tehran: Amir-Kabir.

Mostowfi, Abdollāh. 1944. *Sharh-e zendegāni-e man yā tārikh-e ejtemāʿi va edāri-e dowreh-ye qājāriyyeh*, vol 1. Tehran: Chāpkhāneh-ye elmi.

M. T.T. 1319/1940. "Ling (1776–1839): shāʿer-o varzeshkār," *Āmuzesh va parvaresh* 10, no. 2 (April-May): 15–16 and 58.

Najafi Tehrāni, Farāmarz. 1370/1991. *Ritmhā-ye varzeshi: ritmhā-ye zarb-e zurkhānehʾi*. Tehran: Pārt.

Nejāti, Gholām-Rezā. 1364/1985. *Jonbesh-e melli-shodan-e sanʿat-e naft-e Irān va kudetā-ye Mordād 1332 + annexe: kudetā-ye 28 Mordād 1332*. Tehran: Sherkat-e Sahāmi-e Enteshār.

Niebuhr, Carsten. 1799. *Travels through Arabia and Other Countries in the East*, translated by Robert Heron. Second edition, Perth: R. Morison Jr..

Nikitine, Basile. 1922. "Les valis d'Ardelan." *Revue du Monde Musulman* 49:88–89.

Nora, Pierre. 1997. *The Realms of Memory: Rethinking the French Past*. New York: Columbia University Press.

Pak-Shiraz, Nacim. 2018. "Constructing Masculinities through the Javanmards in Pre-revolutionary Iranian Cinema." In *Javanmardi: The Ethics and Practice of Persianate Perfection* Lloyd Ridgeon, 297–318. London: The Gingko Library.

Partow-Beyzā'i Kāshāni, Hoseyn. 1337/1958. *Varzesh-e bāstāni-e Irān: zurkhāneh*. Tehran: Chāpkhāneh-ye Heydari.

Piemontese, Angelo. 1965a. "La leggenda del santo-lottatore pahlavān Mahmud Xvāresmi 'Puryā-ye Vali' (m. 722/1322)." *Annali dell' Istituto Universitario Orientale di Napoli*, NS 15:167–213.

Piemontese, Angelo. 1965b."La moderna terminologia della lotta tradizionale persiana." *Oriente Moderno* 45, no. 7–9 (July-September): 787–801.

Piemontese, Angelo. 1966. "Il capitolo sui pahlavān delle Badāyi' al-Waqāyi' di Vāsefi." *Annali dell' Istituto Universitario Orientale di Napoli*, NS 16 (1): 207–22.

Piemontese, Angelo. 1967. "Il trattato sulla Futuwwa (Fotovvatnāme-ye soltāni) di Hosein Vā'ez Kashefi. Relazione preliminare." *Atti del terzo confrezzo di studi Arabi e Islamici: Ravello, 1–6 September 1966* (Napoli: I.U.O., 1967), 557–63.

Popovic, Alexandre. 1991. "Quelques réflexions à propos des Zûrhâne d'hier et d'aujourd'hui." In *Jeux et sports en Méditerranée: actes du colloque de Carthage, 7-8-9 novembre 1989*, Tunis, edited by Abdelrahman Ayoub and Adnan Louhichi, 125–32. Tunis: Alif.

Pourjavady, Nasrollah and Živa Vesel, eds. 2004. *Sciences, Techniques et Instruments dans le Monde Iranien : Xe – XIXe siècle*. Tehran: IFRI and Presses Universitaires d'Iran.

Raf'at, Mahmud. 1987. *Takhti: Mard-e hamisheh jāvid*. Tehran: Nashr-e Elmi.

Rahimi, Babak. 2018. "Digital Javanmardi: Chivalric Ethics and Imagined Iran on the Internet." In *Javanmardi: The Ethics and Practice of Persianate Perfection*, edited by Lloyd Ridgeon, 281–96. London: The Gingko Library.

Rahnema, Ali. n. d. "KĀŠĀNI, SAYYED ABU'L-QĀSEM." Encyclopaedia Iranica Online, © Trustees of Columbia University in the City of New York. Consulted online on 19 November 2023 <http://dx.doi.org/10.1163/2330–4804_EIRO_COM_10879>

Rao, Aparna. 1988. "Folk Models and Inter-ethnic Relations in Afghanistan: a Case Study of some Peripatetic Communities." In *Le Fait ethnique en Iran et en Afghanistan*, edited by Jean-Pierre Digard, 109–20. Paris: CNRS Éditions.

Razavi, Seyyed Mas'ud. 1391/2011–2012. "Javānmardi-e zanāneh." In *Tārikh va farhang-e Javānmardi*, edited by Seyyed Mas'ud Razavi, 106–28. Tehran, Enteshārāt-e Ettelā'āt.

Richard, Yann. 1985. "L'organisation des fadā'iyān-e eslām, mouvement intégriste musulman en Iran (1945–1956)." In *Radicalismes islamiques 1: Iran, Liban, Turquie*, edited by Olivier Carré and Paul Dumont, 23–82. Paris: Lmo'Harmattan.

Richard, Yann. 1991. *L'islam shi'ite*. Paris: Fayard.

Ridgeon, Lloyd. 2007. "The Zurkhana between Tradition and Change." *Iran* 45:243–65.

Ridgeon, Lloyd. 2010. *Morals and Mysticism in Persian Sufism: A History of Sufi-Futuwwat in Iran*. London and New York: Routledge.

Ridgeon, Lloyd. 2011. *Jawanmardi: Sufi Code of Honour*. Edinburgh: Edinburgh University Press.

Ridgeon, Lloyd. 2018a. "The Felon, the Faithful and the Fighter: The Protean Face of the Chivalric Man (*Javānmard*) in the Medieval Persianate and Modern Iranian Worlds." In *Javanmardi: The Ethics and Practice of Persianate Perfection*, edited by Lloyd Ridgeon, 1–27. London: The Gingko Library.

Ridgeon, Lloyd, ed. 2018b. *Javanmardi: The Ethics and Practice of Persianate Perfection*. London: The Gingko Library.

Rochard, Philippe. 2002. "The Identities of the Iranian Zurkhānah." *Iranian Studies* 35, no. 4 (Autumn): 313–40.

Rochard, Philippe and Denis Jallat. 2018. "*Zūrkhāneh*, Sufism, *Fotovvat/Javānmardi* and Modernity: Considerations about Some Historical Interpretations of a Traditional Athletic Institution." In *Javanmardi, The Ethics and Practice of Persianate Perfection*, edited by Lloyd Ridgeon, 232–262. London: The Gingko Library.

Rochard, Philippe and Oliver Bast. 2023. "*Zurkhāneh, Akhāṛā, Pahlavān,* and *Jyeṣṭhīmalla*s: Cross cultural interaction and social legitimisation at the turn of the 17th century." *Journal of Yoga Studies* 4:175–214.

Rollier, Paul. n. d. "L'ethos du lutteur: devenir un criminel honorable à Lahore." *Terrain* [online] 74.

Roşu, Arion. 1981. "Les *marman* et les arts martiaux indiens." *Journal Asiatique* 249 (3–4): 417–51.

Sadiq, Mostafā. 1343/1964. "Zurkhāneh va varzesh-e bāstāni." *Honar va Mardom* 26:6–15.

Sadiq, Mostafā. 1353/1974–75. "Gowd-e moqaddas." *Honar va Mardom* 145: 63–65.

Samara, Aikaterini. 2017. "The Characteristic of Hellenistic Gymnasia and Palaestrae in the Ptolemaic Regime as Places of Cultural Blending and Diffusion of Sporting Practices." Communication made at the 21e CESH Congress "Cultural Transfers and cultural mediators in sport" (University of Strasbourg, 7–9 December 2017).

Sarraf, Morteza and Henri Corbin. 1973. *Rasā'el-e javānmardān/traités des compagnons-chevaliers*. Tehran-Paris: IFIR.

Sarshār, Homā. 1381/2002. *Khāterāt-e Sha'bān Ja'fari*. Tehran: Nashr-e Sāles.

Scarce, Jennifer. 1992. "The role of architecture in the creation of Tehran." In *Téhéran capitale bicentenaire*, edited by Charyar Adle and Bernard Hourcade, 73–94. Paris-Tehran: IFRI.

Schayegh, Cyrus. 2002. "Sport, Health, and the Iranian Modern Middle Class in the 1920s and 1930s." *Iranian Studies* 35, no. 4 (Fall): 341–69.

Schayegh, Cyrus. 2009. *Who Is Knowledgeable Is Strong: Science, Class, and the Formation of Modern Iranian Society, 1900–1950*. Berkeley: University of California Press.

Sedigh-Imāni, Mostafā. 1981. *L'institution du Zurxāne à Téhéran dans les années 1920–1979*. Masters thesis, Ecole des Hautes Etudes en Sciences Sociales, Paris.

Seurat, Michel. 1985. "Le quartier de Bāb Tebbāné à Tripoli (Liban): Etude d'une 'asabiyya urbaine." In *Mouvements communautaires et Espaces urbains au Machreq*, edited by Mona Zakaria, and Bachchār Chbarou, 45–86. Beirut: CERMOC.

Shafi'i Sarvestāni, Esmā'il. 1376/1997–98. "Dāstān-e varzesh-e modern." *Sobh* 76 (Āzar): 32–37; *Sobh* 77 (Dey): 58–63; *Sobh* 78 (Bahman): 42–44.

Shamshirian, Saeed, Vidar Halldorsson, and Hermundur Sigmundsson. 2021. "Passion, Grit and Mindset of Iranian Wrestlers: A Socio-Psychological Approach." *New Ideas in Psychology* 62 (2021).

Shāyesteh, Shamsoddin. 1346/1967. *Keyhān-e varzeshi*. Tehran: Keyhān.

Shehābi, Hushang [Houchang Chehabi]. 1387/2008. "Ruyāru'i-e sonnat va moderniteh dar tarbiyat-e badani-e Iran." *Irān Nāmeh* 24, no. 1 (Spring): 81–103.

Showrā-ye Āli-e Farhang va Honar. 2535sh/1977. *Barresi-e fahrangi va ejtemā'i-e zurkhānehhā-ye Tehrān*. Tehran.

Spinetti, Federico. 2021. "Of Mirrors and Frames. Music, Sound, and Architecture at the Iranian Zūrkhāneh." In *Music, Sound, and Architecture in Islam*, edited by Michael Frishkopf and Federico Spinetti, 356–84. New York: University of Texas Press.

Steele, Robert. 2020. *The Shah's Imperial Celebrations of 1971*. London: I. B. Tauris.

Sullivan, Oriel and Tally Katz-Gerro. 2007. "The Omnivore Thesis Revisited: Voracious Cultural Consumers." *European Sociological Review* 23 (2): 123-37.

Taqizādeh, Sayyed Hasan. 1997. "Khiyālāt." *Kāveh* 2 (6). Reprinted in *Kāveh*. Tehran: Vis.

Tehrānchi, Mehdi. 1985. *Pazhuheshi dar varzeshhā-ye zurkhāneh'i*. Tehran: Ketābsarā-ye Moqābel-e Dāneshgāh-e Tehrān.

Texier, Charles. 1852. *Description de l'Arménie, La Mésopotamie et la Perse*. Vol. 2. Paris: Firmin Didot.

Thaiss, Gustav. 1978. "The Conceptualization of Social Change through Metaphor." *Journal of Asian and African Studies* 13 (1–2): 1–13.

Tumār-e afsāneh-ye Poryā-ye Vali. 1337/1958. Published in *Varzesh-e bāstāni-e Irān: zurkhāneh*, by Hoseyn Partow-Beyzā'i Kāshāni, 350–64. Tehran: Chāpkhāneh-ye Heydari.

Vadet, Jean-Claude. 1978. "La futuwwa, morale professionnelle ou morale mystique." *Revue des Etudes Islamiques* 46 (1): 57–90.

Vā'ez-e Kāshefi Sabzevāri, Mowlānā Hoseyn. 1350/1971. *Fotovvatnāmeh-yeh Soltāni*, edited by Mohammad Ja'far Mahjub. Tehran: Bonyād-e Fahrang-e Irān.

Veyne, Paul. 1988 "Conduites sans croyance et œuvres d'art sans spectateurs." *Diogène*, no. 143 (July-September): 1–22.

Vieille, Paul and Kazem Mohseni. 1969. "Ecologie culturelle d'une ville islamique: Téhéran." *Revue Géographique de l'Est* 9 (3–4): 315–59.

Vivier-Muresan, Anne-Sophie. 2006a. *Afzād. Ethnologie d'un village d'Iran*. Tehran: IFRI-Mo'in.

Vivier-Muresan, Anne-Sophie. 2006b. "Le code de politesse iranien (taʿārof) ou la fiction du lien social." *L'Homme. Revue française d'anthropologie* 180:115–38.

Vivier-Muresan, Anne-Sophie. 2020. "Rites d'Achoura et affirmations communautaires." *Archives de Sciences Sociales des Religions* 189 (2): 55–72.

Yaldaï, Sarkhadun. 1965. "Die Organization des Sports im Iran unter Soziologischen Gesichtspunkten." Diplomarbeit, Deutsche Sporthochschule, Cologne.

Yamanaka, Yuriko. 2002. "The Eskandarname of Manuchehr Khan Hakim: A 19th Century Popular Romance on Alexander." In *Iran, questions et connaissances, vol.2: Périodes médiévale et moderne*, edited by Maria Szuppe, 181–89. Paris: Peeters and Association pour l'Avancement des Etudes Iraniennes.

Yeganeh Tabrizi, Farah and Mehrdad Rayani. 2005. "Performing Siyah Bazi/Playing the Black: Satire and Social Relief in Historical Iran." *Documenta* 23 (3): 275–84.

Zarrinkub, Abdolhoseyn. 1951. *Do qarn sokut*. Tehran: Mehrgān.

Zia-Ebrahimi, Reza. "Better a Warm Hug than a Cold Bath: Nationalist Memory and the Failures of Iranian Historiography." *Iranian Studies* 49 (5): 837–54.

Electronic Sources

"Ā'in-e pahlevāni va farhang-e javānmardi." 12 Ordibehesht 1393 (2 May 2014). Retrieved from: https://www.ettelaat.com/archives/49175. Accessed on 26 February 2023.

"Ā'inhā-ye javānmardi va farhang-e pahlevāni dar Irān va jahān-e eslām." 9 Khordād 1401 (30 May 2022). Retrieved from: https://www.ricac.ac.ir/meeting/676. Accessed on 26 February 2023.

"Abdollāh Sajjādi nāyeb ra'is-e federāsion-e pahlevāni va zurkhāneh'i shod." 2 Dey 1395 (22 December 2016). Retrieved from: https://www.borna.news/7/653249. Accessed on 20 February 2023.

"Barkenāri-e zurkhānehdār va morshed beh dalil-e vorud-e zanān beh zurkhāneh." http://varzeshzanan.blogfa.com/post/2278. Accessed on 23 February 2023.

"Bāzdid-e vazir-e varzesh rusiyeh az zurkhāneh-ye Shahid Fahmideh." 26 Bahman 1401 (15 February 2023). Retrieved from: http:// www.izpf.ir/module/news/page-1689/. Accessed on 23 February 2023.

"Doktor Sajjādi: barā-ye defāʿ az varzesh-e bāstāni sokut nakhāham kard." 27 Bahman 1383 (15 February 2005). Retrieved from: https://jamejamonline.ir/fa/news/59108. Accessed on 20 February 2023.

"Doktor Sajjādi dar pāsokh beh enteqādāt-e matrah shodeh: harekāt-e varzesh-e bāstāni-e bānovān hich manʿ- sharʿi nadārad. Salāmat-e nimi az jamʿiyat-e keshvar bā anjām-e harekāt-e varzesh-e bāstāni ta'min khāhad shod." 5 Ordibehesht 1382 (April 2003). Retrieved from: https://www.isna.ir/print/8202–01316. Accessed on 20 February 2023.

"Doktor Sajjādi: varzesh-e bāstāni behtarin badansāzi barā-ye tamām-e reshtehhā-ye varzeshi ast. Gusheh-ye khāneh mitavānad bāshgāh bāshad." 28 Mordād 1398 (19 August 2019). Retrieved from: http s://www.farsnews.ir/printnews/13980528000610. Accessed on 20 February 2023.

"Hafteh-ye tarvij-e farhang-e pahlevāni e'lām shod." 2 Khordād 1400 (23 May 2021). Retrieved from: https://mehrnews.com/news/5218732. Accessed on 26 February 2023.

"Hamid Sajjādi: dar Nikārāgueh zurkhāneh misāzim." 26 Dey 1401 (December 2022). Retrieved from: https://iranwire.com/fa/news-1/112684. Accessed on 20 February 2023.

"Mehralizādeh: az varzesh-e zurkhāneh dar Irān hemāyat-e bishtari mikonim." 21 Farvardin 1391 (9 April 2012). Retrieved from: https://www.asriran.com/fa/news/208620. Accessed on 23 February 2023.

"Mohammad Khoshjān: este'dādyābi mehvar-e fa'āliyat federāsion-e varzesh-e zurkhāneh'i ast." 14 Tir 1392 (5 July 2013). Retrieved from: https://irna.ir/news/80725211. Accessed on 23 February 2023.

"Namāyandeh-ye vali-e faqih dar Māzandarān : akhlāq-e pahlevāni dar beyn-e varzeshkārān taqviyat shaved." 1 Khordād 1401 (22 May 2022). Retrieved from: http://www.shabestan.ir/TextVersionDetail/1177846. Accessed on 26 February 2023.

"Pāyān-e chehar sāl riyāsat-e Jowhari bar federāsion-e zurkhāneh'i." 14 Dey 1399 (3 January 2021). Retrieved from: https://www.isna.ir/print/99101410125. Accessed on 23 February 2023.

"Puyesh-e Irān pahlavān va payām-e doktor Sajjādi, nāyeb ra'is-e federāsion-e varzeshhā-ye zurkhāneh'i." 19 Khordād 1399 (8 June 2020, video length 00:08.38). Retrieved from: https://www.aparat.com/v/ri0SK.

"Qat'i shodan-e vāgozāri-e koshti-e pahlevāni bā emzā-ye suratjaleseh-ye 5 nafareh/Gheybat-e Heydari dar neshast-e enteqāl." 27 Bahman 1397 (16 February 2019). Iran-e Varzeshi. Retrieved from: https://old.inn.ir/Newspaper/BlockPrint/180073. Accessed on 24 February 2023.

"Ruz-e farhang-e pahlevāni va varzesh-e zurkhāneh'i, goft-o-gu bā Abdollāh Sajjādi pishkesvat-e varzesh-e zurkhāneh'i." 20 Khordād 1399 (9 June 2020, video length 00:05.46). Retrieved from: https://varzeshtv.ir/news/172819. Accessed on 24 February 2023.

"Soltān-Ali Tarkhāq mehmān-e Rādio Varzesh," 21 Mordād 1396 (12 August 2017). http://radiovarzesh.ir/NewsDetails/. Accessed on 24v February 2023.

"Tārikhnāmeh: federāsion-e beynolmelali-e varzeshhā-ye zurkhāneh'i." Retrieved from: http://www.izsf.net/fa/post/41. Accessed 23 February 2023.

"Tarkhāq: federāsion-e koshti tafāhomnāmeh'i rā emzā nakardeh ast/pahlevānhā-ye keshvar hamisheh az beyn-e koshtigirān entekhāb shodehand." 4 Bahman 1397 (24 January 2019). Retrieved from: https://www.tasnimnews.com/fa/news/1397/11/04/1929659/. Accessed on 24 February 2023.

"Tarkhāq: federāsion-e zurkhāneh'i, koshti-e pahlevāni rā vāred-e hāshiyeh nakonad/vāgozāri-e in reshteh sehhat nadārad." 28 Bahman 1397 17 (February 2019). Retrieved from: https://www.ghatreh.com/news/nn46313983/. Accessed on 24 February 2023.

Index

abattoirs and butchers 50–51, 54, 58
Abbāsi, Mehdi 87, 222
āb-e ru 18, 177, 187, 192, 193, 203
ābgusht 40, 75, 174, 205
ābji 178
Abrahamian, Ervand 70
ādam-e zerang 177, 181
Adelkhah, Fariba 50, 52, 53, 136, 148
adolescent 10, 137, 143, 172, 219, 234–35
adult men 10, 143, 197–98, 219–21
aesthetic dimension 187, 210–11, 216–18, 228–29, 236
affinities 16, 144, 203
affinity (concept of) 178, 179
Ahmadinejad, Mahmoud 231
Ā'in-e Akbari 114
Akbarnāmeh 114
Akbar Shah 108, 114
akhara 105
akhilik 125
ākhund 115
Alā, Hoseyn 89–90
alaki 190
alam 52, 144–46
alcohol 2, 41, 54, 124, 176, 180, 212
Allan, Graham 178
altruism 13–14, 61, 149, 205, 238
āmājkhāneh 98
A Man for All Seasons 240
amateur sporting status 1, 64, 65, 152, 168, 215
America 23, 47, 53, 69, 76, 79, 154, 210, 218
Amini, Ali 80

Amjadieh stadium 80
Amuzegār, Jamshid 69
andarun 185
Ansār-e Hezbollāh 159, 161
anthropological borderline case 190
Antiquity 2, 92, 109–11
Arabic word and vocabulary 12, 34, 91
Arab invasion 93, 100
Arbāb, Zeyn al-Ābedin (known as Hāji Meyduni) 50
architectural features in question 98, 105–7, 130
aristocrats 78, 111, 136
Asghar Shāter-Rezā 46, 48
āshenā 178
āsh reshteh 153, 155
Āshurā 34, 45, 52, 55, 140, 144–46. See also Muharram
Asian Games 68, 234
Āstān-e Qods-e Razavi. See Imam Reza (Shrine)
athletic public performance 32, 38, 67–68, 78, 101, 108, 111, 112, 121, 124, 135, 176, 210, 239
Attār Neyshāburi 31
Aubin, Françoise 96
authenticity 8, 156, 207, 222, 230
Avicenna 79, 96
ayyār 13, 97, 100, 213, 240
ayyāri 13, 92, 100
az khod-rāzi. See self-satisfaction

badnām 9
Badoft, Hājj Hasan 134

Bahār, Mehrdād 99–104
Bahār, Mohammad Taqi 92
bāj 54, 60
Bakhtiyār, Teymur 97
Balarama 109
baltagi 212
Banā'i, Asghar. See Asghar Shāter-Rezā
bā-namak 176, 214
Bank-e Melli, zurkhāneh 60, 74, 90, 91, 96, 99, 136, 223
Bārāncheshmi, Mehr-Ali 234
bārforush 54
Barnet, Boris 85
bāshgāh 94. See also gymnasium
Basij 12, 159, 161
bāstānikārān 137, 155, 164
bāten 181, 185, 186, 187, 188, 190, 211
bazaar 9, 23, 44–62, 70, 80, 103, 124, 138, 172, 221
bazaari 7, 23, 69–70, 147, 212
bāzuband 62
Beeman, William 169, 185–87, 193
behavior (and misbehavior) 35, 75, 175–77, 184, 186, 189, 195
Behmanesh, Atā 73
Belgium 76
bell 17, 22, 24, 32, 38, 159, 161, 172, 200–203, 227
besāz o befrush 44
bets and betting 42, 108, 111, 125, 134, 212
bi-adab 16, 24
bi-gheyrat 185, 190
bi-khodā 23
bi-namak 189
bi-nāmus 185
bi sar-o-pā 20
bi-tarbiyat 192
blood brothers 177, 179

body 30, 32, 38, 78, 85, 94–96, 109, 112–13, 131, 142, 145, 174, 184, 186, 194–95, 206, 211–13, 228, 234
bodybuilding 85, 108, 194, 206, 210–14, 222–23, 234
bodyguard. See *shāter*
Bolt, Robert 240
Bolur, Habibollāh 58, 68, 88
Bourdieu, Pierre 236
bourgeois 15, 171, 222–23
boxing 221
bozorgsālān (age category) 219
brand policy 205, 237
bravery 118, 124, 240
brothel 49, 54
brother 8–12, 26, 46–47, 50–57, 64, 154, 158–63, 167, 172–174, 178, 185, 193–195, 215, 218
brotherhood 94, 103, 115, 125, 142, 179, 195
Buddhism 109, 126–127
budget 71, 78, 89, 137, 158, 168, 206
buffoon, jester and clown 8, 121, 175–76, 239
Byzantium 110
  military duel with Sasanians 113

calendar of competitions 143, 207
Castiglione, Baldassar 111
catenaccii 145
Central Asia 6, 107–9, 127
chādor 153–154, 176, 185
Chāleh Meydān 8, 23
charkh-e kamān 98
charkh (exercise) 212
chār shuneh 211
chatr 214
Chehabi, Houchang 61, 65
cheshm-o hamcheshmi 96
childhood friend 8–10, 170, 178–80

Index

children 8, 16, 27, 42, 62, 137, 147, 150, 153, 211, 219–22, 234–235, 238
Chizar, zurkhāneh 159–63
chopoq 94
choreographies 215, 218
chowgān (polo) 78
circle of life 219
cleverness 124, 146, 240
clientele 57, 74–75, 103, 158, 198
close friend. See *rafiq*
club. See *bāshgāh*
collective representations of traditional and foreign sporting 129
combat sport 68, 108, 112, 195, 223, 226, 229, 233, 236
compadrazgo 179
Constitutional Revolution 99
Corbin, Henry 12, 13, 100
coup d'état (1953) 23, 51
courier. See *shāter*
cronyism 74, 198–200
Crozier, Michel 148
cultural references 75, 140, 170
cunning 13–14, 67, 112–114, 175–77, 186–87, 212, 240. See also *zerangi*

dādāsh 8, 15, 177–80
daheh-ye fajr commemoration 147
Dāneshsarā-ye Moqaddamāti-e Tarbiyat-e Badani 80
dāng 27, 135
Dārābnāmeh 13
Dār al-Fonun 128, 136
Dār al-mo'allemin-e varzesh 78
darbāghi 53
Darbon, Sébastien 140
Darkhungāh, zurkhāneh 57
Dāsh Ākol 8, 65
dāshmashdi 8, 211

dasteh 10, 52, 55, 145, 146
daughter 50, 134, 149–54, 167, 238
decadence as an argument 84, 104, 118, 125, 195
defeat 38, 96, 125, 213
Degenne, Alain 178–79
disgrace 16, 60, 114, 125, 189, 190
dizi 41
do'ā 15, 26, 35, 36, 134, 197, 218
dojo 226
donation 27, 38, 64, 156–58, 163
dowlat 71, 72
dowreh 144, 151, 155, 170–71, 180
dress 43–47, 86, 108, 176, 200
dumbbells 85, 129
dust 177–81

Ebtehāj, Abolhasan 90
eftār 153–55
eftekhār 73, 220
Elāhi, Sadreddin 97, 101–2
elders 24, 75, 103–5, 140, 146, 197, 205, 213, 219
Elias, Norbert 112, 195
Elqāniān, Habib 69
Emāmzādeh Zeyd (shrine) 147
Ensāfpur, Gholām-Rezā 99–100, 118, 246
Eqbāl, Abbās 92
equality 20, 112, 170, 180
Ershād 137
esfand (*Peganum harmala*) 26–27, 198
esteem 18, 174–76, 214
estekhāreh 116
e'temād o e'tebār 9
E'tezād al-Saltaneh (Ali-Qoli Mirza) 128
etiquette 16, 169. See also *ta'ārof*
Europe 9, 71, 76–78, 91, 112, 129, 178–79, 210

exchange of service. See *pārtibāzi*
exercise pit 3, 10, 17, 43, 93, 104–5, 171, 173, 189, 223, 234. See also *gowd*

face (Goffman definition) 184
Fadā'iyān-e Eslām 34, 51
Fahmideh, Mohammad Hoseyn 57
Farahzād, zurkhāneh 158–63
Farhangdust, Mahmud 172
farhang-e pahlavāni 237
Farhangestān-e zabān 91
Fari Siyāh 54, 240
fata, fityan, javān and *juvenis* 12
father 8, 10–11, 57, 60, 66, 68, 74, 88–89, 144, 150, 157, 162, 172, 173, 185, 198, 220–21, 227
Fatima (Day of) 167
Ferdowsi, Abolqāsem 81, 90–91, 111, 115
fieldwork 92, 144, 149, 153
 anthropologists in 41, 142, 148, 160
 methodological approach 140
FILA (international amateur wrestling federation) 1, 86
football 30, 79, 88, 94, 154, 159, 162, 168, 207, 221
forgiveness 20, 61, 140, 160, 177
Forsé, Michel 178, 179
forutani 107, 173, 174, 189, 204
fotovvat 43, 108, 115, 125
fotovvatnāmeh 13, 119, 120, 127, 254
fozul 186
fraternity 163, 164, 188, 202
Friedberg, Erhard 148
friendship 29, 136, 144, 151, 155, 160, 163, 164, 169–71, 177–81, 188, 195, 197, 202, 204, 212
futuwwa 246, 254

Gaffary, Farrokh 212

Galenic medicine 40, 96
Galenic system (*safrā, sowdā*) 96
Gandhara 109
Ganjineh-ye koshti 128
Ganjineh-ye koshti 105
gardan-koloft 50, 141, 211
Geertz, Clifford , 6
gender 239–40
generosity 13–14, 38, 45, 52, 56, 61, 69, 114, 142–43, 147, 151, 155–56, 163, 167, 170
Gerānmāyeh 77
German Empire 77
Ghafuri-Fard, Hasan 72
Gibson, Thomas R. 79
gift 38, 127, 133, 146, 156, 163, 220
glory 22, 32, 65, 88, 114, 125, 218
Goffman, Erving 184–86, 193
Golden Horde 126
gol-e charkh 156
Gol-e koshti 97–99, 120, 212, 218
gol-e sar sabad 156
gol-e tāj 156
golrizān festival 44–45, 140, 141, 148, 156–64, 204
gowd 1, 17, 18, 20, 24, 30, 34, 35, 36, 37, 38, 75, 92, 103–6, 130, 134, 149, 155–57, 162, 172–74, 180, 189–94, 197, 203, 206–9, 215, 219–29, 234. See also exercise pit
grandfather 157, 220, 221
grandson 219–21
greed 61, 239
Greek 109–13
Gusheh, Hasan 92–100, 105, 118, 119, 248
gymnasium 1, 67, 88, 90, 94, 135, 226, 234. See also *bāshgāh*
gymnastics 1, 2, 76–78, 84, 91, 94, 113, 131, 197, 210, 216, 236

Index 263

Habibi, Emām Ali 65
Hafez 20, 115–16, 185, 218
haft kachal 55
Hājj Rezā'i, Tayyeb 10, 30, 45, 46, 50–60, 67, 73, 145, 240
hāmi 170–71
Hāshemi Tabā, Mostafā 75
Hazhir, Abdolhoseyn 34
Hedāyat, Kamāl 89
Hellenistic period (Seleucid empire and Ptolemaic Egypt) 110
Heracles 109
heroes 13, 57, 65–66, 80, 101, 112–18, 218, 238
hey'at-e azādāri 9, 140, 144–47, 165, 167, 170–75
Hezb-e Sāzandegi 198
hierarchy 16, 18, 35, 56, 70, 79, 101, 102–7, 114, 122, 160, 169, 173, 179, 193, 197, 200, 210, 213–215, 219
High Council of the Cultural Revolution 237
Hinduism 109, 128
historical reinterpretation 108, 115, 140, 237
historiography 1, 6, 75, 157, 91, 93, 98–110, 160, 239
Hitler, Adolf 46–47
Hojjat Kāshāni, Ali 67
homosexuality, passive 192
honesty 14, 151, 237, 238
hoseyniyyeh 145–47
hospitality 14, 143, 153
Hosseini, Amir 232
howz 106
humility 14, 18, 36, 93, 107, 140, 151, 173, 189, 204, 213
hypocrite 152, 173, 179–80, 185, 190

identity construction process 6

Il Libro del Cortegiano 111
Imam Ali 15, 35, 36, 43, 116, 142, 144, 157, 163, 167, 196, 197, 218, 222–23, 226–27
Imam Hoseyn 11, 35, 52, 56, 143–45, 167, 218
Imam Reza (Shrine) 8, 36, 137
income and revenue 27, 49, 59, 69, 78, 124, 127, 134–38, 148, 158, 204, 222, 240
India 6, 82, 96, 108–29, 136, 169, 176, 6
initiation 2, 101, 104–5, 115, 127, 145
innovation 89–91, 196, 215, 223, 240
International Traditional Sports and Games Association 235
interpretive framework 93, 96, 107, 142
intimacy. See *bāten*
Iranian Air Force and zurkhāneh 137
Iranian Communist Party 23, 46, 92, 94. See also Tudeh
Iranian Minister of Public Instruction, Commerce and Mining 128
Irānshenāsi 92
IRIWF (Islamic Republic of Iran Wrestling Federation) 167, 181, 207, 221, 232, 233
Isfahan 41, 89, 98–99, 120, 125, 142, 171, 174, 177, 190–91, 213, 227
Islam 241
Islamic law 42
Islamic Revolution 2, 56, 70, 117, 124, 132, 147
Israel 70, 162, 218, 222
Istanbul 1, 77
IWF (Iranian Wrestling Federation, before 1979) 1, 62, 67, 71, 85, 86, 129

Izadpanāh, Abbās 67, 94
IZSF (International Zurkhāneh Sports Federation) 232–35

Ja'fariān, Mahmud 23
Ja'fari, Sha'bān 23, 27, 30, 45, 51, 56–58, 67, 73, 90–91, 152, 167, 211
Jahān Pahlavān 60, 65
jāhel 8, 11, 14, 54, 57, 65, 123, 161, 177, 240
Jahn, Friedrich Ludwig 77
jaleseh 150
Jām-e Ayyārān wrestling championship 143
Jam'iyat-e gordān-e Irān 81
Jam, zurkhāneh 14–15, 27, 30, 41, 45–51, 60, 81
jānbāzān 172
javānān (age category) 143, 219
javānmard 12–14, 45, 60, 64, 151, 172, 213, 238–40
javānmardi 1, 7, 12–14, 43–45, 53, 66, 92, 94, 99, 117, 118, 125, 157, 196, 205–14, 227–31, 237–39
javānzan 239
jāvdānegi 28
jealousy 61, 96, 188, 204
Jebheh-ye Melli 51. See also National Front
jerid (game) 78
Jewish *luti* 54
jokes 153, 176
Jowhari, Mojtabā 233–34
judges and referees 42, 138, 152, 204, 210, 213, 218
juggling 30, 89, 108, 150, 207, 212, 216, 220
jujitsu 112
Jurābchi Qomi, Mirzā Mahmud Sharif 81

Jyesthimalla 128

kabbādeh (tool and exercise) 35, 38, 57, 85, 89–90, 129, 130, 176, 207, 212, 227–28
kafan 11
kaftarbāzi 42. See also pigeon fancying
kahrobā-ye siyāh 26
Kalarippayattu 112
kalleh pācheh 40, 45, 75, 174, 222
karate 226–28
Karbala 52, 56, 144, 218
Karbāschi, Gholām-Hoseyn 27, 45
Karimi, Ezzat 58, 71–74, 162, 195
Kashan 41, 102, 105, 137, 142
Kāshāni, Abolqāsem 47–51
Kāshāni, Ali Akbar ibn Mahdi al- 128–34
kashf-e hejāb 79
Kasravi, Ahmad 34
Kāzemeyni, Kāzem 99
keneft 96
Kermanshah 50, 86
key moments and methodological problems 142, 149
khāk-e ros 104
khal'at va jāyezeh 134
Khāmene'i, Ali 30
Khāmene'i, Hādi 160
kham-giri. See *narmesh*
khāneqāh 98, 117
Khātami, Mohammad 45, 160–63, 231
khatm 144
Khiva 109, 125, 126
Khomeini, Ruhollah 30, 55–56, 70, 147, 162, 163, 172
khoms and *zakāt* 70
Khorasan 15, 109–10, 137, 142, 157, 207, 219
Khorramshahr 147, 152

Index

Khoshjān, Mohammad 72, 198–206
khoshki-e badan 95
khoshnām 9
Khosravāni, Parviz 102
Kingsley, Charles 206
kohneh-parast 79
kohneh-savār 98–103, 120–21, 127, 134
komiteh-ye varzesh-e bāstāni 68
Koran 116, 154, 186, 198, 218
kot-o shalvāri 45
Krishna and Hanuman 109
kung fu 112
Kurdistan 142, 207, 216

legitimacy 2, 70, 103, 125–26, 132, 202
life-or-death relationship 178
lifestyle 8, 11, 45–47, 75, 115, 125, 129, 171, 204
Ling, Per Henrik 77
long 17, 34, 94, 133, 135, 157
loyalty 9, 30, 50, 54, 231
luti 8, 11–14, 30, 44, 51, 54–56, 66, 80, 92, 101, 120–24, 130–34, 146, 149, 157, 176–77, 188, 211–14, 222, 239–40
luti-acrobats 101, 121, 134, 211, 239
lutigari 92
luti house. See *lutikhāneh*
lutikhāneh 13, 98, 121

mafia 10, 30, 45, 50–56, 157, 161
mahalleh 47
mahram 185
mahriyeh 34
Malāyer 102, 207
management responsability, style and model 133, 136, 150, 172, 198–99, 205, 221, 235
manqal 9, 26

mardānegi 14, 45, 92, 196
Mard-e emruz (newspaper) 46
Mard-e peykār (newspaper) 46
martial arts 68, 111, 114, 195, 200, 214, 221, 223, 228, 237
martyrs, martyrdom and shahids 29, 36, 52, 137, 143–44, 167
masculine identity 42, 219, 238
mashdi 7, 8, 14, 46, 52, 54, 149, 211, 226
Mashhad 8, 36, 137, 142, 207
masnavi 120
Masʿud, Mohammad 46–48
matalak 212
maternal aunt, cousin and uncle 153, 178, 220
Mauss, Marcel 163
Mecca 29, 36, 105
media and audiovisual 9, 46–47, 58, 64, 66, 77, 91, 159, 197, 205–8, 216
Mediterranean 110–111
Mehralizādeh, Mohsen 235
Meydān-e miveh va sabzi 48
Middle Ages 2, 92, 179, 239
Middle East 47, 110–11, 115, 239
mil (tools and exercise) 30, 35, 60, 85, 127, 150, 194, 207, 212, 216
Ministry of Culture and Islamic Guidance 137, 200
Mir-Ashraf, Ahmad 27, 46, 48–51, 60, 67, 71
Mir-Nejāt Qomi (known as Esfahāni) 97, 99, 120, 212, 218
Mithraism 2, 101, 104–11
miyāndār 18, 20, 24, 31, 35, 36, 37, 74, 90, 134, 149, 157, 162, 167, 176, 180, 216
modernization of Iranian society 34, 76, 129, 140, 146

modern sport 1, 2, 75–82, 89, 94, 140, 216
  in provinces 78–80, 87
modesty and its markers 16, 159, 167–69, 173–174
Mofatteh, Mohammad 159
Mohammad Reza Shah 88, 97
Mojāhedin 30
mollā 24, 115, 172
moral dimension 1, 13–14, 20, 42, 43, 60, 66, 77–81, 94, 96, 99, 112, 121, 127, 133, 150, 180, 185, 190, 195–96, 200, 205–13, 222, 231, 236–39
More, Thomas 240
morshed 16–27, 31, 32, 36–38, 55, 68, 82, 91, 94, 98, 103, 115, 119, 133–35, 156–63, 172, 198, 200, 203, 211–16, 223, 227–28
morshed's podium 17, 18, 82, 161, 213–14, 223, 227–28. See also *sardam*
Moses 222
moshkel goshā 26
moshtomālchi 103, 133, 134
Mossadegh, Mohammad 23, 47–52, 59, 64, 66
mostafrang 76
mother and son 55, 126, 145, 150, 151, 154, 167, 205, 234
motreb 98, 103
mourning association. See *hey'at-e azādāri*
mourning ceremonies 144
Muharram 10, 143–48, 155, 165, 171. See also Āshurā
murder and murderer 11, 22, 46, 48, 53, 66
Museum of the Traditional Zurkhāneh and Pahlavāni Wrestling 69

music and musician 1, 16, 17, 62, 94, 98, 103, 115, 116, 154, 186, 203–4, 211, 223
mustache 11, 46, 47, 211
mystic dimension 98–99, 109, 126, 127, 151, 180, 185, 237–38
mythologic dimension 3, 65, 83, 117, 125–27, 140

Nahj al-Balāgheh 36
Najafi Tehrāni, Farāmarz 204
namāz 15, 155
nāmus 42, 94, 185
Napoleon III 77
narmesh 94, 130. See also warmup exercises
Nāser al-Din Shah 69, 134
Nasir al-Dowleh, Ahmad Bader 77
Nāteq Nuri, Ali Akbar 161, 207
National Front 51, 64–66. See also Jebheh-ye Melli
nationalist dimension 46, 77, 117, 121, 128, 129
nazar cheshmi 26
Nazi 46
nazri 155
Nejāt, Mohammad 160
network and networking (private or professional) 7, 9, 50, 66, 68, 69, 93, 137–38, 146, 155–61, 164, 170, 179, 188, 192, 200, 228, 231–32, 238
ney-ye buriyā 104
Nicaragua 235
NIOC (National Iranian Oil Company) 59, 137, 164–73, 190–92
Niru-ye entezāmi 160
noblesse oblige 169
notables and protectors 14–15, 20, 23–27, 38, 43, 51, 57, 58, 74–75, 80, 93, 97, 103, 114–15, 118,

123–25, 134, 136, 156–71, 192
nowcheh 52, 54, 134, 170
now javānān (age category) 143, 219
nowkhāsteh 99, 103
Nowruz 135, 155

obligations of status (high status, low status) 169
official regulations 86, 121, 199, 200
olampik-e Irān competitions 77
Olympic Games 62, 65, 77, 87, 129
Olympic Movement 234
opium 2, 9, 41, 44, 149, 151
oqdeh-ye del 185
Organization of Physical Education. STB (Sāzmān-e Tarbiyat-e Badani); STB (Sāzmān-e Tarbiyat-e Badani)
Ottoman Empire 110

pahlavān 1, 29, 32, 58–60, 66, 73, 82, 86, 88, 96, 99, 101–4, 109, 112–21, 125, 127, 133–134, 149, 161, 172, 196, 198, 200, 211–14, 218–19, 238–39
pahlavānbāshi 103, 134
pahlavān-e keshvar 212
pahlavāni culture 237–38
pahlavān panbeh 211
Pahlavi (regime, era) 64, 80, 82, 91, 93, 108, 115, 123–24, 128–31, 136
Parthian 109–10, 113–14
pārtibāzi 74, 170, 175, 188, 193
Partow-Beyzā'i Kāshāni 97–99, 103, 109, 119
pās dādan 94
passion 9, 41, 73–74, 78, 119, 149, 154, 170, 199
pater familias 8, 149
pātoq 93

patriotic dimension 76, 92, 128–29, 228
patron and patronage 69, 79, 88, 98, 120–21, 125–26, 134–37, 143, 145, 152, 155–56, 164, 169, 171, 193, 232
pā zadan 24, 211–16
pederasty (accusation of) 2, 94, 118
perfect movement 210–16
Persia 93, 109–14, 127
Persian Empire 102, 107, 108, 110
pesar-khāleh 178, 220
photos 11, 28, 29, 47, 51, 60, 73, 79, 82, 96, 190–92, 228
physical education 76–77, 83, 88–89, 94, 128–29, 231
physical exercise 78, 85, 110–11, 129–32, 234
Piemontese, Angelo 98, 125, 251–52
pigeon fancying 2, 41, 124, 170, 212. See also *kaftarbāzi*
pishkesvat 14, 18, 29, 32, 36, 38, 44, 45, 55, 57, 58, 70–74, 82, 90, 92, 103, 115–16, 117, 146, 157–77, 192, 196–205, 210, 215, 219–21
pishkhiz 103
pishkhiz 101
police 11, 17, 22–23, 49–64, 97, 116, 123, 124, 150, 159–60, 176, 228, 238
politeness 20, 36, 39, 169, 191–93, 198, 203
post-revolutionary purge 24, 152
power and influence 11, 15, 26, 45, 50–56, 64, 70, 108, 116–27, 131, 136, 150, 158, 170–74, 179, 187, 203, 219, 232–34
precedence 18, 35, 36, 134, 162, 173, 218
pre-Islamic period (Iran) 1, 26, 83,

91–92, 99, 102, 108–11, 119, 128
pre-revolutionary period 30, 117
prestige 15, 114, 146, 204, 228
Procopius of Caesarea 113
professional treatise 13, 120, 127
professional wrestlers 111–14, 134
profit-sharing question 104, 121, 127, 133, 135
protocol 7, 20, 41, 44, 98, 122–23
public entertainers 121, 176, 212
public homage 24, 56, 173, 196, 197, 205
public humiliation 23, 38, 47, 162, 174, 199, 213
public hygiene 77, 83, 90, 105, 128–31
public speaking 34, 35, 36, 42–43, 64, 147, 151, 156, 162, 177, 180, 196, 198, 203, 208–10, 220, 228–31
Pulād, zurkhāneh 57, 62, 222
Puryā-ye Vali 98, 120–27, 132, 227, 251

qahramān 65, 238
Qajar (era, period or dynasty) 80, 83, 85, 91, 102, 118, 129, 136
qalyān 41, 133
qameh zadan 11
qapān 50
Qazvin 64, 164, 167, 170–74, 207, 221
Qazvini, Mohammad 92
qebleh 29
Qeysar 65
Qom 7, 30, 34, 42, 60, 70
Qotboddin Heydar 132

racketeering 2, 49, 54, 124, 212
radical Islamic group 34
rafiq 15, 149, 175–81
rafiq-e do ru 180

Rafsanjāni, Hāshemi 30, 75, 117, 207
Ra'isi, Ebrāhim 232
rajazkhāni 212
Ramadan 44, 141, 143, 148, 152–58, 163–64, 171
Rastākhiz 23, 102
recommendation letter 74, 152, 169, 193
recruitment crisis and policy 75, 80, 172, 206
reinvented tradition and reputation 114, 117, 140
religious festivals 26, 114, 143
religious minorities 222
renewal policy 161, 205, 214, 219–20, 231–32
respectability 7, 84, 150, 158, 227–28
Révolution 241
Revolutionary Guard 160, 172, 228, 234
Reza Shah 76, 80, 91, 243
rish sefid 93, 103
rituals 2, 20, 101, 108, 121, 127, 144, 160, 173, 179
Rokhsat Pahlavān (newspaper) 58, 162
rokhsat va forsat 20, 221
Rostam 65, 116
rowzeh 144
ru dādan 174
Ruhani, Hasan 231
Rumi, Mowlana 115, 204
rumors 189, 192, 204
runners. See *shāter*
rupush 154, 185
rusari 154
Russia 85, 133, 235
Ruzeh kalleh gonjeshki 153
ruz-e sevvom-e Emām 144

Sa'di Shirāzi 20, 43, 115

Index   269

Safavid 97, 103, 119–20, 125, 127, 128, 134
Safavi, Navvāb 34
Sajjādi, Seyyed Abdollāh 72–75, 159–72, 198–202, 205–8, 231–38
salavāt 17, 24, 36, 69, 135, 161, 172, 197–200
Sālon-e Haft-e Tir 64
Samak-e Ayyār 13
Sanandaj 137, 142, 168–73, 191–94, 207, 216
sanduq-e sadaqeh 149
sangak 41, 154
sang-e na'l 129
sang (tools and exercise) 20, 85, 129, 130, 189, 212
sardam 17, 18, 82, 130, 159–74, 197, 228. See also *morshed*'s podium
sardamdār 228
Sasanian 2, 109–10, 113, 114
sash of honor 52, 60
Sattār al-oyub 43
Sattār Khān and Bāqer Khān 80
SAVAK (Sāzmān-e Ettelā'āt va Amniyyat-e Keshvar) 54, 58, 60, 66, 97
score settling 30, 70, 190
scouting 76–79, 88
Sedigh-Imāni 253
self-flagellating 11, 52, 145–47
self-mutilation 11
self-satisfaction 161, 189
selseleh 204
sense of honor 124, 146
Seyyed 249
Shāh-e Mardān, zurkhāneh 46
Shahid Fahmideh, zurkhāneh 57, 74, 152, 193
Shāhnāmeh 65, 81, 83, 110–16
Shahr-e now 49
Shamanism 126, 127

shāter 14, 98–125, 130, 213
shāterkhāneh 98
Shāyesteh, Shamsoddin 79, 92
shefteh 104
shelang (board and exercise) 104, 130, 214
shenā (board and exercise) 20, 104, 131, 173, 211, 213
Shiism 43, 184, 185
Shiite 8, 15, 34, 56, 70, 77–78, 115, 117, 142, 144, 240
Shiraz 8, 77, 125, 142, 154, 207, 222
Shirgir, Mehdi 75, 199, 206
shirinkār 190, 211–14, 229
shirinkāri exercise 130, 211–16, 222
shirjeh exercise 130, 214
shirzan 240
Shojā'at, Hasan (known as Pahlavān) 57, 82
sibil koloft 211
Siyāh Bāzi 121, 176
social background 71, 149, 212, 221, 240
social conformity 186–88, 195
social eclecticism 236
social groups 90, 99, 140, 195, 236
social interaction 145, 177, 181, 187, 195
social misconduct 124, 191
social practice 75, 115, 141, 222
social rank 7, 102, 104, 111–12, 122, 152, 162, 169, 173, 174, 192, 203
social recognition 125, 138
social relationship 14, 69, 103, 177–79, 186, 189, 193
  egalitarian 170
  unequal 169
social role within Iranian society today 236
social status 18, 111, 114, 171, 219

social values glorified in the gowd 140
sociological objective, profile, study or background 78, 92, 104, 107, 119, 229, 236
sofreh 9, 153–54
sofrehdār 167
solidarity festival. See *golrizān* festival
solidarity values 44, 74–75, 125, 140–44, 149, 155–64, 178–80, 238–39
Soviet Union 47, 80, 85, 92
spinning exercise 35–38, 57, 89, 98, 120, 127, 150, 156, 162, 172, 189, 194, 207, 212–23, 230
spiritual illumination 126, 127
spiritual pilgrim 12
sponsors 91, 118, 136, 166–68, 174, 190, 199, 205–7, 219
Stalin, Joseph 47–48, 94
state ceremonies 121, 122
STB (Sāzmān-e Tarbiyat-e Badani) 1, 57, 66–94, 102, 129, 137, 152, 158–59, 171, 172, 198, 205–6, 232, 242
strategy 14, 141, 171, 177, 181, 186–88, 192–93, 199, 203, 209, 218, 232
street snack 153, 220
Sufi and sufism 18, 36, 77, 98, 103–4, 115, 120, 125–26, 132, 142, 204
Sukhtehsarā'i, Rezā 68
SUMKA 46, 47, 48
sumo and *sumotori* 114, 200
Sunni 142, 185, 240
susul 212
Swedish gymnastics. See Ling, Per Henrik
symbolic dimension 15, 38, 48, 55, 60, 77, 78, 81, 105, 116–17, 123, 125, 136, 140–41, 145, 160, 169, 186, 190, 195, 200, 203, 210, 219, 227, 235

ta'ārof 7, 10, 16, 17, 153–54, 169–73, 190–93
Tabriz 79–80, 92, 105, 120
tactic 199, 205
taekwondo 199, 214, 226
tāj 22, 30
Takhti, Gholām-Rezā 29, 30, 45, 60, 61–67, 88, 161, 172, 196, 222, 238
Ta'lim va tarbiyat (journal) 77
Taqizādeh, Seyyed Hasan 77
Tārikh-e Sistān 93
Tarkhāq, Soltān-Ali 164–75, 190–94, 232–33
tasbih 10, 43
tattoo 22, 30
Tehran Chamber of Commerce 9
tekkiyeh 145, 147
The Wrestler and the Clown 85
Tholozan, Joseph Désiré 128
time limits 86, 210
Tim-e Naft-e Tehrān (VBKP team sponsorised by the NIOC) 165, 172, 190, 194, 218
Timurid (era and sources) 109, 125, 136
titles 99, 102–3, 150, 200, 202
tonekeh-ye Pahlavāni 89, 133
towq 145
traditional sport 1, 2, 6, 29, 34, 42–43, 66, 70–73, 90, 168, 195
 as moral in action 206
traditional wrestling breeches 89, 105, 108, 127, 133, 194, 207, 218, 221
trainer 96, 111, 134, 137, 152, 173
training session 36, 103, 143, 189, 208, 209, 218, 223
transformation process 103, 108, 110,

124, 129, 131, 136, 140, 141, 148, 196, 211, 222
Tudeh 23, 46–47. See also Iranian Communist Party
Tumār-e afsāneh-ye Poryā-ye Vali 97, 119–20, 127
Turkey 109, 211, 235
Turnverein 77
Tusi, Hājj Mostafā 51, 57–60, 70, 73, 88

UNESCO 231–36
United States 9, 58, 70, 222
United World Wrestling 1
unwritten rules and agreement 168, 199, 202
urban factionalism 47, 48, 146
urban subculture 239
Urgench 109, 126
Uzbekistan 126

Vahābzādeh, Rasul 69
vaqf 27
Varzandeh, Mir-Mehdi 76, 89
varzesh-e bāstāni 1, 3, 9, 43, 57, 67–68, 83, 90, 100, 141, 143, 149, 151, 159, 167–72, 198, 207–9, 216–35, 242, 248–50, 253, 255, 256
  competitions 207, 210
  new training space 222, 223, 230
varzeshkārān 30, 32
varzeshkhāneh 90–94, 99
VBKP (Federāsion-e varzesh-e bāstāni va koshti-ye pahlavāni-ye irān) 2, 6, 7, 51, 57–58, 71–75, 92, 116–17, 135–71, 172, 190, 196, 199, 204–12, 215, 221–23, 226–35
  and provinces 77, 90, 97, 142–43, 149, 152, 165, 197, 206–7
  and young athletes 29, 78, 88, 94, 115, 120, 137, 154, 196, 210, 229
vengeance 11, 47, 53
verbal exchange in Iran (the uncertainties of) 187
veteran. See *pishkesvat*
Veyne, Paul 53
violence 11, 84, 96, 112, 145, 149–51, 195, 221
viski-miski pārti 175–76

warmup exercises 91, 94, 130, 194, 215. See also *narmesh*
water pipe. See *qalyān*
weight categories 86, 88, 212
weightlifting (exercise, tools or place of training) 85, 91, 104–9, 127, 129–131, 211, 223, 228
Western practices 45, 76, 78
White Revolution 55, 65
wild rue or Syrian rue. See *esfand*
women 30, 42, 54, 60, 78–79, 94, 131, 145–51, 154, 167, 176, 179, 185, 212, 223, 234–40
women's section of zurkhāneh sport 231–37
working-class 62, 93
working-class district/neighborhood 52, 54, 57, 123, 221–22
World Ethnosport Confederation 235
World Pahlavāni Wrestling Federation 232, 233
wrestling
  khasmāneh 112
  freestyle and/or Greco-Roman 1, 58, 66, 85, 88, 134, 137, 138, 168, 208, 212, 223, 226, 233
  open-handed 111–13, 128
  pahlavāni 58, 62, 66–68, 105, 110, 111, 116–17, 134, 138, 168, 196, 199, 207, 212, 221,

232–33, 236
professional, American style 69

xenophile 240

Yakhi brothers 50, 53
Ya'qub-e Leys (Saffarid dynasty) 93
Yazd 142, 207
Yazdi, Ebrāhim (known as Yazdi Bozorg) 69, 121, 134
yek tigheh 211
Yudin, Kostantin 85

zāher 181, 185, 186, 187, 211
zanbil 133
Zandi, Abbās 68
zang 17, 60, 173, 200
zarb 17, 24, 60, 68, 98, 103, 115, 159, 161, 173, 198, 200, 203, 204, 215, 227
zardāb. See Galenic system (*safrā*, *sowdā*)
zekr 98, 120

zerangi 175, 177, 186, 187, 188, 193–94, 212. See also cunning
Zinnemann, Fred 240
zirzamin 107
Zoroastrian 77, 105, 222
zurkhāneh *passim*
 and *hammām* 11, 93, 104–7
 as subculture 140
 civilian 159–61
 economy of 133, 138
 identity discourse in 148
 Jewish 222
 Marxist interpretation 23, 92–93, 97–99, 118
 military 159
 place of honor in 18, 20, 29, 173
 poetry in 43–44, 115, 151, 156, 171, 177, 180, 186, 218
zurkhāneh'i competitions 206, 211, 216
Zurkhāneh Sport and Pahlavāni Wrestling Federation 231, 237